THE MEMO BOOK

Jim started writing "The Memo Book" in 1966 on a manual typewriter.

Forty years later, Jim finished writing "The Memo Book" in 2006 using a computer to complete his work.

THE MEMO BOOK

Jim Gauger

Copyright © 2010 by Jim Gauger.

ISBN: Hardcover   978-1-4363-8523-7
             Softcover   978-1-4363-8522-0

All rights reserved. No part of this book may be reproduced or transmitted in any form or by any means, electronic or mechanical, including photocopying, recording, or by any information storage and retrieval system, without permission in writing from the copyright owner.

This book was printed in the United States of America.

To order additional copies of this book, contact:
Xlibris Corporation
1-888-795-4274
www.Xlibris.com
Orders@Xlibris.com

Contents

The Rookie Years 15
   1. Me? A Cop? 15
   2. The Paddy Wagon 27
   3. Riding the Ambulance 36
   4. In the Station 49
   5. The One-Man Patrol Car 58

The Early Shift 71
   6. Juveniles and Journeys 71
   7. Civil Unrest—The Riots 79

The Roving Wagon 100
   8. The Roving Wagon—97R 100
   9. Handling Hitches 116
  10. Responding to Calls 123
  11. Emblem of Authority 131
  12. Tavern Trouble 142
  13. Friendly Drunks and Informers 147
  14. Family Time/No Time 151
  15. Crimes in Progress 153

Plain Clothes Detail 160
  16. Plain Clothes—Special Duty 160
  17. Working with the Vice Squad 166
  18. School Kid's Shenanigans 173

The Detective Bureau 180
  19. Making the Bureau 180
  20. TV Shows—Fact or Fiction? 190
  21. Incarceration and Justice 198
  22. New Car, New Partner 203
  23. Interrogations and Arson Investigations 211
  24. Guns Pointed—at Me! 221

25.	More Informers	228
26.	Union Negotiations and The Blue Flu	238
27.	A Made Detective	241
28.	Coppers Down	247
29.	Gin Mills and Struggles	254
30.	District Attorneys and Judges	259
31.	And More Informers, Cases, Partners and Family	262
32.	Con Games	267
33.	A Most Interesting Case	269
34.	Dayshift	279
35.	The Bembenek Case	282

The Homicide Squad 285

36.	The Homicide Squad	285
37.	The Bembeneck Trial	290
38.	Solving the Unsolved ... and More	293
39.	Fresh Murders	300
40.	The Polygraph Test	305
41.	Serial Killers	307
42.	A Quick Resolution Murder	318
43.	A Familiar Face ... Dead	322
44.	Under, Undercover and a Snitch	324
45.	The Bite Mark Case	328
46.	Officers Down ... Again	335
47.	More Interesting Investigations	337
48.	Inside Her Yard, Outside Her Fortress	347
49.	Arson, Drugs and Vagrants	350
50.	Body Dump and 150 Hours Worked in Ten Days	357
51.	Skull Sightings	367
52.	And More Investigations Plus a New M.E.	370
53.	Squad 107M ... Body in a Bag	381
54.	More Murders and Snitches	387
55.	Hospital Operating Rooms	390
56.	Repeat Offender—for Murder	392
57.	Bembenek Publicity and Motions	396
58.	Confession in Colorado Case	398
59.	More Cases ...	400
60.	Sentenced to Death Three Times and a Fresh D.A. Fizzles	410
61.	Another Statistic	414
62.	Continuous Custody	417
63.	Prison Interviews	420

64.	A New Year—Clean Board; First Murder of the Year	422
65.	Tom	431
66.	A Death in Custody	432
67.	Death—A Stinking Disposition	435
68.	Rookie D.A.	437
69.	Verdict: Not Guilty	440
70.	Verdict: Guilty	444
71.	Cab Ride—A Statistic?	447
72.	The Cost of a Murder	450
73.	Whodunit?	455
74.	Discretion with Affair	458
75.	Close Call	459
76.	We-Tip/Crime Line Anonymous	460
77.	Time to Get Out?	462
78.	The Murder of Sara	466
79.	A Phone Call to Retirement	470

To Marlene

My life, my love, my compassionate force behind me, who allowed me to pursue my dreams.

To Karen, Kristie & Jeff

You have given me what every man dreams and hopes for: a loving and caring family. My love for you is everlasting.

Until we all know HIM.

Forward

Every Cop carries a memo book. In this book he keeps such information as a daily stolen car list, "wants" on fugitives or suspected felons and data his Department wants him to keep handy along with details of every arrest and investigation he's involved in. He also makes entries into this book for reference at a later time. For example, if a lady describes a purse-snatcher, this information must be transmitted to other law enforcement that may be able to apprehend the culprit. He cannot always trust to recall every detail, some of which, especially in court cases, might be vital to effective prosecution or defense.

Many Cops are casual in their approach to this book; others are meticulous in detail, including information on clothing, weather conditions and incidental remarks. Some are unreadable by anyone but their owners; others are sparse but neat. Just as Cops vary in their personalities, so do their records. Many of these books are kept carefully preserved for years, while others are considered of little consequence and drop out of sight.

The stories you are about to read reflect a thirty-three year career on a major Metropolitan Police Force. They do more than that, of course. Here you see unfolding in front of you the growth of a human being from young manhood and all its confusion and indecision into the maturity of middle age and then retirement. The patterns of a life are formed, not by one or two incidents but by hundreds of experiences occurring here and there over many years. Television programs and films, which attempt to define a Cop, telling you the reasons he is what he is, are restricted by time. They must tell you the story swiftly, with heavy dramatic highlights. Traumatic experiences, it would seem, directs the life of every Cop, but anyone who has taken the time to peruse the memo books kept by Cops, knows differently.

The purpose of writing these stories are not only to enable the reader to worry with one Cop, rejoice with him, wonder with him, get mad with him, and get sad with him, chuckle with him . . . but mostly to grow with him. His changing, sometimes solidifying thoughts could be yours . . . if you were a Cop . . . . And if you kept a MEMO BOOK!

Author's Note

Because it took me over forty years to compile and finish writing *The MEMO BOOK*, the reader has to take into consideration the different words, slang words and terminologies that were used between 1958 and 1991. *The MEMO BOOK* was written as a Cop would write a report and talk on the streets. Those early years were before hand held two-way radios, cell phones, and computers. D, N, and A were just letters in the alphabet. It should also be noted that all the facts related are to the best of my recollection. Some of the names of victims and suspects have been changed because cases still come through the Justice system to this day. Some of the timeframes written in the book (i.e. "remains unsolved to this day," etc.) may refer to the time period of the writing in that chapter.

A number of people contributed to the material and editing of *The MEMO BOOK*.
My experience on the job as related in the stories to follow would not have been nearly as interesting without the fantastic partners and bosses I encountered throughout my career. I thank my fellow Officers for their support, confidence in me and their comradeship. Family members and friends are to be thanked for their continual support, encouragement and friendship.

A special thank you to . . .

Eric Knutson, who formatted the manuscript into a presentable book for printing. Jeff Gauger, my son, who worked tirelessly on computer issues and teaching his father how to use a computer. Cindy Drida, who spent many, many hours carefully reviewing and commenting on each page—checking and correcting grammar, capitalization, punctuation, and helping to clarify the familiar jargon of Cops that may not make sense to a reader not on the job or experienced with our unusual way of communicating.

And, finally, thank you to Kristie Jorgenson, my daughter . . . who took the original draft of 500 pages or so, broke it down into chapters, read every page and sentence several times, verified facts, edited the book into a final copy and worked with the publisher.

The Rookie Years

1. *Me? A Cop?*

Whatever might possess a man to pursue a profession which leaves doubt in one's mind? A profession filled nightly with despair and degradation and full of seemingly hopeless matters. A job dealing with the side of life which few people fully realize exists, and those that are knowledgeable hope to wash from their minds.

I would like to tell you about the years I have spent in my life trying to realize the imaginary goals I set forth for myself.

It all began many years ago—in 1957—when my sister came home from work downtown and said, "Gee Jim, the Cop on the corner said they are taking applications for the job, why don't you try out?" Little did I realize that with this passing remark lay before me an education that is impossible to attain from any other source than experience itself.

The vocation in which I was about to endeavor was, at the time, merely a means to an end—in other words, a way to make a living. I was, perhaps, too young to recognize that before me would lay the problems of so many and the thanks of so few. I was about to become a Police Officer. This in my mind was a profession that brought with it only respect, glory, grandeur and praise.

It was not until sometime later that I realized I would have to face many good citizens of the community and without revolt or resistance be called a Cop, fuzz, honky, racist, thief, pig, bastard, etc. I would have to face unknown dangers—people with cruel sadistic minds, and individuals that recognize the blue uniform and badge only as a target for their emotions.

Never in my wildest dreams did I possibly imagine spending the next thirty-three years of my life as a Police Officer, or retiring as one of the first Homicide Detectives in a large metropolitan city.

After I pulled my first body from a demolished auto, held a dead child in my arms, delivered my first baby, was shot at and beat up, did I realize that this was a vocation which was beyond my wildest imagination. It still amazes me how individuals can portray cruel, inhumane, and merciless thoughts and desires—not on the individual himself, but on the uniform he or she wears. It is true that I speak of only a small minority, but it is these few that always stand out like thorns on a bush.

I have been told by many that they hate me with such passion and emotion—not because of my race or person, but because I wear the blue uniform, which to them brings out an aversive and repugnant feeling. Many young Officers leave their job after this feeling has been portrayed upon them; they have not learned to harden their minds to these few.

When I speak of the small minority, I of course do not include those good, outstanding, upright, law abiding citizens who sometimes stray from the straight and narrow and get caught in that net of law which they, through legislation, have enacted and I, by oath, must enforce. I speak now of the individuals who for years have always tried to be law abiding, but still have driven a little too fast or not stopped quite long enough at the stop sign. These are the poor souls who feel a cool patch in their stomach when they see the revolving red light, which to them may mean a variety of consequences. But let me start from the beginning.

It began in the auditorium of a school where I found myself with several hundred young men about to take a written test, which is the first of several requirements for the job of Police Patrolman. As I recall now the test was mainly on general knowledge and current events. The test did not seem particularly hard to me, but I presume it was set up as a process of elimination.

Several weeks after taking the written test, I was notified by mail that I had passed, and a date was set for me to take my physical tests. The physical test contained two separate portions. The first part was a physical examination, which I had the fortune of passing without too much difficulty. I found out later that a friend of mine who had been an all-city football player did not pass because of his flat feet. Another friend who failed was colorblind. A panel of doctors, who go over you with a fine toothed comb, conduct these tests. What a change! Now some fifty years later the Police Department accepts the applications of those who have taken drugs and individuals with a criminal history; and they wonder where bad Cops came from.

After having passed the first two tests, and seeing how many had been eliminated, my thoughts turned more towards desire than curiosity. Knowing that the second half of the physical segment of the examination would be to test my physical ability and endurance, I spent many evenings at home running around the block, doing pushups and other physical exercises, much to the amazement of my parents. They did not think it was possible for me to take anything that serious. The previous few years I had been employed in a variety of laborious jobs, and I felt I was in quite good shape. I looked on the next segment of my test as being "in the bag."

I arrived at the gym full of confidence, and suddenly realized that what had started out as over a thousand men had now been reduced to about two hundred. It became clear to me that some of us would not qualify, and the cold feeling of defeat suddenly came upon me. After spending what seemed to me an eternity of running, jumping, pulling, lifting and exerting my body to the point where I was near collapse, the thought entered my mind that I was a complete physical wreck! I remember running the mile with three others and the fellow in front of me was close enough to touch. For a million dollars I could never have passed him.

Once again I was notified by mail that I had passed another segment in the many qualifying tests. Unbeknown to me, at this time the Department was conducting its own investigation into my past . . . interviewing my friends and neighbors, present and past employers, and checking on my own personal integrity. Needless to say my record was not perfect. It had been marred by several traffic violations, which later during my personal interview with the Fire and Police Commission proved to be quite embarrassing. I must say, that the Department does spend a good deal of time and money checking the background and moral character of its applicants. Of course we're talking over forty-five years ago. That was before union input and restrictions because of race and other privacy issues. Because of this, backgrounds have become lax and therefore certain undesirables are entering law enforcement.

My personal interview before the Chief of Police and the Fire and Police Commission was conducted during the evening hours. Dressed in my best suit and tie, and covering my nervousness by chain smoking, I was called before them. Within a few minutes I was standing in a small closed room before a large table around which were seated several men. As far as I could see my attendance before these men gave them neither content nor pleasure. I was just another name and number. Without changing the placid expression on his face, one of the men looked at me and made a fantastic inquiry. "Young man, why do you want to become a Police Officer?"

Any question the man could have asked me undoubtedly would have left me stunned, as I believe I was still in some sort of trance. I gave him an answer which I believe at this time must have been quite standard. I replied that I had wanted to be a Policeman for many years and I felt that I could do an outstanding job. The answer most certainly didn't captivate him, as

I'm sure he had heard it many times before. I started to feel a little more at ease and after a few more questions and answers I almost felt relaxed and thought I again had it made.

The small room suddenly became a closet as an elderly man who was seated in the corner suddenly stood up, grasping several papers in a clenched fist and uttered, "Being a young punk, what's your answer for the heavy foot?" The papers he held were undoubtedly the records of my traffic convictions, which I must confess, left a lot to be desired. I was shocked by the statement and with the feeling that I was about to be chastised, I blurted out "I promise I'll never do it again!" With this statement the interview was completed and I felt sure it also ended my chances of ever coming on the job.

To this day it never ceases to amaze me how several young Officers I have talked to took these same tests three and four times before being appointed. I don't think at that time I could show that much energy or intention. By this time I had met Marlene and hoped she would someday be my wife. In fact, our second date was the night of my interview, after which we went downtown and saw the movie *The Ten Commandments*. Her dad had died in February of 1957, and her mother died in December of the same year. My parents brought a letter to the funeral home, where Marlene's mother laid in state, from the City saying I had passed and supposedly had the needed qualifications to start the much acclaimed and commended Training School of the Milwaukee Police Department.

I can still recall vividly in my mind the morning my class was addressed by the Chief of Police. He not only told us what he expected from us, but also what the citizenry expected, and that above all they would be a harsh Judge and jury. He tried to instill in us a feeling of pride and explained a few of the numerous duties that would be expected of us. The class all rose in unison and with a great feeling of pride and self importance we raised our right hands to the flag of the United States and swore to uphold the laws and ordinances of society with total disregard for our own well-being.

The Training School started and for the next few months my mind would be filled with an abundance of rules, regulations, city ordinances, state laws, federal laws, arrest procedures, searching, seizure and preservation of evidence, testimony, report writing skills, first aid, marksmanship and self-defense techniques. Having hunted most of my life I was pretty good with a gun, but self-defense was something else. Most dictionaries define the art of self-defense as defending oneself without using weapons, depending largely upon the principle of making use of an opponent's strength and weight to disable and control him.

The class, dressed in gym clothes, was seated in a circle. Most were relaxed, but I had the uncomfortable feeling that because of my size, what

I was about to learn, I hadn't really planned on. A gentleman entered our small enclosure and announced that it was his job to show us a few holds to use in case our adversary had a weapon, or it became necessary for us to use physical force when making an arrest. The man was not very large in stature, but by the tone of his voice and being dressed in the costume most generally worn by judo instructors, I got the vague feeling that he was quite capable of taking care of himself. Within a few minutes it became evident that I couldn't have been more right.

After showing us a few come-along holds, one of the more witty men in our class made the classic statement, "What happens if you run into someone the size of Jim?," pointing to me with his finger and wearing a sheepish grin. I knew right then, without anyone telling me, that my six-foot-four-inch body was about to take a beating.

The instructor looked at me with a grin from ear to ear and said in a soft but demanding voice, "Come here young man, I want to show you something." I spent the next few agonizing minutes tied in a proverbial knot where my head was between my knees and my arms were in my back between my shoulder blades. It became quite evident to all present that much could be done to a man my size. Any effort by me to fight back would have been devastating, so I took my beating.

The hours in school were long and the studies hard, but it was very gratifying. Day by day our knowledge increased and the unity and companionship, which is such a large part of the Police Department, became exceedingly evident. We spent numerous hours in the classroom, gym, firing range, and in various courts observing a variety of trials and the tactics both prosecution and defense use. When it was all over we were pronounced fit for duty and placed at the various Police District Stations. We were going to Training School for four hours and then four hours at the station.

I had the extreme good fortune of being assigned to a station which contained the area where I was born and raised. The neighborhoods, business places, and many of the people were familiar to me. This was a distinct advantage and gave me a much more confidant and relaxed feeling. I left for the station with feelings of mixed emotions, not knowing how I would be accepted. Having been fully indoctrinated by the Training School, I saluted everything that moved, even an Auxiliary Policeman who happened to be standing in my way.

I entered the Sergeant's room and after showing my military courtesy, which plays an important part in the discipline of the Department, I was introduced to several other patrolmen. Good fortune was once again with me as I met a patrolman who was familiar to me. I had come in contact with him several times while he was walking a beat in my old neighborhood. When he smiled at me and shook my hand, half the butterflies in my stomach suddenly escaped. I was elated when told I would walk the beat with him that evening. We didn't have our full uniforms yet, so on my first night I wore a Police hat and my civilian gray coat with my badge attached. No gun, nothing. I must have looked like I was going to a costume party. So I started out on my new career, at age twenty-two, not knowing what fate had in store for me in the years to come. I spent the next few months performing various duties, such as walking the beat, riding in a Squad car, directing traffic, and trying to spread goodwill among the citizens of the community.

I can recall one warm summer evening after I had a few months on the street, I had just finished my hamburger and cup of coffee and I felt pretty relaxed. Never realizing that within the next few minutes I would be rolling on the ground engaged in quite a healthy struggle. It began while I was walking in a not too pleasant area on my beat. A young man approached me and since I had not seen him before and his actions showed him to be new in the area, I thought it my duty to question his presence. As this unknown person came near, I said "Good evening, sir."

He immediately replied, "Go to hell." Needless to say this wasn't exactly the response I expected, but I followed by saying, "Just a minute, sir. I'd like to talk to you for a few minutes."

He replied by saying, "Why the hell don't you guys knock it off and leave me alone?" It became quite evident to me that this young man undoubtedly had some previous encounters with the law. Now the object was to get this individual's name, address, date of birth, and get him to the nearest Call box where a check with our Detective Clerical Bureau would reveal whether or not the subject was wanted for anything. And this was about to prove to be somewhat difficult. The conversation between us went something like this:

"What's your name, sir?"
"Screw you!"
"Look, all I asked for was your name, is that so bad?"
"What do you want it for? It's none of your business."
"Look, all I'm trying to do is my job, and you sure aren't making it very easy."
"Okay. My name's Don Mills, I'm twenty-six years old and I live a few blocks down. Now get out of my way, asshole."

At this point the subject turned his back to me and started to walk away. I started after him and he broke into a run. I chased him, and it only lasted about a half a block when he suddenly swung around and grabbed me by the shirt. This action didn't come as too much of a surprise and before I knew it we were on the ground. I was still in pretty good shape physically and it didn't take me too long before I had his arms handcuffed behind his back. I picked the subject off the ground by his arms and said, "Look, wasn't this whole thing kind of stupid?"

To which he replied "I want my lawyer."

I took the subject to the Call box and called for a patrol wagon. After he was taken into the station and booked, I checked Detective Clerical and found a couple of minor traffic warrants open on him. Now besides the warrants, he also had the charges of disorderly conduct and resisting arrest hanging before him.

> Call box. Most people see these blue or red metal items standing on various street corners in big cities and assume they are decorations or remnants of the past. To Officers from my era they were in fact a life-line. They consisted of three doors, one for calling the Fire Department, one for city workers to use and one for Police use. You have to remember this was before two-way radios and cell phones. If I was walking the beat I had to call in every hour. If the operator didn't hear from me he would give me about eight or ten minutes and then turn on the light on top of the call box, or if it was already on, he would make it flash. The flashing light meant I had missed a mark or failed to report in and the Squads in the area would be notified to look for me. Inside the box besides the phone there was also what could be described as a round glass enclosing a disc that was controlled by a small handle. If the beat-man needed help in a hurry and maybe was struggling with a subject he had arrested, he could pull the handle down and this would show his location and help would be sent.

This was commonly referred to as "pulling the hook." Now-a-days these boxes are antiques and collector items, but in those days they were many times a matter of life or death.

Within a half-hour I was back on the street. This is where I started to think of what had happened. The series of events happened so quickly that you react purely out of instinct and self-preservation at the time. I tried to recall what caused all the happenings of the previous hour. Was it my entire fault? Did I do something wrong? Could I have handled the situation a different way? I sat over a cup of coffee and thought about it a long time. I was still very new on the job and didn't realize that this same scene, with just a few variations, would happen many times in the following years.

The next morning I took Mr. Mills to court. He received a suspended sentence on the resisting charge, a fine for disorderly conduct and the traffic charges, and not having money to pay, was sentenced to the House of Correction. To tell the truth, it just didn't give me much self-satisfaction to see this man go to jail. In fact, I had a chance to talk to the man alone the next day before we went into court and I asked him whether he felt any different today. He said, "I sure do." He continued, "I hope I didn't hurt you last night," and after I told him he didn't, he talked further. As I listened, he seemed to be completely unlike the man I had dealt with the previous evening. He said he had lost his job and girlfriend two days ago and was in a very crabby mood when he met me. I can actually say there were no adverse feelings between us by the time we went to court.

Marlene and I had gotten engaged the previous Christmas and were married after I had five months on the job, in May 1958. I had to ask the Captain for a few extra days off, so I had off Friday through Monday for our wedding and had to return to work Tuesday at 4:00 p.m. Our honeymoon was two days in the touristy Wisconsin Dells.

The days turned to weeks, and the weeks to months, and before long I found myself transferred to the late shift—midnight to 8:00 a.m. What an ungodly hour to work. It was a complete transition from my previous shift where the streets were full of people, the business places open and houses full of activity. If you walked the beat during the day you got to know all the neighbors, and if there was a park on your beat with a baseball diamond, you got to watch an inning or two and interact with the kids. It was a beautiful summer and I really enjoyed the job.

It was a cool October evening when I reported to the shift I would work for the next nine years. The majority of the men were new to me, but they were quite friendly and helpful. I started out on the beat and before long the taverns closed, the streets were dead, the air was cool and I was cold. I checked some business places by rattling the doors and then I began to walk, and walk, and walk. I looked at my watch and to my surprise an hour had passed and I had to check in and get my Mark. I reached a Call box, lifted the phone and asked for a Mark. The operator responded with a quick "O.K." I felt so alone that I could have talked to him forever. This was definitely going to be one of the longest nights of my life.

A few minutes later I heard a car pulling up next to me. It was a Squad with its window rolled down and a smiling face looking out. I started to walk towards the car when the passenger said, "Hi there, how's it going—you look kind of chilly." I replied,

"I sure am; I guess I didn't dress warm enough." "Well come on, get in the car and we'll get you a cup of coffee. You can wear my gloves the rest of the night." I know this sounds like a trivial thing, but it was a gesture that I'll always remember. The night came to an end and as I look back I guess it wasn't really that bad after all. The really bad nights were walking the beat in twenty below zero weather when the Sergeant would just say, "Stay warm and out of trouble."

Once again time passed and I began to realize how different my life would be—both on the job and at home. Because of the odd hours and off days, a Policeman becomes somewhat of an outcast with many of his friends. I worked five days and two days off, and then four days on and two days off so I was off weekends only every three months. I know even to the day that I retired, many of our friends would keep a calendar with my off days so they wouldn't even have to ask us out when I was scheduled to work. This usually kept Marlene from having to endure anymore disappointments than she had to. Speaking of my wife, a little later on I'll acquaint you with a few of the problems she has faced being the wife of a Policeman.

I remember walking the beat and how much ground you could cover in an eight hour shift. I would walk and walk and look at my watch and plan where the next Call box would be and how long it would take to get there and would be surprised when I got there I still had ten minutes to my Mark time. I can recall my first winter on the job. I do believe I was never so cold in all my life. You know there's more to being a Cop than enforcing the law. On many occasions I remember it was just a matter of self-preservation from the elements. All night business places such as restaurants, gas stations, and bus terminals became a welcome relief. No matter how cold it would get, you still had to keep your mind alert, for the criminal element never rests.

I remember one very cold winter morning I was walking my beat. The air was still and crisp. I seemed to be the only moving thing in the city. It was time for a Mark and the nearest Call box was situated on a corner by a closed gas station. I looked at my watch and for a second couldn't decide whether to check the station first or get my Mark. I stood next to the box and was about to open it when the still air was suddenly broken by what sounded like a muffled pounding. I listened for a few moments and couldn't distinguish the sound as any I had heard before in that area. The noise stopped, so I opened the box, got a Mark and had a few words with the operator. I closed the box and was about to walk to the gas station to check the door when suddenly the stillness was shattered by the sound of breaking glass. I saw glass flying around in the gas station and realized the back window had just been smashed. A million thoughts flashed through my mind and almost without feeling I had my gun in my hand. I stood motionless for a few minutes with my heart in my stomach, expecting nothing but the worst. The night air once again was still, with my breath being the only visible moving thing. Just then a head peered around the corner of the station and without giving it a second thought, I broke the night air by hollering "Come out you S.O.B. with your hands up or I'll blow your head off."

I guess I must have sounded convincing because a young man emerged with his arms stretched high above his head. I told him to spread eagle against the wall of the gas station, and after I made a preliminary search for a weapon, I handcuffed him and took him to the Call box and pulled the hook. Several Squads arrived within a few minutes. The investigation and report writing lasted the rest of the morning and then I took the subject to court. After the District Attorney issued the complaint for attempted burglary, we went before a Judge and the subject was subsequently given an attorney and bound over for trial. Within a few months the subject was found guilty and sentenced to the State Prison.

There is a lot more to the story than what I just told, but most of it has more to do with my own emotions. I can't help but think whether I would have used my gun or not. The man was caught in the commission of a felony and by law I had the right to use deadly force, but only if I felt my life was threatened. I know if he would have run away from me I probably wouldn't have shot him; but if he had run towards me, I just don't know what my reaction would have been.

I guess that's one of the hardest parts of being a Police Officer. That the decisions you have to make are most generally made in a split second. After it's all over everybody has a chance to second-guess, the Judge, the lawyers, the citizens, and even your bosses. Sometimes they take weeks trying to decide whether you did the right thing when you had but a matter of seconds to make the right move. And quite often it's decided that you were wrong, moved too fast or didn't think fast enough. Many times it's just not that easy.

A crime is committed. If it's a felony you take immediate action, but if it's a misdemeanor you have to decide the many consequences involved, both for the offender and for the Officer, if either is found to be wrong. One of the biggest talents an Officer can have is to have the capability of making the right decision. If you're right, it's taken for granted because this is part of your job and you're trained for it. But if you're wrong you open yourself to more criticism than you can possibly imagine. If only I had the wisdom of Solomon or would be endowed with extreme patience and tolerance.

It is vastly important to plant a good impression in the mind of each person you come in contact with, especially when dealing with a juvenile offender. Many times the result of his first meeting with the law will engrave an image for life. I have always prided myself with having more patience with a juvenile offender than when I dealt with an adult. I can remember being told in training school that the boy of today is the man of tomorrow, the impression you leave with him may last forever.

When working the early shift (also known as the second shift) from 4:00 p.m. to midnight, dealing with juveniles is an everyday occurrence. The streets are full of them. Good ones and bad ones alike. Some like you, some hate you, and some just couldn't care less. I used to meet a lot of nice kids on the beat; most of them treated me with a certain amount of respect. I suppose most of it went back to their first encounter with an Officer.

I remember one instance when I passed a field where a young group of boys were playing a football game. The ball came towards me and I threw it back. "Hey, nice throw Copper" one yelled, "want to try again?" Well, I was still quite new on the job and I suppose I didn't use the best of judgment, for within a few minutes I was involved quite thoroughly in the game. The honking of a horn really snapped me back into reality because it was a Sergeant's car. I said goodbye to the kids and climbed into the Squad. The Sergeant was very nice about it and said he knew how easy it was to get involved with some of the kids, but that I should always remember the watchful eye of the average citizen. He further said someone had called the station and said some Officer in uniform was throwing a football around with some kids and they thought this was a disgrace. Guess it all boils down to who's right and who's wrong and where people place their values.

Needless to say not every night was filled with an over abundance of action. In fact, many nights got quite lonely, especially during the winter when the city seemed to hibernate after midnight. On the really cold nights—in addition to my usual uniform—I would dress in insulated boots, long underwear and gloves, and still carry my gun, handcuffs, ammunition pouch, and memo book. I've stood on numerous main streets in the city and the complete stillness gave me a feeling of almost being in another world. During those times you became acquainted with the night people, as I called them. The people who make their living while the city sleeps. These were the night watchman, the cab driver, the all-night coffee shop, the cooks, waitresses, and the bus driver, to name a few. A friendly exchange of words broke up the monotony of a slow night.

I spent the next five years of my career working inside the District Station. A completely diverse aspect of Police work that I believe the public knows very little about. My duties were distributed between working behind the desk, riding an ambulance, and driving a patrol wagon, which were dispatched from inside the station itself. I truly believe at this time that those five years were a complete waste of my time from the viewpoint of advancing me on in the Department. But I can also say they were extremely interesting years and from a knowledge standpoint, I don't regret them. Working behind the desk and answering the many complaints of citizens by phone and in person is an education in itself.

January 6, 1958 Jim Gauger was appointed a Police Officer for the City of Milwaukee Police Department. Pictured above is Jim's graduating class from the Police Academy. He is in the top row, third from the left.

2. *The Paddy Wagon*

Riding the ambulance brings about a side of life, that most generally I could have done without, if it was not for the humanitarian aspect. Times have changed and now, in 2009, a dispatcher handles all of the citizen calls. The Fire Department or private services handle all of the ambulance calls. Then there's the patrol wagon or what was more commonly referred to as the "paddy wagon."

Let me start with the wagon. The vehicle itself is no more than a van type truck seen many times on the street. The inside is somewhat different and is designed primarily for the transporting—or in Police terms "conveyance"—of prisoners. The doors and windows are covered with heavy metal mesh and the bench seats are bolted to the floor. The actions of a prisoner in the wagon usually differ from the actions of those citizens on the street because generally speaking, a prisoner in the wagon is well aware of the fact that his body is going to be locked behind bars. This thought in itself most generally brings out a very adverse feeling. The only person he can portray his emotions to is the person who locks him up.

I have seen many a grown man sit in the middle of the cellblock floor and cry, plead and pour his heart out. I've also come in contact with a good deal of men who fought so physically hard, that to them, it must have meant a matter of life or death. I have dealt with numerous women prisoners, and that was really an education. After feeling a good blow by a spiked heal or the sharp scratch of fingernails, I realized that those frail feminine individuals were capable of becoming quite vicious. Since the laws based on the Constitution of the United States were enacted for the safeguard of all people regardless of their walk of life, it seemed only natural that these same men and women of every social standing broke these very same laws. I not only closed the cell door on penniless vagrants, but also on well-to-do businessmen—both being given the same kind of cell and the same kind of treatment. Many times the reactions were quite different from what one might expect.

The vagrant, common drunk or habitual law violator, even though he felt wrought over the thought of incarceration, reacted differently because he had probably been through it before. It was not unusual to find a ten dollar bill tucked in the sock, shoe, hatband or underwear of the common drunk. His sole purpose was to satisfy his desire. In other words, to get drunk, and still have enough money to bail himself out before he had to meet the Judge in the morning. The arrest record of some of those individuals may quite often show seventy-five to one hundred convictions; the majority being that of drunk, disorderly or vagrant. They fully realized that an appearance before the Judge may mean a thirty, sixty or ninety day stay in the House of

Correction to dry out. These individuals were a common day occurrence and caused very little disruption in the station. I would say these men averaged in age from their late thirties on up. They usually gave the Officer very little trouble physically because of their condition, which was most generally that of extreme intoxication. The majority of those habitual drunks were filthy and unkempt. They hadn't taken a bath or shaved for weeks. It was not unusual for them to come in with their pants full of human excretion, with the stench being enough to turn over even the strongest of stomachs.

Before placing any prisoner in the wagon, and again before he'd go into the cell, his body was checked for any object with which he may have caused harm to himself or that of the Officers he'd come into contact with. This search revealed a most unusual variety of objects. The searcher might have found a razor with no blades, after-shave lotion, a comb with a few staggered teeth, a half-pint of wine or whisky, and generally a multitude of miscellaneous papers, including their unemployment card, right up-to-date. Very often a there would be a payroll stub which showed they worked three days last month. On a few occasions their wallet may have revealed a picture of a family, which I can only conclude must have been their own. The thought always entered my mind, how can a human being reach those depths of humility and degradation? It was very obvious that it wasn't impossible. A large majority of the drunks carried an Alcoholics Anonymous card with the "Alcoholics Code." I suppose this shows that the mind is willing but the earthly flesh is extremely weak.

I always thought the drunk and vagrant laws were very worthwhile. It got the drunk off the street and the vagrant a warm place for the night. All it cost the taxpayer was a cup of coffee and a bologna sandwich. That was until your "do-gooders" stepped in and said the laws were inhumane and these poor people had rights. Rights are fine except now that there are no drunk or vagrant laws, the drunks lay in the streets and the vagrants die in the vacant cars and doorways they call home. And the liberal society that caused it all, in my opinion, could care less.

Then you have the sophisticate, the enlightened individual that starts out with the classic statement, "Look punk, I make more money in a week than you make in a month." This was most often true because it really wasn't that hard to figure out. Then he'd go on, "I pay your wages and if you lay one hand on me I'll have your badge in the morning." My first contact with these individuals was extremely shocking and unbelievable. You have to take into consideration, of course, that I believed the most obnoxious thing to a sober person was a drunk. A few statements like the aforementioned and you can take all your training in self-control and throw it out the window. My first thought was that, nobody talks to me that way! But after a few years, I don't think there had been anything that I wasn't called. And after all their big talk was done and the cell door was closed, it was somewhat hard to keep yourself from looking behind the bars and saying, "Now who's the better man?"

On a good night I may have gotten as many as fifteen to twenty wagon calls—each one being an experience in itself. After enough time on the wagon, I was on a first name basis with many of the regulars. Some were just like clockwork, every Friday night they'd get thrown in and charged with being "plain drunk" and every Saturday morning their wife would come to bail them out. I would say that the majority of the wagon conveyances were routine. Get the call, pick the subject up, bring him to the station, book him and listen for a few minutes to some annoying and usually meaningless chatter, and then lock him up. One thing I found working the paddy wagon was the night went fast and the work was never boring or dull.

Another segment of the paddy wagon man's duties was the conveying of people who were about to be detained for "mental observation." They were commonly referred to by Officers as "M.O.s." A person might be confined for mental observation when he or she performed some irrational act in the presence of an Officer or if mental observation papers were signed by a doctor and the family. The first thing that had to be taken into consideration was that these people were sick, and their actions were those that a person in their right mind might not have performed. I found that extreme caution had to be used with these people so no harm came to them or the Officers involved. It's completely different fighting someone who has control of their faculties even though they may be somewhat dimmed by alcohol, as compared to someone who cannot restrain his emotions or physical actions.

I can recall one of my first encounters with one of these poor, unfortunate individuals. It happened to be a woman whose physical appearance led me to believe I out-weighed her by at least a hundred pounds. There were five Officers on the scene including myself and before this tiny woman was to reach the hospital, she would cause physical damage to all involved. Knowing my partner and I were sent to make a M.O. conveyance, I was not completely surprised to be met by a young woman in her thirties, dressed in a slip that had just come out of the shower and was dripping wet. She had a wild, unbelievable look in her eyes. Our meeting took place in the living room of her modest home. I'll never forget her first words; she stared directly at me and shouted, "Get out of my house you hypocrite, you worker of the devil." At this she lunged at me and tore my badge from my shirt and knocked my hat from my head. I grabbed her arm and she raked her nails across my arms. There were five huge Policemen, all trying to subdue this one small woman without causing her any bodily harm and all of us were coming out on the short end. She was carried from the house to the waiting paddy wagon, and once inside the wagon she was placed on a cart and strapped down. After the struggle was over we all checked our bruises and scratches and picked up miscellaneous parts of our uniforms and began the ride to the hospital. The woman screamed at the top of her lungs, cursing and damming everyone, continually straining against the straps that held her down. Upon our arrival at the hospital we followed the usual procedures, which consisted of having the woman admitted and turning our guns in at the desk in preparation for our trip to the ward, where these poor unfortunates are kept. This was an education in itself. The door to this ward is kept locked and admittance is gained by a nurse peering through a small portal and unlocking the enclosure. Once inside, the atmosphere became even more disheartening. We started our trip down a long corridor and several times we were interrupted by some obviously mentally disturbed women who would just stare at us or make obscene gestures. Some would even run their hands through our hair and pull at our uniforms. This was one part of the job that I was just never cut out for.

During the period I spent on the wagon I had numerous encounters with M.O.s. In fact, I conveyed the same one three times in the same week. Each time a good fight ensued and each time he was released the next day by the hospital. I suppose doctors know best, but sometimes I wished they would have waited for my off days to release some of these individuals.

I indicated previously that the majority of habitual drunks give us very little trouble even though their dreams may make them out to be fighters; their condition requires very little restraint. The exception to this is the poor soul who sees a violent world through his blurred vision due to an over abundance of alcohol and has delirium tremens, which we more commonly refer to as the D.T.'s. It was described to me as a violent form of delirium, from the excessive use of alcohol, characterized by trembling and by delusions of the senses.

Even though my contact with these people was minimal, they left me with the impression that they were intent on destroying everything, including themselves. I recall an encounter I had with one of these individuals. He had been arrested for being plain drunk a few hours earlier and was apparently sleeping it off in his cell. It was just by chance that I passed his cell and saw his whole body starting to jerk and jump as though his muscles were twitching. I watched for a few moments and then was startled by the man suddenly exploding into a violent, almost inhuman being. He banged the walls and bars with such strength and vigor that he tore the commode right off the wall. I ran for a key and some help, and by the time I returned with several Officers, the man was bleeding from the head and had his clothes all but torn off. The damaged commode had caused a water leak and the cell was filling up with water, which just led to more confusion.

Now the object was to remove the prisoner from his cell, strap him to a cart and convey him to the County General Hospital. Once again all this was supposedly to be accomplished with the least amount of injury to all concerned. I opened the cell door and in this instant it was not necessary to get him out. The man, who incidentally was far from being small in stature, came lunging out like a possessed man. He caught the first Officer off guard and threw a shoulder block into him that sent him flying off his feet and smashing into cells on the opposite side of the room. Immediately five Officers jumped at the man, all trying to grab either an arm or leg. A vicious struggle ensued. This man fought with the strength of ten men. We all wound up on the floor, slipping and sliding in the water. But within a few minutes, we overpowered the big man and got him strapped down. I bandaged the cut on his head and we all proceeded to check over our bumps, bruises, and messed up uniforms. Everyone took a minute to catch their breath and then he was conveyed to the hospital. Nobody seemed any worse for wear and we all chalked it up to experience.

At this particular time, I was one of the younger Officers in the station and the thought did occur to me that I just might have chosen the wrong vocation in life. But the feeling soon passed and I knew more than ever I loved every minute of my new career. Of course, not every night was filled with gloom and violence. In fact, some of the incidents that occurred in the station were quite humorous.

I recall one winter evening when someone had arrested a happy-go-lucky drunk that was sleeping on a bus, and when the driver made his last stop he called the Police. The man had no identification and didn't have the vaguest idea where he lived. So he was given accommodations for the night. He thought the whole thing was funny and didn't care whether he slept in the bus or slept in a cell.

I can't recall for sure whether it was my partner or I that put him in the cell, but whoever it was apparently didn't close the door tight enough and the lock didn't set. A few hours had passed and for some reason I walked through the cellblock. I checked our happy drunk and much to my surprise I found him sleeping very comfortably, only he was covered by two blankets and had his head resting on a pillow. Now I knew we treated our prisoners well, but this was almost ridiculous. I checked with the rest of the Officer crew and nobody admitted giving him any extra room service. So I woke him up and asked where he had acquired the bedding. "Oh," he said, "I woke up with somewhat of a chill, pushed on the door and when it opened I walked over to that cart you have sitting there and grabbed a couple of blankets. You don't mind, do you?" I didn't know what else to say so I told him to make himself comfortable and I would wake him in time to go to work. There was another time the same lock failed and I found the prisoner eating a hamburger that he'd gotten from the corner George Webb's and returned to his cell. Needless to say, not many people heard about this—especially the boss.

Or take the night there was a vagrant in the cellblock. He looked like he hadn't had a meal or a bath in a month. He didn't cause any problem but just sat in his cell with a forlorn look, knowing all he had to look forward to was court the next morning, and the House of Correction for at least the next thirty days.

Now you have to understand that the food in the station is far from being gourmet style or recommended by Duncan Hines. In fact, it consists of rye bread, bologna sausage and black coffee. Occasionally the sandwich might be flavored with some ketchup or mustard that may have been left from some Copper's lunch. On this particular evening a caterer stopped at the station and said he had a lot of food left over from one of his parties and asked us if we could make use of it. After making it understood that we could devour anything this gentleman could afford to leave, he proceeded to unload his truck. He left enough food for us to completely satisfy ourselves and the shift after us. So we decided to share our wealth with the poor vagrant who was still seated dejectedly in his cell. We started him out with a plate heaped with roast beef, potato salad, bratwurst, and various other tasty morsels. Well, let me tell you, the expression on the prisoner's face was unbelievable. This had to be more food than he had seen since his last Thanksgiving at the Rescue Mission. He polished off two big plates of food and two or three helpings of Jell-O and cake. He washed this all down with about six cups of coffee and then fell back into what appeared to be quite a restful and satisfying sleep.

We woke him up in a few hours for his trip to court and there was a marked difference in his physical appearance by the big smile on his face. I remember his parting words as he stepped into the wagon, "Thanks a lot fellas, I'm sure gonna tell all my friends about this and I hope the next time I get thrown in, it's in your station." You know as funny as the whole thing may seem, there's still the tragic side to the story because just as sure as you are going to pay taxes, this man is sure he'll go to jail again.

I recall another night we arrived on the scene of a pick-up with the paddy wagon and the size of the man we were about to convey made me swallow twice. This guy, by his own admittance, was six feet tall and weighed three hundred and forty seven pounds. He was under arrest for plain drunk and causing somewhat of a minor disturbance in one of the local gin mills. The arrest was made primarily because the Officers thought he was in no condition to take care of himself. He wasn't fighting, for which I was very thankful, and went without causing any trouble.

The man was in his early twenties and I'm sure he didn't make it a habit to go out and get drunk and thrown in jail. While I was booking him in the cellblock he just sat dejectedly and then suddenly a few tears came to his eyes. He was very intoxicated and I didn't pay much attention to his emotional state. I finished with his fingerprints and told him he could make a phone call, which he refused. I then took him by the arm and told him he would have to go in the cell for a few hours and sober up. Apparently this is what the tears were all about because he startled me by saying, "How about if I sit out here by your desk?" I told him that was impossible and that he would have to go into the cell. He replied, "You ain't putting me in no cell." I said, "Look, you have to go in there one way or the other, so let's make it easy on both of us." I was well aware of the fact that I wasn't about to put him in there by myself. I called a few more Officers and we sized up the situation of how we were about to place three hundred forty seven pounds of humanity into a cell, without causing anyone harm.

We pushed, shoved and talked the big man into one of the cells and this is where we ran into somewhat of a problem. Standing parallel to the door, his shoulders overlapped each side by about six inches. We pushed and shoved for a few more minutes to no avail and then my partner had a brilliant idea. He squeezed himself into the cell and started to pull from the inside. This finally worked and our reluctant guest was in the cell, but so was my partner. So we let the prisoner out, my partner out, and started all over again. By this time everybody was laughing, including the prisoner. It took us about ten minutes to finally persuade him to sit in the cell for a few hours. And when he bailed himself out in the morning he left by saying, "I hope I didn't cause anybody any trouble, I was really smashed last night and don't recall a thing." We assured him that there were no real problems, but advised him that if it was at all possible not to come and visit us again, unless he came through the front door and was sober.

A few nights later we brought in a young, obnoxious individual, who had been arrested for disorderly conduct (fighting) and resisting arrest. As I recall, he had started a fight in a restaurant and when the Officers arrived he tipped over a table and punched one Copper in the chest. On the way into the station we took the normal amount of verbal abuse from him. He let us know how great he was and if he could take us on one at a time, we'd never stand a chance. He also made it known that he made more money than me and paid my wages. I didn't feel like exchanging words with him and maybe this hurt his tainted ego. We were in the cellblock approaching the booking desk when he suddenly whirled around and sent a "haymaker" to my midsection. The punch was wide of its targeted mark and I was lucky enough to grab his arm and throw him to the floor, with me on top of him.

My partner was behind me, and seeing that I had what appeared to be the upper hand, he didn't interfere. Little did he know that when our reluctant prisoner fell to the floor, he grabbed my tie and hung onto it for dear life. My partner never realized anything was wrong until he saw the back of my neck turning an alarming shade of red. This fellow hung onto my tie so tight it was choking me and I couldn't say a thing. I hit him with everything I had, but he just held on. My partner finally pulled us apart; the knot on my tie was so tight I had to cut it off. We put the prisoner in a cell and after an exchange of a few choice words I went back to the wagon house and tried to repair my tie. Incidentally, this was the last time I ever wore anything around my neck that didn't clip on.

I don't think our young combatant slept too much that night. The cell wasn't strange to him but I think we broke his bubble, and he realized he wasn't as big a man as he thought he was. We gave him his coffee and bologna sandwich and sent him on his way to court where justice was dealt out and he paid for disrupting the normal operation of that restaurant the previous night. He spent thirty days in the House of Correction for striking the arresting Officer. Meanwhile, on my way home I bought a new clip-on tie.

Many people believe that the incidents which occur on the street and in the station, where physical contact is used, are unreasonable and unjustified; that a Police Officer should never use any more compulsion or force than is necessary. I must agree that according to principle this is correct, but it most certainly leaves out the human element and it is my firm belief that no one is more human than a Police Officer. He or she is motivated by complete dedication.

As long as I have mentioned human element, I would like to express my biased opinion on the subject. I believe many people are under the impression Police Officers just aren't human. I mean this almost the way it sounds. They think we're stone, no breath, no life, no feelings, and no emotions, just a substance that has been around for an eternity. If it were just possible to portray to these people the complete human side of an Officer, that his personal feelings and emotions play an enormous part in his workday, maybe they would understand.

A Police Officer most certainly is no special sort of super human being. As an example, after being ridiculed and bantered with disparaging remarks for an extended period of time, it is most natural for him or her to strike back at the source.

I, as an individual, have generally rebelled vehemently against anyone who would make derogatory remarks reflected on my family. This is not unusual, as many people who feel they have been wronged, vent their anger with sadistic expressions. "Hey Copper, I had your wife last night, not bad!"

"Your kids must all be retarded because their father hasn't got a brain in his head." "When I find out where you live, you better not ever leave your wife alone." "Only a bitch would marry a bastard like you." These are light phrases compared to some. I wouldn't consider myself a man, if at times, I didn't rebel against this. I think it's only part of human nature.

If only the bulk of the citizenry would realize that even though the majority of the Officers are dedicated professionals, it is still a way of life and a means of support to his family. I went to work, did my job as best I could and after my tour of duty was done I wanted to go home to my family. Any incidences that occurred on my job should show absolutely no reflection or have any recourse on my family. This was a profession I chose without any influence from those closest to me; therefore, I believe they shouldn't have had to suffer any of the wrath intended for me. Later I will explain some of the inconveniences my family felt with me being a public servant.

3. Riding the Ambulance

I spent about a year on the paddy wagon and then started to ride the ambulance regularly. Even though I had previous experience on the ambulance I was about to get a steady diet of it for two years. In those days there was no such thing as a paramedic or E.M.T. (emergency medical technician). Every Officer took first aid classes during his original training and then took refresher courses. The idea of stabilizing the patient was not part of the protocol and usually it was just a matter of getting the patient to the hospital as fast as possible. As I look back on those years I view them with mixed emotions. I enjoyed the work from the standpoint of helping individuals, but at times it would become extremely gruesome and disheartening. I can honestly say that in those two years I conveyed just about every type of sick or injured person. I went to every hospital in the city and a few in the county. I conveyed those coming into this fascinating and strange world and those that have left for their eternal home. I conveyed the maimed, mutilated, deceased and the hypochondriac, or self-tormented. During those years I delivered seven babies—all which lived. I also conveyed countless accident victims—many of which died. It would be impossible for me to recall accurately the number of conveyances I made, but in those two years I'm sure it exceeded seven hundred.

The first time I delivered a baby, it was a feeling and an experience that is almost beyond description. It gave me an elated sensation of extreme self-satisfaction. To tell the truth, the only concerned party who was at ease was the mother. I was hesitant, and the father was scared. I tried to give the feeling that this was an everyday occurrence for me, but I think the mother understood, and expressed a very warm and understanding feeling to my partner and myself. I took for granted that the training I received when I came on the job was quite sufficient. As I recall, we spent several days on the subject of delivering babies. This included literature, a lecture, and a film of an actual delivery. I had heard many stories of Officers playing the part of a midwife, but there sure is nothing like the real thing. The term used when making an ambulance conveyance for an expectant mother is O.B. (for "obstetrics") conveyance, for which we tried to employ a bit more haste. Not for the reason of it being a vast emergency, but more than anything I don't think any Officer gets particular pleasure out of the thought of delivering a baby. Keep in mind that this was the 1960's, when fathers were not allowed in the labor room or the delivery room, but were left to pace the floor in the waiting room.

Well, on this particular night the phone rang twice, which meant a call for the ambulance. I picked up the phone and the operator said "Ambulance," and gave the address. I asked him what it was, and he replied "O.B. in a hurry." My partner and I ran for the ambulance and I was a bit relieved as it was my turn to drive and my partner would have to sit in the back with the patient. We made good time as it was quite early in the morning, and we had no trouble finding the particular house. As we turned onto the block we saw a man standing in the road frantically waving his arms. I pulled the rig on the wrong side of the road, which brought him on my side of the ambulance. My first observations told me the man was in his late twenties and about to have either a nervous breakdown or a heart attack. He pulled my door open and shouted hysterically "My God! Am I glad you're here; my wife is having the baby." My heart dropped into my stomach and I ran after him into his home, through the living and dining room and into a rear bedroom. There laid this young woman, who obviously was not going to have her baby any place but right there in bed. The blankets were pulled back and I could see the top of the head of her baby trying to enter his new world. The thought flashed through my mind that this wasn't the place for her; she should be in a hospital, surrounded by professional people trained for this, not an amateur like me. I felt a cold sweat starting to form on my forehead. I put my hands between her legs and without really knowing why, told her to push. I wasn't completely surprised, but sure enough out the baby popped, right into my hands.

It's strange what a person's reactions will be when faced with an unexpected situation, for before I knew it, I had cleaned out the mouth of the baby, saw that it was breathing, tied the umbilical cord with two pieces of gauze my partner gave me and cut the cord with my pocket knife. My mind apparently was blank to anything else around me, because my partner later told me the father and a son, about eight or nine years old, were standing directly behind me. The father kept shouting at the son emphatically, "See! See! And you want to be a Cop! See what they have to do!" It was obvious the father was in a state of shock and the son was completely bewildered.

My partner wrapped the baby in a blanket, set it on the bed and we placed the mother on a stretcher. We laid her newborn son on her stomach and started to carry her to the ambulance. The father, who was still a bundle of nerves, followed us to the ambulance and just repeated over and over, "I just don't know how to thank you enough fellas! What can I do for you; anything at all?" To which my partner responded "A cigar will do fine." This, I thought, was a classic statement.

My second delivery was a rare one. In fact, I didn't assist in the actual delivery itself, but the whole experience proved to be quite interesting. I was in the station and took the call myself. The male on the other end of the line said very nonchalantly, "Could you please send an ambulance? My wife just had a baby."

"Right away sir," I responded. And we were there in a matter of minutes. We entered the living room of the home and much to my amazement, found a young woman lying on an open studio couch with a newborn infant lying next to her. The bed and carpeting surrounding it were completely covered with blood, as was the woman. But the infant was comparatively clean. We checked first and saw the baby was breathing regularly and then noticed the umbilical cord had been cut, about two inches from the naval. I tied a piece of gauze around the cord and wrapped the child in a blanket.

I remarked to my partner how clean the baby was, to which the woman replied. "That's probably because it landed in the toilet."

"The toilet," I questioned, almost dumbfounded?

"Yes," she said. "I thought I had to go to the bathroom and the baby just came out, in fact the afterbirth came out too. So I just cut the cord with a scissors, took the baby out of the toilet and laid it on the couch." Even though I was a little confused at this point, I did recall that in training school a doctor had told us that it was important to bring everything along to the hospital in the case of a birth at home. So I rushed into the bathroom, grabbed a towel and started to scoop the afterbirth out of the toilet. What a mess! With all due respect to the situation, this was just about all my stomach could stand. I wrapped the substance in the towel and returned to the living room where my partner had already wrapped the baby in a blanket and placed it on the mother's stomach. We situated the mother and child on the stretcher, placed them in the ambulance and proceeded to the hospital. The ride was quite uneventful; in fact, I checked the newborn several times and could almost have sworn it was sucking its thumb.

We arrived at the hospital, took the mother and baby to the maternity ward, and because the delivery was what the doctor called a spontaneous birth and wasn't delivered in the sterile atmosphere of a hospital, they were both placed in isolation. That's when I called the doctor and my partner over and showed them the substance I had in the blanket. The doctor seemed very pleased, my partner was somewhat shocked that I had thought that far ahead, and I actually felt pretty good about the whole series of events.

My partner and I delivered one baby in the back seat of a compact car. This was a real project. I also delivered one right outside of the hospital where we were going and I delivered two on the way to the hospital. I often thought to myself, why couldn't these women have been a little more cautious, used a little more foresight and left for the hospital as soon as the pain started? Then I would always remember the woman I conveyed three times within a two-week period. Each time she would say, "I felt some pain and I just want to make sure I have my baby in the hospital." Each time they would send her home. Sure enough, one night when I was off, she was conveyed the fourth time and the baby was born a few blocks from the hospital.

The ambulance that I rode in during those years was a big, white, 1957 Cadillac—only two years old. It was equipped with all the necessary paraphernalia, including a resuscitator, first aid supplies, restraints, and what we called puke pans—used when patients felt they had to regurgitate. At the present time, all ambulances are equipped with resuscitators, but at that time ours was one of the very few. We covered the entire district and many times into other districts. A good portion of our area contained the populace that took advantage of the County General Hospital. Not to cast any bad reflection on these people; many were just underprivileged. They would make an appointment at the County General Hospital for some particular day, and not having the necessary means of transportation, they would request our ambulance. It was not unusual for many of these people to be specific with their request. The following conversation typifies many of these requests:

"I need an ambulance."
"What's the name and address, sir, and what seems to be the problem?"
"I got a pain and don't feel good."
"Is this a real emergency?"
"What's the difference?"
"Well, our facilities are limited and we do like to keep the few ambulances we have for emergencies."
"Look, I pay my taxes and you're not a doctor, so how can you tell whether I'm sick or not. And besides that, I think it's an emergency."
"O.K. We'll have one there in a few minutes."

And then would come that passing remark. "Say, could you send that white Cadillac?"

It just never ceased to amaze me how some people take advantage of anything that's free. Even though we are considered public servants, and the services we render are paid for through taxation, the numbers of ambulances are limited by this same budget and their main purpose is for emergency use.

The feelings and emotions that were involved in ambulance work are hard for me to explain and I found it difficult to express them in writing. I don't want to leave you with the perception that I have very little sentiment, sympathy, tenderness, or concern. Perhaps part of that's right, but I believe I hold anguish and affection for all human beings. I've conveyed as many as seven dead people in two days, and if I felt an extreme amount of sentiment and passion in each case, I just don't think I would have lasted.

I will admit that conveying infants or small children that had expired either from sickness or accidents definitely affected me. In fact, a small six-month-old infant expired in my arms. My heart went out to this mother. Then, just a few hours later, I went home and saw my own six-month-old daughter sleeping peacefully in her bed. What could I possibly have told those parents that would have been of any comfort to them? In this particular case it was obvious that the infant was dead and as I held her in my arms, the young mother looked into my eyes and said in a soft, almost pleading voice, "She'll be all right, won't she?"

I've seen death in many forms—the elderly that have expired through natural causes, the sick in mind who have taken their own life, and the accident victim who later just becomes a statistical number in the paper. I've conveyed those that died the violent death of murder and also those who were so close to death that it was just a matter of time before they would go into their last sleep.

Looking at death from a Christian standpoint I don't believe its death itself that people fear, but rather the act of dying; the pain and suffering one may be forced to endure before death itself takes over. Many times I wonder what could have possibly been in the minds of those people who elect to take their own life, and the many who failed in their attempts. Let me relate a few of the conveyances I have made where the party involved completed the act of self-destruction.

It was a cool fall morning when we responded to a call for the ambulance. The operator had told us it was a suicide and that another Squad was already on the scene. We arrived at the home, and as I walked up to the porch I was confronted by a teenage boy who was seated on the steps, his head cradled in his arms and sobbing uncontrollably. I learned later it was he who found his stepmother after she had taken her life. I walked through the house and into the kitchen. A rear door was open which lead into the attic. Silhouetted against the open doorway was a Policeman standing with his head lowered and in front of him what looked like a piece of string dangling from somewhere above. Just beyond the door I noticed an open knife clutched in the Policeman's hand, and at his feet laid the body of a middle aged woman. She was dressed in a robe and slippers and there was a deep crease that ran around the middle of her neck.

Investigation showed the woman had been in a deep state of depression, for the last week, due to an illness which afflicted her. She apparently took clothesline, which was made of wire covered with plastic, went to the attic and tied it to the top of the railing. She tied the loose end of the line around her neck and jumped into the open stairway. Further investigation showed that the line must have broken under her weight and she tied the line together and tried once more. The line apparently broke again and she tied it together for the third attempt. This time rather than jumping and causing the line to snap, she came partly down the steps and then swung the rest of the way by her neck. It apparently was a matter of hours before her stepson found her, and by that time the wire cord had cut its way almost clean through her neck. After finding his stepmother hanging, he slammed the attic door and called the Police. The first Officer on the scene opened the door and came face to face with her hanging body.

After overcoming the shock of this ghastly sight, he opened his pocketknife, grabbed the woman around the waist and cut the cord. Her dead weight was too much for him and he had to let her drop to the floor. She fell to the floor face first and smashed her nose. As she had been dead for quite some time, rigor mortis had started to set in her body and her nose stayed flat up against her face. Her bowels also had let loose and the sight and stench were almost beyond description. What could possibly have gone through this woman's mind to be able to bare such self-inflicted pain is something that is completely beyond my realm of thought. It was evident that she had tried three times before she had completed her act. Her desire for self-destruction must have been overwhelming.

I conveyed another suicide victim from the basement of a very modest home. He had just eaten supper with his wife and told her that he was going in the basement for a few minutes. His wife apparently thought nothing of it until she heard a muffled shot. She called her husband's name from the top of the basement stairs and, not hearing a response, proceeded down the steps. What she saw caused her to faint, and as she awoke she went into complete shock. She ran to her neighbors screaming that her husband had shot himself, they in turn called us.

The sight that greeted her as she entered the basement would have made most anybody lose all sense of reality. Her husband had placed a 12-gauge shotgun in his mouth and pulled the trigger. The tremendous force of the gun took the top of his head completely off (from the bridge of his nose on up). It further splattered the contents of his head all over the ceiling. By the time we arrived and faced this appalling sight, the substance on the ceiling was now dripping to the floor and it was necessary for us to walk through this in order to get to the body. In a situation like this, when it was obvious to us that the subject was dead, we could have called the Medical Examiner. He in turn would call a private ambulance company that conveys mutilated bodies for the county. But the circumstances surrounding this morbid act led us to believe that it would be better for all concerned for us to make the conveyance ourselves. The woman was in a complete state of shock and leaving the body in the house any longer would have just multiplied her grief, so we wrapped the body in a rubber sheet and made the conveyance to the County Morgue.

Of course, these types of conveyances are few and far between; but it does illustrate the appalling and tragic acts people choose to commit which are parts of our job.

I can also recall conveying a man who placed a 22-caliber rifle in the middle of his stomach and pulled the trigger with his toe. The rifle held nine shots and was a semiautomatic. Apparently, what happened is that after he pulled the trigger the first time his body must have kept jerking, causing the gun to keep on firing. The bullets made a pattern on the man's body, with the last one coming to rest directly between his eyes.

I vividly remember entering the bedroom of a home after responding to a call, and finding a woman lying in bed with the blankets pulled up to cover her body from the shoulders down. She had a very pleasant smile on her face and as I looked at her I immediately said, "Good evening." I then noticed that the smile on her face and the stare in her eyes were rigid and unchanging. I pulled the blankets back from her body and observed a hole about the size of a nickel in the center of her chest. There was very little blood but there was also no sign of life. Her husband had just brought her home from the hospital after having serious surgery. The thought of being bedridden and having a lingering illness caused the woman to place a thirty-eight caliber pistol to her chest and pull the trigger. The shot was muffled by the blankets and as she shot herself, her arm fell to the side of the bed and the gun dropped from her hand landing a few inches under the bed. Her husband was in the next room watching television and went to check on her. After getting no response from her, he thought she had passed out or possibly had had a heart attack. He called the Police for an ambulance, and when we told him that his wife had committed suicide, he was overcome with disbelief. Not until we showed him the gun and his wife's body did he fully realize what had happened.

I conveyed a few people who have tried to commit suicide by carbon monoxide poisoning. But only one had actually completed the act. I suppose the worst situation I had to respond to was not an official suicide attempt, but was a young teenage girl who had tried to commit an abortion with an ice pick and died from internal bleeding.

I'm not sure if statistics would bare me out, but I have found that the majority of suicide attempts are made by digesting an overdose of some type of pills. The greater number of these people never completed the act, although after their treatment at the hospital, they sometimes wished they would have. The treatment generally administered to these pill takers is to have their stomachs pumped, which I have been told is a most nauseating procedure.

Another means of suicide, which is quite common, is the act of cutting one's wrists, thereby severing the main artery in their arm. In fact, I recall an instance of this nature which occurred right in the Police station. I was seated at a desk in the station one night when a Squad Officer brought in a juvenile about sixteen years old for some minor offense. In those days we didn't put juvenile offenders in cells unless they were violent, and then they were put in cells in a different room from the adults. Those cells were formerly used for female prisoners, but this practice was discontinued and all females were then held at the main station downtown.

On this particular night, this young man didn't appear to be troublesome, so he was placed in a chair next to me and I was to keep an eye on him. I remembered having come in contact with the boy on a previous occasion and also recalled that he had an emotional problem. I didn't know his complete background, but did recollect that he came from a broken home and was being raised by his over protective grandparents. Besides having an emotional problem, he also had odd tendencies which were pronounced by his false eye lashes, drawn eye brows, long fingernails complete with polish and his hair combed in bangs. Knowing something of his background he was actually a tragic sight. I tried to talk to him as he sat next to me, but he immediately made it known that he had no use for Cops and that as soon as his grandfather would come for him he'd make it bad for us. Having nothing more to say to him I went back to some paper work and didn't pay much more attention to him. He suddenly jumped from his chair and plunged his hand through a window we were sitting next to. In the same lightning fast movement he spun around and sprayed myself, my paperwork, and my desk with deep red blood. It was obvious he had suffered a deep gash in his wrist. My partner was standing just a few steps away and immediately grabbed his arm above the wound and squeezed it until the flow of blood was just a trickle. I believe that fast action by my partner may have saved his life, because in that brief moment the young man had lost a tremendous amount of blood. We sat him down on a chair, applied a tourniquet and prepared him for a trip to the hospital. As he sat there I looked into his very pale face and he responded by saying, "Don't let me die, please don't let me die." This was true fear.

I don't want to leave the impression that every conveyance I made was a ghastly or gruesome event. In fact, the majority of them were just matters of conveying a sick or injured person, very uneventful but yet never repetitious. One of these conveyances that started out to be quite ordinary, but had a very unusual ending was when my partner and I entered a home in response to a call for the ambulance for a sick person. It was a very modest home and the occupants were of oriental descent. A middle aged woman met me at the door and led me at a fast pace to a rear bedroom. There I found an elderly woman, very robust in stature, lying on the floor next to a bed. I bent down next to her and after getting no response to a few questions I asked, I noticed a grey pallor in her face and just a faint trace of breathing. It was quite obvious that the woman was very close to death. We laid the stretcher next to her and fixed our blankets and pillow, and were about to place her on the stretcher when the young woman suddenly stated, "No, no! Don't touch her; the Doctor is on his way".

I told her that it would probably be better if we rushed her to the hospital, but she insisted the doctor was coming, and in a case like this I had found its better not to argue. On hearing this, my partner immediately went to the ambulance and brought the portable resuscitator and applied full resuscitation. The woman seemed to breathe somewhat better with help of the machine, but she still looked pretty bad. It must have taken at least a half-hour to forty-five minutes for the doctor to arrive; in fact, it was necessary for us to change oxygen tanks once during the time we waited.

When the doctor arrived he knelt next to us and my partner removed the resuscitator, which made it evident that the only thing that had kept the woman breathing was the apparatus itself. My partner was situated just to the left of the doctor and next to the woman, and I was bent over at her foot end. The doctor tore open her nightgown and dealt three or four sharp blows to her chest with his closed fist. I had witnessed this act before so it wasn't a great shock to me, but what transpired next was my first encounter with a cardiac injection.

The doctor opened his ever present black bag and removed from it a bottle of liquid, to which he inserted a needle that seemed to be about four inches in length and was attached to a syringe which at first sight seemed to be about six or eight inches long. Just the sight of the needle and syringe sent a chill up my spine. He transferred the liquid from the bottle to the syringe and then suddenly held it in front of us and without changing his sober expression exclaimed, "Have either one of you done this before?"

Well, my partner and I both must have had the same idea, because his mouth dropped open and he moved back about three or four feet to get out of the way of this strange looking contraption. It most certainly wasn't the intention of the doctor, but we had the impression that he wanted one of us to administer whatever he was about to do. In almost the same motion as he had put this thing in front of us, he plunged the needle into the woman's chest where I, without a medical background, would have estimated her heart to be. After the act was completed he looked at us and said, "If that didn't do it, nothing would." He then took out his stethoscope and after finding no response, stood up and stated, "Well, she's passed away." At this point my partner covered the woman's face and body with a blanket and the doctor went to the other room to notify the waiting relatives.

In the meantime, I took the resuscitator back to the ambulance and brought back the necessary paper work, which included a death certificate. The family was going to make the arrangement for removing the body, so we were about to leave when my partner told the doctor that it would be necessary for him to sign the death certificate as it was he that had pronounced her deceased. To this the doctor very flatly stated "I'm not going to sign that paper."

My partner was quite shocked by this and remarked, "Well, why not? It's just to certify that you pronounced her dead and it will be attached to our report." The doctor made no reply and just started to put his hat and coat on. My partner scratched his head for a few moments as though he were deep in thought and then remarked, "Look Doc, I hate to say this, but if you don't sign this certificate I'm going to have to arrest you, because as far as I'm concerned, that woman was alive until you stabbed that needle in her chest."

The doctor snatched his pen from his coat and said, "Well, if that's the way you feel about it, here, I'll sign the damn thing." The doctor seemed somewhat perturbed, but we were satisfied and I could not help but think that that's what makes this job so interesting, something new and something different every night.

The question that has been asked of me many times is, "What conveyances stand out most vividly in your mind?" I never really gave it a great deal of thought, but now that it has been some time since I have been on the ambulance, I would have to say auto accidents—the tragedies on the road, maimed, mangled, mutilated and disfigured bodies. These are events that come into your life in an instant but take an eternity to forget.

One of those tragedies that I will never forget occurred on a cool, crisp morning in March, 1960. My memo book contains just a few lines, the name, address and age of the victim, the place conveyed from and the hospital to which they were conveyed. Then the brief description of: compound fracture of both legs, internal injuries, in extreme pain and shock. She stated that she didn't know what happened, just that her husband is a very careful driver." Unbeknown to her, he was already lying dead at the scene.

This was followed by notation No. 2, which indicated that we had conveyed two parties from the scene. The second person I described as a female followed by her name, age and address, then this depiction: severe lacerations to face and legs, fractured pelvis, skull fracture, subject was in a state of shock and I was unable to converse with her. The notations in my book were made after our return from the hospital, after the doctors determined some of the injuries. This second woman was also widowed by the accident. Earlier in the evening, these two women were the mother and grandmother of ten children, and now these ten children had lost their father and grandfather.

Was this a tragedy? Yes, a tremendous tragedy. What was the cause? Who can ever tell for sure? Six people were involved, two already dead and several maimed for the rest of their natural life, and all it took was a matter of seconds. We found the grandmother in the back seat of one of the autos; jagged bones protruding from both her legs. The mother was under the auto with part of the back seat. Investigation showed that she, along with part of the seat, flew out the back window.

At the time of this writing it has been nine years since I saw this woman, but I'll never forget her. We placed her in the ambulance and there was just nothing I could do for her. The laceration to her face was a long cut across the forehead and it was laid open like you would expect a piece of meat to look after the butcher had cut it with a sharp knife. This particular scene stayed with me for many months.

It was just six days later that I had the unfortunate experience of making another conveyance from an accident scene that stayed with me for a long time. When we arrived on the scene, a somewhat unexpected sight met me. A steam shovel had been parked by the curb during street construction. It was normal in all respects except that a car had wedged its way under the back of it until the rear of the steam shovel was even with the steering wheel of the auto. One ambulance had already been there and left and the driver walked to our rig and sat in the front seat. He had a small laceration to his mouth and while he was being placed in our ambulance, my partner and I were trying to get a young woman out who was being held in by her fractured ankle stuck under the front seat. I felt a lot of blood, but in the darkness I was unable to tell where it was coming from. We got her out of the car, placed her on a stretcher and rolled the stretcher into the ambulance. I got in beside her and noticed that the complete upper part of her body was covered with blood. What was once a white sweater was now, for the most part, crimson red. I removed the pillow from under her head and was met by a hideous sight. She had a deep sever cut right across her throat. I immediately placed a large compress across the opening, but the blood kept oozing out. I placed another compress on top and kept pressure with my hand across her throat. The blood seemed to flow more slowly through my fingers and because of the lack of color in her face I thought we might be too late. By the time we reached the hospital, the blood had coagulated around my fingers and I was afraid to move them for fear that the wound would start to bleed again. It was not until another Officer at the hospital helped us out of the ambulance, and we had her in front of a doctor, that I removed my hand and let the doctor take over. An hour before, this must have been a beautiful girl, but now with her neck as it was, a deep cut to her cheek and the pockets of her eyes filled with glass, I wondered if the miracles of medicine could possibly bring back her beauty.

I took a statement from the driver, and his story was that he wasn't going very fast but that a car came at him and forced him into the steam shovel. At this point I had no reason to disbelieve him, but then I heard the statement from the first party conveyed from the scene. It was very brief, but he told a different story. "He was going very fast and it seemed like he lost control just before the accident, there wasn't another car on the road."

Just the night before, a driver we were conveying made this statement to me: "All of a sudden the car I hit pulled right in front of me from off a side street and I couldn't stop." The disposition of this one? This young gentleman had struck a parked, unoccupied auto.

I mentioned before how involved one can get with emotions and feelings in ambulance work, but I think what concerned me the most was the thought of what I may bring home to my family, almost like being a carrier of some contagious disease.

I recall the first time the hospital called the station after we had made a conveyance, and notified the Lieutenant on duty that the party we had brought to the hospital had meningitis and they considered it highly contagious. The Lieutenant called us in and relayed this information. We immediately took our ambulance out of service and scrubbed it with disinfectants. After this was done, the thought came to us that we also were possibly contaminated with the germ from this disease. We conveyed our thoughts to the Lieutenant and he immediately called the hospital to find out what shots or precautions we should take.

The doctor he talked to may have satisfied some of our concerns, but it gave me very little satisfaction when he said, "We come in contact with contagious diseases all the time and usually don't get sick, so I don't think you have anything to worry about. Tell your Officers to clean all their equipment with a disinfectant and if they become sick within the next few days to notify the hospital of what they came in contact with." This was all fine and well, but what would I tell my wife if one of my children got sick in the next few days, and I told her they might have meningitis because I may have brought the germ home with me? My wife always understood, but I know of a few Officers' wives who gave their husbands the ultimatum of either getting off the ambulance or losing their happy home.

As I went through my memo books, I realized I've conveyed people with measles, mumps, chickenpox, tuberculosis, polio and some afflictions that I can't even pronounce without a medical dictionary. But all in all, I can honestly say I don't regret those years on the ambulance, as they will leave me with many thoughts for the rest of my life.

4. In the Station

After my tenure on the ambulance, I spent about another year just working in the station. It wasn't the most exciting part of my career but it gave me a chance to see part of Police work that doesn't come to the public's eye. And even in the station, the reactions of people just never ceased to amaze me. I would say the majority of people who came to the station, paid their fines or filed their complaints without any adverse feelings. But then there was always that small minority who thought the Officer was definitely getting a percentage from the fine. They felt that as long as it was going to cost them money, they would voice their opinion and tell us exactly how to run the whole show. Most of what these good citizens would say would be taken with a grain of salt, and saying, "Yes sir, whatever you say, sir," would usually pacify them. But on occasion some obnoxious individual would come to the station and express himself so vehemently that he would talk himself right into a cell.

One of these instances occurred, after a young man in his early twenties was arrested for disorderly conduct and brought to the station to be booked and detained. In other words, he was interviewed, searched and locked in a cell. A few minutes after he arrived, two of his friends came in the front door and it was obvious by the look on their faces and the tone of their voices that they were not in a congenial mood. The first youth approached me and stated they came to get their buddy out of jail and asked me how much money I wanted. I told them that their friend had just been brought in and it would be a while before he was processed and bail would be set, to which the youth replied "Look punk, what kind of flunky joint do you run here? Who the hell do you think you are? I've got more money here than you make in a month." At which time he flashed a roll of bills that looked like at least two months of my salary. It became quite obvious from our short conversation that I was about to have somewhat of a problem with these young gentlemen, and I knew from past experience that they would come out on the short end of anything that would transpire.

I most certainly wasn't looking for any trouble, so I let them rattle on for a few minutes and tried to pacify them. When this obviously was not going to work, I told them to sit down and shut up or leave. Their answer to this was, "No punky ass Cop tells us what to do. I pay your wages." By this time I had just about enough, so I gave them the ultimatum of either leaving and coming back a little later or going to jail. They thought for a few minutes and then turned around and left, with the parting words, "Kiss my ass, fuzz."

You know, I think back to when I was their age. I most certainly was no knight in shining armor; in fact, I got in more than my share of trouble, but the last thing my friends and I would think of doing would be to go to a Police station and mouth off. Right or wrong, I always had the greatest of respect for the blue uniform. This was instilled in me as a child, and it was not fear, but genuine respect. My parents taught me from little on that the best friend I had besides them was the Policeman.

Well, it was only about fifteen or twenty minutes later that the two young gentlemen came back and their attitude hadn't changed. A few more words of profanity were issued on my behalf and then the youth with all the money pulled his roll from his pocket and told me that either I let his friend go or he would call his attorney. "You know," he said, "I think your wife goes out and screws at night while you're at work."

This was the statement that did it. I had taken all his guff up to this point, but this was more than I could stomach. There was a desk in front of me and a rail behind that, but I didn't bother to go around either one. Apparently, the sight of me coming over the rail at them must have brought some thoughts of dread into their minds. They turned around and headed towards the door. I must have still been in the air when I hollered out that they were both under arrest. The first youth turned around and took a feeble swing at me and this was all I needed. I taught him a lesson that I do not think he forgot for a long time (still only using enough force to affect the arrest). I picked him off the floor and threw him into the booking room. I then took off after the other individual who I thought for sure I would have to chase down the block. But he had hesitated at the front door long enough to leave the parting words, "I'll get you f—ing Cops for this." As the last word came out of his mouth I was all over him like a blanket. There was little resistance and within a few minutes they were both in their respective cells. Like I said before, I don't get any particular enjoyment out of making arrests, but this one gave me a great deal of satisfaction.

The next day in court I gave my testimony in front of the Judge. After my two degenerate friends gave their side of the story, the Judge gave the following statement: "By oath, Officers of the law have been instructed to enforce the laws and ordinances of the city and state, and in doing so they have also been instructed that they would have to take even more than the normal amount of verbal abuse. But, I feel that from the testimony I have heard, you two individuals surpassed even that which a Police Officer should take." Disposition: fifty dollars and court costs or thirty days in the House of Correction.

Don't people realize we have hearts and feelings, too? That we are not made of rock or wood or some substance that can take constant abuse without damage being done to our inner most self? Just how far can a human being be pushed without striking back?

Of course, not every incident that occurred in the station was of a violent nature. In fact, many of them were quite comical—like the time three young teenage boys came into the station and told me that some guy, who they thought was drunk, had been following them in their car for the last half hour. I asked them when was the last time they saw him, to which they replied. "This guy followed us right to the front of the Police station; in fact he should be out there right now." I told them I would take a look, and led the youths out the front door. Sure enough, there was their car parked at the curb, and another car parked directly behind them, only about five feet out into the street and kind of on an odd angle. I walked to the driver's side of the other auto and observed a man seated behind the wheel with both hands fixed to the steering wheel and his eyes fixed straight ahead as though he was in deep concentration. I opened the car door and asked the man to get out. He looked at me with his glassy eyes and asked, "Am I home now?" This guy was one of the worst drunks I had seen in a long time. I asked him if he had any idea where he was. He blubbered out the following statement, with a very heavy tongue. "I just got done bowling, and didn't know where I was, so I thought if I would follow this car long enough, they would take me home. I wonder what my wife is going to say. Maybe I should call a Cop and let him take me home." I assured him that if he would call a Cop, he would probably wind up in jail for the night, and asked him what he thought of the idea of taking a cab home. He said that would be just great. So the three youths and I helped him into the station and sat him on a bench. The three young men thought this was pretty nice and asked if there was anything more they could do. I assured them I could handle the situation and they thanked me and went on their way. I called a cab for the man and one of the other Officers in the station gave him a cup of coffee. The cab came, I gave the cabby his address and we helped him into the back seat. We all went back into the station and had a good laugh.

The incident was completely forgotten until the next night, when who should I see come through the front door, but our jolly drunk from the previous night. This time he was obviously in much better condition and was accompanied by a woman who apparently was his wife. He walked up to me and said, "I don't recognize you sir, but according to what a cab driver told my wife last night, some of you gentlemen helped me out last night. I found my car in front of your station this morning, and I want to tell you how much I appreciate everything you did for me. I don't make it a habit of going out and getting smashed; in fact, I seldom even drink. But, it was just one of those nights where it all caught up to me. If I would have been picked up for drunken driving, it most certainly would have cost me my job. Once again I would like to thank you and your fellow Officers for what you did, and in the future if you should ever need any assistance, you can be assured of my full support." With this the man pulled out a two pound can of coffee from a bag he had been holding and stated, "This is just a small token of appreciation." I thanked the man for the coffee, and felt the Police Department had gained a friend for life.

This goes to show that incarceration is not the answer for every violation of the law. It would have served absolutely no purpose had we locked this man in a cell. I think he was far more impressed with the treatment he received. Of course, this is only one individual. I'm sure there were many others who received a similar break that were heard the next day telling their buddies, "Boy did I play those Cops for a bunch of fools last night." Many judgments are made in an instant, and when they are made in a brief moment, one is bound to make an occasional mistake. No one is perfect.

There was another incident that occurred in the station, which shows what a fantastic part fate plays in your everyday life. It also shows why Policemen have to be on their constant guard. I came to work one night, completely relaxed, entered the office, gave my greetings to a few fellow Officers, walked up to the rail and stood there quite unconcerned. I even watched a man walk in the front door with his hands in his coat pockets, not thinking a great deal about him except that he may have wanted to pay a traffic fine or ask for some information. What I had no knowledge of, was that just prior to my coming into the station, a teletype had come over the machine to all districts that an individual had just threatened his wife's life with a gun, shot a couple holes in the wall and walked out stating he was going to take his own life. His description was on the teletype, along with his name, and also that caution should be used as the man may have mental problems.

If I had had time to read the teletype, I would have realized, along with two of my fellow Officers, that the man who walked into the station was the same man as described on the teletype. I walked up to him at the counter, and before I could ask him any questions at all, he started to pull his hand out of his pocket and I saw the butt end of a gun. I was completely shocked and the thought entered my mind that maybe this individual was going to hold-up the Police Station. At that point everything started to happen fast. An Officer grabbed him from behind, wrestled him down, pulled the gun from his pocket and before I could really regain my full senses, another Officer handcuffed his hands behind his back. The man broke into sobbing hysteria. After putting together the full story of what had happened, we all realized that the man had come into the station to give himself up and the gun was unloaded. The whole incident couldn't have taken more than five minutes, but it probably took about five years off my life. I can truthfully say the incident left me quite shaken for the rest of the evening. After discussing it and joking about it, everything was chalked up to just another experience.

At this point, it was 1961; I had about three-and-a-half years on the job, and barring any unforeseen promotion or advancement, I was destined to spend at least another twelve years on the late shift.

I suppose anyone reading this book now would wonder what a teletype machine was unless you go back to before computers. The teletype machine could be described as a character printer connected to a telegraph that operates like a typewriter. In other words, communication between Departments that needed a hard copy would use the teletype machine. I see Officers now that have computers in their Squad cars. Years ago it would take many hours to check to see if a person was wanted or if found driving without his license, to check with the state to verify if he had one.

Unless one's family can become accustomed to abnormal working hours, it's most everyone's dream and ambition to work during the day. For this reason, I was quite elated when I was approached by the day shift Sergeant and asked whether I would like to work a few months on the day shift. I related my extreme desire to him with the promise that he would be extremely satisfied with the results that I could produce for him. I came home and told my wife that I was going days. Even though it was just for a few months, this was like giving her a Christmas present. Just the thought of going to work at 8:00 in the morning, coming home at 4:00 in the afternoon; living like a human being, socializing with friends that we had lost with my odd hours, becoming acquainted again with neighbors whom I had lost contact with was something that words cannot explain.

It was quite natural, that several Officers with more time on the job than I were quite disgruntled at the choice the day shift Sergeant had made. I was determined to do everything in my power to stay days as long as I could. For the last three-and-a-half years I had been going to work when everybody else went to bed and coming home in the morning when everybody else was leaving for work.

My first day shift assignment was on the paddy wagon with a day shift man who had about thirty years on the job. I suppose quite naturally he regarded me as a young punk that would be more of a millstone around his neck than anything else. It's also quite natural to assume that the violence that occurred during the hours of the night shift was not as frequent as during the daytime. My first assignment was just a normal conveyance. We were to transfer a MO (a mentally disturbed person) from a private hospital to the County General Hospital. I had made numerous conveyances like this in the past and had a great deal of self-confidence that I could handle this with no trouble at all.

My older partner backed the wagon into the ambulance entrance and with somewhat of a sarcastic note, made it known that my job was just to follow him, keep my mouth shut, and do exactly as he said. We were taken up to the locked ward of the private hospital and there we were met by several interns. In their midst was standing a wild-eyed young man in his early twenties, quite well built, and obviously not having control of his full senses. I made my first mistake by suggesting to my older partner that it would be smart to put the young man in restraints. This obviously was disdainful to him and he let me know by saying, "I'll show you how to handle these guys, all it takes is just a little smooth talk." So we walked up to the young man, gave him a few words of encouragement, told him everything was going to be alright, just to come along with us, and for the next few minutes everything did go fine. We went down in the elevator, walked through the halls, and even though I had the feeling that something was going to happen, everything seemed to go just perfect.

We opened the rear door of the wagon and in the next brief instant I knew what I had done wrong. I had left the front door of the paddy wagon open and as I made a dash for the front door, the young man beat me there. He came flying out, caught me off guard and I went sprawling on the ground. I picked myself up off the ground and the chase started. We ran several hundred yards across the hospital grounds and I was never more than ten or fifteen feet behind him—across a busy street, through a parkway and down a steep hill which led to a flooded creek, maybe twenty yards across. I figured now I had him for sure; but the young man never broke his stride and made one headlong dive right into the creek and started to swim across. I was weighted down with all my gear and I thought it would be stupid for me to dive in after him so I ran for a bridge just a few yards away. Another Officer who had been summoned met me at the bridge and together we pursued the young man, who by now had gained some distance on us. We ran several blocks and by this time my heart was pounding so hard I thought it would break through my skin. As we turned a corner, I caught a quick glimpse of the individual as he ran in the front door of one of the modest homes nestled in this particular area. As we reached the home I was surprised to see a middle aged woman dressed only in a slip and a middle aged man, presumably her husband, dressed in a robe come flying out the same front door our eluding friend had entered. The woman was screaming hysterically that there was a mad man in her house. By this time several Squads had arrived, at the calling of my older partner, who was also on the scene with the wagon. We were informed by the owner of the home that he had a gun collection in the house and a large amount of ammunition. Two other Officers, without fully realizing the danger, and me, stormed through the front door and with as much caution as was permissible started a search of the residence. We checked the living room, bedrooms, closets and basement. We were standing in the kitchen trying to decide whether the young man had crawled into the attic space, when for some unknown reason I opened the closet door in the kitchen and came face to face with the somewhat wild man that I had been chasing. He was dripping wet and in almost a hysterical state. He leaped out at me, knocked me to the ground, and started to claw at my clothing. The other two Officers pounced on top of the two of us and for a few seconds we were engaged in a struggle where no one seemed to have the upper hand. By shear strength we subdued the individual, handcuffed his hands behind his back and cuffed his ankles together.

Unbeknown to us at this time, the roving T.V. reporter who had picked up this activity on his Police radio was stationed outside with his T.V. camera rolling, along with several hundred bystanders. We carried the young man out dripping wet and bleeding from a small laceration he had received from the struggle. All of this, the T.V. cameras, the excitement, my not being able to catch my breath from the previous chase, the wrestling match, and the further thought that everything that had occurred was my fault, left me with the thought that I'd do anything if I could just start that day all over again.

Within a few minutes we had the young man in the wagon and were on our way to the hospital, where I was met by an assortment of comments from my older partner which included, "You dumb asshole, that's all I need is somebody like you around." figured for sure I'd be back on the late shift the next night. But, after everything was over and I related my apologies to the other Officers involved, I was assured that no serious damage had been done and that maybe now I realized that the day shift wasn't all that it was cracked up to be.

I spent three months on the day shift during the summer and it was a real pleasure coming home in the evening, spending time with my family. I was really enjoying my day job. Those three months flew by and before I knew it, I was back on the late shift. It took me a few days to adjust, but soon I was back in the old routine, going to work at 11:30 p.m. and leaving for home at 8:00 a.m.—baring any overtime.

A few months later (I believe it was in December) elections came up for the Police Board of Inquiry, which is a board directed to hear all the testimony at the hearing of a member of the Department charged with any violation of the orders or rules and regulations of the Department. Each year patrolmen from each District Stations elect two patrolmen who, with others elected from the other districts, constitute the panel on the Board of Inquiry along with three other higher ranking representatives. I believe this practice ended when the Police Union was formed.

The Police Department, as I stated previously, is a semi-military organization and as such this Board of Inquiry fell along the same lines as your military court marshal hearing. When I came on the job, I was told to stay away from strange women and booze and I would have a lifetime profession. This by-and-large was very true. There were, of course, rules by which we were governed and which we had to comply with and any infraction of the same could cost the Policeman his job: commission of a felony or misdemeanor under any law or ordinance whatsoever, which covers an extremely large field. Some of these rules were as follows:

Intoxication, cowardice, indulgences in narcotic drugs, insubordination or disrespect toward a superior Officer, overbearing oppressive or tyrannical conduct in the discharge of duty. Neglect of duty. Neglect or disobedience of any order. Absence from duty without leave. Immorality. Conduct unbecoming a member and detrimental to the service. General inefficiency and incompetence. Incapacity for duty, either mental, physical or educational. Breach of discipline. Neglect or refusal to pay just debts. Communicating information relating to Police work without permission. Making a false official statement. Willful mistreatment of a prisoner. Discourtesy or insolence. Untruthfulness. Sleeping while on duty. Uncleanness in person or dress. Smoking while in uniform while in public. Accepting a bribe. Keeping a fee, gifts, or reward. Criticizing Department orders. Aiding persons to escape arrest. Refusing to give badge number when requested. Neglecting to give a receipt for property taken from prisoners. Failure to report any member violating rules or orders of Department. Failure to report known violations of laws or ordinances. Of course these rules were not enforced exactly to the point, as strict compliance would be next to impossible. (The previous rules were quoted from rule 44 section 8 of the Department Rules and Regulations.)

My name was placed on the ballot, and since it was not a most sought after position, I had no trouble getting elected to the board. As of this writing, I had been a member of the board for the past six years in which capacity I have sat in on approximately twelve different trials where a fellow Officer had been charged with infractions of a variety of the aforementioned regulations, none dealing with any type of criminal misconduct that would require an appearance in front of a Judge.

The hearing itself was quite formal. The defendant was charged with an accusation and the necessary testimony was heard to substantiate the charge. After this was all over, the defendant was excused and the board would deliberate on his innocence or guilt. If a finding of guilt was made, the board would then make a recommendation as to the penalty. The penalty may have been an official reprimand, the working of several off days, suspension from duty or dismissal from the force. These recommendations were then given to the Chief of Police who after reviewing all the testimony made the final findings. Even though he took everything into consideration, his word was final, and for this reason it has been referred to many times as a Kangaroo Court—where the outcome has been pre-determined before anything is said or before any evidence presented.

It is impossible for me to relate any of the trials that I've sat in on during this period but I can truthfully say I've witnessed many a good Policeman and his family suffer for some minute offense which if he would have been employed by anyone other than a law enforcement agency, it never would have come to the attention of his employer.

During a John Doe Investigation, I sat in on several trials of Police Officers who had committed infractions, which at the time they happened were not uncommon, but which were brought to light by the ever so perfect citizenry of our community. I might also bring out that under our present administration I truly believe our Police Department is free of any corruption, uncleanness or tainted in any way. I truly believe that the majority of Policemen the world over are as faultless, impeccable, and unblemished as is humanly possible; but there can always be a bad apple in the barrel and for this reason the rules are made and they must be enforced. My membership on this board opened my eyes to the fantastic and intricate workings of this huge organization and I can also say it has been very gratifying. Like I wrote earlier, this was before the Police Union was formed, which is when the Board of Inquiry was disbanded. Some say for the good and some say the bad. The union would always stand up for the Copper, right or wrong, and many times the Copper would come out on the short end. The union decided that a Copper's off days could not be taken away, so instead of the Copper working a couple of his off days for punishment, he could be suspended without pay and this would affect his family monetarily.

5. The One-Man Patrol Car

After my brief tour on the day shift, I spent several more months working nights inside the station. It was then that I started to realize that what I had been doing up until now was very interesting, but was becoming somewhat stale and I needed a change. talked it over with my wife and decided to go on the street. I never quite realized what a radical change this would be. It had been about five years since I had patrolled the streets at night. In those five years, the area had drastically changed. The core area, or high crime area, had expanded quite rapidly in those five years and those areas, which I remembered as being quiet and peaceful, had now turned into the proverbial jungle almost overnight.

I spent the first few nights getting reoriented and adjusting to the change of being on the street and dealing with the citizenry in a different frame of mind than when I worked in the station. Within a few nights I started to ride a one-man car. This was a fantastic experience. It has its good points and it's bad. You were more or less your own boss; you came and went as you pretty well pleased except for your radio dispatches. Any decisions you made, you alone would suffer the consequence, and when you left the Squad for some reason, you were really alone—there were no portable radios or cell phones.

I can remember one of the first accidents I covered. I was sent to a hit and run accident—pole struck. When I arrived on the scene, that's exactly what I found. I found a pole struck, I found a fender of a car, I found a bumper of a car, I found 199 feet of skid marks. The only thing that was missing was the rest of the car and the driver. The operator of this unknown vehicle apparently had lost control around a curve, skidded across the street, struck the pole and left the scene. At this point there seemed to be no witnesses so I was about to write up a simple hit and run accident when three young men came on the scene and said, "Hey Copper, we know where the car is." They had witnessed the accident and had followed the heavily damaged auto and the drunken operator for several miles through the city streets until he finally parked in a tavern parking lot, crossed the street and went into a house. They took me to the car and it was hard for me to believe that this car had been moved by anything but a tow truck. As far as I was concerned, it was a total wreck. The young men pointed out the house across the street and told me that's where the driver had staggered.

I went to the home, rang the doorbell and was met by an elderly couple; the time being about 2:30 in the morning. I apologized for waking them and asked them if they knew who parked the car across the street and who might have come into their residence. They stated their son had come home a short time before and was now in bed. I asked if I could talk to him for a few minutes and they led me to a back room of their home. There I found a man in his late twenties lying on his bed fully clothed. He had a slight laceration on his forehead and apparently was so drunk that he had regurgitated all over the bed. The smell in the bedroom reeked of alcohol and it was several minutes before I could awaken the individual to the point where I could ask him a few questions. About the only thing I could get out of his slobbering speech was that he was driving on some unknown street and thought that he may have bumped into something.

This wasn't his first time through the mill as he had sense enough to say that he had brought his car home, parked it next to the tavern, went into the tavern, had about six or eight quick shots of whiskey, and then came home. This and the fact that there was somewhat a lapse in time, I thought it best that he not be arrested for drunken driving so he was ordered to appear in court the next morning.

He appeared the next day and his arrest record showed that he had a problem with drinking and driving. The City Attorney issued a warrant for reckless driving; the subject went to court and was fined $200.00. I thought this was satisfactory as this violation gave him enough points to lose his driver's license and with the cost of the repairs of his totally demolished car, I felt he might have learned a lesson.

A few nights later I observed my first good drunken driver. I had been checking the rear of several business places on my beat when I came to the rear of a tavern that was just closing and saw a panel truck start to drive out of the parking lot. But, rather than use the driveway, he went over the sidewalk, over the curb, and came to a stop at the stop sign on the corner. The street he was entering was divided by a boulevard and when he was turning onto the street, he went over the boulevard, up on the curb on the opposite side, back down, back across the street, back over the boulevard, and proceeded to drive the wrong way on the street. By the time I got behind him with the red light and blew the siren, he had only gone about two blocks and he made a turn down a side street again going over the curb, across the lawn and down the other side of the street. I continued to blow the siren and he suddenly made a turn into the side drive of a home in the middle of the block. He missed the drive, went up the curb, over the front lawn and came to rest in somewhat of an awkward position—in the middle of the driveway, but facing the wrong way. The door of the truck immediately opened and out stepped a middle-aged man. Nothing was too unusual except that when he stepped out he fell to his knees and started to crawl towards me. I picked him up, set him up against the Squad car, looked into his bloodshot eyes and asked him how he possibly could have considered driving in the state he was in;

to which he replied, "How the hell do you expect me to drive, I've got forty thousand percent alcohol in me and haven't driven in years." I arrested the gentleman for drunken driving. Further checking showed that he had no driver's license at all. We went to court and after two or three adjournments he was found guilty and it cost him a total of $300.00 and thirty days in the House of Correction. The penalty he received I felt was very just for such a serious offense.

This brings me to my thoughts on drunken drivers—the seriousness of the offense, the penalties involved, and the object of proving who's too drunk to drive. This has always been a very controversial arrest and is subject to much criticism by all parties involved. It's my personal opinion that all drivers in the United States at one time or another are potential drunken drivers and it all boils down to a matter of who gets caught. Once they're arrested, it's a matter of what tests they take, what tests they refuse, and many times, how good their attorney is—if they have the funds to afford one or if they have one appointed by the court. Take, for example, a drunken driver arrested who takes all the tests, including the test which determines the amount of alcohol in his blood. He goes to court and if he's not represented by an attorney and pleads guilty the usual fine is approximately $150.00 plus court costs and he loses his license for a year. In ninety days he may apply for an occupational license which restricts him to the use of his auto for the purposes of his employment. Or, the same individual goes to court, asks for an attorney appointed by the court or has his own private attorney, he is granted an adjournment for sometime in excess of a month and then gets his attorney. In actuality all he's doing is delaying the eventual outcome and possible penalty. So now the defendant, the arresting Officer, the witnesses and the attorney appear for the third time. At this time the possibility is that the attorney will ask for a jury trial which, in that case, the trial is set for a future date and which all parties must appear for a fourth time.

Then comes the day of the jury trial and all parties involved are present and prepared to present their case. The jury system, in my opinion, is the backbone of the entire judicial system—where the complete human element comes into light—how good the prosecution presents its case, how well the defense is prepared and how the defendant, Police Officers and various witnesses may testify. All this is then set on the shoulders of the six or twelve citizens who must find this individual guilty or not guilty. If he is found not guilty, he keeps his driver's license but the cost of his attorney may exceed possibly $500. If he is found guilty, he loses his license, must still pay the attorney and the cost of the court. Many times it never ceased to amaze me the cost that individuals would incur for the sake of saving their driver's license. Then when it's all over, I'm sure these individuals still fail to realize how easy it would have been to spend three dollars to take a cab, when they most certainly must have realized they were in no condition to drive.

Cars, cars, cars! I'm sure a great majority of the uniformed patrolman's time is spent chasing cars, checking on cars, following cars and investigating cars involved in a variety of accidents. I can recall one very interesting incident that involved a car full of juveniles. There was a one-manned uniform Squad chasing the car. As it turned out, a juvenile without his father's permission took the car. The juvenile, being only fifteen years old, did not have a driver's license and his driving skill left much to be desired, which apparently was the reason the Police Officer attempted to stop him in the first place.

Once the Officer turned his red light on and blew his siren, the juvenile tried to elude the Officer in the following manner:

He went west on the street that eventually became a dead end and rather than stopping or turning at the dead end, he proceeded over the curb, up the front lawn, coming to rest just inches away from a house. The Squad stopped at the curb and the Officer was about to get out when the juvenile put the car in reverse, came back across the lawn, over the curb and struck the Squad. He then proceeded north down the street with the Squad in pursuit. Back up over the curb, over the sidewalk, down the lawns and in front of a row of houses knocking down several trees, back across the sidewalk, over the curb and once again striking the Squad. He continued north on the street once again, up the curb and driving in a reckless manner, straight down the sidewalk. When the juvenile came to the end of the block he was once again met by the Squad and proceeded to run into it with such force that both vehicles were unable to move.

All the juveniles involved left the scene but the Officer apprehended the driver, and through questioning he related the names of his friends, including his younger brother. The irony of the whole incident is that the juveniles were written up for operating without the owner's consent, driver's license law, reckless driving, and eluding a Police Officer. They went to the Children's Court and received a grand total of one year's probation, which is the same as a light slap on the hand. The father of this individual received the cost, in excess of $1,000.00, for all damage done plus the cancellation of his insurance. Here this poor man was home in bed and yet, because of the actions of his son, he was faced with a great monetary loss.

Chases involving adults are usually somewhat different for the simple reason that they can handle the car better than the juvenile can. I have been involved in numerous chases; but they're never the same and each one has its unusual twist.

I was checking the back of my business places once again early one morning—about 3:00 a.m., when I spotted a truck parked next to a beer depot with two occupants in it. I recognized the truck as belonging to the beer depot and when I approached it from the rear with the Squad, the truck started to move slowly out into the street, which at that point was a boulevard. It had two occupants and I was traveling by myself. The driver made a U-turn around the boulevard strip, still going very slow and I was only maybe twenty or thirty yards behind him. I made the U-turn and the chase was on. It was a late model truck and I had an older Squad that I was using in relief of my regular Squad and I had somewhat of a difficult time just staying with him—through the alleys at a high rate of speed, up and down the side streets, through several stop signs—all with the red light and siren blaring. At one point I attempted to grab the microphone and call for help, but at that particular time I had to make an abrupt turn and my microphone dropped to the floor and was lost for the remainder of the chase. We stayed within eight or ten blocks of the beer depot, just kept going up and down the side streets and through the alleys until finally, much to my amazement, the truck came to rest in the parking lot of the beer depot in the exact spot where I first saw the truck. I jumped from my Squad, my gun drawn, and ordered the occupants of the truck out. They complied with my request and placed their hands on the hood of the truck while I retrieved my microphone and called for additional Squads. I felt sure I had either surprised auto thieves or possibly burglars. But, as it wound up the driver was a young individual in his late teens that worked for the beer depot, had obtained an extra set of keys and made it a habit of borrowing the truck in the early morning hours and going for a joy ride. He was found guilty the next morning of reckless driving, which was amended to imprudent driving and was fined $200, including costs, which he could not come up with so he was to spend the next sixty days in the County Jail. The only thing I gained through the whole experience was about six or eight gray hair and a lesson on how to chase trucks.

It was only a few nights later when I was again involved with a very unusual chase. In fact, this one was of such a reckless manner that it was awarded a small column in the evening newspaper. Once again it was in the early morning hours and I was again traveling by myself and in the process of clocking an auto for speeding, when suddenly this Cadillac passed the car and me that I was clocking at a high rate of speed. I immediately got behind him and got a clocking on him of sixty miles an hour in a thirty mile per hour zone, then he went through a red light and slid around the corner—raising two wheels off the pavement—and coming close to rolling over. By the time I hit the brakes, and adjusted to the fact that he had turned, I slid past the intersection, spun around and raced through a filling station lot to once again get on the street where my elusive friend had gained about six blocks on me. The chase headed straight north through the city with very little turning onto side streets. As the individual went through eight or ten stop signs without slowing his speed much under seventy-five miles an hour, he gained a good deal of distance on me. I was about to abandon the chase when suddenly about three or four blocks in front of me I saw another red light come onto the street—another Squad, not knowing that I was chasing this car, observed it go through the stop sign and took off after it. We entered a housing project, where it was eventually learned that he lived, and the chase was limited to about a ten block area—up and down the side streets, through the parking lots, through the alleys, and finally onto an arterial where the other Squad cut in front of him and ran him onto the curb. I pulled up behind the Cadillac and was so filled with frustration and anger that I leaped from the Squad, ran over to the car, pulled the door open and started to yank on the subject that was behind the wheel. It was obvious at this point that he had been drinking, but not to the extent that he was not in complete control of his combative powers. I tugged long enough to pull the man out of the car and then stood face to face with an individual that must have had at least a sixty pound advantage on me. We traded several punches and finally with the help of another Officer hanging on his back, I was able to knock him to the ground with the other Officer being the full recipient of his weight. We fought on the ground for several minutes until he was subdued with handcuffs. We were all excited, everyone was mad, nothing much was said until one of the other Officers blurted out, "You asshole, look at my hat!" I did not know at first if he was referring to me or to the man we had arrested. It soon became apparent that all three of us had landed on this Officer's hat, which by now looked just like a blob of cloth with a piece of metal hanging on it.

After our arrested subject was taken from the scene in the paddy wagon we attempted to mend the hat to the point where it was wearable and then all sat down and had a good laugh.

The next day in court our elusive friend had sobered up enough to realize how wrong he was and he apologized to the point where we almost felt sorry for him. His arrest record showed he had been picked up in excess of fifty times for a variety of offenses—from drunk to disorderly to battery to resisting arrest to numerous driving violations which had cost him his driver's license years ago and he had never been able to regain it. He pleaded guilty to the charge of eluding a Police Officer and driving without a driver's license and because of his almost appalling record, was fined $250 plus court costs and sixty days in the House of Correction.

It's really funny how the night before, the other Officers and myself were so infuriated with this individual that he could have been sent to jail for life and we probably couldn't have cared less; and now the next morning, talking with him in a sober state, it came to light what a real problem this individual had. He told us he was a full-blooded Indian and that just a few drinks would really set him off. In the last few years he'd lost his home, his wife, numerous jobs, and all for the sake of alcohol. At this point in the story he actually broke down and started to sob. This made me feel completely useless, because by sending him to jail for sixty days all that had really been accomplished was to take him out of circulation for two months. Unfortunately, he most certainly would not gain the needed help he required nor would his life change once he was released.

Here was a human being with a debilitating problem and yet humanity had turned its back towards him and without the proper help and guidance the rest of his life would be filled with nothing but despair. But once again, my thoughts of compassion lasted only for a few brief minutes and by the time I went to work that night I had completely forgotten about this individual. The truth being that your mind must be free and clear at all times in order to cope with the many individuals who seek to make a farce out of the law itself and the uniform of the Police Officer. The very next night, in fact, someone tried to pull the wool over my eyes by pulling a stunt, which I had never run into before.

It was quite early in the morning when I ran across these three young men seated next to their motorcycles. I was fairly familiar with the area and having never run into these individuals before; I stopped and questioned their presence in the area. Since I was alone and there were three of them, they must have felt as if they had the upper hand and my questions were met with several abusive remarks. Taking this all into consideration and after a good fifteen or twenty minutes of questioning the subjects I finally got the story that one of them had run out of gas and the fourth had gone to find an all-night gas station. I checked the identification of two of the subjects and the third one stated he had no identification and he had left his driver's license at home. He gave me a name, address and date of birth and after I compiled the information on all three, I walked to the corner Call box and checked all the subjects out with our Detective Clerical Bureau. I was surprised, but also pleased to find that the individual without the identification was wanted on three minor warrants. At this point I asked for another Squad to meet me and by the time I had gotten back to my Squad a second one-man car had arrived. I told him what I had and together we walked over to the subject wanted on the warrants and I advised him that he was under arrest for the several warrants and that he would have to come along to the station and make good for them. At this point he started to laugh hysterically and told my partner and I, "That's really got to be funny, because that's not really me," at this he reached into his pocket and pulled out a crumbled driver's license, gave it to me and said, "This is really me." Well, to make a long story short, he apparently wanted to be a big man in front of his friends and thought he'd joke around by giving me the wrong name. I failed to see the humorous note of his actions and subsequently placed him under arrest for obstructing an Officer and took him to court the next morning where he was fined $75.00 plus costs. As we left the courtroom the next day the young individual was about $200.00 shorter than when he was arrested the night before and with a sullen look on his face threw one last remark at me and said, "That's a hell of a note when you guys can't even take a joke."

In large metropolitan cities, one-man patrol cars are most generally assigned outside of your high crime areas. But even so, many times an Officer traveling by himself finds himself involved in situations which leave him wide open for possible repercussions and many times bodily harm. The generally accepted idea of a one-man patrol car is that when the Officer comes upon a situation which calls for the attention of more than one Officer, he is to immediately call for additional help. The idea itself is sound but I can recall many times where the situation didn't appear too severe until I found myself several hundred feet away from my radio.

One of these instances I recall, I was traveling early in the morning and came upon an all night restaurant in a generally more quiet and reserved neighborhood. A young man came running out into the street in front of the Squad car. I slammed on my breaks and he hollered, "Go around to the rear, there's a man lying in the driveway!" Without giving it a thought, I wheeled the Squad around to the rear of the restaurant and as I brought it to a halt my headlights showed on the body lying between two parked cars. I leaped from the Squad and not paying too much attention to the commotion in the parking lot, I knelt down next to the body and saw a young man who was in his early twenties with a deep laceration on the back of his head and the blood oozing out. The noise from the crowd suddenly got louder and more severe and as I looked around, I came to the realization that I walked right into the middle of a gang fight. The fellow lying next to me appeared to be in pretty bad shape but a few feet away there was another young man draped over the front of a car in an awkward position screaming for help and from all outward appearances he seemed to have a pretty bad back injury. Two more people came running towards me with blood streaming from their faces followed by a girl crying hysterically with half her clothes torn off. By this time my heart was pumping at a terrific rate and my first thoughts were that I had to get additional help and ambulances. I made a dash for my Squad car and came within about ten feet of the open door when I was met by another young individual wild-eyed and brandishing a tire iron. All I could hear coming from his mouth was, "Come on Copper, let's see how much you can take!" At this point my mind must have been blank for I never broke stride and hit him full force in the chest with my body. He flew up against my Squad car, fell to the ground, and the tire iron skidded underneath the car. I jumped into the front seat, grabbed for the radio and screamed the approximate address and, "Give me some help!" I again jumped from the car and ran over to the first young man I had seen who by this time was lying in quite a large pool of his own blood. I placed my hand over his gaping wound in his head and felt the blood start to come through my fingers. By this time several minutes had passed and I could hear the sirens in the background, which assured me that help was on the way. Within a few minutes there were more Cops there than there were people and the situation was brought under control. We arrested a half a dozen people and conveyed another half dozen to the hospital; and I came out of the whole thing no worse for wear.

That whole situation brought me once again to realize that the best friend a Cop has are his fellow Officers. It's an unwritten law that when a fellow Officer gets into trouble, you drop everything and go. For without each other, you have nothing. In a tense situation, there is nothing more pleasing to the eye than the sight of several more blue uniforms with the assurance that these men will back you one hundred percent no matter what the situation.

Even though this particular incident lasted less than an hour, it took me the rest of the night to write reports and to gain my composure. I spent most of the next day in court, went home, caught a few hours sleep, and went back to work that night with the idea that I could relax for the first few hours, catch up on my books and just generally take it easy for one night.

I was on the street for less than twenty minutes when my Squad was called with the added information—auto struck home, ambulance sent. I was only about six blocks from the address given. I was the first one on the scene and was met by an appalling sight. I immediately called for at least two more ambulances and another Squad to assist me.

I had arrived on the scene only a few minutes after the accident had happened as the dust was just starting to settle. People were pouring out of their houses, there was screaming and moaning and I saw three bodies lying at grotesque angles on the grass and sidewalk. What had started out as a night of merriment for four young males now had ended in tragedy. I learned later that one of the youths had just returned from the service on leave, and that one of his best buddies was going to take him out on the town. They had several drinks and were on their way home when the young man that was driving became confused with the area and, traveling at a high rate of speed, went through a stop sign, up a curb on the opposite side of the street, missed several trees, and struck the side of a house. The auto struck this two-story home with such force that it embedded itself in the outside wall, collapsed the basement stairs and an inner wall and the stairway leading to the upstairs.

Fortunately nobody in the house was hurt, so my immediate attention was focused on the four youths.

Two of the youths apparently had severe neck and back injuries and possibly internal injuries. With the help of gracious citizens, we made the youths as comfortable as we could on the ground and covered them with blankets. By this time several other Squads had responded and our attention was focused on one young man half in and half out of the car and bleeding from almost every part of his body. We tried to stop most of the bleeding with compresses and by this time the ambulances had arrived and he was the first one to leave the scene. We then attempted to remove the driver from behind the wheel but it became apparent that his legs were pinned in and under the dashboard and it would be necessary for the Fire Department to be called to help remove him.

Before the Fire Department arrived, two other ambulances came on the scene and the two youths lying on the ground were gently placed on cots and rushed to the hospital. The Fire Department arrived and with the help of their jacks and hacksaws, the young driver was removed from the totally demolished auto.

After all the injured had been taken from the scene, the investigation of the accident began—measurements, diagrams, pictures, statements—all this taking approximately one hour and a half. Total property damage including the house was estimated at $10,000. But this was nothing compared to the massive injuries suffered by the four young men. Head injuries, chest injuries, broken pelvis, broken back, broken arms and legs, severe lacerations to the entire body. All this for the sake of a few drinks and speed.

At the scene of an accident such as this, it is surprising the amount of help you get from concerned citizens from the area. Blankets and pillows are brought from their homes and none are really concerned of the thought of the property damage involved. Their first thoughts are for the well-being of their fellow human beings.

Once again I spent several hours writing and by the time I was at the end of my shift. I had just completed catching up in my memo book for the last two days. Again I spent the morning in court, came home by 1:00 or 2:00 in the afternoon, went to bed, slept a few hours, got up, etc., back in uniform and then back to work at midnight. Many times it seemed that you only dressed in your uniform and pajamas.

The night after that tragic accident I left the station with the thought that I'd go and get myself a cup of coffee and park for an hour or so to catch up on some of the reports that I had let go for several days. This time I had only gotten about three blocks from the station when a car came by me at a high rate of speed and slid to a stop at a red light about a block ahead of me. By the time I caught up to him, the car once again took off at a high rate of speed and after I had clocked him, I turned on my red light and siren but the auto failed to stop. He was traveling on a boulevard and apparently wanted to make a left turn, but every time he turned, he'd strike the boulevard median strip and kept going straight. This went on for about six or eight blocks until the auto came to stop at another red light. I jerked the door of the car open and an immaculately dressed elderly man turned his head and said "Who in the hell do you think you are you asshole? Close my door." This man looked like one of the best drunks I'd seen in a long time. I asked him to step out of the car, to which he responded "You damn right I'll get out and punch you right in the mouth." The threat didn't scare me too much because the gentleman got out in an unorthodox style by placing his right hand on the pavement and swinging his left foot out of the car. While in this somewhat awkward position he simply rolled out and lay on the road. From the manner in which he was dressed and the brand new Cadillac he was driving, I was quite sure I was about to become involved with some executive who had more influential friends than I would ever hope to become acquainted with; however, I'm a firm believer that the law is not made for specific individuals. After a few preliminary tests I arrested the man for drunken driving. Following are a few of the tests and results that were given to me by this gentleman.

> "Have you been drinking, sir?"
> "You damn right!!"
> "What did you have to drink?"
> "Whiskey and white soda."
> "How much did you have to drink, sir?"
> "Five or six or eight or ten."
> "Where did you drink this?"
> "It's none of your damn business!"

His clothes were orderly; his attitude was talkative, insulting and profane. His eyes were watery and bloodshot and he had a poor reaction to a light test given him. As far as his balance—his walking and his turning—he fell each time. His breath had a moderate odor of an alcoholic beverage and his face was extremely flushed. He refused to give me a specimen of his handwriting but did give me a specimen of his urine. The results of the urinalysis test were .32% BAC (Blood Alcohol Concentration). In this state, in the 1960's, .15% BAC was considered being under the influence. In other words, this man with .32 percent of alcohol in his blood may have had a hard enough time walking let alone driving a car. Urine tests aren't used anymore and I can remember times that the Copper had to hold the urine container because the prisoner was too drunk to hold it himself. By 2003, all states were following the transportation appropriation bill requiring states to lower their permissible BAC to .08% or risk losing federal highway construction funds.

He was then placed in a cell and after sobering up for several hours, he made a call to his attorneys. It was only a matter of a few minutes before two well known corporate lawyers appeared at the station and my previous assumptions of this man's influential standing in society became known. We found out that he was the president of quite a large corporation. His attorneys were quite pleasant and put up the cash bond for the release of their client. Everything went very smoothly but the gentleman made it known as he walked out of the station that this wouldn't be the last that we'd hear about it; and as I walked past, out of the earshot of his attorneys, he told me that by the time he was done with me, I'd be walking the beat out in the boondocks.

We went to court the next day and naturally an adjournment was given to the defendant. This was just the first of seven adjournments, which did not include an affidavit of prejudice being filed against one Judge. It was about nine months later that the case finally went before a jury. I had one good witness that I had obtained on the street who had observed this man's condition and his driving. The City Attorney and I were counting heavily on this outside witness's testimony, but after the fifth adjournment the witness stated that he couldn't lose any more time from his job or he'd get fired so he refused to appear for the jury trial.

The defendant appeared with his two attorneys, his family, numerous friends and business associates who all gave testimony to the fact that the defendant was not a known drinker and further that his status in society was not to be reckoned with. After all the witnesses and I had given testimony the case was given to the jury. Once again justice ran true to form and the jury found the man guilty of drunken driving and he was fined $100.00 and court costs which actually meant very little to him, but he also lost his driver's license for a year.

The culmination of the case in court, where the jury finds the defendant guilty, always gave me a feeling of self satisfaction. It gave me the feeling that I did my job right and further that justice most generally prevails.

Testimony in court can be extremely trying at times. In fact, many times just a slip in your testimony is picked up by the defense attorney and your case is lost. In fact, it's not unusual at all for the Judge to say to the Officer, "Officer, you've had enough experience in something like this; why aren't you more careful in your choice of words?" It's very embarrassing to lose a case because of poor testimony. First of all you get a dirty look from the prosecuting attorney, then you walk from the courtroom past your fellow Officers who are waiting for their cases to be called and then past the crowd of spectators who are usually present. That is why it's so important to give complete and exact testimony in court so that no doubt is left in the mind of the Judge, and the defense attorney can find no loopholes.

The Early Shift

6. Juveniles and Journeys

After a few months, the opportunity presented itself where I was able to express some of my thoughts and desires regarding the Department to some of my superior Officers. At no time in my career as a Police Officer, up until to this point, had I ever fashioned myself as being an unusually over-exuberant individual. Actually my thoughts, actions, and desires had always been more modest. There were countless Officers who had seen and experienced much more than I. I knew this to be a fact and yet I had to consider myself as an individual. I had never cowered from a man or an act, in fact, through all the physical and verbal abuse I had taken, I never considered myself really beaten because I always considered the source. But, on this one occasion, I became involved in a controversial issue with one of my supervisors, and never really being at a loss for words, I expressed myself quite vehemently. Naturally, I lost. And, the next few months I spent as a Police Officer were the most exasperating of my entire time on the job.

I was taken off the Squad and put in the same category as a brand new patrolman. Every dirty job that came up was given to me. It was a form of harassment that was almost unbearable, and through it all I basically had no one to blame but myself. It was not unusual for me to cut off my nose to spite my face. I was extremely discontent at this point and brought my very dejected disposition home with me each morning. I discussed the entire situation with my wife and thought it might be time for me to find a new vocation. However, just the thought of leaving Police work made me very depressed and dejected. So, instead, I decided to change shifts knowing I would change supervisory Officers, thinking that would take care of my problem.

After working practically my entire career midnight to eight in the morning, it was quite a drastic change for me and my family to start work at four in the afternoon. I believe, in fact, that it affected my family the most for my children were now of school age and many times for days on end I'd leave for work before they returned from school and came home after they were sound asleep. I had an ever present feeling of guilt that I was not doing my full share for the family nor completing my act as a father. It practically left all the responsibility on my wife's shoulders, which she bore ungrudgingly and held no animosity in her heart for me.

I faced my new shift, my new partners, my new bosses, with the attitude and idea that I was starting on a new job. The new shift was truly a difference between night and day. I was immediately assigned to a Squad with a very excellent and capable partner in one of the better neighborhoods in the district. I had spent so much time riding the streets after midnight, where at times they became almost desolate, that it was hard for me to become accustomed to the constant flow of people. The majority of stores were open for the first five hours that I worked, and the taverns and restaurants were open for my full tour of duty.

The majority of the time spent on the 4:00 p.m. to midnight shift—or early shift as it was called—was spent taking complaints and dealing with juveniles. Until this point I hadn't felt that the juvenile problem was as great as it was; the only dealings that I'd ever had with them after midnight was in an official capacity. In other words, almost every juvenile that I'd run into after midnight was either arrested or taken home. But on the early shift, the streets were constantly loaded with juveniles. These youthful, immature, undeveloped offspring's of humanity came in all shapes, forms, sizes and dispositions. The majority of them were the epitome of everything that's good and clean and unblemished. But these were the ones that the Police Officer became least involved with. Only the few that were bad did a Police Officer really get to know on a personal basis; and when dealing with these few it was very necessary to keep in mind that they were in the minority. But this small minority sometimes became so ruthless and cruel that a Police Officer could easily lose faith in the majority of the younger generation.

Where do these bad kids actually come from? Where do they actually get the idea that they can twist society to fit their whimsical moods? The problem of the juvenile delinquent is most certainly not a new one. The older generation has complained about the behavior of juveniles since time itself. The juvenile delinquent as such has always been a problem in our society but they most certainly weren't born that way and they had to learn these facts some time throughout their life. The idea that people form in their minds must have a beginning and many times this beginning was brought on by their parents. The love, discipline and attention that parents show (or fail to show) their children most generally make up their character, but I feel the most important thing a parent can show a child is a good example.

Take for example the father who brings a few items home from work, and makes light of the idea that he didn't have to pay for them because the boss would never miss them. His son or daughter would probably see nothing wrong with going to the store and sneaking off with a five or ten cent item. But the idea that a parent's behavior is at fault for the actions of their child is usually pacified by comments such as, "Now where in the world did he learn something like that." Or, "Is that what they teach them at school nowadays?" A child learns the functions and how to get along in society in school, but the difference between right and wrong must be taught at home and this must be taught at a very tender age.

My own personal feeling is that one of the most contributing factors to juvenile delinquency lies in the breakdown of the family structure. Of course, like I have said, this is just my own personal belief and really has no bearing except in my own home.

The majority of juveniles resent a Police Officer, for the simple reason that he puts a restraint on many of their actions, even though those actions may not fall in accord with those of society.

I believe the main objective in dealing with juveniles is to gain their confidence and respect, neither of which can be obtained by use of force. It was not unusual for my partner and me to spend hours on end doing nothing but talking to the young people in our Squad area. We felt it was part of our job and even more our responsibility to close the very evident gap between their generation and ours.

I found it did absolutely no good to relate to these youths the advantages they had being brought up in decent surroundings compared to other young people from the core area. I found that whether the child comes from a wealthy family or from a poor family, the problem he may have is the greatest thing in the world to him. If someone doesn't take the time and patience to help him understand his problem, he will become a lost soul.

Another dealing I had with what one might label a juvenile gang, I came upon quite by accident. I was given information that a forged and stolen check had been cashed at a north side bank in my Squad area and one of the bank clerks was at home and wanted to talk to a Police Officer.

My partner and I contacted the bank clerk and she informed us the boy that cashed the forged checks lived in the next block from her. Being the good citizen that she was, she definitely wanted to give us all this information, but most certainly didn't want us to involve her name in any action whatsoever. My partner and I thanked the young lady for her interest and immediately went to seek out one of our young informers to gain the knowledge of who our unknown youth might be.

It was only a matter of about a half-hour and we knew the name of the individual we were looking for. A check with our juvenile division revealed his date of birth and his past record, which was somewhat lengthy considering the boy had not reached his seventeenth birthday.

We went to the boy's home and were met by very pleasant and concerned parents. They expressed their desire to help us in any way they could to clear their son of anything we thought he may have been involved in. They also made it quite clear that their son had been home every evening for the past few weeks, and they didn't know how it would have been possible for him to get involved in anything.

My partner and I simply asked the parents to see to it that their son was at the Police Station the next afternoon around 4:00 p.m. so we could question him regarding this matter. They once again assured us that they would cooperate in any way possible and would have their son at the station at the prescribed time.

The next afternoon at exactly 4:00 p.m. a young man walked into the station and handed the desk Sergeant a slip with our names on it and announced to the Sergeant that we were looking for him. I recognized the boy from my Squad area but never really had any trouble with him and therefore never got to know him. He explained to us that his parents couldn't come with him but that he wanted to help us in any way he could. We took him into the back room of the station and started our interrogation.

The young boy immediately gave us the impression that he thought as long as he could keep us guessing he would get away with it. It took about an hour just to gain his confidence and try to impress upon him we didn't want to persecute him; all we wanted was the truth. He finally admitted his part in the forgery but denied being involved in anything else and further stated that he wasn't going to be a squealer on any of his buddies. It took us another hour or so before he finally realized that sooner or later everybody would be picked up anyhow and they would probably implicate him in other offenses. Since he was the first one to be arrested, we needed his cooperation and would also make it known to the children's court that he had cooperated with us.

We figured he was probably involved in a few other thefts and possibly may have stolen a few cars. When he started to relate his story to us it was almost unbelievable. He implicated fourteen other juveniles and admitted his part in numerous auto thefts, burglaries, purse snatchings, strong-arm robberies and several more forgeries.

It took my partner and me almost a week to pick up all the juveniles involved. Some readily admitted their part and some denied it all the way to children's court. The thing that amazed me most during this whole episode was the excellent families that the majority of these juveniles came from. When confronted with what their sons had done, most of the parents were shocked and dismayed.

About the only interesting observation I made on the whole incident was that in more than half of the families, both parents worked and supplied their sons with practically anything they wanted. Another interesting point was that none of the juveniles were involved in any sports or other activities in school. And last, but most certainly not least, was the fact that only two of the families regularly attended church.

I only spent a few months on this particular Squad and even though I had a fantastic partner, the work wasn't as exciting and stimulating as I wanted it to be. Like I stated before, I'm not the most exuberant individual, but I felt that as long as this was my career I may as well make the most of it. The only way to really advance to any extent was to be where the action was. I didn't want to cause any hard feelings, but I made it known that I would rather work in the core area. I also had a very excellent boss at this particular time and he saw to it that whenever there was a shortage of men on the more active Squads, he would take me off my Squad and place me farther into the core area.

It was during one of those relief assignments that I encountered a very interesting and unusual episode. The partner I had that particular night was a young Officer, but very capable. I felt we would have no problem handling any incident that might arise.

The first six hours of duty were quite uneventful. We made a couple of traffic arrests; two drunk arrests and served a warrant. We answered several hitches that didn't amount to much and my thoughts were of going home and getting a good night sleep, because I had been in court the last few days and was now starting to feel the stress from the long hours.

Our Squad number came over the air with the added description, "Sound of breaking glass," followed by the address. The call itself was not unusual for the neighborhood and it could have been the result of any of a number of things—vandals breaking some store window, some drunk falling down and breaking his bottle, kids playing in the street, or it could have been a burglary being committed. This was not a case in which to use the red light and siren, but we didn't waste any time getting to the scene.

We arrived and were met by another Squad who came by to see if we needed any help. The address given was a small corner grocery store located in the part of town which contained some of our less desirable citizens. It was close to midnight and the streets were dark and void of any pedestrian traffic. The grocery store was closed for business but contained a residence directly above it. We had just started to check the building when we heard someone call from the gangway adjacent to the store, "Over here Officers!" We ran around to the side of the building and were met by a man who identified himself as the owner. He said he was upstairs watching television with the lights out, and heard glass breaking downstairs in the store. He called the Police and then went downstairs to investigate. On checking the outside of the building, he found a window that was hidden by shadows on the side of the store, broken. We checked the window over and figured out that someone had apparently attempted to burglarize the store, but while smashing the window, the unknown actor had possibly sustained a bad cut to his arm. Pieces of broken glass were lying on the ground along with a sizable amount of blood. The trail of blood seemed to lead to the alley and my partner and the other two Officers followed the red trail. I took the complainant to the front of his business place and left him there while I checked the neighboring yards. I had only checked two yards when I heard someone call from across the street.

"Officer, are you looking for the man that broke the window in the store?" And before I could respond, the woman followed with, "He ran into the house two doors down." Immediately after the woman gave her information, I heard her front door slam and the lights go out in her house. She had apparently become more involved in the situation than she really wanted to be.

My partner wasn't around where I could see him and I didn't want to call him, so I crept along the front of several houses until I was next to the front porch of the house in question. The upstairs of the frame home was dark, but there were lights in what appeared to be the kitchen in the rear of the house, and also in the basement. I could hear voices in the house, but couldn't distinguish what they were saying. I crept along the shadows of the house and peered into several of the basement windows but couldn't see anything moving. By the time I reached the rear door the voices became much louder, but were still undistinguishable except that the parties talking seemed very excited. I was standing by the door trying to decipher what was going on inside when I suddenly got the feeling that someone was watching me. I glanced upward to the rear porch and was somewhat stunned to see a man leaning over the railing and watching my every move. A chill went up my spine and I shouted, "Police Officer! What are you doing up there?" There was no reply, but the man opened the porch door and disappeared into what I assumed was the upstairs residence.

Still feeling somewhat on edge, I heard another noise, spun around to come face to face with my partner. I hurriedly explained the series of events that I had just encountered and he added that someone out in front had told him that the people in the house were known to carry guns. By this time we both had our guns drawn and started to pound on the rear door. The excited voices I had heard previously stopped and a woman shouted out, "Who is it?"

I responded, "Police! We want to talk to you." At the same time I opened the door and my partner preceded me into the back hall. We went up a flight of about four or five stairs and were standing at the kitchen door.

The door opened and before we could say anything at all, a black woman in her late forties shouted, "What the hell you want, pounding on my door at this hour of the night? Ain't you got nothing better to do?" Before I responded to her questions, I looked behind her and got a glimpse of two very large dogs standing in the kitchen.

Now, there is nobody in the world that has more respect for dogs than me, and just the sight of those two dogs made me think twice. She replied that the upstairs was vacant and nobody was up there and she was home alone. She followed by telling us to get the hell out of her house before she would sic her dogs on us.

She barely got those words out of her mouth when we heard a lot of stumbling as though someone was falling down the stairs behind us. We both swung around and were met by what looked to be a wild man. He was holding a young girl around the neck and pushing her in front of him as if to use her as a shield. Everything was happening fast at this point. The man pushed the girl into my partner and ran past him into the kitchen. Almost at the same moment I heard the man shout, "Sic 'em." The next thing I saw was a large amount of teeth, all set in the jaw of a very large dog and aimed directly at my partner's throat. He took one step backward and then I saw a flash come from his gun. He dropped the dog in mid air. Almost in the same motion, I slammed the kitchen door and we both retreated out the back door and over the neighboring fence. I told him I would cover the back door and he should go to the front of the house and call for more help.

It seemed like an eternity that I stayed at the back of the house and all I could hear was the woman's voice coming from inside saying over and over again, "My dog, my dog! They shot my dog."

It actually was only a few minutes before a number of other Officers arrived and we all stormed the house from the back and the front. There was a lot of hollering and screaming, and even above all this I could hear a dog whimpering. We found the subject we had encountered on the rear steps, only this time he had hid himself on the upper shelf of a bedroom closet. We took him into custody and charged him with attempted burglary and resisting arrest. He was also wanted for violation of parole and had a capias (didn't show up for a court appearance) for burglary.

I went home that night and could hardly believe the events that had taken place. Everything became very real when I realized that once again I would be spending the next day in court.

The next night when I went to work I was on the same Squad with the same partner and we were told that it was our unpleasant duty to go and find out what had happened to the dog. As it turned out, the girl that the man was pushing down the stairs was actually his girlfriend. They had planned this all out hoping that he could get to the front door and make his escape. In fact, the whole family had been hiding him from the Police for several weeks.

Well, we went back to the house and were met on the front steps by the same woman we had encountered on the previous night. I told her we were sorry about what happened the night before and wondered how the dog was. She replied, "You dirty white trash, you shot my dog and I'm gonna get your ass! My lawyer is going to see about this. Now get your ass off my porch!"

7. Civil Unrest—The Riots

During the summer of 1967, tensions had grown in almost every city in the United States, and our city was no different. The civil rights movement was in full swing and everybody became involved.

Our city became entangled in the issue of open housing—which gave minorities opportunities to move and to live in any neighborhood they chose. Demonstrations and marches became a nightly occurrence. A Priest who had dedicated himself to the plight of the underprivileged led a majority of these marches. He had recruited a force of followers both black and white that had as their marshals, a young group of black youths who called themselves Commandos. It was the job of these Commandos to discipline the ranks of marchers, and to these youths it was the first position of authority that they had ever held in their life.

Being on the Police force and being surrounded by authority and discipline I was well aware of the fact that in order to enforce obedience and control, one has to endure the chastisement of many of his followers. This in itself was apparently hard for these youths to accept, since they were involved in the same movement and their feelings were mutual.

In other words, the crowds that they led followed them in orderly marches, but also followed them if they became unruly. Naturally, this is where the city Police force becomes involved, and as is most always the case, our position was not welcomed. In fact, we were pictured as fascist racists who were at the bottom of all their problems.

At this particular time the problem of discriminating against race in the sale and rental of property was in the hands of our civic leaders—our elected aldermen. These men had to conform to the whims and wishes of their constituents, as theirs was an elected position. The aldermen who had voiced their objections to the Priest and his followers were the object of demonstrations. The Priest would lead his exhibition of force nightly to the homes of those aldermen, and the majority of these men lived in predominantly white neighborhoods.

Now the problem of the Police became three-fold. We had to keep the marchers in an orderly fashion, protect the rights of the property owners in whose areas these demonstrations took place, and also prevent any violence which might stem from the confrontation of these two groups. Police had to hold a neutral viewpoint and therefore we became the scapegoats for both sides. If we protected the marchers we were wrong, and if we tried to keep the marchers in line, we became white racists.

The demonstrations were held nightly and for the most part were of a peaceful nature. They were also held in several different Police districts, so the

Department felt that several Officers should be picked to follow the marches every night, supplemented by a small force from the district involved.

I was one of ten Officers assigned this task, called the "Dew Squad." We met at one of the District Stations and were commanded by a Sergeant. He outlined what was to be expected of us and what our individual jobs would be. Several Officers were assigned to lead and follow the marchers and several were stationed at the house in question to protect the rights of the occupant. The demonstrators usually came about the same time every night. They would meet at the church the Priest was the pastor at and would then take a bus to the particular aldermen's home, march and sing in front of the home for several minutes and then attempt to have an interview with him in his home. The answers to their attempt at an interview were usually the same. They would be met at the door by the alderman and told that if they wanted to see him they should come to City Hall during his working hours. The marchers would then usually walk around the neighborhood for several blocks, return to the alderman's home, be led in prayer by the Priest and then board their bus for the return trip to the church.

The ten of us would split into pairs. We would patrol assigned areas until the marchers left the church and then proceed to their objective for that particular night. Of the ten of us assigned to this detail, three were black Officers. I was assigned with one of these three Officers. I had seen the Officer on several occasions but being assigned to different stations, I had never become acquainted with him. We shook hands, introduced ourselves and set out on our normal patrol before the marches would begin. The area we traveled in was predominantly black and I was obviously accepted more readily because my partner was of their own race. But, once the marches started it was an entirely different thing. To the white people in the neighborhoods, he was no better than the marchers. Just because he wore a uniform made no difference to them. To the marchers he was an "Uncle Tom." I really felt sorry for him because all he was doing was the job that had been assigned to him.

During the days we followed the marchers, there were only a few incidences that were of a somewhat violent nature. One such incident was caused by the over exuberance of the news media which followed the marchers constantly. Like I said before, tension filled the air and one knew that the slightest spark could touch off a volatile situation.

One of the aldermen came out of his home and became involved in a heated discussion with some of the leaders of the march. At this point, the bright lights of the cameramen flashed and the eager reporters pushed in to hear every word. Several Squads were called in. The alderman was told to return to his home. The newsmen were urged to get out of the crowd and the marchers left on their bus, leaving the air filled with obscenities and the threat that they would return the next night.

Return they did, just like clockwork, but the demonstration was very peaceful and the air was cleared of the tensions of the previous night. The marchers were in the midst of their prayer, which preceded their departure, when through the air flew potential violence in the form of an egg which was thrown by some degenerate, who was not aware of the consequences.

The egg fell in the midst of the marchers and the spark was lit. In an instant the street became mass confusion. The marchers raced across the street to vent their anger and the curious bystander suddenly becoming much more involved than he had ever dreamed of. Once again the men in blue were caught up in the middle. Fists were flying; anger and passion were released from both sides. A marcher was arrested and his comrades felt you're unjust for stopping their retaliation. An onlooker was arrested and you're once again ridiculed for protecting those that have violated the sanctity of their neighborhood. Either way, the Police Officer comes out on the losing end. And who caused all this confusion? A fourteen year-old punk who thought the throwing of a little egg was a big joke. For him it probably was a joke and because of our loose juvenile laws, he never even went to court. He just made an appearance to a Probation Officer that slapped his hand and told him not to get caught again.

Up to this point in my career, my basic ideas on race discrimination and civil disturbances were quite mixed. I had no definite feelings towards the matter one way or the other. The majority of my time at work was spent with either the black populous or the poor white. I was well aware of the filth and poverty that surrounded those individuals, but satisfied myself with the thought that my only job was to enforce the laws of society. The relief of those desperate conditions for those worthy of it was a job for the Welfare Department. This I learned later was a grave mistake.

I lived with my wife and three children in a modest home on the outskirts of the city. The section had an overtone of suburban living with its unpaved streets and no sidewalks. We had a black family that lived to the rear of us and several more in the next block. All of these families were of good moral character and were welcomed in the neighborhood. Our children played together and we exchanged greetings and conversations in the backyard the same as I would with any other neighbor. And I must say that after all the disturbances and unrest our feelings were still the same.

My occupation naturally placed me in a different atmosphere than the rest of my neighbors, but the thoughts which entered my mind at work usually left me by the time I arrived home.

As I said before, I had seen so much slum and poverty living, that my sympathies many times leaned towards the marchers and their quest for better living. These, I am sure, were the goals of the majority of the marchers. The only exceptions were those that did not have the welfare of the poor in mind, but only wanted to satisfy their own sadistic minds through violence and destruction. I also realized that by trying to change a person's way of living, this might also lead to violence. But even in my own mind I could only tolerate violence to a certain degree. The full impact of mob rule never really struck home to me until I was thrust into a mass of humanity that seemed to want to destroy the world and build it anew to their specifications. They even wanted to destroy the means to rebuild. Their similar thought seemed to be that they had nothing, so they had nothing to lose. This was to be their last desperate thrust at a society which they wanted to destroy.

The date was July 30, 1967. This day and more to follow would change the lives of many people. Some would be robbed of their very homes, through total destruction; some by imprisonment, some by life-lasting disfigurement and some by death itself.

The day started out as a bright, sunny, cheerful Sunday. It was also my day off, which added to its pleasantry. After church my family and I went to a friend's home who had a swimming pool. We lounged in the sun all day, taking full advantage of the beauty which God had bestowed on us. We arrived home about 10:00 p.m. that evening. The children were fast asleep in the car, exhausted from a fully enjoyable day. The pleasant feeling of my precious family and the thought of a good night's sleep were foremost in my mind. I had one of the sleeping children in my arms when I entered my home and placed her on the couch, while I answered the phone that had just started to ring.

The voice on the other end of the line was one that I had heard many times in the years past. It was a fellow Officer that I had worked with for a long time. He had always been friendly and cheerful, but this time his voice sounded strange, very hard and very official.

"Jim, get down to the station right away, all hell's broke loose. They're tearing up the city."

All I could say was, "You're kidding! I just got home; what's the scoop?"

He replied, "This is no joke, get down there right away." With this he hung up. stood there for a few seconds with the phone in my hand. I was stunned; I didn't know what to think. There was no doubt that he wasn't fooling, he wasn't the type, and this was for real.

My wife asked, "What happened? What's the matter? Who was that?" I told her who it was and said I didn't know what was coming off; he just said to get down to the station right away. (This was before the days of 24 hours of televised "Breaking News.")

I followed with, "It can't be much though, maybe it's just a test and I'll be home in an hour or so." That turned out to be the understatement of the day.

Within fifteen minutes I was shaved, dressed and out the door. A million thoughts were running through my mind. The streets on the outskirts of the city didn't seem any different than usual. The radio in my car didn't work, so I was still in the dark as to what was coming off. The closer I got to the inner city, the more activity was evident on the streets. Everyone seemed in a hurry. There were lots of sirens and lots of red lights. I was stopped in traffic at least three or four times by either Squad cars or fire engines. Everyone was going like a bat out of hell and all heading for the hub of the city.

Only an hour had passed between the time I had pulled into my driveway and the time I parked my car at the station. This wasn't the station to which I was ordinarily assigned, but because I was a member of the Dew Squad that was the station I had to report to that night.

The station assembly was crowded with lots of strange faces of Officers from other districts. I saw a Sergeant, identified myself and asked him what was happening. He didn't give me much of an answer, just asked me if I was part of the Dew Squad and when I answered him in the affirmative, he told me we were to assemble in the basement.

By this time, I had pieced together enough conversations to realize that the civil disturbances had reached their peak, and all hell had broken loose.

The Dew Squad was a group formed a few months prior to this event. It was comprised of a number of Officers who were to be trained in the methods of crowd control. It was, in effect, the predecessor to today's S.W.A.T. team. We met in the Police gym and received training in the art of controlling and depressing unruly crowds by use of human wedges (many Officers walking in an inverted "V" formation and other formations). The object of this formation was that the lead person in the inverted "V" would approach the crowd first, would make the arrest and pass the prisoner to the rear, through the "V." We also learned how to use a long night stick for self-defense and wore helmets and face shields. The idea itself had many merits, but received a great deal of adverse publicity from several newspapers and civil rights organizations.

I entered the basement of the station and was met by the familiar faces of my partners on the Dew Squad. At this point things seemed relatively calm. The Sergeant in charge told me to sign in. After this was done, he told all of us to take off our badges as they would shine in the dark and make targets to be shot at. We also were told to take off our Sam brown belts, ties and hats. The Sam brown was always a piece of controversial equipment. It ran from mid-back to mid-stomach, over the right shoulder and was attached to the belt. It was about one inch wide and made of leather. It was a sharp looking piece of the uniform, but because of the position in which it was worn, it gave one's adversary in a fight a pretty good handle to throw you around. Ties were also known to be handicaps in a fight.

After we had disposed of our equipment, we were all issued our long night sticks, white helmets and gas masks. By this time our ranks had been filled and we were ordered to assemble in the garage.

I had time to talk to a few fellow Officers and heard a few sketchy stories as to what was happening. No one knew for sure how it started, but it was a fact that gangs were roaming the streets, smashing windows, looting stores, starting fires and shooting at anything that moved. This was a war; not one that's read about in some far off land, but right here at home. This involved not only me but also my family if these actions were to spread throughout the area. No one was safe on the streets.

As I made my way to the garage I was able to grab a phone and call my wife. The conversation was short. I told her it was the real thing and it looked bad. Reports had come through that several people had already been shot and some Coppers may also have become victims. I told her to go to a neighbor's house and wait for my call. I could tell she was upset, but she tried not to let me know. She just said, "We all love you; take care of yourself."

Now it hit me; I was scared. My stomach was in a knot. I had never been in a war and never been shot at, and I wasn't looking forward to it. We assembled in the garage and were awaiting our orders as to where we should go. The sounds of the crowds breaking glass and shooting mixed with sirens were close and real. Our group was ordered to appear at a command post that had been set-up in a garage of a large Department store. We were given a truck for transportation and I climbed in the back with several others.

I didn't realize it, but fate was about to make its move. A small, inconsequential incident was about to take place that would separate me from my group, and place me in an entirely different situation. The truck we were in happened to have four wheel drive, not a big thing at all, except that the Cop that jumped behind the wheel couldn't get it in gear.

Next, I heard, "Somebody get up here and drive this damn thing." Just by chance I had driven this same truck a few years previously on a safety check assignment, so I got behind the wheel and drove to the command post. I arrived and was about to get out when a Lieutenant came to the window and said to go back and get another load. I made two more trips to the command post and when I returned to the station the third time I was told that no more men needed to ride to the command post. I asked a Lieutenant if I should take the truck back to the command post and he said, "Hell no, get out of that truck and into a Squad." So there I was, placed in an entirely different situation just because I could drive a lousy truck. In fact, I found out later that that was the end of the Dew Squad, as any semblance of an orderly formation was of no use when the mob was coming from all directions.

I never forgot that little incident. What would have happened if that first man knew how to drive the truck? Would I be dead?

The Lieutenant handed me a shotgun and a handful of shells, and I jumped into a Squad. There were two white Cops in the back seat and a black Cop was driving. I had seen them all before but only knew the driver by name. Nothing much was said. We pulled out of the driveway and down one of the main drags in the inner city. The radio in the Squad was going mad; everything was at a frantic pace. The radio never stopped—

"FIREMEN BEING PINNED DOWN BY SNIPER FIRE! SNIPER ON THE ROOF! LARGE GANG LOOTING A STORE! ASSIST AN OFFICER! ALARM RINGING! FIRE OUT OF CONTROL! SQUAD CAR TIPPED OVER! CROWD OUT OF CONTROL! BUSINESS MEN TRAPPED IN BUILDING BY GANGS! FIND SOME BLACK MINISTERS TO TRY AND CALM THESE PEOPLE! BURGLARY IN PROGRESS! POLICE STATION BEING ATTACKED! CARS BEING SET ON FIRE! LARGE GROUP WITH GUNS AND CLUBS! INJURED MAN WANDERING THE STREET!"

It seemed like more calls regarding violence were broadcast in half an hour than I had heard in a full year.

Then it came over the air, "Officer shot, need more ambulances, more Squads." The voice was almost hysterical. The location was given. We were only about three blocks away. The driver jammed the accelerator to the floor. One of the streets we sped down was filled with furniture, garbage cans and smoldering fires. We flew past a corner grocery store and I caught a glimpse of a bunch of black youths smashing windows, climbing through and throwing everything out in the street—canned goods, meat, and fruit; even a large scale and cash register.

Another Squad was in front of us and I heard a loud crash. Somebody had thrown a large city trash container at the Squad and smashed the windshield. The Squad swerved for a few feet and then kept right on going.

We came screeching to a stop on the corner where the shooting was taking place. I jumped from the Squad, ran across the street and stopped behind a tree. The air was blue with gun smoke. I couldn't tell who was shooting where. My eyes were attracted to a bright glow in the street just a block and a half away. A store had been fire-bombed and flames looked like they were shooting a hundred feet in the air.

It took several minutes for me to realize the other Cops were shooting at the second house from the corner. From my position I couldn't see the front of the house, and the partial side exposed to me had no windows. I was standing next to the corner house. I peeked around the corner and saw the house that was under siege, but I couldn't do any shooting because I couldn't see into the house.

The Cops that were doing the shooting were at the front of the house, on the opposite side of the street from me and I couldn't get there without getting into a crossfire. A Squad was parked in the middle of the street and I could see the white helmet of an Officer crouched behind it. (Helmets were later painted black because of the target they made.)

The sight of the white helmet moving parallel next to the Squad caught my eye. Suddenly it seemed as if the helmet exploded. It went flying across the street smashing into the curb. My eyes darted back to the head it came from and all I could see was an Officer clutching his face and falling to the pavement. I can remember screaming, "Ambulance! Ambulance! Another Copper's been shot."

I ran back to my Squad and found one of my partners crouched outside the Squad with the microphone in his hand. He was screaming for more ambulances. I tried to get a better position where I could see the front of the house but couldn't without going out into the middle of the street.

More shouting, "There's still a Copper in the house, he's shot, get the tear gas, get the tear gas!"

The Copper shot in the face was lying in the open. Suddenly an ambulance came screaming up, blocking the body from the line of fire. Both Coppers jumped out and opened the back door of their rig. They pulled the cot out and put the wounded Copper on it. He wasn't moving. His hands were still over his face. They put the cot in the rig and one Copper got in the back and the driver jumped in and sped away.

There were hundreds of heroes that night, and that ambulance crew certainly was two of them. By getting their fellow Copper in the ambulance they left themselves wide open. I could see there was never a hesitation on their part. They were brave men.

By this time the tear gas had started. Someone had placed themselves behind the Squad in the middle of the street, and was shooting tear gas from a gun into the front window of the home. It was a long shot and some of the missiles hit the building and bounced back. One such missile came flying towards me. I got out of the way, but it hit the curb and bounced back at my feet. I kicked it away, but not before I caught a good dose of it in my face. My eyes started to water and my throat seemed to tighten up. It wasn't until several hours later that I realized I had a gas mask hanging at my side.

The Copper shooting the gas gun hadn't found the right range and someone was shouting, "You're not getting it in! You're not getting it in!" In the same instant he bolted from behind the Squad and began to run straight towards the house. His hands were full of tear gas canisters and he ran right to the front windows and began heaving them in.

They found their mark because no one from inside shot at him. Smoke poured through the front windows and soon there were a few flames. The flames grew bigger and within only a few minutes the entire front of the house was enveloped in flames.

More shouts from the crowd of Coppers, "Get the Fire Department in here fast," and in reply, "Let the S.O.B. burn."

By this time another Copper and I had gotten the people out of the corner house and everyone in the burning house had run out, including the individual that had been doing the shooting. It wasn't until the fire was put out and the burned out residence was searched that the grizzly results were found. A young Officer, that came to work that night assigned to desk duty, jumped into a Squad and was one of the first Officers to run in the front door of that house. He was shot immediately and died instantly. An old woman that lived on the second floor was found by the back door; she had also been shot dead. It was never determined if she was shot by the people in the house or by the Officers returning fire from outside.

This whole scene started when a call for the Police came from the house in question, and a Detective Squad that was in the area pulled up in front. The passenger happened to be a Detective Captain and when he exited the Squad, he was shot in the face by someone in the house. The driver pulled him out of the line of fire and when other Squads arrived the Detective drove the Captain to the hospital, probably saving his life. Ironically, the Detective Captain became my boss. He always kept a picture in his office that was taken at the hospital, showing half of his jaw shot away.

Back at the scene, one of the first Officers that ran into the house was the one that was killed. The second one in was also shot in the face and was dragged out by other Coppers. This Officer was blinded and went on disability. He subsequently went to law school and became a noted trial attorney. Talk about determination and dedication.

Incidentally, because there were several individuals in the house and no Copper could say definitely who did the shooting, one of the parties was set free many months later by a jury and the rest were not prosecuted.

Several hours had passed now. I don't recall the time, but it had started to rain. The fire trucks came and the Squads started to leave. The four of us were sent to a corner about a block away and told to block off traffic.

Everyone was just about dead on their feet. We parked the Squad on the corner and a Sergeant came by and told two of us to stop the traffic and two of us should try and get some sleep. The shooting had stopped for the time being and the city was relatively quiet.

The thought of sleep seemed like a good idea until a few minutes later when two Coppers walked by, their faces showing the strain of the night. They told us that the body of a Copper had been found in the house, burned beyond recognition; (he was the Officer who had been assigned to desk duty). He was identified by a ring. No one said a word. I felt sick. I wanted to throw-up but I was either too tired or stunned or confused, or a combination of all three. He left for work to answer phones in the station and was now dead.

The Squad radio which had quieted down broke the silence with, "All Squads stand by for the Mayor's Proclamation".

The Mayor had declared a curfew on the entire city. No one was allowed to leave or enter the city limits, and no one was allowed on the streets themselves, with the exception of doctors, nurses, emergency workers and law enforcement personnel. The National Guard had also been called up and was on its way.

It was light now. The air was still. I must have dosed off for a few minutes. The fire trucks were starting to pick up their lines and most of the other Squads had left.

A woman came out of her house carrying a pot of coffee and several pieces of cake. She said, "I thought you Officers might like some coffee and cake. I'm sorry about the Officer that got killed. I heard about it on the radio. How are the rest of them?"

By now it was Monday morning and the thousands of uninformed citizens were rising to begin their normal work day. Those that turned on their radio or television suddenly became aware that their city was involved in a riot. Many left their homes for work and were stopped on the street by Police Officers and told to return to their homes or they would be subject to arrest.

We stopped several autos and when we told the occupants what the situation was, they seemed stunned and almost disbelieving. They all gave us their cooperation and headed back home. At this time we didn't have any trouble with the uninvolved citizenry.

We were told to report back to the station for relief. Everyone seemed to be taking a break. Even the rioters seemed to disappear, but we knew they would return, and next time possibly with more force.

Some catering service donated a large supply of sandwiches and coffee. The Coppers gulped the coffee and tore into the sandwiches as though they hadn't eaten for a week.

Coppers as a whole are an unusual breed. When they're together there's generally a lot of horseplay and joking around. But today was different. For the most part everyone was quiet. Several Coppers had grabbed pieces of cardboard or blankets and spread them on the garage floor, collapsing in near exhaustion. As tired as I was I knew I wouldn't be able to sleep. I got into a corner with a few other Officers; we sucked coffee and went over some of the different incidences from the previous night. Ours had been one of the few Squads left with all the windows in one piece. Those Coppers that had been working when the riot started told unbelievable stories of how they were sent to large groups of youths breaking store windows. When they arrived on the scene, the youths immediately turned their wrath on the Squads. Apparently, several Squads had to flee the area because their partners were bleeding from flying missiles that hit them.

A Commanding Officer addressed us and told us that we might as well make ourselves as comfortable as possible, because nobody was going home. He gave the news about the Copper that had been killed, and we each said a silent prayer.

I found a phone and called my wife. I told her it was as bad as it sounded. I told her that one Copper had been killed for sure and didn't know how many others had been injured. I tried to assure her that I could take care of myself and besides that, everything was out of our hands now anyhow.

By this time several portable cots had been brought from the command post, and the assembly room in the District Stations was converted into a large bedroom. It had been about thirty hours now since I had been to bed, but it still was impossible for me to fall asleep. I went into the garage with a few others and we began to spray all the white helmets with black paint. It had become apparent from the night before, that the white helmets made excellent targets. I knew of one instance for sure, and that was the sight of the helmet flying off that Copper's head. It flashed through my mind again.

Most of Monday was spent getting ready for the impending darkness. The windshields on the Squad cars were taped to prevent the glass from shattering, if it was hit by something. Most of the Coppers were loading up with as much ammunition as they could carry.

A partial report came in regarding the casualties from the previous night. Two dead, including one Officer, at least 67 injured of which 12 were either Policemen or firemen. There were approximately 102 people arrested for a variety of charges ranging from disorderly conduct to murder.

The National Guard had arrived about 8:30 in the morning and we heard there were about 450 of them in Milwaukee. About 1,000 of them were placed in different staging areas around Milwaukee and about 2,300 placed on alert. We also heard that the Guard had brought in six armored personnel carriers—each armed with a 50-caliber machine gun.

It was estimated that the window damage alone that previous night would exceed at least $200,000. It seemed that the only windows left unbroken were those with the word "Soul" scribbled across them. Soul was usually a word used by the black people to describe other black people.

The Mayor called a brief respite in his curfew from 4:00 p.m. to 6:00 p.m. to allow people to go to the store and stock up on essentials. A number of us were sent out to guard the stores. Each neighborhood store was filled with people and outside of each store stood at least five or six Coppers with shotguns. The people didn't speak and neither did the Coppers. It was like the city had called a temporary truce so everyone could stock up for the coming siege.

The early part of the evening was relatively quiet. I found a few pieces of cardboard and made myself a bed in a corner of the garage and dozed off for about an hour. It must have been after 8:00 p.m. when I was again assigned to a four man Squad, this time with different partners, and we set out into the strife torn city. It seemed to start slowly. A few sporadic calls of snipers, mixed with groups looting stores. Most of the calls we went in on were either no cause or there were so many Coppers there, we felt we would just be in the way.

The National Guard made their presence very evident and they were quite impressive. Most of them were stationed on the main drags of the inner city. It was an eerie feeling to drive down the street and see nothing but Squads and army vehicles. An occasional civilian car could be seen coming down the street and seldom could they go more than two or three blocks without being surrounded by Squads and army jeeps. Anyone without a good excuse for being on the street went to jail, and there were very few excuses accepted. The jails were being filled by people violating the Mayor's Proclamation. Even the Priest and several of his Commandos I spoke of previously, found their way to jail because they felt it was their prerogative when to march.

It was dark now and the shooting and firebombing went into full force. Several places of business burned out of control because the firemen couldn't get close enough without being fired upon. The Police radio was once again going full force—"FIREMEN PINNED DOWN! WHOLE HOUSE ON FIRE! SEND MORE SHOTGUNS! CAUTION SQUADS USING CALL BOXES—THEY MAY BE BOOBYTRAPPED!"

We were responding to one of the many sniper calls when we passed a filling station. Much to our surprise an auto was pulling out of the drive.

The driver of the Squad slammed on his brakes and by that time the auto had about a half block start on us. It was obvious that whoever was driving the auto wasn't supposed to be on the street. The chase was on. We headed down a side street that was strange to me. I had the microphone in my left hand and my revolver in my right hand. I was just going to start to broadcast the chase. The car gained some on us and was now about a block and a half ahead. Suddenly there was a big flash and a huge column of smoke. It seemed as if the car suddenly exploded. I soon realized that I wasn't the only one that was new on the side street. The driver of the auto we were chasing apparently didn't realize that the street dead-ended into a house. They must have been traveling at least fifty miles per hour when they smashed into the house. It was an older home that they hit and the basement walls rose up about four feet from the ground. The auto smashed into the home so hard that the front end of the auto knocked over the furnace in the basement.

Our driver handled the Squad beautifully. We screeched to a stop after traveling half a block sideways. I didn't see how it was possible for anyone to come out of that crash alive. But sure enough, the doors flew open and out jumped four youths. All four split into different directions and I spotted one that ran into a yard.

I piled out of the Squad and took off like a streak. This kid wasn't going to get away from me, I thought. I rounded the corner of the house and was only about twenty or thirty feet away from my fleeing friend when he suddenly swirled around and I saw two flashes. I still can't recall hearing any shots, but I did hear them go past the right side of my head. They were awfully close.

I never hit the ground so fast in all my life. I was lucky to be on grass; otherwise I would have scraped the heck out of my nose. In that same instant the youth leaped a fence at the back of the yard and all I could see was his head moving fast across the top of the pickets. I got off two quick shots but I missed my mark and the holes are still in the garage door on the other side of the alley. That had to be one of the closest calls I ever had.

I started running to the back of the yard when I saw just a flash of white out of the corner of my eye. I whirled around and saw a figure lying on the ground about ten feet away, "Get up with your hands over your head you S.O.B. or I'll blow your head off!" I shouted. All I could hear was, "Don't shoot, don't shoot, I ain't got a gun." A young black male stood up and he was really shaking. It was hard to tell who was more scared—him or me. But it's really fast how they gain their composure. I said, "Who the hell was driving that car and who did the shooting?" To which my shaking young friend replied "Screw you, Copper." It took us several hours to straighten the whole mess out. I took another look at the auto and found that the side of the house was even with the windshield. The whole front end was hanging in the basement. The auto wasn't stolen and it was several weeks before the other three youths were picked up. Because I couldn't positively identify the one that did the shooting, all they were charged with was eluding the Police and violating the Mayor's Proclamation. All in all, somebody got away with taking a few shots at me.

By this time it was getting to be early Tuesday morning. The rioting had let up some and I was so tired I could hardly keep my eyes open. We headed into the station to try to get some relief. When we got there, I must have gotten out on the wrong side of the Squad and walked the wrong way, because a Sergeant grabbed me and said, "Go along with those other three guys and take that Squad out."

I said "Hey, Sarg., I just got in and I'm really beat."

To which he replied, "We're all tired; get your ass into that Squad and take off." I climbed into the passenger seat and to this day I can't recall who my partners were. I was just so tired I couldn't even think straight. The streets were quiet and I think everyone wanted to call it quits for awhile. After about a half hour I told the driver to take me back to the station. If we had run into any trouble I would have been useless. We got back to the station and just by luck I found a cot in the corner of the garage and fell on it like something hit me over the head. It had been 47 hours since I got up that previous Sunday morning and in those 47 hours I must have aged at least a couple of years.

It seemed like I only closed my eyes for about two seconds, but actually almost two hours had passed. I was awakened by a lot of moving around. Everyone was breaking down their cots and piling them up. The word spread around that we were going home for a few hours. Even though I was happy to go home I was still too tired to really appreciate it. We all gathered in the assembly and were told by the Commanding Officer that we should report back at 6:00 p.m. that evening. I took a quick look around and could hardly believe my eyes. Coppers are usually a sharp looking group but the hard hours had really taken a toll. There must have been at least a half-dozen guys with their shirts full of blood and the rest looked as if they had been rolling around in the gutter.

My wife had gone to my sister's home the night before so I headed out there to pick her up. I had to travel through the inner city, and the damage from the previous night was almost unbelievable. I went about five blocks before I saw a business place that was still intact. What it all boiled down to was that the black people had torn the hell out of their own section of town. A lot of questions came to my mind. How did it all start? Who started it? What could possibly have motivated them to take such drastic measures? I suppose I wasn't qualified to really answer those questions but one thing I knew for sure was that this wasn't just a war between black and white; they threw another color in there and that was blue.

According to some people that are supposed to know what's happening, the riot itself was started by no more than just a handful of disgruntled youths. The riot lacked the support of the 90,000 black people who populated the city. In fact, there was believed to be fewer than 300 actually involved which included many from out-of-town.

I went to my sister's house, had some breakfast, picked up my wife and children and took off for home. I hit the sack and slept like a baby.

My wife woke me about an hour before I had to leave for work. She had prepared me a steak with all the trimmings. I had supper with my family, put on a clean uniform and took off again. My route to work carried me a few blocks into an adjoining suburb, where I was stopped by a Police roadblock. I talked to a couple of the Coppers for a while and they asked me how it was in the inner city. I told them it was a real bitch. They said they sure hoped it never would get out as far as them, because they didn't have the manpower to cope with a situation like that. I got stopped twice more by the National Guard before I reached the station. It sure made me feel good to see all those uniforms, especially knowing they were on my side.

When I got to the station I was very impressed by my fellow Officers and the city officials. Everybody seemed more confident. A lot of the Coppers had brought their own rifles from home and everyone was well armed and felt they could handle most any situation. The Mayor had lifted the curfew from 6:00 a.m. Tuesday until 7:00 p.m. Tuesday. There were no major incidents, due mainly to the Police and National Guard. The Mayor also issued an order that all taverns, liquor stores and beer depots were to remain closed and were prohibited from selling intoxicants. All the stores were prohibited from selling firearms, ammunition or weapons of any kind. Service stations were also limited to pumping gas directly into autos, and no gas or oil could be sold in any containers.

The positive action taken by the Mayor, city officials and the Chief of Police, along with the cooperation of the hundreds of thousands of citizens not involved, helped keep the injury total and property damage from getting out of hand.

This particular night I was assigned to an ambulance with three more Officers. You have to remember, back in those days, an ambulance was just a station wagon with a rollout gurney and the Officers had not much more training than basic first aid. There was no such thing as paramedics and private ambulance service. We set out onto the street and awaited the darkness, which we were sure would bring further violence. We drove around the first couple of hours and answered a few hitches of looters and snipers. The sniper situation was being well taken care of, because the city had requisitioned the use of several Brinks armored trucks, and the Police had placed in them several sharpshooters—rather than having Coppers hiding behind trees and autos trying to get close to a building that held a sniper. If the structure was a small building or a house, the Brinks truck would simply pull right up in front of the building and that was the end of the sniper situation.

About 10:30 p.m. we had just returned from taking an O.B. patient (woman having a baby) to the hospital when we heard the call, "ALL SQUADS STAY AWAY FROM THE COMMAND POST, THEY'RE BEING FIRED ON." What apparently happened was that a sniper got on top of one of the higher buildings surrounding the command post, and he fired a few shots at the hundreds of Coppers and National Guardsmen that were there. What a lot of people—including Coppers—didn't know was that the National Guard had some big weapons and really looked the part, but they had no ammunition. I was shocked when I was standing next to a guard man, that was also an off duty Copper, and he told me the only armament they had was what they brought from home.

The sniper position had been narrowed down to the roof of a large building that covered almost a whole block. By the time we got there the shooting was going full force. The first thing that went was the street lights which illuminated the Coppers on the ground and made them better targets. I was driving the ambulance and pulled across the street from one of the corners of the building under fire. My three partners took off for better positions and where they might possibly have a shot at the sniper. I stayed crouched outside the ambulance door to handle the radio if needed. The gun fire was really getting heavy, and to add to the confusion, some of the Coppers that were trying to put tear gas on the building were arching the missiles too high and they were going over and landing on the Coppers on the other side. Suddenly, there were three gunshots—Bing, Bing, Bing! They seemed to come from a small caliber gun and were awful close. I crouched a little lower next to the Squad and then I heard them again. Bing, Bing, Bing! Only this time I saw the bark come off a tree across the street from me. That was close enough for me. I couldn't see anyone firing so I figured the best place for me was flat on the ground. So there I was for the second time in two days, lying face down and not knowing what in the hell to do next. I laid there for a few minutes and then they started to bang us on the radio for another conveyance. I reached in the Squad, grabbed the microphone and told the dispatcher that I was pinned down and didn't know exactly where my partners were. He responded by saying we were one of the few ambulances left and would have to make the conveyance. Just then my partners came back and the shooting seemed to let up. Apparently, the sniper got off the roof and was now in one of the apartments.

We left to make our conveyance and all I can say is, the sniper was really lucky because from the way the street lights looked hanging by wires and all shot up, these Coppers really meant business. The conveyance was for a woman who had taken an overdose of pills. We made a couple more conveyances after that. One was a woman hemorrhaging and one was an injured child brought to a firehouse. After one of the trips out to the hospital, we were just leaving when they brought in a youth on a stretcher. It was obvious he was expired and I was told he had been shot by a Policeman after the youth threw a firebomb. The riots had claimed another victim.

We worked until 8:00 a.m. Wednesday, and during the early morning hours things quieted down. The few hitches we went to were well covered. That's one thing I have to say about Coppers. When there's a fight, shooting or another Copper in trouble, you have to go like hell or you'll be the last one on the scene.

The curfew was lifted Wednesday morning again and went back into effect at 7:00 p.m. I still say that the curfew was one of the main reasons we were able to keep an upper hand during the riots.

I was back on the ambulance Wednesday night and we started out with quite a few conveyances. Another woman hemorrhaging was taken out to the County General Hospital. A girl struck by an auto earlier in the day was taken out there also and then we had a cancer patient, an O.B. and an injured child. These and a couple of looting hitches took us until about 1:30 in the morning.

We went back to the station, had a cup of coffee and then started to patrol the deserted streets. It was unusual to see a car come down the street with its head lights on, as we had had ours off the last few days to avoid becoming targets. We stopped the auto and were confronted by a young gentleman about thirty years old. He had quite a few drinks in him and we asked him what he was doing on the streets. He said he got out of work about 7:00 p.m. and was just on his way home. We asked him where he had been drinking and he told us he had to go out of town for his drinks because we had closed up all his gin mills. That cost him $50.00 and the next day in court for violating the curfew.

We arrested another man about 4:30 a.m. after the National Guard had called us and told us that the man had been walking around the last hour or so, and kept telling them that the curfew didn't include him because he wasn't one of the rioters. I spent the next morning in the crowded court room listening to a variety of excuses why the curfew shouldn't have affected citizens. The pressure of the curfew was really starting to take its toll. People were starting to realize what it was really like to lose their freedom.

I remember one young man that came into court with his arm all bandaged up. A reporter asked him what happened and an Officer escorting him said, "Go ahead and tell him how your arm got cut."

The youth replied, "You damn right I'll tell you. I got it by putting my arm through a store window, and if I get out tonight I'll do the same damn thing. We're out to destroy your racist society." The Judge took the young radical out of circulation for sixty days. But after the sixty days one could count on him coming back for more because he was thoroughly convinced that society owed him plenty for the abuse he had received the past one hundred years. I could have sympathized with his cause much better if he hadn't been twenty years old, unemployed and very capable of working. Of course, this is just a personal opinion.

I spent the next five days working 7:00 p.m. till 7:00 a.m. on a ten man detail. We patrolled on foot about a six block stretch on one of the main drags. By the end of the five days the National Guard had pulled out, the curfew was lifted and things were starting to return to normal. The apprehension of further rioting stayed with us the rest of the summer and the Priest didn't exactly help matters when he began his marches again. In fact, there were incidences almost nightly that could have really erupted into something big.

The Father and his followers carried their marches to the predominantly white Polish section on the south side of town, and were met by extremists from the opposite side. By this time I had been sent back to my own station so I didn't become that involved. But I'll never forget a classic statement made to me by one of the Coppers who was caught in the middle of one of the clashes. "I couldn't understand it," he said, "I'm white, I'm Polish, I was about six blocks from home, my partner was black and we were getting stoned by both sides." The one thing he forgot was that he was wearing that magic color—blue—that made him game for anyone's fury and rage.

My return to my own station was a welcome relief. During the first week of the riots I put in one hundred hours. I talked to several Coppers who put in more than one hundred thirty hours. That had to be pure dedication, because I don't think anyone else would do that for straight pay. But like I said before, Coppers are a strange breed; they almost seem to strive on action.

It amazed me to find out how many Coppers returned early from their vacations just because they knew their fellow Officers needed them and were counting on them. My partner was one of them. He left his wife and family in a trailer at a lake where they were camping, and drove into town the minute he heard about the riots. I talked to another Officer that drove straight through from Canada.

We stayed on twelve hour shifts for the next several weeks which didn't include court time. The command post had moved to the Safety Building and a certain amount of Officers were always on alert at the command post so they could squelch any potential disturbance before it got out of hand.

It was at this time that the Department organized the highly controversial Tactical Enforcement Squads. They traveled four men to a Squad and patrolled the high crime areas of the city. Naturally, the populous of this area complained bitterly that they were being flooded by Police. But it was mainly the habitual law breaker that did the complaining. It seemed that they were being arrested more often than usual. Now that was a real shame! I myself had nothing but the greatest respect and admiration for those Officers on these Squads and the good people of the community can thank them for putting down many volatile situations by their quick action and show of force. In fact, in the next few months they saved my hide from taking a beating on several occasions.

I spent the next four weeks on my old Squad in a quieter area of town and it felt good riding down the street without a shotgun on my lap. It was during this brief period that I had a funny incident happen to me.

It occurred right after I started my shift. It was a nice warm pleasant evening and my partner and I were dressed in short sleeves, just enjoying the peace and quiet. I noticed a car had been following us for several blocks but didn't pay much attention to it. I stopped at a house to make a notification and when I returned to the Squad, I noticed the same auto was parked right behind my Squad. I waved to the driver and he waved back. I thought he was just being friendly and was parked there waiting for someone. But, the minute I drove away he was right back on my tail. I made a few turns and then stopped at a Call box to get a mark. When I hung up the phone I went to the driver's side of this strange car that was now parked right up against my rear bumper.

I said, "Good evening sir, are you looking for someone?"

The young man seated in the auto said, "No sir."

I said, "Do you have some kind of problem that you keep following me?"

He said, "No sir."

By that time I was becoming somewhat irritated and said, "Well, just what the hell are you doing?"

To which he replied very readily, "Well, you guys are always following me so I thought I'd follow you for a while."

I said, "What are you, some kind of a nut? Let me see your driver's license."

"What for?" he asked.

"So I can identify who's following me," I replied. I read the name, address and date of birth on his driver's license and when I got to his description my mouth dropped open. It read six feet six inches and two hundred and sixty pounds. He was twenty years old and looked in pretty good shape. I gave him his license back and told him that I worked until midnight, and that if he wanted to follow me, I hoped he'd have a good time. I could tell by talking to him that something was not right.

I went back to the Squad and told my partner what had transpired and all he could say was "That's pretty big!" We got a check on him over the radio and neither he nor the auto was wanted.

We drove around for a while with our friend right behind us, planning our strategy because we knew we had a problem on our hands. We decided the best thing to do was to call another Squad and a wagon and meet someplace where we could find out if this guy's problem was mental or if he was just a joker. But either way, he was probably going for a ride in the wagon unless he stopped his foolishness.

The Squad and wagon arrived and after we talked our giant out of his auto it was obvious that his problem was mental. He talked very irrational and after every few words he would flex his huge biceps. And they were really big! It was quite evident that he was very impressed with his size, and so was I. After about twenty minutes of talking we finally convinced him that if he came with us we would take him to someone who would listen to his problem with the Police Department. The ride to the hospital wasn't too bad but the minute we arrived, our friend took one look at the sign that said County General Hospital and announced very emphatically, "I'm not going in there!" At the same time he started to walk away. I jumped on his back and grabbed him around the neck and for a few seconds, I felt like a bird, the way I was flying around! One of the other Coppers grabbed his legs and down he went, fighting like a mad man. It took four of us and a hospital guard to hold him down while a nurse tried to put restraints on him. My arm was still around his neck but it was also being ground into the cement and I felt the skin being ripped from my forearm. I also felt the back of my shirt tear.

All the while the struggle was going on, I could hear some women in the doorway of the hospital saying, "Look what those Policemen are doing to that poor man, why don't they leave him alone?"

I couldn't help but reply, "Hey lady, I hate to tell you but I think we're coming out on the short end of this deal." By this time we were able to lock the restraints on his wrists and legs, and he was strapped on a cart and taken into the hospital. It's a shame that such drastic means had to be taken, but many times it's necessary just to prevent any serious injury. A check of the young man's record showed that he was released from another hospital a few weeks prior to this and that he hadn't shown up for his out-patient treatment. It turned out that it was all for his own good and the only real casualty was my shirt.

The Roving Wagon

8. The Roving Wagon—97R

I took one week's vacation sometime after that last incident and when I returned to work, I was given a Squad change that I believe had an effect on my entire Police career. As I stated before, I had made it known that I wanted to get assigned to a more active Squad, so when a Sergeant called me at home and asked me if I wanted a particular Squad, I jumped at the opportunity.

This new assignment was a roving wagon. It's a panel truck that is closed off in back and was used both as a Squad to take hitches and to convey prisoners. Its main purpose was to get a prisoner off the street faster to avoid any repercussions that sometimes occur from crowds that gather, and also to prevent any possible injury to the Copper making an arrest of a subject prone to resist. This Squad also was sent to any shootings or armed men in the entire District.

The working hours of this particular Squad were from 7:00 p.m. to 3:00 a.m. weekdays, and until 4:00 a.m. Saturdays. This was designed with the thought in mind that these were the most active hours on the street. Taverns close in the city at 2:00 a.m. on weekdays and Sundays, and at 3:00 a.m. on Saturday nights. This was also an active period because of the influence alcohol has on many individuals. This particular Squad overlapped two districts and its boundaries included a predominantly black section of the city. When I had asked for a more active Squad, I never dreamed of something like this. In the next sixteen months I answered 656 hitches (not including the hundreds we went to when we were not sent) which were everything from parking troubles to shootings. I made 521 arrests, which varied from plain drunk to first degree murder. I also made 643 conveyances—many of these being multiple conveyances in which as many as six or eight are conveyed at one time. Those sixteen months were the most exciting and fun-filled months of my career.

Because of the unusual hours that this Squad worked, there were three men assigned to it and by alternating off days we very seldom worked with anyone else. It was also my extreme good fortune to have two fabulous partners. I had known both of them previously but only to the point where we exchanged greetings. But in the months that followed we became very close. In fact, our families became very good friends.

It became a necessary asset to be on good terms with one's partners. Not only for physical reasons in which they can make the difference between being the victor or the victim, but because of the many hours that are spent together both at work and in court.

Dave was about 5'10 or 11 inches and weighed about 235 pounds. When we started together he was about 26 years old, an ex-marine and had about five years on the job. Bob was about 6'3 inches and weighed about 235 pounds, was 28 years old and had about six years as a patrolman. Because of their size I never felt the least bit of hesitation going in on any kind of call. We all had families to support and a good way to pick up a little extra money was to go to court. We never paused going in on hitches because one of us would always be able to take it to court in the morning. One would be amazed at the many minor violations that go untouched because the Officer doesn't want to get involved in court the next morning because of some previous commitment. No Officer can be criticized for not wanting to go to court after a full night's work. Sometimes it's a simple matter of going to court or losing your happy home. An individual can only spend so much time on the job. The first night I spent on the wagon was with Dave. We were still working from 8:00 p.m. until 8:00 a.m. because of the threat of possible civil disturbances. If that first night was any indication of what working on that Squad was like, I was in for a lot of work. We made twelve wagon conveyances, answered seven hitches and even managed to squeeze in an arrest for disorderly conduct. The arrest was kind of funny.

We were riding down the street when we saw two young black males swinging away at each other. We jumped out of the wagon, broke up the fight and were just getting their names when one broke away and punched the other fellow right in the mouth. The blood spewed out of the victim's mouth and we had no choice but to throw his assailant in jail. I really got a bang out of those people. They didn't care whether they went to jail or not, as long as they came out the victor.

The next few nights were a real rat race. All the big wagons from the different stations were being used to follow the Good Father and his followers, so we had to take all the wagon conveyances in three districts.

Besides making the conveyances itself, every time a drunken driver was transported we would have to make notations in our books regarding our observations of him for possible use in his prosecution in court. Some of those notations were quite amusing and showed the extremes alcohol will create in a person. "Subject very intoxicated, strong odor of alcohol, helped into wagon, helped out of wagon, swaying, staggering, mumbling, falling, insulting, and profane"—and the next day they don't remember a thing.

I hadn't had a chance to work with Bob yet, but if he was anything like Dave, he would be a real worker; always going. Within the first three days we even managed to get in a chase between all of our hitches. This was a relatively short chase but it was the first of many that we would eventually be involved in.

We saw this car blow through a stop light and gave chase down a main drag of the city, with red light and siren traveling sixty miles an hour—up and down a few side streets and through a couple of alleys. We turned a corner and there the car was sitting. We got the driver out of the car and asked him why the hell he didn't stop. His answer, "I didn't know who was behind me; I thought it might be some of my friends fooling around. If I knew it was a Police Officer I would have stopped right away." Penalty: $150.00 and court cost or sixty days in the House of Correction. I'll bet he stopped the next time he saw a red light.

Two days later we had another chase. This time the auto went around the same six block area three times—running the same stop sign each time. This driver at least had a little better reason. He said he was trying to drag race with another car and that when he saw the red light he just panicked.

The most common arrests that were made were for plain drunk and driving without a driver's license. In this particular section of the city there were several Super Bars that catered to your habitual alcoholics and derelicts. It was a common occurrence to see a man stagger down the street and suddenly just topple into the gutter. Naturally, the best and safest place for him was in jail. This was called a plain drunk arrest. It was a violation of the city ordinance to be intoxicated on the street to such a degree that one is unable to care for himself. A habitual drunk was a pathetic sight, but he could also be extremely humorous and amusing. It was not unusual to throw the same man in for drunkenness three or four times within a month. Usually after six drunk arrests in the same year, they weren't allowed to pay a fine but were forced to go to court where the Judge would send them to jail for thirty, sixty, or ninety days to dry out. I found most of these derelicts to be over fifty years old, either single or without a family, and usually on some sort of small pension—either from the government or some place of former employment. We often wondered how they could afford to get loaded so often, but after dealing with them for a period of time we realized that they could get drunk beyond imagination on a buck and a quarter.

The other arrest that was very common was driving without a driver's license. As precious as a driver's license is to most people, that's how little it means to many. The reasons for not having a license were as amazing as the people themselves: "I just can never pass the test!" or, "I've only been living here a few months and haven't had a chance to get one." It was not unusual to stop ten cars in an evening and find three of them without licenses. It got so that we could almost pick out the cars with the unlicensed drivers. So far as the license plates went, it was more unusual to find them properly registered than not. In general, the people in this area and cars just didn't get along.

As I think back, I can recall many incidents that I became involved in just by stopping a car. I remember one time when Dave and I were just cruising around. It was a real quiet night and I think Dave was half dozing on the passenger side. A car pulled out in front of me and I clocked him at sixteen miles over the speed limit. I turned on the red light, blew the siren and the car pulled over. Dave asked how fast I had him and I said sixteen miles over. Dave got out of the Squad and walked over to the car. Because of the area we worked, we generally made it a practice that the passenger would get out of the Squad so that the driver could cover him and have a better view of him when he walked up on a car. In fact, if there were three or more males in the auto, the driver usually opened his door slightly and kept his gun on his lap. This all may sound very senseless, but I can also remember several times when I'm thankful we were prepared.

Dave talked to the driver and came back to the Squad with his driver's license. I asked him what the driver had to say. Dave said, "Oh not that much, he didn't think he was going that fast." Dave finished writing the ticket and walked back to the car. I had my window open so I could hear the conversation. It went like this: "This is a ticket for auto speed, sir. You have three days to pay it or make arrangements to go to court. Would you like to see the clocking we got on you?" I didn't hear any response from the car, but the door opened and the driver got out. I thought he was coming back to look at the clock, but instead he headed across the street. Dave looked quite surprised and said, "Hey, here, take the ticket and your license." Dave followed the man half way across the street when the man suddenly swung and nailed Dave right in the chest with a full fist. Being as big as he was, Dave didn't go down, but he did lose his breath for a minute. I was only about fifteen feet away and when the man swung I was out of the Squad and heading toward him. By the time I reached him, Dave had him in the air and threw him over the hood of his auto. The guy was really going wild, kicking and swinging and cussing us out.

After we had him handcuffed and in the wagon, the man gave us one last shot by saying, "Wait 'till the next riot, I'll get a few of you." All I could think about was how this all erupted because of a lousy speeding ticket? We took the man to the station and booked him for disorderly conduct, resisting arrest and, of course, auto speed.

Up to this point, Dave seemed to be unusually quiet. When we left the station I asked him what was the matter. He gave me kind of a funny look and said, "Just who in the hell do you think you were punching at out there on the street?"

I said, "What do you mean?"

"What do I mean?" He went on, "Hell, that was my leg you were punching and it's still sore!" After that we both had a good laugh and I told him that was one he owed me. Actually, I think he was really teed off because when he got hit by our friend, he broke his flashlight that he just paid $7.00 for.

It's not unusual to get into a fight and catch a stray punch. In fact, now that I think back, the hardest I recall ever being hit was by another Copper by accident. At least I think it was an accident.

About three or four days after we had our little encounter with our reluctant speeder, Dave and I got involved in a pathetic, heartbreaking and yet very interesting case. It had been a relatively quiet night; we answered one call that turned out to be no cause. We threw in one plain drunk and issued one citation for no driver's license. It was about 9:25 p.m. and we were just having a cup of coffee when we heard a Squad get sent to "Shooting, ambulance sent!" We were parked only three blocks away, so it was a matter of seconds before we were pulling up in front of the address given. Dave ran up the front steps and stood alongside the front door while I covered him from the bottom of the steps with a shotgun. The inner front door opened and a boy about thirteen years old opened the screen door. He was standing in front of a man which I assumed was his father. It seemed as though the boy was about to speak, but the man blurted out "I shot my wife accidentally while I was taking my gun outside." It was obvious that he didn't have a gun in his hand, and as I entered the house I asked him where she was, and at the same time Dave made a quick check of his person for a weapon.

He said she was in the kitchen and we should follow him. Before we reached the kitchen we walked through the living room and dining room. It was a typical home in the area. It wasn't a slum dwelling, but it was less than middle class. Seated on a couch in the living room were five more children besides the boy that answered the door who seemed to be the oldest. The other five looked as if they ranged in age from ten years old down to two or three years old.

I only had time to give them a quick glance, but except for the two smallest ones, the tears on their faces reflected that a tragedy had struck their home. We followed the man and boy into the kitchen. I was apprehensive as to what we would find and I was also trying to be careful because we still didn't know where the weapon was.

My apprehensions weren't disappointed. Lying on the floor in the corner of the kitchen was a woman clothed in a white blouse and tan skirt. Her eyes were open and there was movement in her chest to indicate she was breathing. The only visible wound was a small red spot about the size of a quarter on the right side of her abdomen. I've seen enough people either dead or dying and knew she was drawing her last breathe.

A shot gun was leaning up against the wall next to her and Dave grabbed the gun and shoved it under the kitchen table away from everybody. By that time the ambulance was arriving and I took the young boy into the dining room—he was obviously in shock. I learned later that when I left the kitchen Dave and the woman's husband bent over her body and she looked at her husband and said, "He shot me." (At the time, these three words seemed very inconsequential, but a few months later during the court trial they were considered a dying declaration.) She then lapsed into unconsciousness and never came to. Just before the ambulance crew lifted her body onto the stretcher, I used a piece of chalk and marked off on the floor where she was lying, which is necessary to ascertain at a later time the position of the body.

The woman was carried out and Dave and I took the husband into the dining room. Dave asked him if he shot his wife and he stated he did, but it was an accident. Dave then said, "Sir, you are under arrest for attempted murder, I'm advising you of your constitutional rights: you may remain silent, anything you do or say may be used for or against you in a court of law. Further, you may stop talking any time you so wish. You have a right to an attorney and if you can't afford one, an attorney will be appointed to represent you. You also may have this attorney present during questioning regarding this matter if you so desire. Do you understand this sir?"

The man seemed very unemotional and answered with a very definite "Yes." I placed my handcuffs on the man and told him to sit down next to Dave in the dining room. By this time the Detective bureau had arrived and taken over this investigation. The Police photographer came and took pictures of the crime scene. I was instructed to go in the living room and interview the children. This was rough. All six children were seated on the couch in the living room. The three year old was sitting on his brother's lap. It must have been a very close family because the children seemed sincere and concerned for one another. It was an extremely emotional scene.

The eight year old was the first to speak. He looked up at me and, with tears in his eyes and a quivering mouth, asked me, "Is my mom dead? Did my dad kill her?" All I could say was that I didn't know, but that she was taken to the hospital and they would do everything possible for her. It was a stupid thing to say because I was told she was pronounced dead on arrival. I just couldn't bear to be the one to tell those poor kids.

I asked the eight year old, whose birthday was just ten days away, and the thirteen year old if they thought they could tell me what happened. The youngest one, apparently either in a state of shock or not fully aware of the seriousness of the actions of his father, started to talk right away. He related to me how his father was seated on the couch next to him with the shotgun wrapped in newspaper lying behind them. His mother came home and a violent argument ensued. The boy talked very fast and it was hard to understand him. But I soon became aware that this little fella was standing in the kitchen and saw his father shoot his mother. What a tragedy—this was bound to leave a scar on his mind for the rest of his life.

The thirteen year old said about the same thing as his brother except that he had stayed in the living room while his mother, father and brother went to the kitchen. He said he heard a lot of arguing and then silence for a few minutes. He said suddenly he heard his mother scream and then heard a shot. His brother came running towards him and said that dad had shot mom. His father came into the living room and told all the kids to shut-up, sit down, and then he called the Police. I didn't see any point in questioning the boys any further. A neighbor lady came to the house and said she would take care of the children for the night. Dave and I were instructed by the Detectives to convey our prisoner to the Detective Bureau and start writing our reports. This we did until about 5:00 in the morning.

I got home about 5:30 a.m. and was up again at 7:00 a.m. to get ready for court. Dave and I got back to the Detective Bureau about 8:30 a.m. and were sent by a Detective Sergeant to go and get a cup of coffee as it would be a while before the autopsy was completed and we could take our prisoner to the District Attorney and apply for a warrant.

We went across the street to a coffee shop and I drank a cup of coffee and ate a hard roll, while Dave had the works—bacon, eggs, ham, coffee and a sweet roll. We got back to the bureau about 9:15 and again were met by the Sergeant, who, this time said very nonchalantly, "You fellas better hurry up and get down to the morgue—you have to witness the autopsy." This was our first autopsy and neither one of us were quite sure how our stomachs would react.

We went down to the morgue, which was in the basement of the Safety Building, and were met by one of the Detectives from the previous night, the Detective Sergeant, a stenographer, a photographer from the Bureau of Identification and the Medical Examiner. The whole scene was informal yet very professional. The body of the woman was lying nude on a table in a room that looked somewhat like an operating room. The only thing about the room that still stands out in my mind was the flooring which consisted of small black and white tiles.

The Medical Examiner introduced herself to the stenographer and all those present and then began the autopsy. She stated that the victim had received a round entry wound seven eighths in diameter to the lower right quadrant of the abdomen. She further stated that she diagnosed the cause of death as a shotgun wound to the abdomen which resulted in massive internal hemorrhaging. She then took a scalpel and made an incision in the woman in the shape of a Y that ran from just below both shoulders and met at the middle of her chest and continued to her abdomen. All during this time she was dictating to the stenographer in medical terms. She then opened the section she had cut and this revealed the entire chest cavity and stomach. It was at this point that I noticed the black and white tiles on the floor starting to move. I looked around at Dave and he had lost all his color and looked pale as a sheet. I looked back at the body and by now the doctor was removing the blood from the victim by the same manner as one might ladle soup from a kettle. She poured the blood into a container and I could hear the sounds of metal. These turned out to be the shotgun pellets. She removed fifty pellets and five pieces of shotgun wadding. In fact, the entire shotgun load must have stayed right in the woman. I looked around again but this time Dave was out of sight. I walked into the next room and all Dave could say was he shouldn't have eaten such a big breakfast.

The entire autopsy took about two hours and Dave and I spent the majority of the time in the adjoining room listening to the doctor's description of what she was doing. It's really hard to explain my feelings about that first autopsy. I knew it was part of the job but I also knew I could never get used to it.

It was afternoon by the time we finally got to see an assistant District Attorney. After listening to our description of the offense, he issued a warrant for first degree murder. We took the subject to court and he was bound over to Circuit Court for appointment of an attorney. He had pleaded not guilty. The Judge set bail at $25,000 and the date for the preliminary hearing was set for seven days later.

Relatives had brought the two oldest boys down to the District Attorney's office as their testimony may have been needed for issuance of the warrant. I talked to them several times in the hallway and was still very impressed by their politeness and good manners. In fact, this is what made it even more of a tragedy because children aren't born this way; they learn these things from home. At one time they must have been part of a very close family because even after this extremely painful experience they still talked to their Dad and held his hand as if they were seeking comfort and guidance from him.

The preliminary hearing was held the next week and the defendant was in court and represented by a very capable attorney which the state had provided. The testimony was very brief. I remember the Judge asking the younger boy a few questions to qualify his competence as a witness because of his age.

The last two questions he asked were, "Do you know what a lie is?"

To which the boy answered, "Yes."

The Judge then said, "What happens when you lie?"

The boy responded confidently, "God will punish me."

The Judge then turned to the District Attorney and defense attorney and stated, "I believe this young man will make an excellent witness." The Judge found that there was probable cause that a crime had been committed and bound the defendant over to Circuit Court for trial.

It was several months before I saw the two boys again. The next time I saw them was in Circuit Court and the trial was about to begin. This trial could send their father to jail for the rest of his life. I talked to them briefly and they said they had visited their dad every week in the County Jail.

The trial began and after the twelve man jury was picked the defendant pleaded not guilty and not guilty by reason of insanity. The trial lasted the better part of three days, and both the defense attorney and the assistant District Attorney who were prosecuting the case did an excellent job. At the end of the trial they both gave their summations. The one statement that I do recall made by the prosecutor came after he had just finished telling the jury how the state had proven its case beyond a reasonable doubt. He then added, "And in conclusion, I would just like to say that nobody, for any reason, shoots his wife!"

The Judge charged the jury (gave them their instructions) and they went into seclusion to deliberate on their verdict. Dave and I left the courtroom and met the two boys and their relatives in the hall. We thanked them for their cooperation and made them promise that if there was ever anything we could do for them, they should never hesitate to get a hold of us. That was the last time I ever saw the boys. I've thought of them many times. I'll always wonder what affect that tragic experience would make on the rest of their entire lives.

Dave and I were contacted later that evening by the Detective Sergeant and he told us that the jury had come back with a verdict of guilty of murder in the first degree. The Judge immediately followed by sentencing the defendant to life in the State Prison. Justice was once again meted out by a fair and impartial judicial system.

When I look back at that homicide, I think it might have been a turning point in my career because it changed what I looked forward to doing. I never really envisioned any type of promotion, and was just looking forward to someday going on the day shift. But what really made an impression on me, were the Detectives that were assigned to the case. Dressed in their suits and ties, they were extremely professional and thorough yet compassionate. I was impressed with the way they handled the case from the very beginning until the trial ended. How they collected the evidence and processed the scene. How they talked to the witness, especially the children. I found out later, that after the trial, they went to see the children on several occasions and took them to a ball game and out to eat. What was also impressive was how the Assistant District Attorney handled the case. He was one of the main attorneys in the office and handled most of the violent cases. He ran for District Attorney one time and when he failed to get elected, he went into private practice and became one of the top criminal lawyers in the state. It was evident that homicides brought out the best in everybody.

I think one of the reasons that Police work is so fascinating is that each and every night brings a new experience of some sort. Each time I thought I had heard every excuse for some violation of the law, someone would pop up with a new one. As common as it was for us to arrest people for driving without a driver's license, I never thought I could arrest the driver and the passenger for not having a license. As I said before, the violation was so common that we could almost pick out the driver just by his actions. It was also quite common for the driver and passenger to switch places when they knew they were going to be stopped; depending upon who had a license or who had the best record and could afford to be arrested.

The arrest in question started when I spotted a woman driving a car in the opposite direction we were traveling. It was obvious she was learning how to drive and the man seated next to her was very intent on giving her instruction, at least that's how it looked because he was almost on her lap. I made a "U" turn and thought we would make a routine stop to check her temporary instruction's permit. By the time I turned the wagon around, the car was about half a block ahead and pulling toward the curb. Then, by the time we got behind the auto it was pulling away from the curb, and to my surprise the driver was now a man. I pulled the auto over and had the following conversation with the driver and passenger:

> "Good evening, sir. I don't mean to bother you but could I see the young lady's driver's license please?"

To which she made the logical reply, "What do I need one for, I'm not driving."

"Look," I said, "Let's not play foolish games, I saw you driving and for that you need a license. As long as I'm checking licenses, let me see yours, sir!"

"I left mine at home," was his reply.

"You mean neither one of you have a license?" That has to be a first. "I suppose you have a logical explanation?"

"Well, sir, you may not believe this, but I really don't have a license and neither does my girlfriend."

"No kidding?" I said.

"You see, I lost my license a few months ago for drunken driving and I was just teaching my girlfriend how to drive so she could get a license and I wouldn't have to take a chance on getting caught for driving without one. You believe me, don't you?"

All I could say was that a story like that I had to believe. The next day he was charged with driving without a license and permitting an unauthorized person to drive, and she was charged with driving without a license. He got sixty days in jail and she was fined $50.00.

I think that's why Coppers are many times classified as being hard-headed and thick-skinned. You hear lies on top of lies on top of lies and pretty soon it's hard to distinguish the lies from the truth. Therefore, someone who may really deserve a break doesn't get it. I truly believe that some people lie just for the sake of lying. Many times it's a lot easier to convince an individual to accept a lie, because a lie many times is more logical than the truth.

A very predominant business in our Squad area was the taverns. In fact to be exact, there were fifty-eight of them. They were all just about the same. Neighborhood taverns in neighborhoods where the people many times didn't have money for food on their tables or clothes for their children, but they always had money to lie on the bar.

Besides dealing with the problems that stemmed from these gin mills, it was also part of our job to keep the taverns in line. We made it a point when we first started working together, to stop in every tavern in our area and introduce ourselves. We also made it known that we would check them at least twice a month, and as long as they ran a clean place and didn't give us any grief, they wouldn't have any trouble with us. I must say that the majority of the tavern keepers gave us their complete cooperation. At least to our face they did, what they said after we left was immaterial.

Then there were the few that were real dens of iniquity—those were the ones where a Copper doesn't walk in alone. They were also the ones that got that little bit of extra attention that may have bordered on harassment. I remember one night right after Dave and I started working together, we decided to see how many taverns we could check before we found a violation. This wasn't the main part of our job, so we could only spend about 10 minutes out of the Squad and away from the radio. We picked one at random and walked in the front door. There were about twenty people in the bar and we immediately saw a young man at the end of the bar that didn't look quite old enough. The city ordinance in our city states that one must be twenty-one years old to be drinking an intoxicant in a tavern. I asked the young man for his identification and after fumbling in his wallet for a while, he came up with an identification card that made him twenty years old. I asked if the bartender had asked him for his I.D. and he said no. The bartender, when questioned, said he thought the boy was old enough. The owner of the tavern wasn't on the premises so he was contacted and all the parties were ordered into the District Stations on another day to see our Commanding Officer. The procedure was for the District Captain to review the case and if he felt the violation was serious enough he would send us to the City Attorney for issuance of a warrant.

In this particular case the bartender was fined for selling a malt beverage to a minor, and the owner was fined for permitting the minor to loiter on his premises. Even though he wasn't in charge himself, the law states that the owner is still responsible for action in his tavern. The minor was fined for loitering on the tavern's premises. The fines themselves were quite minimal, but each violation is recorded and when the owner of the tavern makes his application for renewal of his liquor license, if there are enough of these violations, it could be a reason for him to lose his license.

Dave and I left the tavern and felt quite pleased, and yet concerned that we found a violation on our first try. Maybe our taverns needed a little more attention!

We drove around for a while, not really looking for anything in particular when I spotted a real young looking guy going into another one of our taverns. We parked down the block and waited for about ten minutes. The youth emerged carrying a bag and got into an auto. We stopped the auto a few blocks away and questioned the driver, who was seventeen years old. We then questioned the young man who came out of the tavern and after initially denying he was there, showed us the bag which contained a pint of rum and six pack of beer. He said he was twenty-one years old, but didn't have any identification with him.

One must understand that a good majority of these people in this particular area have arrest records, so it was just a matter of checking with our Bureau of Identification to find he was only eighteen years old. We took him back to the tavern. He said he was afraid to go back inside, so he pointed out the bartender who sold him the beer and rum through the front window. I went inside and questioned the bartender and he vigorously denied selling anything. This, as I learned later, was my first mistake. I should have taken the youth inside to make a positive identification. All the parties were ordered to the District, and from there we went to the City Attorney who issued a warrant.

We went before the Judge and I gave my testimony. The tavern keeper denied the sale, and when it was the youths turn to testify he said nobody sold him the rum and beer but that he had gone in and stole it while the bartender wasn't looking. The strange thing was that besides the rum and the beer, he also had a cash register receipt in the bag. The youth was fined, but the case against the bartender was dismissed. I learned a lesson from this and it definitely wouldn't happen again. One thing was for sure, though, the tavern would get some special attention, and it would only be a matter of time before we had a good case against him.

I had a long talk with the minor after court. He said he had received several threatening phone calls from unknown individuals regarding the way he should testify. We didn't push the case any further and just chalked the whole thing up to experience. Better preparation on our part would have resulted in a conviction. But a sure way to learn is to do it wrong once—chances are good you won't do it wrong again.

It was just three days later that Dave and I were driving past the first tavern we had knocked off, when the door swung open and out came a drunk. We stopped and talked to him and came to the conclusion that this guy was really smashed, besides that, he was only twenty years old.

Back in the tavern we went and sure enough there was the same bartender. He gave us the same story that he thought the youth was old enough. In fact, everything else was also the same, including the fines in court.

All told, within the next few months we knocked this same tavern off five times. Three times for serving minors, once for operating after closing hours and once for having an unlicensed bartender behind the bar. The strange thing was that the owner was never on the scene during these violations. After our last appearance in court, we finally convinced the owner to fire all his help and start spending some time on the job himself. He took our advice and we never had trouble at his place after that.

Because of a conflict in our off days, it was several weeks before I actually got to work with Bob. I found him to be a hard worker just like Dave, and I knew our working relationship was going to be very pleasant.

I recall one of the first nights we worked together. Bob was driving and we had just pulled up to a red light at a busy intersection in our area. I glanced at a car parked across the street. Suddenly the passenger door flew open and a woman jumped out and started running towards us screaming for help at the top of her voice. I jumped out of the Squad. She ran up to me and said that the man in the auto had just beaten her up and robbed her. The car she had just left turned the corner and headed into an alley.

I hollered to Bob that it was a robbery and he took off with the Squad to cut the car off at the other end of the alley. I ran up the alley after the auto and saw our Squad block the other end of the alley just as the auto reached it. The driver jumped out and started running towards me. When he saw me, he tried to change directions but by that time Bob was on top of him.

We handcuffed him and while searching him I found a switchblade knife in his pocket. We went back to the woman and had another Squad bring her into the station where she could file her complaint. We conveyed our prisoner to the station, and while booking him we found over $500 in cash along with some identification. I went out and questioned the woman and told her who the man was. She then told me I had the wrong name. After about an hour we got the whole story straight. The man was her boyfriend and when he found out how much money she had on her, he punched her in the mouth and took it.

We charged the man with battery, carrying a concealed weapon (the knife), driving without a driver's license under his proper name and operating an unregistered vehicle. We also discovered he was wanted on two warrants by the sheriff's Department. Things became a little more complicated when he insisted that the $500.00 was his. They became very complicated when, as a routine thing, we checked the woman out and found that there was a state warrant out against her. We looked her up and decided that the next day the Judge could decide who the $500.00 belonged to. The climax to the whole affair came when the woman called a friend to come down and bail her out. The friend came to the station and sure enough, we checked him out and he was also wanted.

The next day the battery charge was dropped, naturally, because this was her boyfriend. He got one year in the House of Correction stayed to one year probation for the carrying a concealed weapon charge. (Meaning, if he stayed out of trouble during his probation period, the one year sentence would be dropped. If he committed a crime during his year of probation the one year that had been stayed, could be enforced and he would have to serve that time.) He also got six months in the House for the driver's license law and thirty days for the unregistered vehicle. We never did find out who wound up with the $500.00.

It was amazing how many good pinches we came up with just because of a person's guilty conscience. If we had nothing to do, many times we would just start to follow a car. If the car kept going straight for six or eight blocks we would just turn off and follow another one. On the other hand, if the car made a couple of turns down side streets and then went back onto a main drag, it usually meant that he was trying to either lose us or see if we were following him. And if the driver was that interested in us, it usually meant that he either didn't have a driver's license or he was wanted for something.

Bob and I started to follow a car one night and after three or four turns decided to stop him. I turned on the red light and it was just as though I waved a green starting flag. The driver trumped her down and away we went. It was 1:30 in the morning on a Saturday night and the speeder reached seventy miles an hour down a main drag of the city. Bob was broadcasting the chase over the air and it sounded just like a stock car race. I still think he was doing it with his eyes closed and one hand on the dashboard, bracing for a crash. I was just about ready to give up the chase because it was getting too wild when, believe it or not, he turned the corner and his car stalled. When we turned the corner I was so surprised to see the car in the middle of the road that I almost ran right up his rear end.

Bob and I jumped out with our guns out and Bob told the driver to come out with his hands up. The driver emerged and we placed him in handcuffs and put him in our wagon. A check of his car revealed that he had a sheathed bayonet with a seven-inch blade lying on the front seat next to him and another knife with a six-inch blade under the front seat. Naturally, he didn't have a driver's license and that was the reason he gave us for trying to get away. We asked him what the knives were for and he said he had borrowed the auto and didn't know the knives were in there. We checked the ownership of the auto and discovered that it was reported stolen. That went out the window when the owner found out who had the auto. He suddenly remembered that he had borrowed it to someone while he was drunk and had forgotten who.

I took the subject to court the next day and the District Attorney issued three state warrants—one for eluding a Police Officer, one for carrying a concealed weapon, (knife), and one for driver's license law. After a couple of adjournments the subject was tried and found guilty on all three charges. He received thirty days for the eluding, sixty days for the driver's license and one year for the carrying a concealed weapon. The sentences sound kind of stiff but the individual was only twenty-three years old and had been arrested no less than thirteen times for a variety of offenses. All three sentences were to run consecutively, so he would have to serve the full fifteen months, less time off for good behavior. About a month and a half after he was convicted, Bob and I received a subpoena to Circuit Court. Apparently, the individual had hired an attorney and was appealing the conviction of carrying a concealed weapon.

We went to court and the defense attorney immediately asked that we be sequestered. In other words, if Bob testified first I would not be able to hear his testimony and vice versa. This is done many times so that the attorneys might find discrepancies in one or another's testimony.

The basis for the appeal was:

1. We didn't advise him of his constitutional rights;
2. He had no knowledge that the knives were in the auto;
3. That the search of the auto was illegal; therefore, anything we found in the auto could not be used as evidence—namely the knives.

Bob testified first and after he was done I testified. The only discrepancies in our testimony was that Bob said the dome light of the car was on and I said it was off, and Bob said the sheathed knife was on the seat and I said it was under the seat.

The defense attorney made quite an issue of these two things in his summation. I was very pleased by what the Judge had to say when he made his decision. He stated that it was hard for him to believe that the subject didn't realize that there was a large knife sitting on the seat next to him. He further stated that he didn't feel it made much difference whether the dome light was off or on, nor did it make a difference which knife was on the seat and which was under the seat. He also believed that the subject was fully advised of his constitutional rights. As for the differences in our testimony he felt we had testified to the best of our knowledge and recollection and the slight discrepancies showed that we hadn't fabricated the case. He therefore upheld the subject's conviction and sentence.

I think some of my finest moments have been when I can match wits with attorneys in court, especially when I have been on the winning side. No one enjoys losing a case, especially when you know that the defendant is definitely guilty. It's amazing how many cases are lost in court through poor case preparation and poor testimony on the part of the Officer. I have found that most good defense attorneys will cross examine an Officer and really try and shake his composure. But I have also found that, these same attorneys will shake your hand after the case and tell you, win or lose, if you did a good job.

9. Handling Hitches

So far the stories that I have been relating have been more or less isolated incidents. When in actuality every night a Police Officer spends on the street can be a story in itself. I'd like to relate in sequence some of the actual arrests, conveyances, hitches and happenings we became involved in over a two-week period, with a brief explanation of each incident.

ACCIDENT, AMBULANCE SENT

Red light and siren used to get to the scene. The extent of the injuries and severity of the accident is never known until you arrive. In this case the injuries were minor—a few band-aids and compresses were applied and two parties were conveyed to the hospital with minor lacerations and bruises. We handled the scene of the accident and wrote the report.

FAMILY TROUBLE

Husband came home from work drunk and started an argument with his wife. She called the Police. We had been to the home on several occasions. Husband was advised to either go to bed to sleep it off or he would have to come along with us. In cases of family troubles, we always made it known that if we had to come back the second time, someone would go to jail.

SUSPICIOUS AUTO AT A FOOD STORE

By the time we arrived the auto was gone. We interviewed the proprietor of the food store and he stated that an auto had gone past his store several times and it looked like they were casing the store for a holdup. He didn't get the license number so there was nothing we could do or follow-up on. We checked the store throughout the night just in case.

FAMILY TROUBLE

Another husband came home drunk and struck his wife in the mouth. Since we didn't witness the striking we asked the woman if she wanted to meet us in the morning at the District Attorney's office for a battery warrant. She said her husband had been beating her for the past eight years whenever he was drunk. All she wanted was for him to go to bed and sober up. He was also given the ultimatum of either bed or jail. He decided he needed some sleep.

FLAGGED DOWN BY A BUS DRIVER AND TOLD THAT ONE OF HIS PASSENGERS HAD JUST BEEN BEAT UP BY A GROUP OF BLACK YOUTHS

He gave us a description and we found them a block away and brought them back to the bus. The youth that was struck decided not to complain and we had to kick the whole group loose, but not until they had taken our badge numbers and threatened to report us for harassing them.

ARREST FOR DRIVING WITHOUT A DRIVER'S LICENSE

Car full of seven young black males stopped because they looked suspicious. Driver had no license. He was given a ticket and ordered to appear for court. They had to let the auto sit because none of the seven had a driver's license.

TROUBLE WITH A CUSTOMER

One of the Super Bars in our area was having trouble with a regular customer. He walked in, ordered a glass of wine and fell asleep at the bar. One arrest for plain drunk.

CONVEYANCE One plain drunk to the station requested by a patrolman walking the beat.

THEFT COMPLAINT

Three black youths walked into a shoe store, grabbed three pair of shoes and ran out. A description of the young thieves was obtained from the complainant and a report was filed.

CHILDREN STARTING CONSTRUCTION EQUIPMENT

All parties were gone when we arrived.

ARREST FOR DRIVER'S LICENSE LAW AND MUFFLER ORDINANCE

Stopped auto for having a loud muffler. Driver didn't have a license but had proper identification and was a resident of the city. Ordered to appear for court the next morning. He didn't show up, I obtained a warrant and arrested him at his home two days later.

TROUBLE WITH A JUVENILE

Complainant stated that unknown black males threw a bottle at their house. She gave us a description and we knew who it was. We went to the boys' home and after we talked to their parents, they went back and cleaned up the glass.

CONVEYANCE

One plain drunk to the station for a Squad.

CONVEYANCE

One disorderly white male to the station for a Patrolman walking his beat. This one turned out to be a fighter. He wound up with a cut on the back of his head and I wound up with another ruined shirt.

TROUBLE WITH A DRUNK

A bartender had served the subject a glass of beer. After he drank it, he became loud and boisterous and knocked over a few tables. The bartender called the Police. A check revealed the drunk was only twenty years old. The bartender and owner were ordered to appear for serving a minor. The drunk was arrested and conveyed to the station. He stated that the bartender asked him for some identification, and when he showed him identification indicating he was only twenty, the bartender said that was old enough.

CONVEYANCE
A white male prisoner transported from the District Station to the Detective Bureau.

CALL FOR POLICE
Complainant stated that two black males and three white females had tried to get into her house. We broadcast a description and another Squad saw them standing on a corner about two blocks away. One of the black males was arrested by them for disorderly conduct (urinating on the sidewalk). They called for us and when we searched the subject before we put him in our wagon, we found a loaded 38 caliber revolver stuck in his belt. He also had a switch blade knife in his pocket. In addition to the disorderly conduct charge, he was charged with carrying a concealed weapon. The original complaint of them trying to break into the house was dropped. The second male lived at the house and was the husband of the complainant. He thought his wife was gone to work and he was bringing his girlfriend to his house for a little party.

CONVEYANCE
Two drunks to the station for a Squad.

CALL FOR POLICE
Six young black males (the oldest being thirteen) charged into a filling station and began throwing cans and bottles at the proprietor. He took refuge in his back room and from there called the Police. By the time we arrived all the kids were running down the block. We chased and caught two of them and brought them back to the station. The damage these young kids had caused was tremendous. After leaving the station they had picked up rocks that were lying around outside and broke every window in the place. The damage to the windows alone was over $1,000. The two that we caught gave us the names of the other four. They were all picked up and turned over to juvenile authorities.

The filling station owner was responsible for the complete loss. He said his insurance had been canceled because of the area his station was located in. The juvenile Judge ordered the parents to make restitution, but they were all on county welfare and didn't have any money.

ARREST FOR AUTO SPEED
Subject was from out-of-town and was taken to the station where he posted bond.

HOLD-UP IN PROGRESS
A liquor store was held up by three masked men. We were the first Squad on the scene. We got a description from the store owner and broadcast it to all Squads. The Detectives arrived on the scene and handled the investigation. We checked the area for the suspects with negative results.

CONVEYANCE
One white male for drunk and disorderly to the station for a Squad.

ASSIST AN OFFICER
Even though we were only about six blocks away we were the fourth Squad on the scene. A beat Cop had gotten into a fight with a drunk and a citizen had called for help. By the time we arrived the fight was over and we conveyed the subject to the station. He was charged with resisting arrest in addition to the drunken charge. Instead of it costing him ten dollars, it cost him thirty days in the House of Correction.

DRUNK ON THE PORCH
Woman came to her front door and found a man lying on her front steps. The man was very drunk. We searched his wallet and found that he was one block west from where he lived. We put him in the wagon and took him home. We turned him over to his wife, and considering the size of the man and the size of his wife—he probably would have been better off in jail!

PURSE SNATCHING—AMBULANCE SENT
Two elderly women were standing on the corner waiting for a bus when two teenagers came up behind them, knocked them down and took their purses. It looked like the one woman may have broken her hip. We broadcast the brief description they gave us and then began to check the area for the actors. We didn't find the youths, but we did find the purses about two blocks away in an alley. Everything was still in the purses with the exception of the grand sum of three dollars and eighty cents.

CONVEYANCE
Two drunks to the station for a Squad. The two were twin bachelor brothers in their late fifties. Their being arrested for drunk was as common as the sun rising.

FAMILY TROUBLE—SECOND CALL—MAN MAY HAVE A GUN
The second call meant that a Squad had been there before and apparently had advised both the husband and wife, and felt the situation had been taken care of. We were met at the front door by the wife who said her husband had threatened to shoot her, and were now in their bedroom with the door closed.

Two other Squads had gone with us to the hitch, and after checking over the house carefully and not finding the subject we went to the closed bedroom door and kicked it in. The man was lying drunk on the bed with a rifle lying next to him. We found the gun to be empty and arrested the man for being drunk. The next day the wife met us at the District Attorney's office where we were going to apply for a warrant, for reckless use of a weapon. But the wife wouldn't testify that he pointed the gun at her, and he was released after stipulating to the drunken charge. It's interesting to note that the very next night we were called back to the same house on another family trouble call. This time the husband had packed his clothes and left the house, but not before he had given his wife a good beating. She went down the next morning to the District Attorney's office, and a battery warrant was issued against her husband.

MEET A SUBURBAN SQUAD, MAN WANTED ON WARRANT

It's a matter of courtesy that when an outlying jurisdiction comes into the city to serve a state warrant they call for a local Squad to assist.

CONVEYANCE

Three drunks to the station for a Squad.

CONVEYANCE

Juvenile plain drunk to County General Hospital to be examined and then back to the station. Any time a juvenile is arrested for being intoxicated, he has to be examined before he is turned over to juvenile authorities or is released to his parents.

CHECK FOR SICK MAN IN A PHONE BOOTH

The man was drunk and had called the telephone operator and asked her to send an ambulance. She couldn't understand him so she switched the call to the Police Department. We arrested him for plain drunk and conveyed him to the station.

MEET A CITIZEN REGARDING FAMILY TROUBLE

We met a sixteen year old girl who related that her mother had died about six months ago, and ever since then her father had been coming home drunk. She said she was the oldest of five children, and it was very hard for her to care for the younger children when her father was in this condition. She seemed like a very responsible young girl who was dealing, as best she could, with a tragic situation.

We followed her home from the corner phone booth where she had called from, and she led us into the living room where we found her father in an extremely drunken condition. There was more to this than just arresting the man for drunk. We spent several hours talking to the children and feeding the man black coffee in order to try and sober him up. We also contacted several relatives to find out how responsible the oldest daughter actually was. After discussing the whole situation, we talked the man into committing himself into a hospital where he could find help. We then notified the relatives and they said they would make periodic checks at the home to see that everything was going alright. In fact, we checked back daily for better than a week. After this time the father was released from the hospital and at least for the present, seemed to have a completely different outlook.

ARREST FOR DRUNKEN DRIVING

Dave and I observed an auto go through a stop sign. We turned the Squad around and followed the car with red light and siren for several blocks before he finally stopped. I got out and went to the driver's side and told the driver to roll down his window. He just stared at me with blood shot eyes with his head leaning up against the window. I opened the door and the subject fell right out. We picked him up and leaned him against his auto and ran him through a few tests. When asked whether he had too much to drink, he stated yes, at a party on the south side of town. I asked him if he knew where he was and he stated he was still on the south side and just three blocks from home. He apparently got his directions mixed up and was now approximately six miles from home. We advised him that he was under arrest and started to help him back to the wagon when I looked down and saw the front of his pants getting wet. I asked him what was happening and he said, "I'm pissing in my pants, what you think I'm doing?" We took him to the station, ran him through all the tests and placed him in the cell. As I was closing the door he said to me, "Hey Copper, how the hell are you going to prove drunken driving when I wasn't even driving a car?"

TROUBLE WITH A CUSTOMER

One drunk asleep at the bar, walked home.

STOPPED AUTO FOR GOING THROUGH A RED LIGHT

Talked to the driver and after asking him a few personal questions regarding his driver's license, he admitted that he had none and when he got stopped he asked his buddy to let him use his. Both subjects were on leave from the army and had just come back from overseas. As is usually the case when dealing with service personnel they were both very polite and answered all questions with a, "Yes sir" and a, "No sir." Both were released with a verbal warning.

SOMEONE MAY BE IN THE BUILDING

A cleanup man came to a factory and found the rear door open. The building was checked by us and the owner contacted. He stated that he probably left the door open. No cause.

TROUBLE WITH A JUVENILE

Woman came home from work and when she went to the basement to do washing, she found a young girl sleeping under the basement stairs. Interviewed the girl at the station and found her to be a runaway from home. She said she knew a girl that lived at the house and when she found the back door open, she went to the basement to sleep for the night. Contacted the parents who stated the girl was uncontrollable, and they didn't want her at home. She was turned over to the juvenile authorities.

FAMILY TROUBLE—THIRD CALL

We weren't sent the first two times, but we made sure that nobody would have to go back for the fourth call—at least not for the rest of the night. One arrest for plain drunk.

CONVEYANCE
Three white males for drunk and disorderly conduct to the station for a Squad.

MERCHANT POLICE ALARM
Building checked with owner, no cause, faulty alarm.

THEFT COMPLAINT
Complainant had picked up an unknown female at a bar. He took her to his house and after he had relations with her, he took her to an address that she stated was her home. When he returned home, he found that she apparently had unlocked his back door and while they were gone, some unknown persons had cleaned him out. One color television, one black and white television, one stereo set, the rest of his living room furniture and even his bed.

Complainant could only give a brief description of the woman as he was quite drunk. We checked the address where he had dropped her off and an elderly couple lived there. The complainant was apparently the victim of a pretty neat scheme. I wonder what his wife said when she returned from visiting her folks down south.

CONVEYANCE
A prisoner who had been confined at the hospital was brought back to the station.

That just about completed the activity over a two-week period. The only things that I left out were a few arrests for vehicle equipment violations, the follow-up investigations on complaints from previous nights and the nightly interviews of numerous people on the street which constitute field interrogations.

10. Responding to Calls

Bob, Dave & I had been working together now for about four months. We had gotten used to each other's misgivings and all-in-all seemed to make a good team. In fact, it was almost a disappointment when occasionally two of us would be off at the same time and a relief man would be assigned to the Squad.

It was with a relief man one night when I encountered an unusual situation. We were just going to get a cup of coffee at one of our usual restaurants. As we were about to pull up in front, we noticed two young, suspicious looking black males going into the restaurant. We decided to drive past the restaurant and make a U-turn. By the time we got back to the restaurant the two were coming out. We saw them walk down a side street and get into an auto with several other youths.

What had actually happened was that the two had gone into the restaurant with the idea of holding it up, but as they were walking in the front, a Copper was walking in the back door to get a cup of coffee.

We followed the auto for several blocks until we got to an area just off the expressway that was surrounded by vacant fields and cyclone fencing. This is where we liked to pull over autos, just in case the auto was stolen and everybody started to run, we would have a better chance of catching one or two.

When we stopped the auto, all four doors opened up and six young black males and one black female emerged. By the time my partner and I got out of the wagon all seven of them were coming towards us and started to give us the business verbally. "Hey man, why you following us? Just because a black man has a car you think it's stolen." The driver seemed to be the oldest and really worked up his passengers. "Man get off my back, I been stopped three times already today. This is my mother's car and she's going to sue your ass." We checked out the plates and they weren't reported stolen, but the identification tag from the auto was missing and it would take quite a bit of time to check the engine number. We told the group that they should all get back into the car and follow us to the station. They all started to walk away and just then one of the four-man Squads pulled up and asked if we needed any help. We told them we would lead the way and they should follow the other car.

Twice on the way into the station the car stopped and everybody jumped out and started to walk away. Each time we had to get out of the Squad and round them all up. Each time we were lashed with more verbal abuse. We finally got to the station and started to check out the car more thoroughly. First, we found the identification number and found that the auto was stolen almost two months prior to this date. Then we found that the plate was stolen off a car that had been parked in a garage for several months and the owner never realized it was gone.

This was all we needed and we placed all seven of them under arrest for auto theft. Once the booking, searching, interrogation and report writing was done we added up our total:

> One adult for operating an auto without the owner's consent; five juveniles and one adult passenger in a stolen auto.
>
> One adult for armed robbery (he was picked out of a lineup after we found he matched a hold-up description).
>
> Two adults and four juveniles for possession of marijuana (their pockets were loaded with the stuff).
>
> One juvenile for theft of license plates and one adult on three separate warrants that were outstanding on him.

Not bad for stopping one car.

It was now the winter of 1967 and emotions from the previous summer's riots were still running high. I was working with Bob one night—in fact it was the day before New Year's Eve. We were traveling down in the lower end of the inner city when an auto passed us with one tail light out.

We weren't going to stop it, but it pulled over to the curb in front of us so we pulled behind it. The driver got out and started to walk towards the passenger side of the wagon. But instead of stopping, he walked right past. Bob called out the window, "Hey, come here, I want to talk to you." The minute the youth turned around I recognized him as one of the leaders of the group that followed the Good Father that I spoke of previously.

"Hey man, what do you want with me?" the young man said as he walked towards Bob. By this time Bob was out of the wagon and standing between the sidewalk and the curb. Bob said, "I just wanted to let you know that your tail light is out."

"Don't tell me, man, tell the driver."

"I am talking to the driver, and besides that, let's see your driver's license."

"Look man, no punky ass Cop is going to tell me I was driving when I wasn't—all you want to do is rap me for driving without a license."

By this time I could tell that Bob was getting teed off, and the exchange of words between the two of them was getting pretty vehement. The whole thing was positively ridiculous because we had the car in our sight the entire time, and saw the young man get out of the driver's side. Besides that, there was nobody behind the wheel even now as I looked at the car.

I figured Bob could handle himself with the young individual so I stayed in the wagon and listened to the shouting match. In fact, it got so loud that soon they had accumulated three or four bystanders and then four or five young black males got out of the car we had stopped and came toward Bob. I figured it was about time I gave him a little moral support so I got out and stood next to him. Bob was trying to get some identification from the young man and he, in turn, was trying to convince Bob that he wasn't driving.

Before I realized it the crowd of bystanders had swelled to about thirty or forty and it was obvious from their remarks that we didn't have a friend among them. I got back into the Squad and called for a few more Squads to cover us because I figured that if anything broke loose, I could handle one or two of them, but Bob was going to have a hell of a time with the other thirty or so, and I just didn't feel like getting my tail kicked that night.

Two or three Squads responded, and by this time Bob had gotten the information he needed and ordered the young man to appear in court a few days after the New Year.

We all climbed back into our Squads and started to leave the area amidst the cries of "white honky, racist," etc. We could hear a few bottles smash in the street and a good sized brick bounced off the side of our wagon.

The young man never showed up in court and Bob got a warrant. He was arrested a few nights later driving the same car, and after several adjournments he was sentenced to ninety days in the House of Correction. His attorney asked the Judge to let him serve his sentence under the Huber Law, which entitles the offender to spend his nights in jail but allows him to work at his job during the day. The Judge denied the request because of his record and ordered him to spend his entire time in confinement, even though his attorney tried to convince the Judge that the young man was an outstanding citizen, serving the community as a whole in his profession.

His profession? He was employed by the state to attempt to rehabilitate those that were recently released from the State Prison and Reformatory helping them to adjust to civilian life. I can imagine what kind of advice he gave.

A few nights later Dave and I were working together when we received a call: SHOOTING, AMBULANCE SENT—MAN WALKING DOWN THE STREET WITH A SHOTGUN. We checked two or three of the streets around the address of the shooting for the man with the gun and then headed towards the house. By the time we got there three Officers were coming out of the house with a man in handcuffs. I went into the house and saw a man lying on the floor in the back hallway in a pool of blood. There were several other Officers and Detectives in the house taking care of the scene, so I went back outside. By this time Dave already had the man in handcuffs in the back of our wagon so we conveyed him to the Detective Bureau. Once at the bureau we asked him for a statement, after advising him of his constitutional rights, this is the story he related:

"My wife and the woman that lives downstairs from us had an argument today and the woman downstairs says to my wife that she's gonna kick her ass. Well, I don't want anybody to do any beating on my wife, so tonight I went downstairs to talk to her husband. I had gone out earlier in the day and bought a gun and had it in my back pocket, because the man downstairs is big and I heard he had a gun.

I met the man in the back hall and I told him that I love my wife and know how to handle her and he ought to know how to handle his wife. I also told him that he should keep his wife away from mine. This big black ape started towards me, so I pulled my gun and shot him, because he's too big and I didn't want him beating on me. He fell to the floor and I was still mad, so I fired two or three more shots into the wall.

His wife came out into the hall and told me that she also had a gun, so I chased her through the house and into the street. I fired a few more shots at her as she ran down the street and into some house.

Then I went back to my house and the Officers were there. I told them I was the one they were looking for and that I did the shooting. The reason I carried the gun downstairs was that if there was going to be any trouble, I was going to shoot the black bastard. I didn't want to kill him; I only wanted to shoot him."

Apparently most of the story that he gave us was the truth, except that when he went downstairs and pulled his gun, the other man got on his knees and begged him not to shoot. So the little man put the gun up to the kneeling man's head and pulled the trigger.

The next day in court he was charged with attempted murder on the man he had shot, and endangering safety by conduct regardless of life, for shooting at the victim's wife. Several days later the man who was shot died and the charge was changed to first degree murder. The little man with the big gun got life.

I worked with Bob the next two nights and besides being in court all day, we got nailed with about a dozen hitches each night that involved a lot of writing. So by the end of the two days I was pretty well worn out and really appreciated my two off days.

When I came back to work, Bob was off so I worked with Dave, and he told me that he and Bob hadn't had much action the previous nights, so he was really ready to hustle tonight and find some court time.

Well, it didn't take us very long to get involved. We started work at 7:00 p.m. and at about 8:00 p.m., we were just returning from taking a prisoner to headquarters, when we heard a description broadcast over the air about an armed robbery that had just occurred in our area. The description was of three black males armed with a sawed off shotgun and fleeing in a black 1959 Cadillac.

I was driving and was just watching a car go wheeling out of a filling station when Dave suddenly shouted, "There it goes!"

"There goes what?" I asked.

"The black Cadillac from the holdup," he said.

"What are you talking about?" I said, "That's a Chevy." I thought he was looking at the same car I was.

"No, no," he said, "The other way! Turn this damn thing around." It took me a second to realize he was talking about a car that had passed us going the other way and I had never seen it. I whipped the wagon around, but by this time there wasn't a car in sight. We went for a couple of blocks and I could tell that Dave was really pissed-off that I didn't see the same car when suddenly, there in front of us, was a 1959 black Cadillac parked at the curb. Dave was like a little kid, "There that S.O.B. is! They probably abandoned the thing when we turned around," he said. We pulled up in back of the car, wrote down the license number and then got out and started to check the auto over. The door was open so we made a fast check of the inside when just then an older black male shouted from the other side of the street. "Hey man, that ain't the car you're looking for." He came over to us and I asked him what the hell he was talking about. He then told us that he had just come from home a few blocks away and that just as he was taking his car out of his garage, he saw a black Cadillac like the one we were looking at. It pulled into his alley and three or four black males jumped out and started running through his yard. He also stated that one of them was carrying either a shotgun or a rifle.

Dave and I looked at each other and at first didn't know what to say—the story sounded so weird. By then the man said he thought he recognized one of the men fleeing from the auto, and said he would get a hold of us in about an hour and see if he could find out where the man was.

Dave and I figured we didn't have much to lose so we gave the man our Squad number and told him to call the Police Department in about an hour and we would meet him some place.

The man took off. We checked on the Cadillac and found that it belonged to a patron in the tavern on the corner, and that the patron had been there all day. We started to check the neighborhood where our unknown informer said he lived. We didn't have any luck and, sure enough, in about an hour we were sent to meet a citizen a few blocks from where the man said he lived. We picked him up and he rode around in the back of our wagon for about fifteen minutes pointing out where he said the men ran through his yard and where he thought they lived. He then asked to be let out and that he would get in touch with us a little later.

By this time we figured we had played his game this far and might as well stick to it for a while. We dropped him off on a corner and he disappeared into a corner gin mill and we took off. About forty-five minutes later we got another call to meet the man and this time we called a couple of Detectives that are assigned to the Hold-up Squad to meet us also.

We met the man and he gave us the name of a man he thought was one of the ones we were looking for, and stated that he was in a tavern just a few blocks away. The four of us headed for the tavern and called for another Squad to meet us there. Four of us started to go into the tavern and two stayed outside to cover us, when out of the front door came a young black male that fit the description of one of the hold-up men to a tee. We asked him for identification and sure enough, he was the one we were looking for. We put him into the wagon and went into the tavern where we found another one that was wearing clothing identical to what one of the actors from the hold-up was wearing, so we arrested him too.

We were just putting the second man in the wagon when we heard that the Detective Squad had the Cadillac stopped two blocks away. We went down there and there was the Cadillac with the driver already in handcuffs. Two of them were positively identified as being the actors involved in the hold-up. The third man was a suspect in a previous hold-up, and he was also identified by a complainant and charged with armed robbery.

As of this writing, all three men are now serving sentences in the State Prison. In fact, one of the men received an additional sentence when he was convicted of performing an act of sexual perversion on a fellow inmate in the County Jail, while awaiting trial on the robbery charge.

Dave and I checked for several nights after the arrests to try and find our unknown witness. We never went to his house because he was quite emphatic that we should never try and contact him there. We knew that there must have been more to the story than what he told, but it was not until almost a year later that we realized what happened.

A young man was picked-up for robbery and attempted murder, and we found out that he was the son of our unknown informer. Further, he was the third man involved in the original hold-up. The father had tried to protect his son by giving us the names of his accomplices. As it turned out, he would have been better off giving us his son also, because now his son is serving forty years.

By this time, I had spent enough time in the inner city to realize that it was a world within itself. A world built on violence, hatred, passion and strength in numbers. Naturally, the good outnumber the bad, but like I have said before, it is only the bad that a Police Officer most commonly comes in contact with and when a half dozen or so of these hate-minded individuals get together, they become a strong body.

I remember one night shortly after our incident with the armed robbers. All three of us were working so I was put on a Squad with someone else. For several hours we had been looking for a young white boy who was wanted for a variety of offenses including burglary, auto theft, resisting arrest and escape from custody. He was a fairly intelligent individual in that he not only would steal a car, but he would then change the license number with black paint by making a one into a seven or a six into an eight, etc. It was a crude form of deception, but at a glance it was enough to deceive.

His only downfall was that he had a girlfriend who he could not stay away from. We planted (meaning surveillance) on her house for several hours and sure enough, he drove up in his brand new stolen auto—changed plates and all. The trouble was that he spotted us at the same time and away he went, with us right on his tail.

It was the end of January and the roads were a sheet of ice. He had the advantage over us because he didn't care if he piled up the stolen auto, where we had to be a little more cautious with the Squad.

He slid around a corner, lost control and wound up in somebody's backyard. By the time my partner brought the Squad to a stop the young man was running up the alley. My partner ran up the alley after him and I ran along the front of the houses hoping that he may cut through a yard. I heard my partner fire a shot and later learned that he threw one into the air hoping to scare the kid. All the shot did was light a fire under him and after that there was no catching him.

My partner met me back at the Squad and he told me that he had chased the individual for about four or five blocks. He said he came through a yard and out onto the street with his gun still in his hand. He was just trying to decide which way the young man ran, when about six or seven young black males came up the street. My partner said he was just about to ask them if they had seen anybody running, when one of the youth asked him, "Hey white honky, what you doing out all by yourself with that gun in your hand?"

Another said, "Yeah man, why don't you take that gun and shove it up your ass?" The taunting kept on until my partner turned around and walked away. He told me he never felt so useless in his entire life. He said there he was a grown man, standing in front of a bunch of teenagers who were cussing him out, and all he could do was walk away. He said he knew that if he tried to arrest one or two of them he would have gotten his can kicked. He also knew that the gun he had in his hand wasn't worth a damn in a situation like that, and besides that, the kids knew the same thing. You've got to remember that in those days there was no such thing as a handy talky or portable radio. If you got in trouble you had to rely on your instincts or physical abilities, remembering you would probably get another chance when the odds were different.

The more he talked, the madder he got. He had almost piled up the Squad, chased a kid we had been looking for quite some time, and then to top it off, was humiliated by a bunch of young toughs who thought he had invaded the privacy of their own little world. As individuals they probably would not have said a word, but because of their number and being surrounded by their own environment, they had the mental strength of a giant.

The funny thing about that night was that a few hours later we met up with this giant once more. But this time it was on more even terms. We had been sent to investigate a false fire alarm and were just standing on the street corner talking to the firemen. Along came our giant and out of the center spewed the declaration, "Hey there's that same white M.F. Cop who's going to get his gun shoved up his ass."

That's all that my partner needed. He charged into the crowd of youths and when they realized that the odds were in our favor rather than theirs, they all took off in different directions. The young man that my partner grabbed was a real fighter. He was only seventeen years old, but was about six feet tall and about two hundred pounds. It took both of us and a couple of firemen to subdue him. By this time Dave and Bob arrived with the wagon and took him away. He was charged with disorderly conduct and resisting arrest. The juvenile authorities released him the next day with a slap on the hand, but at least my partner got some personal satisfaction out of it.

If these kids would only realize that the majority of Coppers can take a tremendous amount of kidding and good natured ribbing, but when they get so downright profane, obnoxious and repulsive night after night, it's bound to take its toll on even the most even tempered individual.

11. Emblem of Authority

Speaking of being antagonized by verbal abuse, it was about this time in history that the phraseology PIG became a household word when referring to a Cop. I can honestly say that of all the degrading names that I've been called, that is the one that hurt me the most. Most Coppers passed it off as just being another form of harassment, but that was one that I couldn't shake.

One night four of us were standing outside our Squads when a bus load of youth came by. Suddenly the air was filled with 'PIG, PIG, OINK, OINK." The rest of the Coppers just ignored it, but it hurt me so deep that I could feel a burning sensation in my stomach. It hurt me so much more when I realized that the youths in the bus were from a church in our Squad area. I had spent many hours with these youths trying to inspire a friendship. A few days later when I approached several of them and asked them about the remark, they said that they didn't realize that I was one of the Cops standing there. I tried to explain to them that it didn't make any difference that I was there or not, they were degrading the uniform that I was wearing and was so very proud of. It had nothing to do with race, color or creed; they just felt that everyone in a blue uniform that bore a badge was considered a pig. They seemed to understand my feelings and I was sure that I would never hear it from them again. But it brought to mind something I found very predominant in the inner city, and that was guilt by association. We weren't bad because we were black or white, but we were unsuitable for their society because we wore a blue uniform and an emblem of authority.

I recall being sent to a neighbor trouble call one time. The home was a modest duplex located on the fringe of the inner city. The landlords, who were black, lived in the lower unit and a young black couple with a small baby lived upstairs. It was the tenant who called so we interviewed them first. The young couple was very pleasant and when I asked for his name I recognized it. I asked if he had any brothers or sisters that I may know. He told me the names of two of his brothers and I immediately recognized them as being leaders in the group that followed the Good Father. He explained to me that he got along with his brothers, but he wasn't involved in any of the demonstrations because he was working two jobs trying to support his young family and save enough money to purchase his own home. He was what one might refer to as a very outstanding young citizen.

My partner and I then asked what his problem was and he explained that he had had some words with the landlord regarding leaving too many lights on in the basement, so the landlord turned off the tenant's electricity and padlocked the basement door. They were concerned about their young baby and said it was time for her to eat, and they had no means of warming her bottle.

He asked us if we would go down and talk to the landlord and explain the situation and tell him that they would move out at the end of the month, but until then they particularly didn't enjoy living in the dark. It seemed like a reasonable request so my partner and I went to talk to the landlord. We were met by an extremely hostile man and wife in their early thirties who immediately asked who the hell called us, and questioned who gave us the right to be in their house.

I tried to explain what the circumstances were and at the same time I was able to survey the inside of their living quarters. It was immaculate. It was very obvious that the occupants took great pride in their dwelling. Between the man and woman giving us a hard time, we tried to explain that they had no right turning off the electricity and locking the basement door. The woman immediately looked me in the eye and stated that I was the last one in the world to be talking about rights. It was obvious she had absolutely no use for me, but I disregarded the remark when her husband told us that he would put things back in order as long as his tenants were moving out at the end of the month. My partners and I were satisfied and we left.

We drove for a few blocks and both of us made a comment on how spotless the house was and also on the feeling of hate that was conveyed by the landlord's wife onto us. Just then the dispatcher called our Squad again. He gave the same address we had just left and added that it was a second call on a neighbor trouble and this time one man had a gun. We swung our Squad around and by the time we reached the house, two other Squads were there waiting to cover us. We were met outside by the young tenant from upstairs and also by two men who I recognized as being his brothers. He quickly related to me that his brothers had come to the house, and all three of them went to the basement to turn on the electricity. When they started back up the stairs the landlord met them at his rear door with a shotgun in his hand. We learned later that most of the tenant's story was true, except he left out the fact that they had broken the basement door open to get in.

My partner and I went to the rear downstairs door with our revolvers drawn and were followed by two Officers with shotguns, meanwhile, two other Officers went to the front door. I knocked on the rear door and announced that it was the Police and that they should open up. I could hear the woman inside hollering that we should get the hell out of their house, that they didn't need us or call for us. A few seconds later the door opened and the man of the house asked what we wanted. I told him that we had a report that he had pointed a gun at someone and at the same time the four of us more or less squeezed our way into the kitchen. The woman was in an outrage, screaming at the top of her voice. To make matters a little touchier, the Officers on the front porch had opened the door and when they entered, they saw the shotgun lying on the dining room table and came into the kitchen with it. So now there were six of us in the kitchen along with the couple, and a lot of guns.

The woman was almost out of her mind by this time, hollering at the top of her voice that as long as we were treating them like animals, we might as well shoot them down like dogs. To make matters worse, the brothers of the tenant were standing at the door and demanding that we lock the couple up for threatening them with the gun. It took about five minutes to get things somewhat calmed down. We explained that we were going to take the shotgun along with us for safe keeping and the young man from upstairs said he would take his wife and baby and stay someplace else for the night.

We then gave everyone a referral memo to meet us the next morning at the District Attorney's office to hash over the whole situation, and see if there was need for issuance of a warrant. Within a few minutes everybody else had left the house and my partner and I were getting a little more information from the landlord. We were still standing in the kitchen and he asked us if we wouldn't like to sit down. He hardly got the words out of his mouth when his wife retorted with, "No M. F. Cop is sitting in my kitchen!"

I turned around and said, "Look lady, I'm not going to sit in your kitchen—after we have the information that we need we'll be leaving your house, and you won't see us again until the morning. But just for my own satisfaction, I'd like you to tell me why you hate us with such deep passion. I realize that we may have disrupted your normal way of life somewhat, but I'm sure it was necessary to prevent any bodily harm." I also said, "It can't be a matter of race, because you're black—the people upstairs are black and two of the Coppers that were here are black."

Then it came out. She hit me with a flurry of words that lasted for almost ten minutes. She started out by saying that the black Coppers were nothing but Uncle Toms that they had turned their backs on their own people and were no better than the white racist pigs that had kept her people in slavery for the past two hundred years. She said that wearing a uniform was just a disguise we used to keep her people suppressed. She also said she taught her children to abide by the laws of the land merely as a means of survival because they were written by white men as a means to obliterate the blacks from society. She further stated that if any of her children would dare bring a white friend into her house they would be severely punished.

I could hardly believe what I was hearing. This woman was so full of hate that it was beyond my imagination. I knew that at this point anything I would say would be misconstrued and I would only be adding fuel to the fire. I did tell her that when I had time some night I would like to sit down and discuss some of her thoughts with her. To this she replied that the next time I—or any Cop—step into her house they better be carrying a big gun and be prepared to use it. At this my partner and I left and there was little doubt in our minds who was the racist.

The next night I worked with Dave and told him I'd met the most prejudiced woman in the world. I felt that her judgment was so warped and twisted that she was almost injurious to her own race. We talked about it for a while and then got involved in a couple of arrests and a tavern violation.

I never met that woman again, but I've often wondered what values her children are growing up with.

Dave and I worked together for three nights in a row and each night we ran into an interesting situation. The first night we got sent to a fight in a tavern. This was a common hitch for us and we averaged at least two or three a week. Walking into a tavern and finding the floor covered with blood, a man lying in a heap with blood pouring from a gash in his head was not unusual. But the reason for him being in that position was somewhat uncommon.

He had the misfortune of trying to break up a fight between two women. The tavern was in shambles—chairs smashed, bottles broken and the two fighters were standing nose to nose and cussing each other out with a choice of words that almost made me blush. The ambulance was called and after they had taken our Sir Galahad away to have his head patched up, Dave and I tried to settle the fight. The reason for the fight was almost unbelievable. One woman had accused the other of wearing a wig, and the other made the accusation that the first woman wore falsies. After a brief exchange of words the one woman grabbed the other by the front of her dress and tore it down to her waist. This was done apparently to prove that what she had was false. The other woman, with her dress torn, grabbed her assailant by what she thought was a wig and pulled a clump of hair from her head. The clump was big enough to make a four inch paint brush. When our hero stepped between them and told them they weren't acting like ladies, they each broke a beer bottle over his head. The disposition on this one was quite simple. Both women were thrown in for plain drunk and battery. The next day when the man with the headache refused to prosecute, the battery charged was dropped. Unbelievable!

The second night Dave and I were sent to a noisy party about 1:00 a.m. We were met there by a couple of other Squads who told us they had been stopping young people all night who were on their way to a party at this address. They told us someone had made an anonymous complaint that there were drunken juveniles at the party.

The house was a duplex and the party was on the second floor to which the entrance was in the back. Two Coppers watched the outside and four of us made our way up the dark back stairs.

We listened for awhile at the back door and I must say that it wasn't a very noisy party. All we could hear was soft music, a little giggling, a little moaning, and the sound of glasses. Now the idea was to get in the door. Nobody had any brilliant ideas so we just knocked. To our amazement a young female voice from inside said, "Come in, the doors unlocked." Well, when we opened the door and walked in, I never saw such a shocked look on anyone's face before. Apparently, we were the last people in the world that the young girl thought was going to walk through the door.

Once inside we could tell that it wasn't the most lavishly furnished place. The first room we entered was the kitchen and the only thing that occupied that besides young people was a half barrel of beer. The next room was the living room and that was furnished with a couch that someone got out of a junk pile, a couple of beat-up old chairs and a whole mess of drunken juveniles. The next room was even worse, which was the bedroom. In it was one bed with a mattress and about eight kids on it. Some dressed and some half dressed. And last was the bathroom. When I entered that, all I found was one girl putting on lipstick. She looked at me and said, "What the hell's the matter with you, can't a girl have a little privacy?" Her boyfriend behind the shower curtain was an added attraction.

Well, I can't say that the party was noisy, but it most certainly was disorderly and that's what they were all arrested for. Those over eighteen were arrested for disorderly conduct and contributing to the delinquency of a child, and those younger than eighteen were charged with disorderly conduct and drinking. We never did find out who was throwing the party and nobody would admit to living there, but it sure must have been well advertised because as we were loading the wagon with the people we arrested, one car after another was stopping and a few young people stopped and called out the window, "Well, I guess the party's over for tonight."

The juveniles were turned over to the juvenile authorities. The next day in court the adults were fined $50 each and were turned over to the court Chaplin for a little counseling.

The third night we worked together we decided that we were going to take it easy and not get involved in anything, because we had both spent the last two days in court and we both just wanted to relax for a change.

Well, we lasted until two twenty in the morning. All we had to do was stay out of trouble for another half hour or so and we could go home. We had just finished taking a prisoner downtown and we figured that by the time we got back to our area and checked a few places, we'd be all done for the night.

But that wasn't to be. We were stopped at a red light when we suddenly saw a Squad chasing an auto on the street that we were about to enter. We spotted them two blocks away and from the looks of the smoke coming from the cars they were really traveling. When the car reached the corner where we were sitting, the auto being chased suddenly screeched to a halt. The chasing Squad was out in front of him to block his path.

Dave was driving and he headed towards the auto because we figured that the occupants would run for sure. All of a sudden the driver put the car in reverse and started backwards at a tremendous speed. The only thing wrong was that he didn't have any place to go. His path was blocked by parked cars and he smashed right into them, knocking one of them all the way up on the sidewalk.

By this time we were right next to the auto and everybody was climbing out. A Copper from the other Squad and me grabbed the passenger and Dave and the other Copper took off after the driver. The last time I saw the three of them was when they ran between two buildings.

I put the cuffs on the prisoner we had and was about to put him in the wagon when the early morning air was shattered by a shot. It came from between the buildings and the thought of Dave or the other Copper getting shot brought my heart into my stomach. I pulled my gun and started running towards the gangway (a small space between two buildings) where the shot came from. Before I had gone more than a half dozen steps or so, Dave and the other Copper came out of the gangway. Now I was really shocked. They had the driver between them—one by each arm. His face was completely covered with blood. Dave hollered to me, "Get an ambulance here in a hurry."

"What the hell happened?" I said.

Dave replied, "I hit the guy over the head with my gun, it went off and I shot him."

All I could say was, "You've got to be kidding."

I ran back and called for an ambulance and then we applied a compress to the top of the man's head where the blood seemed to be coming from. The ambulance came and we laid him on a cot and they sped off for the hospital.

To say the least, we were both pretty well shook. It had only been a few weeks since a black man had pulled a gun on a Copper and after a struggle the man was shot to death. The incident occurred in the heart of the inner city and even though the shooting was completely justified, inner city groups were trying to press for a murder warrant on the Copper. I figured that if the guy that Dave shot died, even though it was an accident, we would be in for a whole lot of criticism and harassment.

The four of us conversed and tried to piece together what happened. Dave said that as he was chasing the fleeing driver of the auto the other Copper was in front of him and as they turned the corner into the gangway the other Copper slipped and fell. While he was on the ground, the man they were chasing picked up a piece of concrete and was about to throw it at the fallen Copper, when Dave got to him first and hit him over the head with his gun. The man went down for a second and when he got up he punched Dave in the chest. By this time the other Copper was at Dave's side and they both hit the man over his head again with their guns. Dave said all he heard was a loud bang and a big flash of fire right in front of his face.

While Dave was talking he opened his gun, which was all full of blood, and suddenly realized that he had six live rounds. He looked at the other Copper and with almost a sigh of relief said, "Well I'll be damned! You shot him. I didn't." I think at about that time, the other Copper would just as soon have been someplace else.

As it turned out the man wasn't shot and all he had was a large cut on the top of his head. By the time we had finished all our reports it was five in the morning and by eight-thirty we were back in court. The passenger was charged with being drunk in an auto and was fined fifty dollars plus costs.

The driver, who had been released from the hospital, was charged with eluding a Police Officer and battery to the Officer. The latter charge had just been made a felony with a mandatory jail sentence. This was done to try and cut down the large number of Police Officers that get their teeth kicked in every year. An undesirable would probably think twice about striking a Copper when the consequences meant sitting in the can for a few months rather than a fifty or one-hundred dollar fine.

Well, that completed my three days of so called interesting situations and after that I took a sick day and two regular offs to recuperate.

That's one of the many things that make this job so fantastic. After being off for a few days I would come back all full of vim and vigor and I would never be disappointed. I could always count on being involved in some situation that set my profession apart from everyone else's profession in the entire world. Be it tragedy or comedy, it was always something different.

Speaking of comical situations, I can recall when Dave and I were involved in something that was absolutely hilarious. I don't know whether I can make it sound as funny as it actually was, but I'll try.

We were sent to help four or five other Coppers who were trying to catch two supposedly vicious dogs. By the time we got there the other Coppers had the two dogs cornered in a fenced yard. They were both German

Shepherds—one male and one female. They both appeared to be excited from being chased by the neighbors and the Police. Several of us had dog ropes that we fashioned into short lassoes and it was our intention to try and play dog catchers. Well, after two of us threw our ropes and missed, and two more jumped over a fence to get away from their charge, the two dogs pranced merrily down the street.

Dave and I jumped in our wagon and chased the large male dog several blocks down an alley that was bordered by fences. Dave drove the wagon next to the dog singing "Hi Ho Silver" while I hung out the window and tried to get the rope around his neck. After several blocks the only thing we had caught was a picket fence, so we decided to give up and try something else.

We parked on the street contemplating what our next form of attack would be, when the big dog trotted to within ten feet of our truck and sat down. Just for a joke I opened the door and called out, "Here boy," and to my tremendous amazement the dog made two giant leaps and the next thing I knew he was flying over my lap. Well, you never saw two Coppers move so fast in all your life. We jumped out, slammed the doors behind us and stood there with foolish looks on our faces surveying the situation.

There laid this enormous dog across the front seat of our Squad. In fact, he looked very complacent. Dave looked at me and said, "Alright smart ass, you got any more brilliant ideas?"

I reached through the wing window of the Squad and grabbed the Squad's microphone. (Back then the cars had little windows on the side which opened independently of the big window in the door of the car.) I told the dispatcher that we would be 10-7 (out of service) for awhile and would he please have the humane society meet us. He asked if we had caught the dog, and all I could say was that I wasn't too sure who caught who but the dog was locked in the Squad and we were out.

A few minutes later a Sergeant pulled up, looked in the Squad and with his hand on his forehead and a comical grin on his face said, "Unbelievable, absolutely unbelievable! If I didn't know you two better I'd wonder how the hell something like that could possibly happen."

I said, "You probably won't believe this shit."

He held up his hand and just said, "Don't even try." With that he shook his head, got into his Squad and drove off.

Now that I've thought it over, I've had quite a few dealings that have involved dogs besides this last one, and the one where my partner shot the dog. I remember going to several family troubles where huge dogs were mastered by one of the parties involved. The first thing we would invariably do was determine who the boss of the dog was and then have him or her lock the dog in another room, or, if that wasn't possible, we would probably be forced to take the master's side.

One such family trouble was resolved by the dog and his master agreeing to leave the house, but only under the condition that he go by cab. This was agreeable to us, but after the cab arrived the cabbie didn't want to take the dog along as a passenger and this infuriated his master. Then, instead of having just a family trouble, we also had a cabbie having trouble with his fare. This one we had to resolve by threatening the man with the idea that we would shoot his dog. After we convinced him of that, he locked his dog in the basement and went along to jail with us for being drunk.

Another time, Dave and I picked up two large German Shepherds for a Squad and were taking them to the station. We had to travel through a predominately black section and as we did, the dogs became excited from being locked up in the back of the wagon, and they began to bark and jump at the back wire meshed window. A large group of black youths were standing on a corner and when they heard and saw these huge dogs they went running down the street hollering, "They got dogs! They got dogs! The white honky M.F.'s got dogs!" By the time we reached the station our lieutenant told us that he had six calls from citizens and one call from a black newspaper criticizing the fact that the Police Department now had a dog patrol.

Another time we had a huge Collie in the back of the wagon and when we got to the station we couldn't get him out. He wasn't mean, he was just comfortable back there and wasn't about to move. We got a stretcher from one of the ambulances and carried him out of the wagon on that. In order to get to the basement where we had a dog cage we had to go through the main office. As we carried the dog through on the stretcher I remember some man standing there waiting to pay a ticket. He looked at us and then exclaimed, "My God, what is this place? A Police station or a dog hospital?!"

But the one that I remember most, but which I denied having any part in, was when a huge Labrador was brought into the station and somehow he turned up in the lieutenant's clothes closet. The shocked look on the lieutenant's face when he went to get his lunch was almost unbelievable. It's a good thing he had a sense of humor!

A few nights after we had the dog in the front seat of our Squad Dave and I got sent to "A GUN FIGHT IN THE STREET." It wasn't the first call like that we had ever had but this one had an unusual twist. We were only a few blocks away so we were first on the scene. It was a lower class neighborhood with factories on one side of the street and two story flats on the other. There were a couple dozen people standing in the street and two cars—one parked behind the other—at an odd angle.

As Dave came wheeling up I jumped out with the shot gun. A young man and woman came running over to us and the man, who was quite pale, shouted, "Some asshole just took a shot at me."

This was followed by the woman pointing an accusing finger at the man and saying, "This guy tried to pick me up and my husband shot at him in self-defense." At this point we weren't that interested in why the shooting took place. It was obvious that nobody was injured and what concerned us most was where the man was that did the shooting and where was the gun. The woman seemed to read our minds and said, "My husband ran back into the house with the gun to call the Police." At the same time she pointed to an upper flat where they lived.

Feeling a little uneasy I pumped a shell into the shotgun and Dave and I proceeded up the stairs of the flat. As many times as I had had that shotgun in my hand, I never really got used to the idea. I had never had to use it and there was absolutely no doubt in my mind that I would if the situation called for it, but just the thought of all that power. A short barreled twelve gauge with three double O buck magnum shells followed by a slug. Wow!

Well, anyway, I was up about five or six steps with Dave right behind me, when suddenly a young man came flying around the top of the stairs. I hadn't heard any noise from up there before so he really startled me. In that first flash that I saw him I also saw that both his hands were empty and there was no weapon in sight on his person.

"Get the hell out of my house," he shouted "What the hell you doing in here? The guy you want is outside. He tried to pick up my wife." I told him to calm down, that there were other Coppers outside and the man he was talking about wasn't going any place. I told him that as soon as he handed over the gun we would all go outside and talk the whole thing over. He said, "Look, none of you bastards are coming in my house! I don't have a gun so get the hell out of here." It was obvious that the guy was really shaken! He was shaking and almost in tears.

I said, "Look, let's be reasonable about this. Either you tell me where the gun is or we'll come up there and tear the place apart."

"You can't do that" he said.

To which I responded, "Try us." Whether we would have or not was immaterial. Apparently he thought we would and that was the main idea.

"O.K.," he said, "It's in my bedroom. Come on I'll show you."

We followed him into a bedroom and he pointed to a drawer in a dresser. "It's in there," he said. Dave opened the drawer and sure enough there was a thirty-two caliber automatic with one in the chamber and six in the clip.

"O.K.," I said, "Now let's all go downstairs and talk this whole thing over." We didn't arrest him or advise him of his rights because we still didn't know what we had, and the man apparently was now going to cooperate.

We got all three parties together and this is the story that came out: the young woman was a housewife and mother and had received two obscene phone calls the day before. Each time the caller tried to make a date with her. When her husband came home he told her that the next time she gets one of those calls she should make a date with him and he would be waiting for him. The next day she got another call and this time arranged to meet the man in front of her house.

At the arranged time her husband waited in his car in a parking lot a few doors away. She said she saw this car go around the block a few times and then stop across the street. She went up to the car and the driver said, "Are you sure you want to go with me?"

At this point the husband came screeching up behind the man's car, jumped out and ran up to the car, gun in hand. He shouted, "Get out of the car you S.O.B. or I'll blow your head off." Either because he was excited or he wanted to emphasize his point, he blew a shot off into the ground. The neighbors, hearing all the commotion, called the Police.

We arrested the one man for disorderly conduct—making obscene phone calls, and the other man for reckless use of a weapon. The next day in the District Attorney's office the man charged with disorderly conduct emphatically denied making the calls and since there was no way we could positively prove it and he had no record, the warrant was refused. The District Attorney told us this while everyone was out of the room except for Dave and me.

Now all we had was the guy for reckless use. We had a good case on him, but after a good night's sleep he turned out to be a real nice guy who apologized over and over again for giving us such a hard time. He said that he was so upset with his wife getting those phone calls that he didn't know what he was doing.

The District Attorney, Dave and I talked the whole thing over and decided that the best thing to do was not charge either man and make the man who we knew did the calling but couldn't prove it feel fortunate that he didn't get his head blown off. That's exactly what we did. Not everybody was pleased, but I think everybody involved got the message.

12. Tavern Trouble

Things slowed down the next few days so we figured it would be a good time to check a few of our gin mills. They were always sure to turn up a few pinches and a few comical drunks, especially when we hadn't checked them for awhile and they started to hedge a bit on the violations. Under our city ordinances, a person one had to be twenty-one years or older to enter and loiter on a premises licensed to serve liquor. Closing hours were 2:00 a.m. Sunday through Friday, and 3:30 a.m. on Saturday nights. These were the most common violations.

The first tavern we checked was one of our regulars. It was almost 2:30 in the morning and we noticed for the past couple of weeks that the bartender or owner had made it a little farther past closing time each night. Dave and I were working this particular night and after checking through the front window we saw six or eight people at the bar. We entered through a small hallway leading into the main tavern area. Much to our surprise the softness under our feet as we entered the hallway wasn't carpeting, but rather was two stoned drunks that had been thrown out earlier, but never made it through the second door.

The one was so smashed that he never felt my two hundred pounds walk across his chest. After Dave and I placed our two sleeping beauties in the wagon, we went back in to see what other choice items we might find. By the time we got back in, a few of the customers had made it out the back door. All we had were a couple that apparently didn't even try to leave and the bartender and his wife.

The licensee wasn't on the premises, but he had to suffer along with the misfortune of his bartender. I say misfortune, because this is one that I felt a little bad about. The bartender had a Police record that was almost unbelievable. He had served time in the State Prison, and in his lifetime had been arrested for everything from robbery to drunk and disorderly. The only thing was that in the past three years since he got married, his record was perfectly clean. I hated to get him started all over again. As it was, I apparently did, because within two weeks he was arrested for drunk and disorderly and another week later we had him for another tavern violation.

A couple nights later Bob and I were working together. It was a Saturday night and unusually warm for the time of year. It started out as a typical Saturday. We made a few arrests for drunk and made a few conveyances for other Coppers.

About 10:00 p.m. we were sent to a noisy tavern. The call wasn't uncommon and due to the weather most bars had their front doors open. This particular tavern had a black owner who had never given us any trouble.

Although he had a couple of bartenders who had been quite hostile towards us on previous occasions, and never hesitated to show their dislike for us. Naturally, with that attitude we made our presence known more than usual. We were a block away from the tavern when we heard the loud thumping music. By the time we pulled up in front we realized that whichever neighbor called, we felt they had a perfect right to do so.

We figured just closing the front door would cut down the noise sufficiently. As we walked in the tavern there were four or five couples dancing. This we also knew was a violation because he had no dance permit. We talked to the owner for a few minutes and explained our being there and he was very cooperative. He stopped the dancing, closed the front door and turned down the juke box. All these actions brought on hostile looks from his patrons as well as his bartender who was one of the guys who hated Coppers. We told the owner we were satisfied with his actions, declined the drink and cigars he offered, and left.

Within an hour and a half we were sent back to the same tavern on the same noise complaint, but with the added information that the desk had received numerous calls. When we pulled up in front, the music was just as loud with several of the same customers, plus a few new ones who were dancing.

We entered and were met by not only the loud music, but they had changed the words to the song and were chanting in unison, "The honkies are coming, the honkies are coming!" We knew without asking that the owner wasn't around, otherwise this probably wouldn't have been going on.

Before we could say anything to the bartender, he pointed his finger at us and said, "Say what you got to say and then get the hell out because you're driving my customers away." The customers thought this was great—"Yeah, yeah, you tell 'em man!"

Little did our obnoxious friend know that he had just guaranteed himself and the owner a tavern violation. While I went to the phone to call a Sergeant, which was required in tavern violations, Bob started adding fuel to the fire by checking all the licenses, which have to be displayed, and after that he checked all the identifications of the patrons.

By the time I returned from the phone, Bob had really been rattling cages. He made it perfectly clear that either they keep the noise down or he would close the place up tighter than a drum. Knowing Bob as well as I did, I knew that he didn't make idle threats, only promises.

When the Sergeant arrived we gave the bartender and the patrons involved referral slips to meet us in a few days in the Captain's office, where the violations would be reviewed and then possibly sent to the City Attorney for issuance of a warrant.

As we left the tavern Bob let the bartender know that if we came back to check—which we planned to do and found the same thing going on, all hell would break loose. The bartender didn't answer, but let us know by the expression on his face that he hated our guts with a passion.

We went outside and wrote in our books for awhile, also making our presence known by parking right in front of the door. After a half hour we started to go around the block with the intention of parking at the corner, waiting for the loud noise we were sure was coming, and then calling a few Squads and really cleaning house.

Just driving around the block made us forget all about our troublesome tavern. In fact, as it was, it took us almost two hours to make it all the way around the block.

As we turned the third corner and were heading for the curb to park, Bob suddenly stopped. I asked him what was the matter and he said, "There's a pickle laying over there; let's see if he lives there." I looked over and sure enough, there was some poor guy laying on the front steps leading up to a porch.

It may upset someone to see a body lying on the sidewalk, but in this area of town it wasn't that unusual. Although on closer inspection, it was more obvious that he wasn't one of the run-of-the-mill drunks. My books showed that he was a black male about thirty-five years old wearing a brown plaid wool jacket, dark pants, blue dress shirt, brown sandal shoes and white socks. Actually, he looked quite neat considering the area where he was and the position in which we found him.

He was lying on the side of his face with his arms wrapped around a cardboard box. We rolled him over and saw that his eyes were glassy and he seemed to be in a dazed condition. While Bob tried to talk to him and sit him up, I started to go through the box he was cradling so carefully.

The first thing my flashlight shown on was enough to make my eyes pop out. Lying right on top were two empty money bag pouches stenciled with the name of a drugstore. Under that were several hundred cancelled checks from the pharmacy, several hundred empty capsules, syringes, pills, sun glasses, a hat, jacket and shirt.

By this time Bob had the man on his feet, but he was completely incoherent. Recalling that the pharmacy, whose name was printed on the money bags, was held up earlier in the evening and the subject we had was apparently under the influence of drugs, we called for the Vice Squad and the Detective bureau to meet us.

By the time they arrived it was obvious that the man we had was starting to go through withdrawals. While the bureau men were going through the box, Bob and I started to search the man. In one pocket we found a black plastic pouch which contained needles, syringes, eye droppers and a burnt bottle cap. Another pocket contained a woman's nylon stocking and in another we found a plastic bag containing unknown pills and a torn prescription. As soon as we finished our search we put the man in our wagon.

This was the first time I had seen anyone go through withdrawals from drugs. It was absolutely pathetic. His whole body trembled, his eyes watered and he thrashed around and screamed as if he was having a horrible nightmare. Then suddenly he would lapse into a semi-conscious state and just lay there muttering.

We conveyed him to the Vice Squad and from there he was taken to the County General Hospital where they would help him through his withdrawals.

Bob and I spent the next two or three hours inventorying all the items found on his person and in the box. Eight-thirty the next morning we took all the pills and syringes, which contained an unknown substance, to the city chemist to be analyzed. From there we took our man, who by this time had come out of his withdrawals but would be ready for another fix shortly, to the District Attorney who issued warrants for armed and masked robbery, possession of narcotics, use of narcotics and possession of narcotic paraphernalia. The Judge placed $50,000 bail on him, and his preliminary hearing was set for a week later.

Bob and I felt pretty good about the whole thing. We cleared an armed and masked robbery and got a good narcotics pinch out of it. But before the preliminary hearing came up, we learned that the man we arrested had cooperated with the Vice Squad. All the narcotics pinches had been combined, and he was placed on probation with the stipulation that he commit himself to a hospital for drug users.

The information he gave was good enough to make several arrests for the sale and use of narcotics. Also, the armed robbery was dismissed when he gave the whole story, signed affidavits and named the persons involved.

What really happened the night he was arrested was that three other black males had held up the pharmacy and on their way to a tavern where they were going to split the loot, they met this individual walking the street looking for a fix. Knowing him to be a drug addict they gave him a ride to the tavern which was close to his house, let him shoot himself full of drugs and then gave him the box with the worthless canceled checks, empty money bag, a few pills to keep him high and some of the clothing they used in the robbery. They dropped him off in front of his house and told him to burn all the stuff. Before he got into his house he passed out on his front steps and that was where we found him.

The funny thing about the whole affair was that the tavern in question where the loot was to be divided was the same tavern that Bob and I had knocked off for the loud music and dancing. In fact, all three holdup men were probably in the tavern when we were there. Kind of ironic, I guess.

13. Friendly Drunks and Informers

And so it went, on and on and on and on. Night after night—family troubles, men with guns, women with knives. It's a fascinating and yet vicious world we live in. It seems like an endless circle and inside is nothing but violence and bitter hate. Just when I felt it was almost more than I could stand along would come some friendly little drunk who could change my whole disposition and give me that one little moment that would keep me going for months.

Like the little old drunken junk man that we found in an alley starting a fire in a barrel next to a garage to keep him warm. We thought we might do him a favor and let him sleep it off in a nice cell. For as uncomfortable as a cell might be, it still had to be better than a rat infested alley. The only thing we forgot to do was take his matches away, for right after he was locked in the cell he immediately stripped off his clothes and started a bon fire right in the middle of his cell. His reasoning? He said the last cell he was in was a lot warmer than this one and besides that, he had been wearing the same clothes for three weeks. He figured that if he burned them, the county would provide him with something to wear, because they wouldn't let him on the street nude. In fact, he was ready to spend thirty days in the House of Correction to prove his point. That is exactly what he did, after he spent five days at the County General Hospital for mental observation.

It's been said many times by some of the greatest investigators that a Cop is only as good as his informers. An informer is simply one who gives information on another, which supposedly leads to arrests or seizure of unknown property.

Dave, Bob and I had developed several informers—some good and some bad. The good ones were protected very carefully. The bad ones were only used once or twice and if their information didn't develop, they were dropped from their roll.

Many informers are developed by catching them in a minor violation or in a violation that would be hard to prove in court. We had to make it sound like we were doing them a great service by letting them off, and for this they owed us some information we might seek at a future date.

A good deal of these people were found in the various gin mills that we checked. And like I said before, some would come through almost every time, whereas some really threw us some bad curves.` For example, there was one young man we had given a break for loitering on a tavern premises after hours. We took him outside and told him to go on his way with no further action taken on our part, but leaving in his mind the thought that he owed us a favor. Little did he know that we also gave the tavern keeper a break, and had no intention in the first place of even charging him. Several days later he came up to Dave and me and said that he had some information on an after-hours joint. This was a place that operated outside the limits of the law, because their business was done after taverns closed. This was usually set up in some house and most anything was available—liquor, gambling, hookers, drugs, etc.

Our young friend, who I'll call Andy for the time being, told us that he had visited this after hour's joint the previous Saturday night. After having several drinks and going to bed with one of the patrons, he was rudely dragged from his bed, beat up by persons unknown, robbed of his money and thrown out on the street. He further stated that the majority of the people there were from the tavern where he hung out. Since they offered him no help when he was being hustled, he felt his ego would be satisfied if the placed was knocked off.

This was a Thursday night; we told Andy that we would be in touch with him before the weekend and that he should be sure and not say anything to any of his friends.

We got in touch with a couple of guys from the Vice Squad (one who was Carl, my partner in future years and is still today a very good and personal friend) that we knew were assigned to gambling and told them what we had. They said it sounded good and told us that the raid would probably take place on Friday night.

On Friday, Dave and I had court all day and we met our informer and Vice Squad Coppers about 4:30 p.m. We took our informer into one of the Judge's chambers where he gave testimony for a search warrant. The testimony he gave the Judge was basically what he had told us, which was enough evidence to qualify for a search warrant. The Judge then, feeling that everything Andy testified to under oath was in fact the truth, issued a search warrant for the entire premises where the offense had occurred.

This search warrant was good for the next forty-eight hours and gave us the right to break into the home, confiscate all gambling paraphernalia such as dice, etc. and also arrest everyone on the premises we could prove were involved in any illegal act. This meant that at the least everyone would be charged with being inmates of a disorderly house and the owner would be charged with keeping a disorderly house, along with other misdemeanor charges which usually occurred—such as resisting arrest, etc.

In other words, if we found a dice game going on and could confiscate some money and dice, the parties in the home would be charged along with the owner. The same would go if liquor was being served; naturally they had no license and would be charged with same. Usually this was accomplished by getting an undercover Copper into the house to make a buy. This time we were more interested in the gambling.

This was completely different for Dave and me because we had never worked in plain clothes before. In fact, I really felt strange going to work without my uniform on and I still remember the look on Marlene's face. It was as though I was doing something just a little special and she was just a little more proud of me.

Well, anyhow, Dave and I met the two guys from the Vice Squad about midnight and they said the raid probably would take place between 3:30 and 4:30 a.m., and would start planting on the place around 2:30 a.m. or so. So they suggested that we go have a couple of bubbles (drinks) and relax for awhile. This was my first taste of working with the Vice Squad and I really liked it.

They took us to a couple of their spots where they are known and the drinks are free, and by 2:00 in the morning I was half in the bag, but still very much aware of what was going on. It amazed me to see how these two Vice Squad Coppers operated. They both had twice as much to drink as Dave and I, and they appeared to be both as straight as when we started. Either they both had dumped their drinks on the floor or they had strong constitutions. I asked one of them and he said if I ever got to work on the Vice Squad and wanted to do a good job, I would have to learn how to not only drink, but to handle situations while being under the influence. All part of the hazards of the job I suppose.

By now it was 2:30 a.m. and they told us we had better start planting on the house. We went back to the Police garage and picked up an old beat-up panel truck the Vice Squad uses in their raids and plant jobs. We took the truck out and parked it across the street from the house in question—in a vacant field. The back of the truck was empty except for a couple of folding chairs and the only vision to the rear was through two peep holes in the back window.

Well, that first night we sat there from 2:30 a.m. to 6:30 a.m. and all that happened was eight or ten people would walk into the house, stay for a few minutes and then leave. This went on all night and by early morning at least 50 or 60 people had gone in and come out. It was obvious to all except Dave and I what had happened.

The boss in charge of the raid said we wouldn't go in unless there were at least fifteen people in there so at 6:30 a.m. we called the plant off and decided to try again the next night. I never realized until later what the expenses of a raid like this cost. There must have been at least 25 Vice Squad Coppers waiting in Squads at a parking lot several blocks away for our raid to go off, and all these men had been kept over from their regular quitting time and had to be paid overtime.

As I look back now, I think the Vice Squad Coppers were just doing us a favor, and they knew full well that there had been a leak. We just weren't going to get any sort of crowd in that house.

Saturday night went just about the same except we didn't start the plant until 4:00 a.m. and finished about 7:00 a.m. The only thing that happened that was the least bit exciting was that a holdup occurred about two blocks from where we were planted. When Squads were searching the area they came upon this old panel truck, saw movement in the back and surrounded it with drawn guns. My heart skipped a few beats before one of the Vice Squad Coppers leaned out the door and call them off.

Morning came and nothing happened. Carl and I snuck up on the house and looked in a window. All we saw was a guy laying on a couch and a woman knitting. Dave and I could do nothing but tell the Vice Squad that we were sorry it turned out that way. They were real nice about it and told us that it happened all the time and not to feel too bad about it. They also told us to find our informer and give him their thanks.

That's exactly what we did. It took us a few days to find him, but once we did, he admitted that right after we got the search warrant he went back to the tavern and told everyone not to go to the after-hours spot because he heard they were going to raid it. Dave and I told him thanks a lot and just by chance we ran into him about three days later. He got boisterous and wound up in jail for drunk and disorderly for which he received thirty days in the House of Correction.

I was kind of disappointed with how things worked out, but I learned one thing for sure—I had to start working in plain clothes. There was nothing like it!

Several years passed. Then while attending a monthly class in the Police Academy, they were showed pictures of various people wanted for an assortment of narcotic violations. Sure enough, there on the screen was a picture of our old so-called informer. He was wanted for violation of parole and for use and sale of dangerous drugs. I actually chuckled to myself when I saw his picture.

14. Family Time/No Time

Previously I mentioned how important an Officer's wife and family's attitude means towards his Police work. I think it is proper that I mention something on this. I truly believe it would be impossible for me to appreciate all the pain and suffering I brought on my family—mainly my wife, because of my occupation. I really never heard them grumble or complain. The only thing I occasionally heard was a confession that my family would like me home evenings and weekends and holidays like other husbands and fathers. And yet, I am constantly assured that my family realized that this was my profession—the only thing I knew—and they would never stand in my way or alter my decisions. God bless them all!

I came on the job in January of 1958, and was married four months later in May. I had not accumulated enough time to get a vacation. Our wedding and honeymoon consisted of four regular off days—Friday before the wedding, Saturday the day of the wedding, Sunday, Monday and back to work Tuesday at 4:00 p.m. Everything was fine the first year except that my wife worked days, I started at 4:00 p.m. and I only had weekends off every three months. Our marriage had to be compatible because we seldom saw each other.

We had our first child in April of 1959, and by this time I had been transferred to the midnight-to-eight shift. I had two-week's vacation coming and took it during the time my wife was supposed to have the baby. Naturally, the baby was late and came the day before I went back to work. I should have realized that was only the start. I also didn't realize how emotional women were after having a baby, and my being gone every night and many days in court was almost too much for her. It wasn't until several years later that she confessed to me how she would not sleep at night, while it was dark, but would only lay there and shake with fright. She also told me that she never let on to me, because she thought I would quit the job. I wonder if I can ever repay her those years. I worked nights for twenty-one and-a-half years. Nine of those years were midnight to eight and twelve years 4:00 p.m. to midnight (or 1, 2, or 3 a.m.); then court the following day.

I also realize that for her, it was more than just being alone. It was also the anxiety. I could see the hurt in her eyes every time a report was on television or in the paper that an Officer was hurt or killed. (During my years on the Police Department, twenty-seven Officers were killed and many injured.) There's nothing written that I can refer to, and when I ask my wife she simply says it wasn't really that bad. While on the Police force, I decided that if or when I retired and got another job, it had better be days, with weekends and holidays off, or that would be grounds for divorce.

Its funny how people take so many little things for granted—like being able to see your child on their birthday, being home on a holiday, not falling asleep in church because you've been up for the past 30 or 40 hours. I'm not complaining mind you, I'm merely pointing out a few things that the family of an active Policeman has to look forward to.

In my first ten years on the job I had seven Christmas Eves off and one Christmas Day with my family. Those were more or less by choice because the Department liked to give everyone at least one of the days off. I also had five New Year's Eves off and several Thanksgivings and two Easter Days off. I only had one 4th of July off because that's the day of the big parades and fireworks, so everyone works.

Now that I look back I did have almost every Arbor Day off, and I suppose to some people that may be important. It's just that planting trees never turned me on. Yet through all those missed birthday parties, anniversaries and other festivities, there was never a grumble from my family—only admiration. I may never be rich monetarily, but my wife and children make me the wealthiest man in the world.

Besides the lousy hours and off days, it seemed that at least once a year, usually around late spring or early summer, I would go through a few weeks where I would be completely fed up with my job and plan to quit. It seemed that it would usually happen when we would start to plan our vacation and I would have bad weeks, or the neighbors would plan parties and cookouts for the holidays and I didn't have any of the days off. I talked to a lot of Coppers and they all seemed to go through similar periods. Sometimes I would even go out and look at different jobs. When I did this I soon realized that usually once a Cop always a Cop. It not only gets into one's blood, but besides that it's a good steady job and offers just a hair of prestige that's important to me. I guess I liked being a Cop.

15. Crimes in Progress

It was the summer now of 1968 and we had been hearing rumors that one of us would start working special duty out of the Captain's office as soon as there was an opening. This meant working plain clothes. Following-up on complaints, and checking for tavern violations; it was a real plush job! Between the three of us I had the most time on the job, and it was more or less by mutual consent that if we were given the choice, I would go first. That's the way Dave and Bob were—very, very unselfish individuals.

The stronger the rumor got, the harder we worked. We stopped everything that moved and went in on every hitch of importance that occurred in our area. The idea was to really produce activity that the bosses couldn't overlook.

That reminds me of the time Dave and I were riding around early in the morning. We were discussing that what we really needed was a good pinch. Something like a burglary in progress, but those are almost too much to ask for. The words were barely out of my mouth and we must have both been looking down the same alley at the same time. Dave slammed on the brakes and said, "Did you see what I saw?" I said I thought so but someone must have been joking around.

Dave shut the lights off, backed up and pulled into the alley. Sure enough, there was a man with half his body into a building through a window and half hanging out. The window was about 15 feet off the ground and he had apparently climbed on the roof of an auto and boosted himself to the window. We immediately called for more Squads, stating that we had a burglar in the building. Dave covered the window and I started to run to the other side of the building and cover any possible escape route. I turned the corner of the building at a full run and almost ran right past a man standing in the doorway smoking a cigarette. I don't know who was more startled—him or me. I said, "What the hell are you doing here?"

To which he replied, "Smoking a cigarette, what the hell does it look like?"

He further stated that he was working and that there were two more employees inside. I told him what Dave and I had seen, and he said all that was on that side of the building were the locker rooms. By that time several other Squads arrived and a few of us went inside to check the locker rooms. Sure enough, there was our burglar, drunker than hell.

As it turned out, the guy got smashed and thought he would sleep it off in one of the factories in the area. That little escapade cost him one hundred dollars the next day for disorderly conduct.

Talk about odd burglaries. Dave and I were working together one day and were cruising the alleys in our area. It was a very poor section of the city and there were a lot of kids. But much to our amazement, rather than the kids playing with their usual rocks and sticks and broken bottles, each one had at least one brand new toy. Besides the toy, most of them also had a new wallet, watch, radio and fishing rod. They all seemed to be enjoying their new found toys and upon questioning they were more than willing to name their benefactors.

In fact, after a week of investigation in between our regular hitches, we came up with a total of fourteen kids that we arrested for a variety of charges including burglary and receiving stolen property. This was over and above all the kids with the toys who were never charged. It seems three or four kids climbed on top of a garage and got into an unlocked window at a wholesale supply warehouse, which was like a dream to those kids. Naturally, they wanted to share their new found treasure chest, so they unlocked a basement window and told all their friends. They, in turn, each made their own midnight requisitions. In fact, they did it with so much care that the store owners never knew what happened until we told them.

By the end of the week we had recovered enough property to fill two cells in the station, not including the toys which we let the kids have because we felt sorry for them. One of the boys was even sent to a boy's home during that week on some other charge. We heard he took a suitcase full of goodies with him. Sure enough, a Detective team went to the boy's home and came back with a whole slew of watches, radios, wallets, etc.

One thing that really didn't impress me was the attitude of the store owners. They told us that they didn't care about the recovery of the property because they had already collected from their insurance company. They further stated that if they were called to court as complainants, they would refuse to prosecute because it was a waste of time.

After we heard that, Dave, Bob and I decided that we should have let the kids have a ball. Burglarize the hell out of the place and listen to the owners cry when their insurance got dropped. Actually, I bet big insurance companies don't really know the half of it—regarding false claims, that is. But, that's something else again and probably none of my business. Looking at those store owners who thrive on the underprivileged, one can soon get sick of our pious self-centered society.

In the time that I spent on the wagon it never ceased to amaze me how much brute force could be shown and damage caused when the wrath of a frail woman was raised. One such incident occurred a few days after our burglary investigation, on a hot muggy Friday evening. Dave and I were sent to a fight in a tavern; not too unusual a call and the location was even more indicative of the problem. An inner city tavern that catered to not only poor black and white folks but also to a few hostile Native American Indians that were still left in the neighborhood.

When Dave and I pulled up in front of the tavern it sounded like Custer's last stand. Hollering, screaming, glass breaking and very colorful language filtered out the front door. Dave was the first one in and I was only a few feet behind. The first thing I saw was this little five-foot-one-inch Indian lady with a bar stool stretched out over her head taking aim at the bottles on the back bar. She let loose with the stool and threw a couple of glasses and ash trays after it. Then she ran behind the bar, where the white owner and his wife or girlfriend, were trying to get out of the line of fire.

Everything was happening fast and at first I didn't realize why Dave was climbing over the bar. His reactions were fast, but not quite fast enough to prevent the little lady from smashing a beer bottle over the head of the white woman behind the bar. All you could see in the air was brown pieces of beer bottle and bright red blood gushing from the gash on the woman's head.

By this time Dave was over the bar and had the assailant by the arm and I had come around and grabbed her by the neck. We dragged her from behind the bar and bent her over a pool table to handcuff her. She bit my arm and when I let go she pulled on what little hair Dave had left on his head. I was holding my arm and Dave was holding his head and the little Indian lady started to play the war drums on our chins with her pointed toed shoes. I figured that was about enough so I belted her in the mouth, handcuffed her and that seemed to be the end of it, or so I thought. Just then her big, and I mean big, Indian boyfriend grabbed me by the back of my shirt, spun me around and without a sound, reared back and was going to take my head off with his fist. Dave then sapped him and that was the end of the fight.

We wound up arresting six or eight people on various charges ranging from aggravated battery to a minor we found loitering on the tavern premises. Just before we left for the station with our load of prisoners, we made one last survey of the damage. It was incredible. There was hardly a bottle or glass left unbroken. Every ash tray was busted, every bar stool and table were either busted or tipped over. Two pinball machines were smashed, the back bar was in shambles and everything was covered with blood including our uniforms. The majority of the damage was done by the little five-foot-one-inch lady. Incredible!

It was right about this time in the summer of 1968 that a state law was passed requiring the operators of motorcycles to wear protective head gear and goggles. While this law at first received a great deal of publicity, it really didn't matter to a great number of people. It was definitely for the protection of the riders and the majority of them obeyed the law.

For those that thought rules were meant for others, we enforced the law with a court appearance. Whether the law was right or wrong, this was another way of filling the few empty spaces in our court calendar. In fact, at this particular time we were having trouble with a motorcycle gang and this served as a catch-all for them because they always defied the law. This same gang later gathered national publicity because of their brutal and uncouth acts. By their own admission, they had great respect or fear for our city Police and usually stayed clear of it.

Because of a missing helmet on a biker, I got into one of the wildest chases I can remember. Naturally, Bob was driving and I must say his judgment was from another century. In fact, I think he thought our Squad was invincible. We spotted a violator going in the opposite direction and by the time we got turned around and put on the red light and siren, the cycle was two blocks away. Well, I thought the chase was futile from the start but not Bob. Up and down streets and alleys we went at incredible speeds. In fact, we made so many turns that during my broadcast on the air we would head north and I would broadcast east. This thing went on for about five minutes, which seemed like an hour. Bob did a fantastic job of driving, in fact at one point in the chase we were so close behind the bike rider that when he would occasionally glance back, I'm sure he thought we would run right over him. The motorcyclist finally tried to negotiate a turn too fast, hit the curb and took off like a rocket, landing unhurt in someone's back yard.

As I think back, very few cars got away from us when Bob was driving. We were never involved in an accident during a chase, but I can remember a few that we helped investigate, including one fatality. After each of them we would naturally receive abuse from several organizations and also the press. But once again this criticism would fall on deaf ears, because it was pure simple logic that once it would become known that the Police were not allowed to chase anyone, every violator would attempt to elude them.

I would have to say up to this time in my career, the months I spent on the roving wagon were the most pleasant and memorable. I do regret not having kept better track of the numerous incidents that occurred, because so many were humorous and heartwarming. Naturally, the ones that stand out most in my mind are the ones that involved a lot of action, whereas the humorous quotations that people blurted out escape my mind. I think if there was ever a talk show with just Policemen present it would have to be the comedy of the year. That's one of the qualifications of being a good Policeman—having a tremendous sense of humor.

Two other incidents that stand out in my mind took place while working on the paddy wagon. The first occurred in the later part of September 1968. Dave and I had been in court all day, in fact, the last two days. It was a Friday evening and Fridays were usually wild. We tried our best to stay out of trouble because neither of us particularly wanted court the next day.

We did pretty well until tavern closing time. Then it was just by chance or possibly fate that Dave drove past one of our regular trouble spots. In fact, now that I think back, fate had nothing to do with it at all. The patrons of this particular place were well aware of whom we were and many knew us by our first names because of previous personal contacts. There was absolutely no love lost on either side—them or us.

As we drove past the front door everyone was leaving as it was about 2:10 a.m. Dave noticed that one of the drunks was staggering down the street with a glass in his hand. He told me to holler out the window and tell him to take the glass back. My window was rolled down and I very nonchalantly called out and said, "Hey fella, take the glass back." Apparently he wasn't very impressed.

He turned around and said, "Screw you, Copper—you want the glass—here it is." With that he smashed it on the side of the Squad.

Well, within about six seconds our hero was in the back of the rig under arrest for plain drunk. With the arrest came a lot of cat calls from the thirty or forty people who had emerged from the tavern. Needless to say, there was no backing down now. We told everyone to move on or stand the chance of going for the ultimate ride.

The cat calls and profanities kept up but everyone kept moving except one smart ass that stood with his arms crossed and said any M.F. Cop that wanted him would have to move him himself. Naturally, I felt I was just the man to do it, so I placed him under arrest. The minute I touched him the fight was on and this guy was no slouch. We traded a couple of good punches and I was lucky enough to get him on the ground and put the handcuffs on him. Meanwhile, Dave went running across the street into the crowd to try and snap up some smart ass punk that was trying to incite the people to charge us.

As best I recall, I had my man in a headlock with his hands cuffed behind his back and I unlocked the wagon door with my free hand. Just as I heard the lock on the door snap, I knew I didn't do something right because the original drunk we had arrested came flying out at me.

I let loose of the guy I had in the headlock and drew back with my sap to lace the guy coming out of the wagon. But as I brought my hand back the sap flew out of my hand and landed in the street. At the same time the guy was on top of me and we rolled into the gutter. The last I saw of my handcuffed prisoner was when some of the upstanding citizens in the crowd were helping him over a few fences.

Everything was happening fast. I was having a rough time trying to overpower this drunk for the second time and then to really complicate things I looked up and saw the wagon drive away. I thought, "Oh boy, that's all we need is to have our Squad stolen." What I didn't know was that Dave had dragged some guy from the crowd, threw him in the wagon and was going after our handcuffed fugitive.

The minute Dave got in the wagon he called for help. Dave figured I had my man under control so he went after the guy in handcuffs. Apparently, each time he would get close to him someone would help the guy over another fence and someone else would try to open the back door of the wagon to let the one prisoner we still had, escape.

Well, while Dave had his hands full, I was left alone sitting in the gutter on the chest of my prisoner looking across the street at about 15 or 20 people who had just made up their minds to clean my clock. I was contemplating whether to pull my gun on them when I heard a noise behind me. Help had arrived in the form of two tactical Squads—four Coppers to a car who flew over a hill and charged the group like the cavalry. That was a beautiful sight for me and for Dave.

It took them about thirty seconds and the whole thing was over. I lost a couple of buttons, a piece of my shirt and my Green Bay Packer tie clip but otherwise neither Dave nor I were any worse for wear.

The next day in court we wound up with four disorderlys, two resisters, one drunk and one escape from custody. Even though it took a few months, we got convictions on all of them. Dave and I still talk about that one because if someone could have taken movies of the whole incident it must have looked real close to the old keystone Cops.

The last event on the wagon occurred just about a week later when I had a relief man with me. We were on our way to a hitch when some idiot ran a stop sign doing about sixty miles per hour and hit us broadside. My partner for that night went through the windshield and flew about ninety feet through the air and landed on his face. He was off work for almost a year and came close to dying.

I bounced around in the cab of the wagon for awhile and flew out the passenger's door and landed on my head. I remember a city sign clanging on the pavement and people coming out of the houses and running toward us. I was able to grab the mike and call for help and then passed out. This is another one of those experiences that my wife had to endure when the Sergeant knocked on our home door and said I was in the hospital and he didn't know how bad I was hurt.

She told me later on that her heart and stomach were tearing apart, but she knew she had to keep her composure because that's what's expected of Copper's wives.

Fortunately, I was able to get a Copper at the hospital to call her when I was being wheeled in. He told her that I was conscious and didn't appear to be hurt too bad. I think one of the most ironic things about the whole accident was that during all the fast driving we did in chases and responding to emergencies, we never sustained even a dent. And here I was only going twenty-five miles an hour and I got wiped out. The other oddity was that Dave and Bob were both off and out on the town with their wives, and were just coming out of a restaurant when the tow truck came by with the wagon hanging on the back. Dave's wife was the first to spot it and they all laughed because they thought it was broken down, but I remember them telling me how their hearts skipped a beat when they saw it was a total wreck. Just to show how close partners get, they and their wives immediately went to the hospital and sat with Marlene and me until 5:00 a.m.

 I was off work for the next eight weeks and when I came back I was informed that I had been taken off the wagon and was to work in plain clothes out of the Captain's office. Little did I know that a whole new career was about to begin.

Plain Clothes Detail

16. Plain Clothes—Special Duty

Wearing "plain clothes" and working out of the Captain's office is a far cry from the Detective Bureau. To be in the Detective Bureau is the ambition of most Officers, including myself. At that time it most certainly was a step in the right direction. In fact, as I look back now, it wouldn't be a bad idea for young Officers to realize when they get disgusted, to take note that I spent a good deal of time being one of the forgotten ones. But, being in the right place at the right time and really being active in everything you do can sometimes bring results. I would imagine that most Coppers don't realize that there are so many that are really qualified for advancement, but so few are chosen because many times the positions are just not there.

I fully realized that there were many others who were just as qualified as I and many who were more qualified, but I most certainly was not about to look the proverbial gift horse in the mouth and give the chance to someone else. That ridiculous I'm not.

I do think we all have to realize, and this I believe, that the men in blue are not only the backbone of any Police Department, but they alone stand between law, order and humanity, and that great chasm of chaos which we are on the brink of.

I worked special duty at the District Station from January until the first part of August and what I experienced in those eight months would undoubtedly fill another book!.

What I intend to do is just give a brief depiction of what occurred, not in the order of its happening, but rather as it comes to me. I really am grateful that I was fortunate enough to experience all these most unusual ways of life. To say the least, I do believe I've seen a good deal more than most people.

Take for example prostitutes. That's a word that might come up when a bunch of guys are joking around, telling old war stories, or at a party when a few off color remarks are made. But in fact, how many inhabitants of this great mass of humanity have actually had a chance to really see that side of life? That may sound funny to many who have dealt with them or who see nothing wrong with them or don't particularly care. But to me, it was another chance to see a completely different way of life, one that I hadn't been exposed to before.

In the following pages I'll refer to the prostitutes as "hookers," which is the most common reference that I heard when describing these young women of, shall I say, less than desirable repute. Don't get me wrong—I place the entire blame for this commodity on the opposite sex, for if there wasn't the market, the product wouldn't sell as well as it does. I also don't want to give the impression that I am holier than thou. But, I have always been fortunate enough to resist the many temptations that I have come in contact with, and for this I am eternally grateful to my wife. She has never ever nagged me or pushed me to the point where I may, shall we say, look for something strange!

I recall the first time I went to the Vice Squad to work on hookers. Bob and I had gotten involved in a few raids because of a couple of good informers we had. The Sergeant from the Vice Squad asked us to come down there for a few days to act as whore bait. In other words, most of the regular Vice Squad Coppers were known to the local talent, so they would get Coppers from the District Station for a few days at a time until they, too, became known.

Getting back to our first night. I believe it was late in February on a Wednesday night that we were notified to report to the Vice Squad at 7:00 p.m. In fact, I know it was Wednesday because it was the day before pay day and I had to send my wife to the bank to draw out fifty dollars because I was broke. Now that's what I call an understanding wife. She drew out almost all of our meager savings so I could pick up a hooker.

We got down there about a half hour early and found that we would spend the night with two regular Vice Coppers, making it a four man Squad. They would show us the places to go and act as our covers in case we got into trouble.

I recall that Bob and I were nervous and it must have been apparent to the regulars, because they said the first thing we would have to do is get "loosened up." Little did I realize how loose I could get!

The first order of business after joining the Vice Squad was to relieve ourselves of our gun, handcuffs, callbox key and all identification that mentioned or could be attributed to Police. These two Coppers were so thorough that they even checked to see if our wallets had holes in them from pinning the badge there when off duty. They said that was one of the first checks that a good hooker made. After that we were supplied with out-of-state driver's licenses and other identification. We even thought up fictitious occupations.

Now it came time to get us loosened up. We hit a few bars that they knew and a few that Bob and I knew, and between all of them we got so loosened up I thought I was floating.

The object behind the whole sequence of this event is probably hard for anyone but a Copper to understand. Sometimes I don't even understand it myself. But the best way I can explain it, is that for someone like me, and apparently I was no different than the rest down there, it was really not in my make-up to go out and pay to take some gal to bed. So they figure, and quite rightly so, that if you drink and relax you're less likely to be spotted as a Cop. That's also the main reason for the covering Coppers, because sometimes you drink too much and relax once too often and the troubles one can get into need no explanation.

Well, I drank, was relaxed and was all set to give it a try. They took Bob and me to a downtown spot and dropped us off two blocks away. They said we might have a little harder time at this time of the year because no conventions were in town. Believe it or not, the teacher's convention and nurse's convention were the most active.

Joe and Bill, our covers, and Bob and I followed separately a few minutes later. I walked in and moved about half way down the bar where an attractive young white girl was sitting. After a few minutes I struck up a conversation, bought her a few drinks and suddenly realized she belonged to the bartender and all I was doing was feeding her and the house.

Naturally, the more I drank the thicker my mind and tongue got but I really didn't care at this point because I knew we were covered by Joe and Bill. Even if they wouldn't be there, I wasn't particularly worried.

Then she came out of the back room. She looked so much like a prostitute that I think she had a dollar sign on her forehead. She was black, about 35 years old and really not a bad looking gal, as that is what my condition related to my brain. She slithered right by me and plunked herself down right next to Bob. I kept telling him later that it must have been his bald head that turned her on.

Well, my condition once again got the better of my mind and I came to the conclusion that Bob wasn't working fast enough, so I butted in between them, sat down and sputtered out some small talk. I think back now how ridiculous I must have sounded, but I contribute most of it to my condition of stupeficaction, if that's a word. We did have a few drinks, which at that point I most certainly didn't need, and I had a hard time trying to convince her that I wasn't a Cop. I later learned that she was a pro.

All my false identification that I pulled out of my wallet and dropped all over the floor apparently didn't faze her in the least. She offered all kinds of things, but never an exact price.

I learned later on, that several times I had enough to make the bust, but either it was my condition or my inexperience that at those times failed me. Anyhow, we settled on the fact that I would give her ten dollars at the bar, drive my car to a given location and wait for her. I gave her the ten, staggered out the door and once the cold air hit me, I realized that I had been taken for ten bucks.

This really teed me off so back into the tavern I went, grabbed the hooker by the arm, spun her around and said, "Give me my ten, bitch." By this time I must have had Copper written all over my face because she threw the ten bucks at me, headed for the back room and I walked out. Joe, Bob and Bill met me at the car and they all thought it was hilarious! I didn't see the humor in it at the time.

We spent the next few hours hitting a few more spots. Thursday was about the same, check a few spots, hit a few known taverns, have a few drinks and shoot a couple of games of pool. Not a bad job at all. The rest of the night we hit most of the regular spots where hookers hang out but apparently Bob and I either were not appealing or we were so out of practice that we couldn't get a tumble.

Three o'clock came and Joe and Bill said they would take us to a spot where all the hookers and pimps go after the taverns close. It was an all night restaurant downtown and apparently they came there for either one last try if the night was bad, or if it was good, a cup of coffee; and, rest if it was exceptional. What they forgot to tell us was that this same restaurant was the last stop for all the Vice Coppers before they checked in and went home.

We walked in and I took a separate stool from the rest of the Coppers and Bob. No one paid any real attention to me. I took off my sport coat and put it on the back of the chair. I looked over the crowded restaurant and there had to be at least a dozen hookers sitting around tables with either pimps or clients. I figured this was where I was going to make my really big play. I figured that I would walk back out, stay in the lobby for a few minutes, come back in, sit right down with a hooker, order a cup of coffee and give her my pitch. I was sober by this time so I can't blame what happened on my intoxicated condition.

So I walked out, paid for my cup of coffee, put my jacket back on and went to the basement wash room. I stayed there for a few minutes and then went back up the stairs to the restaurant. I got half way back up the stairs when I was met by Bill, who was laughing so hard he had to hang onto the railing to keep from falling. I started to explain my plan to him and at the same time he reached behind me, under my jacket and pulled out my handcuffs that I had forgotten to leave in the assembly. Well, let me tell you, I got flushed, weak in the knees and felt like the perfect fool, even though I wasn't perfect.

Bill told me to come back upstairs and he'd buy me coffee and see how good I could take a ribbing.

We walked back into the restaurant and all eyes were on me. Coppers, hookers, pimps and waitresses and they all began to laugh. I never felt so humiliated in my life. I guess those are the breaks, and one of the reasons I never got assigned to the Vice Squad. But I have to admit, even though it was embarrassing at the time, now that I think back on it, it must have been pretty funny.

Friday was our last day at the Vice Squad and I must say that I was looking forward to going back into my own district. It wasn't that I didn't enjoy the work, but I felt out of place.

The whole three days weren't a complete failure. About 1:00 a.m. Saturday morning Bob picked up this tall black hooker. She said she would give him a straight lay for thirty dollars. I was covering Bob at the time and before I realized what was happening, Bob had her by the arm and was heading out the door. It wasn't the slickest operation that the guys in the Vice Squad had ever seen, but it did hold up in court. She was fined fifty dollars and put on probation for a year.

The only time I ever picked up a prostitute was when I wasn't looking for one. We had spent the whole day in court and had invited one of the City Attorney's that we knew real well to have a drink with us and play a game of pool. We took him to one of our favorite joints in the inner city and had just started to play a game when this slim good looking black gal came slithering up to the table and said, "Is this game just for men?" Well, about that time our City Attorney friend made a quick exit via the rear door as he didn't want anything to do with that, and I said that as long as our friend had to leave, she may as well be my partner.

We shot about three games of pool and beat Dave and Bob all three games. During this time we made small talk. She said she was going to a party and could fix my two friends up if we took her there. That seemed at the time to be a problem because all we had was a plain Squad car parked out front. So I told her that my friends weren't interested and that if she wanted to she could take care of me. She said I could have whatever I wanted for thirty-five dollars and at that point I helped her on with her coat and we walked out the door. On the way she was more explicit in what I was about to purchase, so once we got outside I placed her under arrest for soliciting.

She later pleaded not guilty to the charge and was found guilty by a jury and placed on two years probation.

Now that I think back on those days, I would have to say that I wasn't cut out for the Vice Squad. Even though it was fun, interesting and good overtime, I think if the opportunity had come—which it didn't—I would have to have passed up that particular faze of Police work. I'm also glad I never had to make that decision.

I spent approximately nine months working Special Detail with Bob as my partner. Those months were indeed something special. Not only was the work fascinating, but the money was great. We worked an average of sixteen hours Monday, Tuesday and Wednesday; twelve hours on Thursday and Friday, and were off on the weekend; unless something real good came up—and then we worked seven days a week.

All the hours gave us a chance to catch up on some past due bills, of which there were many, and the weekends off gave us a little social life for a change. Not to say that we didn't get a lot accomplished in those nine months, to the contrary! Let me give you just a little list of the arrests we made: three drunks, sixteen for disorderly conduct, twenty-nine for auto theft, two for hit and run, eight for robbery, twenty-one for theft, thirty-four for burglary, seven runaways, seven truants, ten for uncontrollable, two for resisting an Officer, fifteen for possession of marijuana, one issue of a worthless check, one fraudulent use of credit cards, four for contributing to the delinquency of minors, three for possession of dangerous drugs, two prostitutes, two for indecent behavior with children, one false fire alarm, sixteen for permitting minors to loiter on a class B premises (tavern), twelve for selling intoxicating liquor to minors, five for battery, one for carrying a concealed weapon, four forgers, eight for criminal damage to property, one for forging a prescription and one person for shoplifting. Besides these arrests, we would clear approximately two hundred offenses a month just by arrest and interrogations. It was more than just putting in the time for those nine months; it was also a lot of hard and diligent work.

17. Working with the Vice Squad

During this time I must have talked to and interrogated several hundred individuals both adult and juvenile, and from these interviews I developed some pertinent information. I just can't emphasize enough how important informers are. It never ceased to amaze me how much the right people on the street know about what's really happening.

Take for example a young boy we arrested several times for driving a stolen car. He came from a broken family and Bob, Dave and I used to take him for rides in the wagon, try to give him part of a father image and something to grasp onto. We took him to several youth gatherings and a couple of shows, but even his mental attitude was scarred and diminished from living in a home that showed nothing but degradation and despair. It was hard for us to ever really get close to the boy and try to extract information from him, but I remember on one occasion when I came to work he was waiting for me. He asked to see me in private and when we were alone he told me that the only real friends he ever had were Dave, Bob and I, and that he was being sent away to a state school for boys the next day. He wanted to tell me everything that he had been involved in, and we must have cleared a dozen auto thefts, several burglaries and a few purse snatchings. I really felt sorry for the kid, but I could tell he was actually enjoying clearing his mind because he thought he was doing us a favor.

If I've said it once, I've said it a thousand times, how thankful children and parents can be that have a mutual understanding and can communicate with each other. For every well adjusted child and parent there is, there has to be a thousand that fight each other daily, bringing nothing but despair, misery, anguish and pain.

Speaking of broken families, Bob and I got sent to talk to a woman who wanted to report her missing sixteen-year-old son. Ordinarily we would not be taking such a complaint, but she apparently told the Lieutenant that she also suspected him of dealing drugs and cashing some of her personal checks. We met with her and she told the age old story that her son was an only child, and that her husband and her had parted ways several years ago. She tried to raise him by working two jobs and giving him everything he wanted. Apparently, he wasn't getting enough because she showed us several of her own personal checks that had been returned from the bank marked insufficient funds, and not a known signature on them. In fact, she said the signature on the checks was not even that of her son.

We got a good description of the boy and some of his close friends. After questioning several of them, we found a young lady that he apparently had been seeing quite a bit of, and even his mother did not know this. In fact, this young lady had been in daily contact with the boy by phone. We assured her that it was in his best interest to turn himself in to the Police, and when he called her that night she should get in touch with us.

We had just gotten back to the station when the young lady called us. She informed us that she was to meet her boyfriend in a food store on the west side of the city. Bob and I planted in the store and we could hardly miss the kid because he was about six-feet tall and two-hundred-fifty pounds.

I approached him at the checkout counter and after he denied being who I said he was, he gave me a false name to go along with the check he was trying to cash. He apparently realized that things weren't going exactly his way so he tried to make a quick exit out the side door. Unfortunately for him it was right into Bob's arms. The struggle lasted for about fifteen seconds until he realized he was no match for Bob.

We put him in handcuffs and placed him in the back seat of our unmarked car and amidst all the stares from the curious onlookers, he immediately broke down into tears. We asked him who was with him, and he pointed to a car that was just leaving the parking lot. We radioed to a uniform car and they stopped the auto a few blocks away.

Inside the auto were two white males about nineteen and twenty and a white girl about eighteen. It later turned out she was only fourteen and also a runaway. All three were obviously from the hippy community and all three were strung out on drugs.

All three were placed under arrest for contributing to the delinquency of the minor boy and all three told us to get laid when we asked their whereabouts for the last several days and questions regarding their drug use. This was not an unusual response from these long haired sons of who knows what. In fact, all three came from very influential families in the suburbs and made their home in the lower east side of the great metropolis.

Bob and I then turned our attention to the young boy. After gaining his confidence and assuring him that we would try and help him straighten out all the problems he got himself into, he gave us a full statement.

The account of his presence in various places for the past month included being picked up by a bunch of hippies while hitch hiking, and being taken to their apartment and being allowed for the first time to try marijuana. He further related that they told him to go back home and steal his mother's checkbook and credit cards, and they would show him how to make a fast buck.

By the time we had arrested him he had used his mother's cards and checks to run up a total bill of almost eighteen hundred dollars, of which he bought about twenty-five dollars worth of records. His mother got all the bills and she was later held accountable for almost a thousand dollars worth.

(This was before the credit card companies had the present rule on reporting stolen credit cards and restricting spending.)

He also told us that besides the three others we had arrested there were about six more hippies living at the east side apartment and that they dealt heavily in drugs. In fact, he said they got a whole shipment that day from an eastern state and all the drugs and grass were in a suitcase in the apartment. Now this is what we wanted to hear.

We immediately got a hold of a few vice Coppers and they also interrogated our young friend. They agreed that the story sounded good. In fact, they had information that a large supply of drugs was supposed to come into the city during this week.

By this time it was almost midnight and we had to find a Judge that would hear the testimony necessary for the search warrant. This was always a project and since then, the Chief Judge assigns one Judge per week that is available at any time—day or night. We took our young confidant to the Judge's home and after about a half hour of testimony, we were issued a search warrant for the east side apartment which turned out to be a two-story flat.

Prior to the taking of testimony we took the young man past the flat and he pointed it out. We were able to get a physical description of the building and the address. It was then planted by two Vice Coppers. We proceeded to get the additional information we needed about who resided there from as many sources as were available at that hour, which was by now early morning. All these things were necessary and demanded by the Judge before the warrant is issued.

As in every case preparation, it is extremely important to prevent a possibility that later on the case will be thrown out of court because of some small technicality in the original issuance of the search warrant, which I might say happens all too frequently. Anyhow, by two-thirty in the morning we had the search warrant and Bob and I along with about ten vice and special Coppers hit the hippy pad.

As per the information we received from our friend, the best way in was through a back door after entering a small hallway and proceeding down a few steps. We had gotten together at the corner of the block prior to the raid and it was mutually agreed that several Officers would surround the house. I, along with two others would go through the front door and the rest would hit the back.

The front and back door were supposed to both go down at approximately the same time, but because all good plans of mice and men sometimes go astray, the guys going in the back found the door open and also found no resistance from the occupants and just at the time myself and another Copper were putting our shoulders to the front door—you guessed it—someone from inside opened it up and we fell on our can!

After our initial embarrassment had left, I observed how well these Vice Coppers operated together. They already had about eight persons in several rooms all spread—eagle up against various walls and were doing a body search of them. At the same time they were making notes in their official memo books regarding what they were removing from their bodies, including knives, razors, and an assortment of various drugs and the paraphernalia used by these poor souls to shoot this crap into their bodies. I helped search the rest of the house which I can only describe as being so filthy that even a stupefied derelict might hesitate stepping into.

Along with a lot of the property that was purchased with the stolen credit cards and forged checks, I found a good amount of marijuana, several small packages of pills and some coke. It once again amazed me the thoroughness of these Vice Squad Coppers. Within one hour the entire home had been searched, all the proceeds had been photographed where they had been found and once again when they moved them to a central location. All the physical damage done by us during the search and making the entry had been photographed. The residence had been secured and we were on our way to the station to start processing the prisoners.

The Vice Squad Coppers said they were satisfied with the way things turned out, but were a little disappointed that they didn't get the big haul. In fact, we did find the suitcase that our friend said the drugs were in, but it was empty and no signs of any residue or anything else were inside the case.

By the time we had booked, processed and questioned all the prisoners it was almost eight o'clock in the morning. We barely had time to run home, shave, shower and grab a little breakfast before appearing in front of the District Attorney for warrants.

The total activity for the evening resulted in the arrest of four juveniles on various charges including runaway, uncontrollable, possession of marijuana, etc. Seven adults were arrested and charged with contributing to the delinquency of the minors, possession of marijuana and dangerous drugs, some with intent to deliver, forgery, fraudulent use of credit cards, carrying concealed weapons and disorderly conduct—the latter resulting from one of the nice young girls placing a glob of spit on a uniform Officer's shirt while he was guarding her.

Now for the swift and dooming results of justice in action: The juveniles were all placed on informal probation without ever seeing a Judge. The cases against the adults were handled somewhat differently. The largest fine paid by anyone charged with a misdemeanor was fifty dollars, and that was the disorderly conduct. All except one of the adults were placed on probation and this occurred because the one adult stated the residence was his and took complete blame for everything that occurred there. His case was adjourned for almost two years and after numerous adjournments, the state let him plead guilty to one count of delivery of a dangerous drug and contributing to the delinquency of a minor. He was fined the exorbitant amount of two hundred dollars and also placed on probation for two years with the first six months to be served in the House of Correction under the Huber Law, which allowed him to leave jail during the day and early evening to work in his father's factory.

In fact, after his guilty pleas to the lesser charges, I had an opportunity to talk to him for a few minutes. I asked him how we had missed the big load of drugs that was supposed to be at the house the evening of the raid. He said just between him and I and the bed post, the Coppers that had come in the back door and walked down those four carpeted stairs thought they were stepping on carpeting that had padding beneath it when in fact several hours prior to our arrival they had placed all their hash and cocaine under the carpeting and nailed it down. How's that for being ingenious!

Bob and I had several good raids in the nine months we worked Special Detail together, and one of the most unusual ones happened just a month later. We once again had one of our informers in a crack where he needed a favor. He told us that he had been going regularly to a pot party on the north side, and that there was supposed to be a good one going on this particular evening. He also volunteered to take an undercover vice Copper along with him to the party.

This sounded pretty good so we got hold of the Vice Squad once again, who by this time were getting pretty used to us, and they agreed to supply an undercover Copper to go along with our informant to the party. They made a few phone calls and about a half hour later a long haired, unshaved, sloppy looking individual came to our location dressed in army fatigue clothes and looking like he either was strung out or hadn't slept for the past few days or both. This turned out to be the Copper and I must say he really looked the part.

Our plan of attack was that the two of them would go to the party and when the Copper figured it would be a good time to hit it, he would let us know by a predetermined word that he would say over the two-way radio we had him wired with. We also had all the windows of the apartment covered and if anything went wrong, he would try and throw something through the window. Little did I realize that the next thing flying through the window would not be an object, but a body.

We surrounded the apartment from a good distance away in about six Squad cars, including some vice women. Bob, I and two Vice Coppers sat in one car trying to monitor the two-way radio. After about forty-five minutes we realized that it just would be impossible to hear anything distinguishable on the radio either because of a faulty radio or some other interference.

We were just deciding whether to hit the place by chance, as we had observed a good amount of young people entering the apartment building, when the Vice Copper came out of the building and started to walk down the street. We followed him for about three blocks where he entered a tavern and came back out a side door with a six pack of beer.

He related to us that the party was going strong and everyone was getting high and that there seemed to be a substantial supply of drugs and hash to go around. He further stated that he had given the password several times and then realized that he must not have been getting through to us so he said he was going out to buy some beer. We later learned that about six people didn't like the idea of him leaving the party so they also left.

The method we now were going to use was that we would give him fifteen minutes back in the apartment and then we would hit it. This sounded good and after fifteen minutes about ten of us crept quietly up the apartment stairs to the second floor. I was the second man, being led by the hammer man who was carrying a twenty-pound sledge. The Copper inside said the door was kept locked and looked to be solid.

The party apparently was going strong as we could smell the weed in the hallway. On a given signal the man with the hammer knocked on the door and a girl questioned, "Who's there?" He mumbled some garbage thinking that she may open the door, but when she responded by saying, "Who?" he gave one mighty swing with the sledge hammer at a point right above the lock and below the door handle and the door went flying in.

There was immediate massive confusion with everyone yelling and screaming and running around and just as I had entered the dining room and was headed for the living room, where all the action seemed to come from I heard a loud crashing noise. To my utter disbelief, I saw this huge guy diving through the window, taking all the glass, frame, curtains and shade with him. I also realized in the brief moment that he wasn't just jumping through the window, but that he actually dove. We were on the second floor and that particular window overlooked a rear driveway.

I immediately looked out the window and sure enough, there was this body laying spread-eagle face down on the asphalt pavement below. He was immediately surrounded by several uniform Coppers and realizing there was nothing I could do, I went back into the room and assisted with once again the act of trying to organize the arrests and searches as much as I could. By this time, after having been on several raids, I felt I was somewhat more of a help than I had been in the past. But it still amazed me how well these Vice Coppers worked together.

One typical example was that it had never occurred to me to head for the bathroom. That in itself was one Copper's job and, sure enough he had to knock some guy on his ass and then reach in the toilet and come out with a bag of various drugs, just as they were going down the drain.

I think we arrested about fourteen people in the raid for various charges of either use of drugs, use of marijuana or use with intent to sell or deliver. One person had actually sold some hash to the undercover Copper and the Copper himself had actually witnessed the use by the rest of the apartment occupants.

The whole raid had turned out good with the exception of the individual that thought he was superman and tried to fly away. In fact, he sustained multiple fractures.

His first appearance in court was some six months later, and at that time he was still confined to a wheel chair. His case was ultimately disposed of by placing him on probation. The Judge felt that even though he had a prior record for drug use, he had suffered enough with all his injuries I learned that both he and his wife were at the party. Both were in their early twenties and both held decent jobs. In fact, while talking to his wife I found out that her husband had become hooked on drugs at some company party and he then got her started. She later told me after the trial, that both she and her husband had been off drugs since the raid. She also said he may be crippled for a long time and both of them had lost their jobs. She actually thanked me for what had happened. She said it was a shame it took such a tragic experience for them to see the evils of their drug orientated society that they had latched onto.

18. School Kid's Shenanigans

Bob and I kept pounding away, day after day, and were getting a good reputation at the Detective bureau as not only making a lot of arrests, but clearing a lot of offenses, which means much more. Clearing offenses means a lot because it causes the local, state and national statistical figures to look good. Later I found out that it's a big part of the whole law enforcement game.

We started to hear rumors that either Bob, I, or both might get a chance at the bureau. In order to get there you have to be recommended by your Commanding Officers and we both had been recommended at least six or seven times in the past.

We also had a good working relationship with the day men at the bureau who sometimes were looking for some younger Coppers to give information to. Not saying that these guys weren't hard workers, on the contrary they were exceptional, but some had been on the job for twenty some years and one can only keep up the rat race pace for just so long.

We had an interesting burglary case given to us by the day shift. They had received information that several young boys were leaving school between classes, pulling burglaries and returning to school. Not only establishing an alibi for their presence, but they also hid their loot from the burglaries in their school lockers. This was the early part of 1969, when cooperation by the school officials was more or less the rule rather than the exception. The courts had ruled that a juvenile could not be removed from school merely on a suspicion and questioned regarding crimes committed possibly by them. In fact, teachers were more fearful of law suits than anything else and made it almost a constant practice of not allowing the removal of students without either their parents' permission or an order by the court. This put a tremendous stumbling block in the way of good Police investigations and interrogations. Getting back to the case itself, we questioned the boys one at a time in the principal's office with the principal present. After advising them all of their constitutional rights, to which even the principal shook his head, all the boys admitted their part in numerous burglaries.

The principal accompanied us to their lockers and both Bob, I and the principal were amazed at the loot they had accumulated in their lockers. It included several guns, including one twenty-two caliber rifle, whiskey, money, watches, jewelry, radios, binoculars, and even a bottle of champagne. Not recovered at that time were all the items that they had sold out of their lockers to fellow students. Selling stuff out of their lockers was apparently their downfall, because we later learned that it was from a student that the original information came.

We questioned the juveniles for several hours and thought we had just about all the burglaries picked out, either by going past the houses or out of our burglary book, when one of the youths asked if we knew of a house that had been damaged a lot while the people were on vacation. Even though it was in another district, we had heard about a house being completely ransacked while the owners were gone for a few days.

It turned out that it had been these same four boys that caused the damage. The reason given was that one boy had been seeing a girl that lived there and her parents had told her not to see him anymore.

We got the report and started to read it and also looked at the accompanying pictures. We could hardly believe our eyes. The boys had apparently broken into the home on a Sunday, the day after the owners left. They cut and slashed all the furniture, clothing and any other fabric material they could find. They broke every glass and bottle in the house, threw all the food from the refrigerator up against the walls, urinated on the bed and floor and smeared human excrement on the walls and mirrors. As a final last bit of ingenuity they plugged all the drains in the sinks, bathtub and basement floor and turned on all the faucets. This water, I was told by the owners, ran until the following Saturday when they returned home. In fact, one of the owners was a waitress at one of our eating places. Needless to say, she was shocked at her daughter being involved.

The total damage caused by, how should I say, 'misfits?' was settled by the home owner's insurance company, which came to almost sixteen thousand dollars. Just for being turned off by a girl—WOW!

It's amazing how much property damage was caused by juveniles during both burglaries and other offenses, and it is the exception rather than the rule that the parents of the actors are held responsible, monetarily speaking.

I can recall one instance when we had been plagued by false fire alarms on the corner of one of the local schools in our area. Apparently, the kids would set off the alarm on the way to school in the morning, home for lunch, back to school again and then again on the way home at night. It was usually one of four call boxes in a six block area where the hook was pulled calling for a fire engine.

Our Captain told us he had a complaint come down right from the Chief; we should see if we could nail one of those little misguided brats. We figured the best way would be to plant on the boxes in plain clothes instead of our uniforms. I found that one was across the street from a tavern. I conveniently sat myself on a stool next to the front window, stared at the Police and Fire Alarm Box. While I was doing this, two other plain clothes Coppers were in cars watching two other call boxes.

It only took a little while to watch about a hundred young teenagers walk past the Box, when about four boys came bounding by, slapping hands and all the while looking around. I knew I hit pay dirt.

Before I got my hand on the front door, the one youth had the Box open and had pulled the alarm. I jumped down a flight of stairs and at the same time they saw me. And me being the only white one in the neighborhood with a short hair cut, they figured that I was "the man."

The month was February and the weather was cold and slippery and within a block they had me beat. But then fortune fell my way. The one kid that was caught with his arm in the Call box slipped on the ice, fell on his ass and I was all over him. He was only fifteen, but his first reaction was to punch me in the chest.

I got his arms behind his back and then realized that I had lost my handcuffs in the chase. I struggled with the youth back to my handcuffs, had the kid pick them up and I cuffed his arms behind his back. I dragged him to the Call box while at the same time listening to the fire truck sirens coming because the alarm had been pulled at the Box.

The firemen, I, my prisoner and about seventy-five juveniles all arrived at the Call box at the same time. By this time the kids had gotten over the initial shock of the chase and realized that I was "the man," so the taunts started. "Hey white honky mother, let the little kid go," along with other varied, rude comments.

The pushing and shoving started and I had the uneasy feeling that I just might get my tail kicked, when about four firemen jumped off the rig with their ventilating pike poles, and the threat was over.

I think the fact that the kid was caught by a plain clothes Copper coming out of a tavern must have put the fear of God into the juveniles for awhile, because there wasn't another alarm pulled around the school for the rest of the year.

Meanwhile, when talking to the kid at the station he not only wouldn't kick into (or admit to) setting off other alarms, he even denied setting off the one I saw him pull!

He was released to his parents and about three weeks later, I was subpoenaed to Children's Court where the boy's family had hired an attorney. He was pleading not guilty. After about an hour of testimony by me and the Fire Captain, who was called as the complainant, the Judge found the youth guilty. Then came the astonishing part; the Judge called the Fire Captain to the witness stand and asked him numerous questions regarding how much it cost each time a false alarm was pulled and how he felt about the burden this placed not only on the taxpayer but on the safety of the people who may need the Fire Department while they were away on a false call.

The Captain not only had done his homework, but he must have stayed up several nights coming up with all the figures he did. When his testimony was finally over the Judge not only placed the boy under strict probation until he was eighteen, but he also told the father to make restitution in the amount of five hundred dollars for the actions of his son. This sum was only a small part of what a false alarm really costs a taxpayer. All parties involved on my side were satisfied because very seldom was restitution ordered in juvenile cases.

It always gave me a little bit of satisfaction when I could do the Fire Department a little extra, because I could always remember the cold winter nights after midnight while walking the beat that the most welcome site was a fire house. Several times in my career I counted heavily on the cooperation of other Departments in the city besides the Fire Department, but I think a little more closeness was felt with the Fire Department because of the type of service the men on both Departments had—lousy hours and close family ties.

I used to always tell the kids I talked to, that the best friends they could have besides their parents were their teachers, firemen, Policemen and ministers. Speaking of ministers, I remember getting called to the home of a minister at one of the churches in the inner city. He was white and all his parishioners were black. He said he came to this particular church about a year ago from a farming community, and prior to his coming here the only black people he knew were a couple he went to college with. He further related to me that when he came to this particular parish it was his intention to not only minister to those underprivileged, but also to save them from the ravenous jaws of society, which were depicted to him by the black youth as being the men with the blue uniforms. In fact, he stated that his idea of a good Cop was one that he never saw.

I asked him what his particular problem was, and with that he took me into his church. He showed me where the kids stashed their weed, whiskey, knives and stolen loot. He also pointed out that it was impossible to keep a "poor box" nailed to the wall, nor was it possible, he felt, to get through to some of the kids he was working with. He felt that at first they were placing their trust in him by telling him about their sordid deeds of sex and crime. Then he realized they were only taking advantage of both him and the church, because it acted like a sanctuary when running from the Police. He felt they were making a fool of him, the decent parishioners, and God.

He asked me what he could do about the situation he had gotten himself into and we talked for several hours. In the end, it was agreed that he would face the teenagers he was having trouble with and tell them that this was the end. Any further trouble would be turned over to the Police.

Several months later, the minister told me that he not only felt relieved but he felt he was doing the whole black community a favor by ridding them of the sickness these kids had brought to their parish. As a matter of fact, he later became one of my more reliable informants and I sorely missed him when he moved to another state a few years later. It was a strange relationship that we had, but I think we were both satisfied.

When I speak of citizen cooperation, I speak not only of citizens telling what they see and hear, but also that they follow through on their complaints. A typical example of this is an incident Bob and I got involved in.

We were told to meet several owners of equipment rental agencies who were having a meeting to discuss a very serious situation that had arisen. It seemed that there was a group of black men that were going from one agency to the other and after placing a deposit in cash—usually a small amount compared to the rented merchandise—gave false information from stolen identifications, and took the rented items with them. They took these businessmen for property valued as high as twenty thousand dollars.

The only additional information they had of any value was a license number and a few first names that the men used when discussing what they wanted to rent. It also seemed that most of the items taken were commercial cleaning equipment and various items used for bands, such as large amps, speakers, etc.

Bob and I worked on that for about two weeks, off and on between other jobs, but we must have put in at least twenty or thirty hours on this case. We finally came up with a private black club that was going to be opening up soon. While gaining the confidence of a member that was disgruntled, we came up with all the parties involved and also the location of almost all of the property.

At this point we approached the District Attorney. He stated that after we had completed our investigation, we should order all the complainants in and he would then issue warrants on the actors involved.

Apparently the word got out, possibly from the member we had talked to, and they realized what we were up to as far as the warrants were concerned. Just as we were about to make the notifications to the businessmen as to when we wanted them to appear, we were contacted by them, one at a time relating that almost all of their property had been returned. Not only was the property returned but any late charges that were due were paid.

Bob and I told the business people that apparently the actors were worried about the warrants and wanted to stop the issuance by returning the property. Bob and I both told all the business people involved that even though they had been satisfied by the return of their property, they should still appear at the District Attorney's office to discuss the matter and prevent any future thefts by fraud.

Would you believe that after getting almost sixteen thousand dollars worth of property back, they had the nerve not to appear with us, but one of them, in fact, rented the same property back to the same individuals? How's that for citizen cooperation!

Following that, we had the most unusual pleasure to get involved with some young burglars from the south side of town, which was predominately Polish. We approached the arrest of the youths with the same type of attitude that we were usually faced with, and that was not too much cooperation from the parents. We made our first stop, and after identifying ourselves and being admitted to the home, I informed the mother we had information that her son had committed several burglaries, and we would have to take him with us.

At that point she startled us by saying not only were we perfectly right in taking her boy from her house, she insisted that we first have cake and coffee with her and her husband. This did not turn out to be an isolated instance. We received the same cooperation (except for the cake and coffee) from the parents of the other three boys involved.

I know for a fact the statement I always make, regarding how hard it is to please the public and how cruel they can be, but least I forget that I, too, am part of that sect. How soon I forget, when I get a particular bill that upsets me, how quick I am to call the main office and jump all over some poor girl working there who has to take the brunt of my frustrations. Or, how often I have become aggravated at a clerk in a store when she or he did not bend to my particular whim? I think we can all gain a lesson when dealing with the public. I've learned that frustrations beget frustration and tolerance often times brings courtesy. Who do I think I am—a philosopher?

I wonder if I gave a false impression in the last few pages. I don't want to give the impression that I spent nine months, morning to night, dedicated to work; quite the contrary. I really believe I could count on one hand the nights that we didn't wind up in some gin mill. In fact, before I went Special Detail my tolerance of liquor was not the greatest in the world, but I sure learned how to drink. At that point in time, our Police Chief believed that crimes were solved by associating with people in the know. Getting into the gin mills was imperative to developing good informants.

In order to knock off a tavern for a violation or gain the confidence of informers, it became necessary to identify one's self with the particular crowd that patronized that particular establishment. In other words, if we were trying to knock off some skuzzy gin mill in the ghetto area we would look completely out of place in a suit, tie and clean shaven. And the same went for the higher class establishments in our area. I became quite proficient in the art of shooting pool, bar dice and pinball machines.

I can say this, though, that a bunch of Coppers relaxing after a particular bad night or week are something else to behold. I would imagine the only possible people that would understand are other Policemen or those odd members of society that become acquainted with them.

I did find at the time and even now that a Policeman can and will become your greatest, closest and most intense friend. But on the other hand, they show just as much intensity in handling the tough parts of their job.

I watched a television program last night about a uniform Policeman stopping a particularly obnoxious citizen and after he had given him a ticket, the citizen told the Copper and his partner that he was going to report them to their Commanding Officer. Then, the Copper took the man's drivers license, smeared it with peanut butter and ate it. He politely told the man that he should also tell his boss that the Officer smeared his driver's license with peanut butter and ate it—a very funny story that sent me into hysterics. Do you know why? Well, I've never eaten a driver's license, but I bet the story was true.

I remember a few instances when, just because a ticket was given, that individual thought he could discuss and berate not only myself and my partner but also our families.

I recall the startled look on several people's faces when they would say, "Give me my G.D. license you lousy asshole." At which time I would politely hand him back his license, which by now was in several pieces, and then thanked him kindly for his thoughtful words. I imagine a book could be written on just those types of instances, and only Cops would believe it and find the humor in it.

Those nine months have always left an impression in my mind, even to this day. I recall experiences with some of the Coppers I worked with at that time and we find a lot of humor in the past excitement. We all agree that they were great times.

During the three or four decades that have passed since writing *The Memo Book*, times certainly have changed. Drinking alcohol on the job (as well as consumption of alcohol by society as a whole) has come under public scrutiny and certain guidelines regarding what is expected of special Squads has changed.

The Detective Bureau

19. Making the Bureau

By this time it was the early part of August, 1969 and rumors were circulating that one of the Special Detail men from the station was going to the Bureau. There were five of us, with me being the oldest and with the most time on the job (eleven years). I would say the average time spent in uniform for those who went to the Detective Bureau varied anywhere from eight years to twelve or thirteen years, depending on your activity and being in the right place at the right time, and by all means knowing the right people that are going to push you.

The statement has been made that the only way to get to the Bureau is by having a hook. In other words, someone personally that will get you down there because your good friend is on the job or is a member of the same lodge or whatever else you might have. And I do suppose and would be rather ignorant in my way of thinking if I didn't think this was so in a few of the cases. But I would have to say the majority of times I have seen advancements, it's been mainly by merit and hard work.

I don't want to sound vain or conceited, but I would have to say that the reason I was sent to the Bureau would have to be contributed to a great deal of work, arrests, clearances, time on the job, and some boss downtown at the Bureau recommending me at that particular time and moment, when the names are put into a so-called hat.

I have to admit that I have had suspicions of who the boss downtown was, but I have never found out for sure. I also had a great deal of push from the station. We had, at that time, a tremendous Captain, who we made look very good at his weekly meetings, and we also had several uniform bosses that pushed for us. All in all, I can honestly say that I deserved to go to the

Bureau as much as a great deal of others—no more and no less. It's just that I was picked.

Also, I know a great deal of uniform Officers that have turned down advancements to plain clothes, because they like uniform work and wouldn't consider giving up certain advantages that I'll try to explain later.

The particular time was on a Wednesday afternoon when a boss from downtown that I knew called me at the station. He said that an order was coming out on Friday transferring me to the Detective Bureau on the following Sunday.

My first thoughts were mixed. I was pleased that I was going to the Bureau and not the Vice Squad. It had been a pattern in the past that new men would spend some time on the Vice Squad before going to the Bureau, and if that would have been the case, I do believe that I would have turned it down. Not that I'm a prude or anything, but that way of life was just not my cup of tea.

Bob was my partner that day and we had planned on working to midnight, and during the day Thursday and Friday, so this was our last night of working together. This was to be a night of celebration. We started out with a good meal at a fancy restaurant in our area that Bob paid for, and then proceeded to hit all the gin mills in the area that we were known at.

By this time I had called Marlene and she was pleased with my promotion, or at least she said she was. She never really made her true feelings known about the job in general, and it probably was best that she didn't, because in my opinion it sure isn't much of a life to be a Policeman's wife.

For example, my transfer to the Bureau came exactly one month prior to my turn to go days in uniform. That meant who knows how many more years of night work—sort of starting all over with shift seniority on the Bureau. As it turned out, I'm writing at this time some almost eight years later and am still on nights.

It also meant a new wardrobe, because I was expected to wear a sport coat and tie every night. It also meant a great deal more of lonely days and even more lonely nights for Marlene. I told her not to wait up for me because Bob and I were going to celebrate a little. All she said was to be careful driving. She was well aware of how Policemen celebrate anything; it's with the same enthusiasm and spirit that they do all things. You can imagine, knowing all the people that we did know and all the places that we were trying to visit and all the bartenders and patrons congratulating me, that by four o'clock in the morning I had had a few drinks.

The next day was Thursday and neither one of us made it to work before noon. Nothing was said and the other Special Detail men covered for us. I really don't think that was necessary because the bosses knew what had happened the night before. I would assume some of what happened was known and am grateful that they didn't know all!

Well, here it was, Sunday and my first day at the Bureau. It was almost like starting a new job all over again. Dressed in a new suit and tie I made my grand entrance to the hallowed ground of the Detective Bureau.

I was greeted by one of the bosses who gave me the standard introduction with the statement that I should feel proud that I had been hand-picked to serve in the Bureau, and that possibilities of farther advancement were all within reach. He further stated that after spending a year at the Bureau as an Acting Detective I would be eligible to take an exam for Detective and after that, barring any further promotions, it would just be a matter of a few years and I would be working days.

The exam didn't come for three years, and it was another year before I was promoted to Detective. That is a total of four years that I worked in the same capacity as a Detective, without the same pay; same responsibilities and same ass chewing.

It was unfair at that time and to my knowledge it presently has not changed. Our union, that's what they call it, finally did get the exam open to the whole Department but that still has not come to pass. No other exam has been written since I took mine almost four years ago. In fact, there are some Coppers at the Bureau still with the fictitious rank of Acting Detective that have been there for as long as twelve years.

I was pleased that first day at the bureau because I was told that I would be assigned to a Squad that covered the same district that I had come from. At that time I believe there were only about fourteen Detective Squads to cover the entire city. And that only occurred during the week when everyone was working and no one was sick or injured or on vacation. I recall several nights when there were only six Detective Squads on the street to handle the major crimes. In 2009, there were dozens of Detective Squads. Speaking of major crimes, that is what the Bureau is all about. It's the follow-up of the investigation of all the major crimes that occur in the city which, when I was on the Bureau, numbered in population about eight hundred thousand, with a minority population of about twenty to twenty-five percent. In eight years I did everything from handling the most gruesome homicide to handling the most complicated internal theft in a large corporation.

I can honestly say that barring a few days that I'd been disgusted by working lousy hours, there weren't many days that I didn't really enjoy my job. Not in the sense of relish or delight in the blood and guts of a homicide, but rather pleasure in the fact of getting involved in a difficult case and seeing it through to its resolution or conclusion.

The first few nights were rather slow and I more or less was feeling my way around. I had been assigned with two excellent partners: Dick and Jerry. They showed me a lot of the finer points. I kept Dick as a partner for several years, but Jerry for only about six months.

As I recall now, and it really hasn't changed that much in the past years, the bosses usually gave a new man a few months to get used to the new system and then everything is the same for everyone. When a hitch comes in and you're available—you get it.

There were special Squads, that at that time, only handled robberies and shootings, but those were only two Squads and the majority of the time they were busy.

The bosses also felt that most Coppers coming to the Bureau were seasoned and knew how to take care of themselves—in regard to handling crime and also their personal conduct; on and off duty.

I recall being down there for less than a month and both my partners were working so I was put on another Squad. This particular partner had very unusual working methods. Shall we say somewhat unorthodox—to say the least. I still recall Dick telling me before I went on the street with this other Copper, "Jim take care of yourself and don't let this guy get you into a crack." Very wise words, but apparently they fell on deaf ears.

Once on the street, my partner for that evening told me that he had been involved in a special assignment that involved following known criminals in the city. He further said that the assignment was now complete and that he had caused some hard feelings among these thieves and in fact a week ago his car had been fire-bombed.

Well, I knew about the fire-bombing of the car and I also knew that this guy had been involved in some other assignment, so I had no reason to disbelieve him. He also told me that he understood that I had a lot of friends and informers in this one particular tavern where the clientele did not have the best reputation in the world. In fact, this particular place seemed like a clearing house for all the criminals that came out of the State Prison. They would check there first, either for a quick loan from the owner or to find out how things had changed since their incarceration and what was happening on the street.

I not only was well known at the tavern, but also had gained a good deal of respect; I conveyed the thought that I and my partners would treat them as men as long as they stayed within the law. They knew from actual occurrences that I would not hesitate to arrest any one of them. I can't count the number of good arrests and clearances I got from informers in that tavern over the years.

Anyhow, back to that particular night. This Detective, let's call him Pete, wanted me to take him to this gin mill and introduce him to a few people he thought had information regarding his car. I agreed and we entered the tavern about five o'clock in the afternoon—right after coming out of roll call. I recall introducing him to several people and also asking him several times during the night if it had been cleared with the bosses that we were staying out of service so long. He gave me full assurance that the information he was getting was extremely valuable and he had called the bosses and everything was taken care of.

Well, between five o'clock and eleven-thirty when I walked—and he staggered out, I must have shot thirty games of pool and another thirty games of pin ball. All this time he went from person to person trying to extract the information that I thought he was getting.

I should have known better because several days later I was told that he was spotted as a phony as soon as he walked in the door of the tavern and the only information he received was what he already knew and the rest was useless. They also assured me at that time that no one in that tavern had anything to do with his car and that the word on the street was that he actually torched it himself.

Anyhow, we walked out of the place at eleven-thirty and I stayed back a little to make my apologies for his conduct. I then went to the Squad and much to my surprise there was a young woman sitting in the front seat of the car next to Pete, who at that time was trying to find the car keys. I knew this gal well and also knew that if he thought he was going to get anything of value from her he was mistaken. This gal wouldn't tell a Copper the time of day if her life depended on it.

By this time he had the keys in the ignition and was attempting to get the windshield wipers going. I reached over from the back seat, started the wipers and also turned the key in the ignition and at almost the same instant the radio blared our Squad number about four times in a row very emphatically. I knew then that they must have been calling us for a good deal of time. It turned out that they called us on and off for three hours.

I had that uneasy feeling in my stomach that my tenure at the Bureau was going to last just a little less than a month. I give the guy credit for one thing—he kicked the gal out of the car and made a quick call to one of our bosses that we were just checking out and going home. They told him that both he and I were in a hell of a lot of trouble and should put our actions for the evening on paper.

We drove around for about half an hour to make sure all the early shift bosses had gone home and then went in and wrote what I thought was a stupid excuse for where we were, but Pete insisted on it and I—being gullible and new—went along with it.

I was off for the next two days and I told Marlene that when I went back to work I wouldn't be surprised if I was sent back into uniform.

The first person that I saw when I came to roll call two days later was the same boss that had originally greeted me on my first day at the Bureau. He immediately called me to a back office and held my report in his hand. He merely looked at me and said, "I know everything that's on this report is a crock of shit and I hope you realize that I have that much intelligence to see through it." He went on to say, "We know you're new down here, but you're also supposed to take care of yourself. Pete took advantage of a new man and for that reason and that reason only, you're getting a pass." With that statement he tore up my report, threw it into the wastebasket and said, "Now get the hell out of here!" That was it and I never heard another thing about it. I sure learned a valuable lesson.

This was a dog-eat-dog job and I had to learn to take care of myself or be eaten up, even though up to this point in my career I had been involved in several homicides and a good number of serious shootings and cuttings. The mere fact that I was now an Acting Detective made the entire investigations different from an investigative standpoint. Up to this time my investigations had been limited to making usually the first appearance at the scene. Now it seems on most occasions we arrive after the initial excitement was over, and most usually after the victim had already been conveyed. Again, in uniform we made a lot of arrests and wrote a good deal of reports regarding our actions, but we really never got into the more detailed part of the investigations such as the intense, deliberate and exacting interrogations of not only the actor involved but also the victim and witnesses.

In fact, up to this point I don't believe I ever had the somewhat dubious pleasures of trying to question either a victim or sometimes a reluctant actor in the hospital while half a dozen nurses and doctors are trying to save his life by shoving tubes in his mouth, nose and other cavities, pumping blood into them, cutting, bandaging, compressing and x-raying them. To say this causes mass confusion is to put the facts in a very mild sense.

I recall the first shooting I had while at the Bureau. It wasn't much of a case by difficult standards. It was probably just as well, because I could really take my time and more or less set a pattern for future such investigations.

This shooting was a simple one in that when we got there the victim had been conveyed to the hospital. The actors had been arrested at the scene and the gun had been recovered in the actor's pocket.

The investigation still took several hours. We first carefully looked over the entire house so we could better relate to the incident later on. We then arranged for the photo car to come and take pictures of all the rooms in the lower portion of the house and take pictures of evidence which we had found and left lay in its place so it could be photographed. This included several spent shells, blood stained clothing and other miscellaneous articles that either my partner or myself thought may be of use later on in the investigation or possibly be important in case of a trial.

Several things go through your mind during those first few hours, because once the original phase of an investigation is completed, it is almost impossible to reconstruct the scene or evidence in the exact manner as it was originally.

After all the photos were taken and the evidence was identified, everything was measured and later a complete diagram was made placing the victim and evidence in as an exact a position as possible.

In the case of a more serious shooting or other offense, the City Engineer is called to the scene and a detailed diagram is then made.

After all these things were completed it became apparent that the other cars at the bureau were busy and that we would also have to handle the hospital end of the investigation. Once again, because of the less seriousness of the offense, the victim had merely been shot in the leg and would soon be released; the hospital end of it was also quite simple.

After questioning the victim in detail and taking his pants with the bullet hole as evidence, we notified the doctor that we wanted the slug when and if they took it from his leg. After being assured of this and concluding our investigation at the hospital, we proceeded to the bureau to question the suspect and file all of our reports.

The suspect was intoxicated when we questioned him but the story he related was that he and his roommate, who was the victim, had been drinking all day long. He further related that he went home with some gal he met at the tavern and they went to bed. A short time later his roommate came home and also tried to climb in bed with him and his lady friend. When the suspect protested and his friend wouldn't get out of bed, the suspect got his gun from his dresser and before his friend could get out the front door, the suspect fired six shots at him, hitting him once in the leg.

The story sounded reasonable and the next day the suspect was charged with endangering safety by conduct regardless of life. He sat in jail for a total of seven months because he couldn't make bail and after that period of time the victim again failed to appear in court as he had several times in the past. The case was dismissed because the victim failed to appear as the complainant. In offenses involving girl friend/boy friend, husband/wife or friends, that disposition is many times the rule rather than the exception.

I would imagine the most boring jobs not only at the Bureau but also in uniform are the many plant and surveillance tasks that come about. They are usually not only dull and annoying, but they are also dangerous in most instances because one is usually lulled into complacency by the lack of activity.

I can recall while in uniform, I planted every night for a week from midnight till eight in the morning, locked in a loan office waiting for someone to break through the roof. The reason being that someone had received information from an informer that someone recently released from the State Prison was planning that particular job. The roof never came in and it was one of the longest weeks of my career.

While at the bureau we had several plants—Judges, the Mayor, the Police Chief and other political individuals—for a variety of reasons. Some I fear were just because they were either lonely or wanted to show how much influence they had. Some of the plants would last for several days, weeks, months, or in some cases for an entire term in office.

One of these plants had been going so long that I saw an individual go from playing in the street to getting married to bringing his first child to his parent's home. Who knows, if it went on long enough I might have seen his grandchildren! This was the exception rather than the rule and it was alternated so that your turn usually only came up once a month or so.

One of the first plants I had in the Bureau was to try and catch a holdup man that had been terrorizing the dry cleaning establishments in our city. The plant was for four hours a day and it was on overtime so that made somewhat of a difference. But, trying to hide in a small cleaning shop and still maintain a good view of the store front and be within reach of your shotgun, was sometimes a problem.

I was sitting on a chair for the full four hours up against a wall with a full clothes rack pushed up against me and trying to peer between a suit coat and several pair of pants. Good thing this was on overtime because I needed the money.

During one of the days of this particular surveillance, one of the Officers involved called in sick and I was sent to another dry cleaning location. The store that I originally was to be at—but was changed to a different store—actually got held-up. When I heard about the hold-up a thousand thoughts went through my mind. I couldn't help but wonder what action I would have taken. The store had a peculiar setup and once I would have come into the open, I would undoubtedly have been face to face with the hold-up man.

What became even more astonishing was the fact that this same hold-up man was arrested after a stickup and chase several days later and I had the chance to question him.

After he had admitted his part in all the dry cleaning offenses, I asked him what he would have done had I been in the back room on that particular day and had come out with a shotgun in my hand. He told me that he was a coward and would probably have dropped the gun and tried to run.

Would I have taken the chance that he would drop the gun? Would I have said "Police" at the same time I was pulling the trigger? Would I have shot him as he was running out the door? Would he have panicked and shot me or the clerk? There were a number of questions that will never be answered.

POLICE DEPARTMENT
CITY OF MILWAUKEE, WISCONSIN
CERTIFICATE OF PROMOTION

To all who shall see these presents. Greetings: Know ye, that reposing special trust and confidence in the integrity and abilities of _JAMES O. GAUGER_

He is hereby promoted to the rank of _DETECTIVE_ in the Milwaukee Police Department.

This elevation in rank imposes upon the recipient a profound obligation to discharge the duties of his office diligently and in an exemplary manner as prescribed by Department Rules and Regulations.

In dealing with citizens and co-workers, he shall always strive to be courteous, tactful and fair and so discharge his duties that he will inspire public confidence and create respect for the police profession.

It is required that all officers under his command obey his lawful orders, if his rank is supervisory, and that he be obedient to such lawful orders and directions as he may receive from his superior officers in the Police Department, in accordance with the Rules and Regulations of the Police Department, the ordinances of the City of Milwaukee, and the laws of the State of Wisconsin, and of the United States of America.

Effective this _17th_ day of _June_, 19_73_.

Chief of Police

Jim was promoted to Detective June 17, 1973.

Harold A. Breier, Chief of Police, congratulates Jim on his promotion.

20. TV Shows—Fact or Fiction?

Speaking of holdups and homicides, it was only a matter of about two months and in two successive days that I got involved in one of each that were straight out of a *Kojak* program (a popular T.V. Detective show in the 1970's). That sounds funny to mention his name. I started to write these memories before he was on television. In fact, I started this book before Wambaugh wrote *The New Centurions*. I guess I'm either a slow writer or maybe it takes a little bit longer to actually get involved in these situations.

Everything you see on television is not all that far-fetched. The only difference, besides that glory and glamour, is that an hour case on television may take six months in real life. In fact, I've related myself to quite a few Cop stories.

Anyway, by this time I had gotten well acquainted with my partners. Jerry and I were to be partners for only about six months but Dick would be my partner for several years.

Dick had to be one of the coolest, calmest, impassive and most composed people I have ever met. He was straight out of one of those television series or movies—a good looking guy who was a four-letter man in high school with a very attractive wife. He had made it to the Bureau after spending a good deal of time on the Vice Squad. He was not only a good Copper and an excellent investigator, but he was also a nice guy. And man, could this guy drink. His passion was Manhattans and he drank those things like water. I guess it was his practice from the Vice Squad because I sure couldn't keep up with him.

On this particular night we got an arson complaint right out of roll call and after getting all the information we went to one of the District Stations to write the reports. While doing this we heard a Squad car get sent to a hold-up of a bakery on the south side. The description came over the air and it was only a matter of a few minutes and another Squad got sent to a second bakery on the south side and in the same vicinity of the first one. When the description came over the air from the second hold-up it was obviously the same actor.

By this time we had just about completed our reports and were ready to leave when we got sent to investigate the second robbery. The offense occurred on the south side of town and I was driving. I always got lost on the south side; I took off like a streak toward that side of town but didn't have the vaguest idea where I was going. Dick was sitting looking out the window and I felt if I was going the wrong way he probably would have said something by this time. I was looking for a particular cross street, when Dick said, "Hey, stop. That guy just ran out the back of that bakery." Most guys, including myself, would have been getting somewhat excited by now, but not Dick; it was just a very calm and natural statement.

Well, let me tell you, if he wasn't excited—I sure was. I slammed on the brakes, threw it in reverse and backed up to the alley behind the store. I looked down the alley and saw a figure that by this time had reached the other end and was now turning out of sight. I wheeled the Squad down the alley and out on the adjoining street and then nothing. Not a thing in sight except one lonely car parked toward the end of the block. I thought sure as hell we had lost this guy when suddenly the parked car started to slowly move down the street. I got right on his tail and with the red light on, he immediately pulled over to the curb and got out.

He was a white guy, about twenty-four or five-years-old, stocky build and a pockmarked face. There was no doubt from hearing the description on the air from the previous two hold-ups that we had the right man. Both of us had our guns drawn and had him spread eagle on the trunk of his car. My heart was going a mile a minute. No matter how often you get involved, it's the initial excitement that's the most exhilarating. The guy kept saying, "Hey, what's going on? Who are you guys? I was just on my way home."

By this time Dick had the guy handcuffed and I opened the driver's door to see if anyone else was in the car and guess what was laying right there on the floor of the driver's side? There was a nice small thirty-two-caliber automatic and a stack of cash. All I could say was, "Dick, we sure as hell got the right guy." At the same time we heard another description come over the air, but this time it was in reference to a hold-up that occurred in an adjoining suburb.

When I heard the brief description and the address where it occurred I watched the eyes of the guy we had, because he matched the description to a tea. But I also realized that by chasing to the south side of town I must have wandered into the adjoining suburb by a few blocks and just by some quirk happened to be going down the right street at the right time. I guess that's the name of the game. Being in the right place at the right time.

Dick immediately got on the air and said very, very calmly that we not only had the guy from the suburbs but we also had the guy for our two hold-ups, the weapon and the cash. It was only a matter of seconds and the suburb's uniform Squads were converging on the scene. If I thought that I was excited, this was their first hold-up in the last six months and the guy was already in custody!

I had the guy in the back seat of the car and after advising him of his constitutional rights he absolutely refused to say anything except his name, date of birth and "I want a lawyer." This guy was real cool.

As long as we had arrested him in another jurisdiction and for an offense that actually occurred there, we conveyed him to the suburban Police station. Once there we got all the witnesses from all three hold-ups and conducted a line-up. It was obvious that the Coppers from the other city hadn't had much experience at line-ups so Dick took over and conducted the entire viewing. Not only in a very professional and legal manner but also putting the other Coppers at ease and never once giving them any reason for embarrassment. That's the way Dick operated. Never put anyone down. Always treated the other guy with respect.

I can't put into words the many things I learned from Dick. Things that I use every day. One of the biggest lessons I learned was to treat the uniform men with respect and consideration. The uniform men can make or break you. They can really make you feel and look foolish if that is their wish.

The suspect we brought in for the hold-ups was positively identified by all three clerks but he still refused to say anything except that he wanted a lawyer. He was given the opportunity to call one and he called one of the most well-known criminal lawyers in the city. He talked for a few minutes on the phone and then said that the lawyer wanted to talk to me.

I knew the lawyer from a few cases I had with him and I told him that this guy's been positively identified by three different clerks in three different stores and besides that, we got the gun and all the money. In fact, some of the money was even marked and was identified by the owner of the store.

The lawyer said, "I know it sounds like a good case but I'm telling you I don't want my client saying anything—no statement, nothing—am I understood?" All I said was "See you in the District Attorney's office in the morning."

We finished all the reports and the inventorying of the evidence by ten o'clock and then got sent to question a suspect they had picked up from our earlier arson. I got home about three in the morning and back to court by eight thirty a.m.

The hold-up man was really a sort of likeable guy, never arrested before, married with two kids and another one on the way. I guess he just got into a bind and took the only way out he could find at the time. He sure didn't remind me of the typical hardened criminal that you find pulling armed robberies.

Another thing that wasn't true to form was that he still refused to say anything at all. Usually when we have that good a case the actors are looking for a break and some cooperation from the District Attorney and investigating Coppers; but not in this case.

I even told him that the lawyer he hired was going to cost him a hell of a bundle and with the evidence that we had, I didn't think it made that much sense to have a lawyer. Even after the lawyer told him that his usual retainer in these type cases was five thousand dollars, he still insisted that he wanted him.

The lawyer represented him during the issuance of the warrants, but before the preliminary hearing it became obvious that the guy had no money, so the lawyer asked to be relieved from the case.

The Judge granted the lawyer's request and then appointed another lawyer who was also very capable, but who would now be paid by the State as our holdup man had taken a pledge of indigence.

The case lasted several months and his attorney filed just about every kind of brief and motion that he could think of. He challenged the arrest, lineup, search of the vehicle, and questioning of the suspect even though the suspect didn't make any statements except those at the original time of arrest.

Failing in all these motions before the court, the lawyer finally agreed during a pre-trial conference that his client would plead guilty to one count of armed robbery and the other two offenses would be read into the record for consideration by the Judge at the time of sentencing.

It was only after all this time, and facing the Judge and pleading guilty, that the suspect finally admitted that he had pulled the hold-ups.

The Judge held open the sentencing for a pre-sentence investigation to be conducted on the suspect and it was after this time that I got a chance to talk to the suspect in the back room of the court. I told the guy he didn't have to answer me if he didn't want to, but I was really curious about why he kept quiet for so long. He then told me that he was so ashamed about what he had done that he could not even face the reality and fact that he had actually committed the crimes. In fact, up to this very day he had insisted to his wife and family that he was innocent.

He came up for sentencing several weeks later and he had his wife, parents, minister and employer in court to give testimony on his behalf. After hearing it all, the Judge sentenced him to five years in the State Prison, stayed that sentence and placed him on probation for five years with the first year served in the House of Correction under the Huber Law so he could still support his family.

Dick and I thought that the sentence did fit the situation and felt sure that the guy would probably not do the same thing again. But you never know. In fact, about one year later, I heard a description of a hold-up man on the south side and when they said pock-marked face, I immediately thought of our friend the bakery man.

Getting back to that period of time, I now had spent the whole day in court and came to roll call only to find out that Dick was on a plant and Jerry was off so they had me working alone. The evening started out quiet enough. I got sent to a simple burglary and was just finishing up. In those years we didn't have portable handy talkies to carry with us so I couldn't hear what was going on in the streets.

I called the boss back on the burglary hitch and he asked if I was busy with anything else. I told him no, so he told me to meet another boss on a corner on the far north side of town—not that far away from where I lived. I arrived at the corner and turned going south and was looking for the boss's car when I happened to look in my rear view mirror and saw about six Squads parked at the other end of the next block behind a large business building and across the street from a large vacant field.

I turned the Squad around, pulled up behind a uniform car and about four uniform men came towards me. Looking at the big building, I asked them if they had an alarm there or was somebody trapped in the place. "Hell no!" the one Cop replied, "We got a body in the field." Body in the field? That's all I needed! Of all the times to find a body in a field I thought, this was not the right day. I was not only tired but I also suddenly realized that I was the only Bureau man on the scene and was actually in charge of the situation and was being flooded with questions from the uniform men.

Taking a quick view of the situation and trying to comprehend a lot of facts at the same time I tried not to make any fast decisions.

The ambulance was there and they were anxious to convey the body. I told them no, that as long as we were sure she was dead a few more minutes wouldn't make any difference. I also saw that a lot of Coppers were walking in the field, probably getting a quick look at the body. There's nothing wrong with that, but because of the high grass, they were probably trampling on what I thought might later be evidence.

I also observed what appeared to be drag marks from the curb through some dirt to the sidewalk and then across the sidewalk and into the field. Blood was pointed out to me in the gutter right next to these marks. I immediately instructed a uniform boss on the scene to assign men to stop any traffic on the street, guard the drag marks so no one would step all over them, call for equipment to rope off the scene and also call for the picture car. He informed me that everything had been called for and about that time the picture car came on the scene.

I then proceeded with the Copper from the picture car into the field and there, lying in the dirt on her back, was a white woman. From first look I would say that she was about twenty-five or twenty-six years old, five-feet-five or six-inches and about onehundred-twenty pounds. She had one shoe on, no under clothes from the waist down, her skirt was pulled up but she was clothed from the waist up. She also had a black fur coat covering most of her body and also her face.

The coat had been removed from her face and upper portion of the body by the first Squad on the scene and it was obvious that she was dead so I had the coat placed back over her face and a great number of photographs taken.

By this time only fifteen minutes had expired but it seemed like a lifetime. I was just trying to correlate in my head what the next plan of action would be when several other bureau cars arrived along with my boss. My boss took over the decision making. It was both a relief to see them and also a funny feeling because by now I figured I had the immediate situation under control, and actually had done a pretty good job of analyzing and handling the original scene. This, as I stated before, is ever so important.

After the boss had asked a few preliminary questions and gave a few orders to the uniform Sergeants regarding the scene, he must have realized that I already had taken care of most of these points so he then simply said, "Let's take a look at the body, get some measurements and get it out of here."

Looking at the body the second time—this time more carefully—I noticed that the cause of death undoubtedly was caused by several wounds in her side and back. The blood already had coagulated and it was obvious that she had been there for some time.

This is when investigations of this sort differ from television. In a case like this it was several hours before we even knew who the woman was. We were all given different assignments—some to gather evidence at the scene, some to start a group of Officers searching the complete field with large search lights looking for, among other things, the murder weapon in case it was thrown away in the field. Others were to question neighbors and I was given the job of thoroughly questioning the man that found the body.

I took the guy to my Squad and started my questioning. He seemed like a real nice guy. He was my age and a little shocked at what he had just witnessed. He related to me that he came to this field several times a week to run his dog and on this particular night after coming home from work and playing with his three kids, he took his dog to the field and unleashed him. He further stated that he was giving the dog commands by whistle, when it suddenly began to bark and act strange. He went into the field and saw what appeared to be a body. He said he thought at first that it might have been a manikin from the store across the street so he touched the body on the thigh, lifted the coat from her face and then stated he saw her finger nails at which time he knew it was a human body. He further related that he then returned home, called the Police and when they arrived took them to the body in the field.

I must have talked to him for about an hour, getting his whole and complete statement and then spent several hours with other Coppers canvassing the entire neighborhood—talking to as many people as possible.

If this had been television, somebody would have seen or heard something, but I could not find anyone who had been in the field since three days prior to this date.

I returned to the scene and by this time the Officers there had just about completed their investigation and the whole area had been roped off waiting for the City Engineer to arrive and make his detailed drawing.

At this time I was informed that the body had been identified from a missing person report and that the victim was a white female, twenty-six years old, divorced and the mother of two children and that she lived about a mile from this spot. I was further told that a friend of hers had identified the body and also had given the name of a male associate of hers that was last seen leaving with her the night before from a local tavern.

With no real leads, this looked like another one of those homicides that would take days and weeks of questioning and re-questioning a hundred people.

I had just arrived downtown and started to write my reports when I heard someone say that they had picked up the woman's boyfriend at his place of work and were bringing him downtown for questioning. A few minutes later the boss said that the boyfriend had kicked in (or confessed) to the murder. I couldn't believe it! Six hours hadn't passed yet. Now it was starting to sound more like a television series.

Another Copper and I were sent to meet the Squad that had the suspect. When we arrived they had a white male, twenty-seven years old, in the back seat of their Squad. The suspect was handcuffed. One of the Detectives came over and said that it took them only about fifteen minutes of questioning and the guy admitted everything; he was even laughing about it. He had stated that she was his girlfriend and that after leaving the tavern the night she drove him—in her car—to the rear of his house and was about to drop him off. He further stated that he tried to have sex with her, as he had done in the past, but this time she refused and he, for no real reason at all, reached under his jacket, pulled out a knife and stabbed her several times.

He stated that he then drove to the field—where the body was found—and dragged the body to a patch and laid it down. He then returned to the car, got her coat, took it back to the body and laid it over her face. He then drove to a housing project in the area of his home, parked the car in a lot and then, after walking between several apartments, threw the knife to the ground.

This guy was unreal. He actually thought the whole bizarre event was a joke. In fact, I can recall even during his week-long trial he always had a smile on his face.

After hearing the whole story my partner and I went and recovered the knife, had it photographed and then proceeded to get his car. The car was parked exactly where he said it was—blood stained seat and all.

The car was towed and we went back to the Bureau to fill out all of the reports. This took until about four in the morning. This sure wasn't bad considering the whole case was completely wrapped up.

Incidentally, he did get sentenced to life in prison and I believe he's still locked up. What a tragic and complete waste of human life.

21. Incarceration and Justice

It had now been several months since I was assigned to the Bureau and the vast difference in work was almost overwhelming. Practically every investigation was of a major proportion and concern. There were criminals of somewhat major dimension who usually could afford their own attorneys and who would be able to get their cases adjourned for considerable periods of time. Then there were the poor indigents who many times had no idea of what the whole system was all about and who would probably become a statistic and wind up in the State Prison for a period of five years for not having at his disposal, the vast means available to many criminals.

I'm talking about everywhere from working a deal with the Police so we could make a bigger arrest and clear offenses, to plea bargaining with the District Attorney's office—many times because they were unsure they could win a conviction in court.

To this day I believe that is one of the biggest fallacies in the judicial system. The prosecutors pick and choose the cases they wish to handle in court. Naturally the ones that are solid and sound are the ones that get the most attention. The ones that lack certain aspects of a good case are either held open for further investigation or warrants are simply refused. I think they, the prosecutors, are trying to eliminate or subdue the Judges and jurists position under the guise of expediency. I firmly believe that the majority of the cases brought before District Attorneys should be decided by courts, rather than decided in their particular offices and many times at their own whim or inclinations.

Don't get me wrong. Just as there are good and bad Cops, so it goes in any profession including lawyers and jurists.

A particular case that may show the natures and proceedings of a court came up about that time.

It involved the wife of a well-known adult burglar, having a falling out with her husband. She had complained to us that he had been beating her and seeing other women and for this reason she was going to see to it that his parole would get revoked.

She had approached Jerry, Dick and I and it immediately was of concern to us because we had experienced a large amount of burglaries in our and adjoining areas in the last few months. In fact, the information she gave us indicated that she, her husband and another couple, were pulling the majority of these jobs.

The one adult was known to me by name but I had never had any dealings with him. The second adult that she named immediately struck home. I had arrested him several times both as a juvenile and as an adult for everything from burglary to battery to auto theft. I hadn't seen or heard from him in several years—partly due to the fact that he had been incarcerated in our State Prison.

We requested and received permission to set up a team of uniform men and ourselves to put these individuals under surveillance to see if we could catch them in the act of committing a crime.

We couldn't use the one man's wife because by now she had become separated from her husband and they no longer would allow her to go on any jobs with them. She had stated that their method of operation was to travel in one car as couples through a particular neighborhood between the hours of seven and nine at night—when people are generally shopping or visiting.

They would find two dark houses in a row and would sit in their car down the block acting like lovers. When the time appeared to be right, one of the couples would go to the side door of the home that seemed to be protected by the other dark house and they would then use various methods of breaking into the home.

Once inside they went mainly for small items of jewelry and cash. Occasionally they would take a camera, radio or some other items that caught their attention.

We already had checked with the District Attorney's office and they did not think that she could testify against her husband. In fact, they did not want to give her immunity to testify as a co-conspirator against the others until we had more information or actual physical evidence. This is what we were trying to accomplish by the surveillance. After about a week it appeared to be fruitless and almost seemed like someone had tipped them off that we were following them.

We had just about given up when we received information that after one of the burglaries in our area, the complainant and his wife drove by their house before putting their car in the garage and actually witnessed a man and woman come out of their front door, cross the street in front of their headlights and get into a car. They tried to get the license number of the auto, but failed.

Jerry and I went to the house and showed them a series of black and white photos and they immediately picked out the pictures of the second couple we had suspected. Armed with this information and a second witness seeing two people come out of the house but not recognizing them, the District Attorney's office agreed to issue burglary warrants on the couple and also warrants against the original informer and her husband using her as the main witness.

A top criminal lawyer was hired to defend all the parties. The woman informer was separated and later given immunity to testify against the rest.

Her husband, who had been on parole, pleaded guilty and his parole was revoked. He was sent back to the State Prison without ever making any kind of statement.

The second couple had numerous adjournments and finally a two-week jury trial during which the complainants in the burglary spent several days on the witness stand under vigorous cross examination. The whole crux of the defense was that they had been mistaken when they picked out the defendants pictures and could not have actually seen them the night of the burglary because of the poor lighting and because of their age. The couple was in their late fifties.

The couple handled themselves marvelously through the whole trial and was satisfied when the jury came back with a finding of guilty. The disposition being that the male defendant be sent to prison for a period not to exceed ten years and the female receiving probation because of her not having a past record and being pregnant.

These particular civilian witnesses had put up with many harassing phone calls and letters and several appearances by the pregnant girl coming to their door and pleading that they not send her or her husband to jail.

After the trial I had a chance to talk briefly with the male defendant and he told me, off the record, that he may have pulled as many as two hundred jobs, but he swore that the one he was convicted of was one he did not do.

The irony of this whole case came approximately one year later when the State Supreme Court over-turned the conviction of the one adult male who had the jury trial. It was their contention that during the original interview of the complainant and his wife they had made a statement to the investigating Officer that they did not think they would be able to identify the two people that they saw coming out of their house. They also concurred that the report with this statement on it was not given to the defense in time for him to use it at the trial.

The District Attorney's office thought it would be to no avail to appeal the case to a higher court or try to get it reopened so once again a guilty man, like so many others, was free to roam the streets again.

Fortunately or unfortunately, whose ever eyes you might look from, his freedom only lasted a couple of years. This time the crime was more severe and he was convicted of rape, robbery and false imprisonment. He abducted a woman on the street, took her money and purse and then drove her to an unknown location where she was drugged, raped repeatedly and held prisoner for several days.

The way I look at it, this was just another valiant effort by the justice system to protect the criminal from any remote possibility that his character might be dishonored—all at the expense of the ever so trusting current and future victims. I wonder what that rape victim feels about justice.

As far as I know he may be on the street at this very time, possibly the product of a society that feels incarceration is not the answer.

Many times an Officer finds it necessary to make a deal with a criminal, usually when he has a weak case that looks doomed already in the District Attorney's office. Such a case came a few days later when I was informed that a day shift Squad had picked up three black males fleeing from a burglary of a grocery store. A witness had seen three black males come from the side of the store and get into a maroon Pontiac.

Several blocks from the scene the car was stopped and all three occupants were arrested for burglary. All three being street wise and having records for burglary refused to make any statement at all regarding their involvement. The witnesses were brought to view the car and its occupants and they did identify the car, but none of the black male occupants. The auto was searched with the permission of the occupants and nothing was found.

The next day I went with the uniform Officers to the District Attorney's office and after hearing our weak case, the District Attorney called me out in the hall and said he was going to have to release them because of lack of evidence.

Just then, one of the prisoner's attorneys came down the hall. He had been late and didn't hear exactly how weak our case was. I told him that we could probably work a deal with him because his client was on probation, and with the help of the District Attorney we could talk to his probation Officer and possibly get him released on his own recognizance. In order to do this, he would have to cooperate completely and not only testify against his co-conspirators, but also help us in recovering the stolen property that included a large supply of blank money orders, a check writing machine and some other small miscellaneous items.

The attorney asked to speak to his client alone. After a few minutes he came back and said it was a deal. Now what had started out to be a weak case turned into a very interesting situation. We immediately separated all three parties and interviewed the one that now had become cooperative. He related that they had committed the burglary and that after they realized there was a witness across the street, they disposed of the check writer and other small objects by giving them to a friend they saw on the street and told him to take the items to one of the suspect's home.

I then asked him about the blank money orders and to this he stated that he had put them in his shorts and after being placed in the paddy wagon, he observed a small slit in the roof liner. He stated he slid all the money orders in there and as far as he knew they were still there. This was indeed verified by a quick call to the station and much to the amazement of the wagon driver and attendant, they found all the money orders exactly where the kid said they would be.

He also gave us enough information to obtain a search warrant on one of the other actor's house and we recovered not only the check writer but a couple of thousand dollars in stolen property from other offenses along with some drugs and weed.

Burglary charges were issued against all three and were subsequently dropped against the one for his cooperation. In fact, the other two defendants were later sent to prison for crimes they had committed while out on bail on my charges and mine were read in at their sentencing. That is just an example of how one had to fight the criminal element by every means at hand.

22. New Car, New Partner

In the beginning of February, 1970, Dick and I were transferred to another car. We stayed in the same general area that we had been in, but were assigned to somewhat of a more active Squad that was put on the street every night no matter what. This is where I first came in contact with Ernie. Ernie had only been on the car for a few months and one of his partners went days, and the other got transferred to the south side, so Dick and I took their places.

I had worked with Ernie only one or two times in the past and really didn't know him, mainly because he was so quiet. However, our relationship would soon change and in the next seven years we would become extremely close—not only at work but also in our family lives. He was one of the most tremendous partners one could ever ask for.

The quietness that at first mislead me also would, in the future, mislead many others. This seemingly modest gentle manor was only a cover-up for what I considered a brilliant mind. He had a fantastic and extremely thorough way of conducting investigations that led to numerous arrests and convictions of a variety of crimes.

In seven years we never had a cross word—except one time—and that was when I had had a particularly bad day and I took it out on him. After several minutes of my ranting and raving and realizing that I had made a fool of myself, his only comment to me was, "Forget it, you're probably just having your period."

We had a working relationship that I think was unbeatable. At the scene of a crime it was almost like two minds and bodies working as one. There was absolutely no one that I would rather conduct an investigation with than Ernie. He was thorough, complete and always thinking. And besides all that, his small stature was merely a cover-up for a well-conditioned athlete. I could always count on Ernie in a time of need. Well, enough about Ernie because if he ever reads this, it would probably go to his head. All in all, the next seven years were enough to fill an average life time.

I think what I'll do is go through those seven years and try to pick out all the highlights, leaving out the many hours in seven years that we spent just riding around, talking, or going to some gin mill and shooting pool. Or the many hours our families spent together. Or the hundreds of hours in court or sitting on plant jobs. Seven years of activity have to bring a million memories.

It would be absurd to think that every night was filled with crime fighting and clearances by the same Officers, as it was on television. But, there was always enough action, excitement and stimulation to fill anyone's fancy.

I might have mentioned an experience with my first autopsy, but at this particular time I not only attended one of the many autopsies performed but was also the recipient of a lesson in biology. I had been assigned to attend a post (autopsy) being conducted by the Medical Examiner on a white male who had been found dead laying in an alley in the rear of his home. The only unusual aspects to the death were that he had scraps and lacerations to his knees and a cut to his head.

It had also been noted by his wife that the subject was an alcoholic and frequently came up the alley and in through his back yard when returning from the corner tavern. Robbery was suspected because the subject had been paid a large amount of money that day and nothing was found on his body. However, it was later discovered that the subject had deposited some money in his bank and had spent a very large amount buying drinks for the house at his local gin mill. The autopsy was being performed mainly to discover the cause of death and to possibly rule out any foul play.

In matters such as these it was necessary that an Officer witness the post so he may later testify in court, not to the medical aspects of the case, but to collect evidence that may be recovered from the body. Also noted were any unusual signs on the body such as holes, cuts, bumps, bruises, etc., that may help in a future investigation in case the death was caused by an unnatural means.

The Medical Examiner began by cutting back the subject's scalp from his skull in a manner that would expose the top portion of his head. He then took an electric saw type instrument to cut through the skull across the top from ear to ear and then across the back of the head. He removed the portion he had cut and this appeared to me to look somewhat like a quarter shell of a coconut.

He then reached into the brain and began removing the contents, placing them in a bowl. All this time he was talking in medical terms into a tape recorder. Every once in a while he would say something to me that he thought might interest me, both as a Police Officer and also as a spectator.

After removing the portions from the skull, he cut several small pieces away and placed them in separate receptacles to be tested in a lab, in order to determine if the subject had possibly suffered from some sort of disease.

He then placed all these objects back into the man's skull, presumably not in the same manner or location as they had been removed. He replaced the piece of skull, pulled the scalp back into place and sewed it together with string along the back hairline so it would not be obvious in a casket.

He then proceeded to open the man's chest cavity—split his chest bone and he again began removing various objects, cutting small pieces away and once again placing them in some jars. "A-ha," he said, "This must be it." From the subject's chest cavity he pulled an object that most certainly did not look the least bit familiar to me. "Come over here," he said to me. Placing an object on a metal table he began to dissect the object with a very sharp knife—all the while talking into the tape recorder. "This," he said, "is the cause of death. This man not only suffered a massive heart attack but he had suffered several slight ones in the past."

With this statement he showed me what I assumed was his heart. He sliced away at it very carefully showing me what he called scar tissue from his milder heart attacks and a large line that was discolored from the rest of the tissue as being the actual cause of death. He stated that further results of the autopsy would be pending further microscopic tests of the tissues that he had removed, and also tests done on the blood that he had sucked from his chest cavity. He stated that I could put on my report that the cause of death was coronary thrombosis.

I put all his remarks and my further investigation later on in the evening into a report and came to the conclusion after interviewing several witnesses, that the man was extremely intoxicated when he left the tavern. In fact, at one point he had been crawling on his hands and knees. I also talked to a young boy who stated that he had seen an unknown man crawling in the alley behind the man's home.

What could have been an armed robbery and murder turned out to be nothing more than a sudden death, that rated about ten lines in the paper and one full night's investigation.

Of course not all deaths, either natural or unnatural, are that easy to handle, nor do they come to a definite conclusion where the case is closed. In fact, I wonder just how many homicides are unsolved in America and are simply forgotten or the investigation has ground to a halt because all possible leads have been exhausted.

One such case was assigned to Ernie and me just a week after we had been partners. We had been standing in front of one of our bosses' desk, who was arranging to change an off day, when the phone rang. He talked for several minutes and then asked if we had anything going at the present time. We stated no, so he told us that they just found the body of a young girl under a car in a garage, and that we should take the scene and he would send someone else to the hospital.

The ride to the scene was quiet because we both had in the back of our minds the idea that the hardest cases for a Copper to handle are those that involve violent actions committed on a youngster.

Up to the time we arrived at the scene we still thought that maybe a child had been hit by an auto or that some other sort of accident had transpired—knowing in the back of our minds that the scene we were to cover would, in all probability, be ghastly and grotesque.

No truer words were ever spoken, because the setting that appeared before us was one that would affect even the hardest Detective. Apparently what had happened was that a small girl had been abducted, taken to an unknown location, raped, beaten to death and then brought to this spot where her body was thrown under an auto in a closed garage.

Naturally, the first Officers on the scene were excited and somewhat confused because this most certainly was not a run of the mill assignment and for some it might be their only contact with such a crime in years.

It was obvious that the child was dead so her body had not been removed as yet. In fact, her identification up to this point had not been made, but several minutes later a Sergeant told us that she matched the description of a missing girl from about twenty blocks away.

We stood back and tried to get adjusted to the whole situation and focus our thoughts and ideas, as once again it came into my mind how important the first hour of an investigation of this sort is.

The body had been found by the resident of the adjoining home and occupant of the garage. He was getting his car from the garage when he saw what appeared to him to be two small legs sticking out from under his car. He screamed and ran back into his house and told his wife to call the Police because he just saw a body under his car.

Ernie and I got on our hands and knees and looked under the auto. What we saw was enough to make an ordinary man throw-up. It was a small child, about nine or ten years old and she was partially clothed from the waist up. Her long blond hair was straight away from her head and her face was full of grease, dirt and blood. She apparently had been slid under the auto from the rear, as there were marks on the cement floor that would indicate such an act.

After making all the observations of the body that we felt was necessary we jacked up the car, marked the area of the body and checked the area for any evidence. We then had her conveyed to the hospital and then to the morgue, where by now her parents had come for the identification.

Uniformed Officers were summoned from surrounding districts and a thorough search of the neighborhood was conducted as various articles of her clothing were still missing. It was not determined at this time what her actual cause of death was. As it turned out the actual cause of death was due to strangulation by a belt type object and also a severe beating.

Ernie and I spent several hours in the garage, which by now had been roped off and huge searchlights had been brought to the scene. We covered every inch of the three car garage and had thirty or forty photos taken of the scene and the surrounding area. We took scrapings of different parts of the floor and also separate scrapings from the floor where the body had been placed. We determined at this time that the actual offenses of rape and murder must have occurred in some location other than the garage.

By this time the area was loaded with citizens, reporters and anyone else you could possibly imagine, and we even had to chase some bosses out of the garage for fear that they may trample on some small article of evidence.

Having completed our investigation at the scene, we met at the morgue with the Squad that had viewed the body and had also interviewed the parents. They stated that the girl was nine years old and she lived with her parents and several other brothers and sisters. They said that at about 5:10 p.m. on that particular evening her mother had given the girl some money to go to the bakery, which was about two blocks away from her home. That was the last time she was seen by anyone except a few friends that had seen her come out of her house and go through an alley next to a large food market. The girl apparently had been abducted somewhere in the alley as she did not get to the bakery and was not seen by anyone between the alley and the bakery. We know this for a fact because every possible party living and working in a five block area surrounding her home was interviewed and shown a current picture of the girl.

All the reports on the original investigation were now being typed out and at this time Ernie and I decided that we should take another closer look at the body for any evidence that might have been overlooked. This was something that I didn't really relish but was a necessary part of the investigation.

What we found was a hair that may have been a pubic hair that may have come from the actor as it was foreign to the victim. We also discovered that there appeared to be some unusual discoloration on the skin that seemed to be some foreign substance. This was pointed out to the Medical Examiner for future reference.

That particular substance was never again mentioned in the Medical Examiners report and we feel that it may have been some sort of auto body paint. We felt the offense may have taken place in an auto body shop close to the scene and also may have been committed by one of the workers. Whether this particular piece of evidence would ever have been important we will never know.

The next day Ernie attended the autopsy and that was where the final determination was made as to the cause of death. Those last few hours of that poor child's life must have been like hell.

We stayed on the investigation for the next month covering every square inch of the area surrounding the twenty blocks between the victim's home and garage where she was found. Along with uniform Officers assigned to us, we scoured through every garbage can, garage, yard, roof top and basement in the area and the only thing we found were the missing articles of clothing that had been shoved in a garbage can a few blocks from the scene. We even planted at the funeral home to watch for any suspicious characters that might come around. Who knows?; anyone with as warped a mind as the individual that committed this act may just further his gratification by coming to the funeral. We spent one whole night questioning everyone that went in and out of the food store hoping that they might have seen something on that particular night. Everything proved fruitless.

Several months later, after we had talked to every person in our city that had any record at all that included sexual offenses against young children, some Officers learned that one of the men had been sentenced to the State Prison on a sex offense. They went to the prison, talked to the subject and found that there was a good possibility that he could have been in the city and in the area on the date of the murder. In fact, after further checking it was found that he worked in a body shop just a few hundred feet from where the body was found. This is where that piece of evidence that Ernie found may have come into focus, but it was never removed from the body.

After several meetings with the subject at the prison he finally agreed to take a polygraph examination at the State Crime Lab, the results of which were inconclusive because of his mental condition.

That's where the case ended. The suspect still had some ten years to serve and there just wasn't enough evidence to convict him, so the case was placed on the side and only received occasional follow-up work because by now there had probably been another twenty homicides that took precedent.

I wonder if the families involved and the citizens in general ever know things like that go on. I truly feel that when that man gets out of prison should revert back to the biblical times and brand him for life.

It always seems that absolutely every possible chance is given to the accused to prove him—or her-self innocent. I do believe that this is the true democratic process. In fact, many times we have to spend as much time working for the defense as we do the prosecution.

One of these instruments used by the defense is the alibi witness. It is an act in which a defendant notifies his lawyer that he or she has certain people that they can rely on as witnesses to say that indeed they were somewhere else when the crime for which they are charged occurred. It is the duty of the defendant's lawyer to then notify the District Attorney's office of these facts before the trial. The District Attorney in turn notifies our Department and the Officers involved in the case are given the assignment of interviewing these witnesses to see what their testimony will be.

I have found it to happen more often than not that the witnesses usually are lying for the defendant, and usually don't know what they're getting themselves into, until perjury is explained to them. Then they usually either come around and tell the truth or simply say they don't want to make any statement without their lawyer. In most cases, if it is found that they have been lying, they never show up in court but in some instances the prosecution has called these very same people as adverse witnesses and under oath has found that they were asked by the defendant to supply him or her with an alibi.

We were still involved with the homicide investigation when one night, while assigned with a different partner and on the way into the bureau, we spotted an auto that we had information may have been involved in a recent rash of tavern hold-ups.

We stopped the auto, questioned the four black male occupants and upon searching all of them, found one to be carrying a gun and one of the others carrying a can of mace. The subject with the gun was arrested for carrying a concealed weapon, but the one carrying the mace was let go because he was a juvenile and he let us dispose of the small can. All the occupants were checked out and none were wanted, so the others were let go and we filed a report on the occupants. We described them in detail for use by the hold-up cars, which by now had been working day and night with Special Details because of the large number of hold-ups.

The next day I went to court and was confronted by the boss of the Hold-up Squads. He chewed my ass out for not arresting everyone in the car. He further berated me by saying I let all the hold-up men get away. All this was done in front of my partners and several other Officers. At first I took great offense with his remarks but later, after thinking the whole situation over, I realized that he must really be in a crack over all the hold-ups and was probably getting some of the pressure off his chest.

I told Ernie I was taking this whole thing as a personal challenge and that we were going to catch these assholes ourselves. We must have spent at least a week looking for that juvenile. Numerous calls and interviews with his parents proved negative. They said he had run away from home and they didn't have the vaguest idea where he was. Finally we checked, just by accident, at the Children's Center and sure enough the kid had been arrested two days prior to this for a residence burglary.

We immediately went to the Children's Center, got the kid out and took him to the Bureau where we were going to question him and have his photo taken. We started the questioning on the way into the station and realized that after bringing up the subject of armed robberies and indicating that he may have been put down by some adults, the juvenile just may crack if we treated him right.

Here was a boy, barely sixteen years old, who had spent almost three of those sixteen years in boy's schools for offenses of burglary, robbery, auto theft and third degree murder—the last stemming from a purse snatching in which the old woman had died. In fact, that offense was committed by him and several other boys when he was only twelve years old.

One would think that by now this kid would be a hardened criminal, but he wasn't. Sitting there in the back seat of the Squad he looked like a frail, scared sixteen year old kid, not a punk or smart ass—just scared.

We realized that the whole thing may be an act on his part, but after talking to him for several hours at the Bureau, he not only confessed to about eight or ten hold-ups that he had participated in, he also implicated seven other adult males. He gave us information on practically all the taverns and small grocery store hold-ups in the past two months.

He also related to us that prior to every hold-up, the actors involved would go to a specific apartment where they kept their guns. After the hold-up they would return to the apartment, drop off the guns and money and go to their homes, which were nearby.

Once the kid started to talk we could hardly shut him up and we started to realize that some of the information may not be accurate, as now he was just trying to please us. After the interrogation we charged the juvenile with several of the robberies and then took him back to the Children's Center.

We then wrote a complete report on the information we received and turned it over to the same boss that had chewed me out. If this wasn't poetic justice, I don't know what is. The very next day a hold-up occurred in a tavern and part of the special unit that was working on hold-ups planted themselves at the apartment building and sure enough, the three hold-up men showed up and were arrested. Once they were positively identified in a few of the hold-ups they talked their fool heads off, clearing all the offenses our juvenile friend had told us about.

It wasn't but two days later that I was again going to court and the same boss got a hold of me and again in front of several other Coppers apologized for chewing me out and also said Ernie and I had done a hell of a job. I thought at that time, and still think today, that particular boss's actions were exactly the way they should have been.

23. Interrogations and Arson Investigations

I cannot fully visualize all the prisoners I talked to in the first nineteen years on the job, but the figure has to be close to a thousand—maybe more. (The year now is 1977.) As in every other faze of Police work, each Officer and Detective has his own way of talking to a prisoner.

Some come on hard at the beginning and expect answers to their questions to be brought on by fear. Others start out slow and build up to a climax. Still others use the partner system in which one guy comes on hard at first, then leaves the room and his partner takes over trying to instill the thought that something is wrong with his partner and that the prisoner should be careful and not get him too excited. In fact, if the prisoner wishes to make a statement he would be better off talking to the second man. Still others start out almost invariably by slapping the prisoner in the mouth, thinking they have to get their attention; this means has practically disappeared in today's Police work.

I would be lying if I said I never struck a prisoner. I've probably laid a few out, usually in self defense. But, as the years go by and one tries to be more professional about it, one realizes that the only thing that is gained by a fight is the possibility of getting hurt, ruining your clothing, and also leaving yourself wide open for a lawsuit.

I pride myself in the fact that I feel I can talk to, interrogate or question practically anyone. The method I used was developed over a good many years. It starts out with the conception and feeling of self-confidence that I can do any of the above.

I always started out the interview with a feeling of self-confidence and tried to portray this feeling to my captive audience. I tried to make it a relaxed atmosphere and try to get the subject not only to trust me but also to have the feeling that everything I said was in his or her best interest. I insisted on conducting my interrogations by myself—if for no other reason than that I tried to gain total control of the subject's concentration and found that an interruption by a partner, even if it was a good question, could totally destroy the whole situation.

Different Coppers use different small techniques that they have developed and many are actually funny, but if they work—more power to them.

It reminds me of one of my favorite sayings, especially if I was talking to a juvenile. I had the habit of saying, "Do you realize that I have been a Policeman longer than you are old?" Or, "There is nothing that you're going to tell me that is going to shock me, and if you think I haven't heard it before, you're mistaken."

I think one of the funniest sayings I have heard was the one used almost invariably by a partner, Carl, who I have all the respect for, but who would put me into stitches every time he would use it. Sometime in his conversation he would invariably say, "When push comes to shove." It may not sound funny, but when you hear the same thing a hundred times, it does start to become amusing.

Every interview I conducted started out the same way. It was not only required by law, but it served the purpose of breaking the ice of a first introduction. It went as follows: "You realize that I'm a Police Office don't you? And that anything you tell me is going to be held against you in court. And that you don't have to talk to me at all if you don't want to. And if you want an attorney, you know what an attorney is, don't you? You can get one for nothing if you or your folks can't afford one. And you can stop this interview and ask for an attorney at any time. Do you understand everything I have said?"

Now the above statement is all that is required by the Miranda Decision but I usually add that they can pick and choose any questions they wish to answer, stop the interview at any time and also have the right to make a phone call.

The magic behind a good interrogator I feel is that after you tell them all their constitutional rights, they still make a full and complete statement which would convict them in most any court in the United States.

I imagine most any lawyer will tell you that the original statements by their defendants are the most damaging evidence that can be produced. This is because most people realize and believe that a defendant's first statement that implicates him is usually the truth.

I've had interrogations that have taken as long as six hours, and after six hours of talking and making any variety of statements to the prisoner—a sign of a good interrogator is the response the defendant gives the next day in the District Attorney's office. When the defendant is asked if any threats or promises were made to him and he actually answers no and thoroughly believes it.

I have been accused of lying, threatening, coercing, promising, and beating a prisoner. But when we walk into the District Attorney's office the next morning and I say that the subject gave me either a written or verbal confession, and he sits there without a complaint, that to me is not only self satisfaction but actually what the whole game is all about.

Speaking of professional, it was about that time that I really had my first dealings with the local F.B.I. office.

I had been sent to a hotel to meet with several agents who were trying to apprehend a subject wanted for impersonating an F.B.I. agent. They merely wanted me and my partner there so that the local authorities would be involved. After a surveillance of the subject's hotel and room for several hours, he did appear and the agents in charge approached him The agent immediately identified himself by producing a large leather pouch from his pocket that contained a very impressive gold badge—the other side of the leather pouch contained a picture of himself and what looked to me like very impressive credentials signed by J. Edger Hoover, Director of the F.B.I. I thought of the small black imitation leather holder that I carried in my back pocket that contained a dirty silver and gold badge along with a funny picture of me and several band aids.

After searching the subject for any weapons the agent produced another leather folder that contained the Miranda Decision typed out on very legal looking paper that was read to the subject and then signed by him in the presence of witnesses.

After all this exhibition of authority and professionalism I was almost ready to confess myself! All kidding aside, they were impressive and did handle themselves in a very business-like manner.

I recall the night with the F.B.I. agents, because it was right after we left their building that we received a call that a ten-year-old girl had been reported missing. This girl lived in the very same block as the murdered nine-year-old girl found in a garage under a car that I previously wrote about.

By the time we got to her house at least a dozen Squads were already on the scene. We immediately organized a house to house search beginning with the girl's own house. We then interviewed the hysterical mother, who at first questioned our actions of searching their own house.

It was necessary for us to tell her that a good deal of missing youngsters are often found hiding in their very own homes—sometimes because of fear of discipline and sometimes just as a game.

After determining that the girl had not been punished recently by her parents, and they could think of no reason why she should be missing, we started to interview neighbors and kids on the street.

It was at this time that some Officer found a small friend of the missing girl who said he had seen her talking to a stranger in the alley behind her home Ernie and I immediately not only thought, but were sure that this would wind up being another murder. We were just going to send out a description of the stranger when a call came in that a citizen about six miles from the missing girl's home found her hiding in his front yard bushes. We immediately picked up the girl and thanked the citizen who stated he had heard about her being missing on television. We returned her to her parents at once.

After the parents were able to control their emotional joy, they questioned the girl regarding her absence. All she could say was that she went for a bus ride and when she got off the bus she was lost so she thought she would sleep in the bushes until morning.

The whole episode took about five hours and when it was all over we estimated that approximately fifty or sixty Officers took part in the search, not counting the next shift from three separate stations that were called in early and prepared to make it an all night effort.

Since I was the newest and had less seniority on the Squad, it was I who usually worked another Squad when all three of us were working.

I never minded this because it gave me not only a chance to get familiar with to the entire city, but it also gave me an opportunity to work with a variety of Detectives who all had different methods of doing their job.

It was also my pleasure at this time to work with one of the three black Detectives that were assigned to the bureau. I was always under the impression and belief that I knew a lot of people, both in the white and black community, but I was rudely awakened to the fact that the black Detectives knew practically everyone. There was not a business place that we entered or a street we drove down that either of them weren't recognized by someone or they knew someone—usually either by name or by what they had been arrested for. These guys were not only a credit to their race but also to the Police Department as a whole.

The next couple of days I spent on another couple of cases, either one of which would probably cover an entire chapter of a book but which I'll try to summarize concisely.

The first was one of the worst arson murder cases that I have ever encountered. Dick and I were sent to it late one warm August evening. Besides the heat and humidity from the outside, we also had to contend with the stifling stench of a burned out house and the dripping water from the recently extinguished fire. It started out to be a miserable scene and atmosphere for an investigation of any sort.

We were met at the scene by the head of the arson Squad of the Fire Department. He related to us that when they arrived at the scene the entire two story single family residence was completely enveloped in flame. He also stated that several panic stricken people on the street indicated to the first firemen that there was a teenage girl on the second floor. He then led us through the smoldering wreckage of what was once a home, to the second floor which was illuminated by the moon shining through several holes in the roof. He then pointed out a corner in one of the two bedrooms and also pointed out a blanket that was lying next to the wall. He stated that the first firemen to get into the bedroom immediately began to search for the girl and it took them several minutes to find her because she was huddled in the corner covered with a blanket. He further related that it appeared that the girl was breathing and when they carried her out of the home she was immediately given mouth to mouth resuscitation and conveyed to the hospital in a rescue Squad.

We went to a neighbor's home where we called our office and were told that the girl had expired upon her arrival at the hospital and that the pending cause of death was smoke inhalation. They further stated that it did not appear that she was burned in any way. She was described to me as being a black girl, very small in stature, seventeen years old, wearing a flowered blouse, blue jeans and one pearl earring in her left ear. They further stated that the entire area around her nose and mouth was covered with black soot.

We were informed that the girl's father was also conveyed to the hospital suffering from burns to his arms, hands and face. After having viewed the entire scene we sealed off the area and continued our investigation by interviewing the victim's mother, brothers and sisters. They related the following story.

It appeared that the father, even though he held a regular job and supported his family, was a drunk and while drunk he would repeatedly beat his wife. After putting up with this for several years she finally served him with divorce papers and got an order from the court restricting him to the times he could visit his children and also ordering him from the house.

Well, it seems on this particular evening the victim's mother had gone to visit friends and was not at home when her husband came there in a drunken stupor and indicated to his children that they should all get out of the house because he was going to burn it down. With that statement he went to the basement of the home and returned with a gas can and began dumping gas on the living room and dining room carpeting. Prior to him going to the basement all his children had been on the first floor, including the victim. When he made his announcement they all fled out the front door with the exception of the victim who, for no reason known to them, ran to her upstairs bedroom. Apparently in the confusion that followed she was not missed by her brothers and sisters who had gone to a neighbor to call the Police.

When the father returned from the basement one son stated that he observed him dumping gas from a can in both the living room and dining room and then lighting this fuel with a match. He stated that as soon as his father dropped the match the entire room seemed to be enveloped in flames and his father ran from the house engulfed in flames. He stated that his father rolled on the ground and put out his flaming clothes and at the same time they heard the victim screaming from the interior of the home.

The son said that he tried to get back into the home and at one point thought he saw his sister at the bottom of the stairs, but both he and she were turned back by the intense heat. At about that time the Fire Department arrived and removed the girl from her smoke enveloped bedroom where she had gone and hid, probably out of fright and probably for a feeling of security. It must have been a horrible death.

We finished our investigation at the scene recovering the partially filled gas can along with pieces of a book of matches. We then had several photos taken of the interior of the home and also the corner where the young girl had died.

We finished about five in the morning and I went home for a couple of hours and then met the City Engineer at the scene who made a complete and detailed diagram. While I was at the scene Dick took the father of the victim, who had been released from the hospital, to the District Attorney's office where warrants for arson and second degree murder were issued against him.

Dick said later that while talking to the mother in the District Attorney's office, she said what was doubly sad about the tragic incident was the victim was the favorite of her husband, and that she usually stood up for him—even when he was drunk and beating everyone. He got thirty years in the State Prison after pleading guilty.

It was odd that we were involved in an arson and murder at that particular time because Dick and I had been working on another arson complaint which occurred a few weeks prior to this case.

That particular one was at an eight family apartment building and was deliberately set in three separate areas of the hallway and caused in excess of ten thousand dollars damage, but there was no personal injury involved.

The lack of personal injury was due in part to the fact that a Fire Department dispatcher had received a phone call from an unknown person stating that he had just set a fire in an apartment building and they should get all the people out. The Fire Department did respond immediately and did have to rescue several people from their second story windows.

When we interviewed the owner of the building he stated that there was a former tenant who, he believed, had a mental problem and was currently being sued for divorce by his wife who still lived in the apartment building. We learned his name and ascertained that he had been released from a mental institution and had been convicted for setting fires in the past. We interviewed his wife and she stated that he again was being confined in the County General Hospital for psychiatric care.

We contacted the District Attorney's office and received permission from them, along with the subject's attorney, to take him from the hospital and allow him to call the fire dispatcher from several public phones so that voice prints could be made. These prints would then be checked against the original call, which also had been taped.

On this particular day we, along with a member of the arson Squad, got the guy from the hospital. We took him to four different public phones where he made calls to the dispatcher, and made statements that the arson Squad members told him to make in order to compare the tape from the original call. The dispatcher was the same one who took the original call and felt reasonably sure that it was the same voice.

Then we took the man back to the hospital, which incidentally Dick and I both agreed he really belonged there. After dropping him off, we returned to the Bureau where we carefully packaged and shipped all the recordings to a place in Philadelphia that specialized in this type of voice comparisons.

We waited anxiously for their response because it was the first time this type of evidence was to be used by the District Attorney's office. It was several weeks later when we were called to the District Attorney's office. We were told that they had received a letter from the institution in Philadelphia, and that the Director had stated that a fee of one thousand dollars would be required for their findings. Also, if he was needed to testify in court he would require a payment of five hundred dollars a day plus expenses. The District Attorney's office had written him back stating they thought his fees were extravagant. The Director replied by sending the tapes back.

So there we sat. The District Attorney's office wouldn't pay. The evidence couldn't be used. The man wouldn't confess, so the whole case was dropped and as a result, a precedent was set.

We also learned that the man already had served time in an institution for the criminally insane and had been judged a pyromaniac. So, because of a few dollars, the subject was again on the streets and we would simply have to wait until he set another fire, which he surely would, and hope that he would get caught in the act and that no one would be hurt.

About two days after our disappointment over the voice prints, Ernie and I got involved again with the Fire Department. It seemed these things ran in streaks. We might go a whole six months or a year with hardly any dealing with them, and then in the next month we would be sent to investigate three or four fires.

At that time the Fire Department had their own arson Squad but this was discontinued and all the investigations are now left to the Police Department. It makes for a lot of disgruntled firemen who feel, and rightly so, that they know a good deal more about fires than we do.

By the time we arrived at the scene of this call, which was just to meet the Fire Department, we realized that something must be wrong. The building was a huge brick building that covered an entire square block. All the fire trucks and several Squads were toward the front of the building, but all were at least a hundred feet from the main entrance.

We were told that a pipe bomb had gone off, malfunctioned and had seared the front door of the building. We crossed the street for a better look and saw what appeared to be some paper lying by the front door. Ernie said we should take a closer look and I figured he knew what he was talking about. So amid the glare of the television cameras that by now were on the scene, we walked slowly to within a few feet of the bomb.

Ernie had some training in demolition, but this was my first time and I wasn't too sure that I was doing exactly the right thing. What we saw was a brown paper bag ripped open and a piece of cardboard about one foot by six inches. On the cardboard was a "C" cell battery which was wired to a West loc alarm clock and also wired to a piece of galvanized pipe about six inches long and one-and-a-half inches in diameter. There was a small hole in the top of the pipe, and this I assumed, was where the fuse was inserted.

I later learned that the bomb had gone off, but the charge blew the fuse from the end and all the powder came out the little hole like a flare gun. This flash had caused a large glowing light that scorched the wall next to the front door.

I also noted that on the side of the pipe was a quaint little message left by the benefactor who must have manufactured this little firecracker. Painted in bright red letters was "Power to the people." People being spelled "peple." Maybe the guy ran out of room and should have used a longer pipe.

I was just going back to a safer vantage point when Ernie said, "Hell that thing's all spent. Let's kick it and see what happens."

I said, "You're nuts; if you're going to kick that thing let me get out of the way."

"I'm only kidding," he said, "But what we really should do is get a long piece of rope, lay it around the pipe and then from a distance give it a good pull." That sounded more logical but by the time we got back across the street a boss had arrived and told us that an army team of demolition experts were on the way to check it out. I could tell Ernie was somewhat put out that they didn't let him handle it. He was even more put out when the experts had arrived and after taking the bomb apart they told us that if they were not available at some future time, we could wait for them or take a long piece of rope, place it around the bomb, get to a good distance and pull the rope. Maybe Ernie would try that, but I knew damn well that I never would.

We took all the pieces of the bomb to the bureau and after a closer examination, we discovered that a flash bulb was used as the fuse and this apparently fell from place when it went off, causing the malfunction.

The experts told us at the scene that if the bomb had been constructed properly, it could possibly have taken off a good portion of the front of the building.

The Memo Book

The building in question was a laboratory supply house that just happened to be located in the hippie section of town. This was also during the Vietnam Conflict when bombings and protests were common around the country.

We did not have a bomb Squad at that time, but that incident is one that led to the forming and equipping of one.

I recall going to any number of bomb calls where they were just telephone calls indicating that a bomb was in such a place and would go off at such a time. The method of operation that we normally used was to evacuate the building, wait for the time period to expire and then search the building. When these calls became more common and the store owners or managers railed they were losing business, we let it up to their discretion as to whether the store, factory or business place was to be shut down or not. As years passed, the fad wore out because the bomb calls were few and far between.

The bombing of the laboratory, or the attempted bombing, was somewhat different because we took the cardboard box into the bureau and had a technician spray it with an adherent solution, which produced a fairly decent latent finger print. We received a call later in the week from a girl who stated she knew who the bomber was, and would give us his name if we met her.

The girl turned out to be a real diehard hippie. It was quite a shock to me because I never knew any of them before that—she not only talked to us so-called "pigs," but would also give us information.

This girl was about twenty-years-old, tall, long straggly hair with deep set eyes and a pock-marked complexion. It was obvious that she was on some kind of drug because at times she would become completely incoherent.

She related to us that she came from a very affluent family in one of the suburbs and her father was the president of a local business. She stated that she came in contact with drugs at her high school and after graduation moved with her friend to the east side and worked part time at a local hospital. She also stated that she was at a pot party a couple of nights before the bombing and heard three or four white male hippies talking about the bomb they had, and how they were going to blow up a laboratory to protest the war in Vietnam.

I remember we got in somewhat of a discussion about values and what the lab had to do with Vietnam. We could tell by her responses that she had been completely indoctrinated by that particular group in our society that she chose to associate with.

After questioning her for several hours we took her to the bureau to view photos. When she was finished viewing photos we dropped her off at her so called "pad."

We followed up on her information for the next several weeks and even went so far as getting permission to show her photos kept at the Subversive

Squad. Those were pictures taken at meetings and rallies of any group that might be linked with parties known to be subversive and radical in nature. Even I was amazed at all the photos they let her see—and we saw only a few of what they had. They had pictures from rallies, parties, demonstrations, etc. Usually on all of these group pictures you could pick out the same familiar faces in the crowd. It was explained to us that at most of these demonstrations, numbered in the hundreds, it was usually just a handful of semiprofessionals that got the whole thing started and then when things got moving towards violence, they would slip into the background.

This was a completely different side of Police work that I, like most other Coppers, knew existed but never paid much attention to because they were always very low key and almost clandestine.

About six months later we learned that the finger print on the bomb was finally identified and the Subversive Squad handled the whole case. We later learned that the culprit was given immunity from prosecution in return for what they considered very valuable information. Naturally, they didn't tell us what the information was, and we never did find out.

I think that's one of the biggest mistakes made in Police work, and it was done almost every day—that being the withholding of information amongst Coppers themselves. I suppose I've done it myself; it seems that every Copper—especially the working ones—want to make that big arrest. One would be surprised how many criminals get away with a variety of crimes simply because of the lack of communication within the Department itself.

24. Guns Pointed—at Me!

I look back in my memo books and recall most everything that happened. However, there are many good cases that I was involved in that are just no longer fresh enough in my memory to recall accurately.

I was involved in a large forgery investigation about this time; also the thefts of numerous snow mobiles that had just caught on as the craze. I do recall that those thefts even involved an attorney who was buying them. But like I say, to write about them would only lead me to half truth and half fiction which none of my prior, or future, writings are.

I just wish I could have kept either more accurate books or continued writing during my whole career. Instead, it seemed the only time I wrote was when I was off sick or injured, and I'm actually a very healthy person.

I also went through several memo books without taking any stories from them—not that it wasn't busy—but if I wrote on every incident it would not only be boring but would be very repetitious. It got to the point where I handled at least one or two burglaries every night when I wasn't involved in some other investigation that took precedent and besides that, how many burglaries can I write about that are different?

I suppose that is where this job in reality is so entirely different than those you see on television. Not that I don't enjoy television, but more times than I can count I have seen a situation on television that has been very close to an actual case that was involved in, but the outcome was always different.

You would be surprised at how many people relate television above actual life experience. It was not uncommon at all for people to follow me through a house pointing out all the places that Kojak and his helpers found fingerprints. Or they'd tell me about all the information they got from the numerous neighborhood witnesses.

When, in reality, the finger print is left on relatively few points in a burglary, and these are usually at the point of entry or where things were ransacked. Too often we have to tell the complainants that we could stay at their house all night dusting objects for prints, and the results would just be a fantastic cleaning job for them in the morning.

As far as witnesses go, especially in the black community, it's not rare at all for a youngster to approach us and say, "We know who burglarized the house," and at the same moment finds the boy or girl's parent pulling him or her away and saying that they didn't see anything. Who do you blame? The parent or society?

The parent has probably learned that the thief in question will probably get probation and will undoubtedly beat the hell out of their son or daughter for squealing. Their reluctance used to bother me, but now I can actually sympathize with them. I told my own children that if they see something happen, tell me first and I'll Judge what to do with the information.

Almost a year had passed since I was assigned to the bureau and I handled most of the usual major crimes. I also thought that being in plain clothes was a lot more desirable from the mere fact that the current times had produced a good majority of people who hated Cops more now than they had before. In fact I felt considerably more secure in plain clothes than in the uniform, which was continuing to be a prime target of the radicals.

However, being out of uniform may make one relax a little too much and many times that is all that is needed in this profession to cause an injury. For example, I never thought twice about talking to someone on the street while sitting in the Squad car. In plain clothes, in an unmarked Squad, it took the following incident to put me back on my guard.

I was with a different partner other than Ernie or Dick, and we were just cruising in the black community on a quiet summer night, when we spotted a young black male coming out from between two business places. He spotted us and continued to walk slowly down the street. This leisure attitude by him is what may have lifted my guard somewhat. As I approached him, he suddenly turned and crossed the street directly in front of the Squad. I didn't have to slam on the brakes or anything, but by this time he was toward the driver's side of the car so I pulled up next to him, rolled down the window and announced, "Police."

He immediately came to the window of the car and before I could open the door he was leaning on the window with both his hands. I asked him what his name was and then attempted to open the door but realized that he was not only holding the door with his hands, but was also pushing on it with his knees. I then realized that something wasn't right, but I didn't want to say anything to my partner for fear that I would excite the youth.

I pushed harder on the car door and then suddenly realized that one of the hands I was watching on the window was now in the subject's jacket pocket and was pulling out a dark object that I knew, without fully seeing it, had to be a gun. My partner was getting out of the passenger side and didn't realize what was going on. I grabbed the boy's hand while it was still partially in his pocket and could feel the barrel of the gun. All this was done while reaching out the window, but now the door was starting to open. At that same moment the subject started to pull away from me, but my grip was so tight that I wound up with the gun in my hand and the gun was now pointing at him.

By now my partner had come around to the driver's side and was shocked when he realized that I was pointing the gun at the youth and the kid was hollering, "Don't point that S.O.B. at me, it's loaded."

The Memo Book

It turned out that the kid was only fifteen years old and had been missing from home for the past several days. He hadn't burglarized the business place, but when I questioned him he said he panicked when we stopped him and he automatically reached for the gun.

Would he have shot me? Who knows? But to this day I've never talked to a person through a window again. Come hell or high water I always get out of the car, and if the weather is that miserable that I can't get out, I just simply pass them up and wait for the next time.

Several months prior to this incident Bob had been assigned to the Vice Squad, and after spending a few months there he was transferred to the Bureau. This was the first opportunity I had to work with him since we were both assigned to special duty at the District Stations.

It was a particularly quiet rainy evening in November and we spent practically the whole night just driving around and going to all our old haunts, and getting reacquainted with a lot of people we hadn't seen for a while. It got to be about eleven o'clock and we started to head into the bureau. We were stopped at a stop sign and through the rain we could see a car next to us, and we heard a horn blowing.

Bob rolled down his window and an attractive black woman told him that the guy he was looking for was at her house right now. Bob looked at me, and I at him, and we both shrugged our shoulders. She apparently thought we were someone else. If we had simply told her we didn't know what she was talking about, we would have undoubtedly been home by midnight. Instead Bob told her to pull across the street so we could talk to her, and by doing so, we wound up working straight through until six o'clock the next evening.

The woman said that two Detectives had told her that they were looking for her cousin for some armed robberies, and that he was at his sister's house with a bunch of property taken in a burglary. She further related that the burglary was at the home of one of her friends and that she had seen all the property including a television, stereo, speakers and several guns in her cousin's living room. She also stated that her cousin owed her twenty dollars and for that reason she was going to put him down.

We got his name from her and checked with our clerical bureau and found that he was not wanted. By this time it was almost midnight and the robbery detail from our shift was going home. We couldn't find anyone that wanted to talk to the subject in question. We almost said the hell with it and went home, but then decided that we could maybe get a search warrant and get a couple of hours of overtime.

We took the woman downtown and found the burglary complaint of her girlfriend's house. After being assured that she had seen the property in the home of her cousin within the last twenty-four hours we got a Judge out of bed and obtained a search warrant.

By this time it was three forty-five in the morning and we hadn't served the warrant yet. We contacted a late shift Hold-up team and the four of us, along with several uniform cars hit the house about four-fifteen a.m.

The house was dark, and because of the hour and the fact that we didn't think they had anything they were going to flush down the toilet or throw down the sewer, we banged on the door several times rather than breaking it in.

A few minutes passed before a sleepy-eyed young black woman came to the door. I announced we had a search warrant for the premises and at the same time we all pushed past her into the house. I took the time to read her the search warrant after ascertaining that she was the party in charge of the house and contents.

The search only took a matter of minutes before we got results. The television, stereo and speakers were all in the living room plugged in and all set to be used. A further search of the home revealed several other televisions which were stolen along with about five or six hand guns. We also found several stocking masks and some checks and other miscellaneous pieces of paper from several hold-ups.

We then asked the woman of the house, who by this time had aroused her small children and had become hostile and belligerent, where her brother was. She said she hadn't seen him for the past several days. At almost the same instant, a small child that was across the room, pointed to the wooden seat which was in the front room by the front windows covering what I assumed was the radiator.

I walked over and picked up one corner of the lid and immediately slammed it back down again because I was looking down the barrel of a 357 magnum gun. I was as surprised as her brother, who was scrunched in the window cabinet. I don't think he could have pulled the trigger anyway because of the way he was stuck in there. I yelled for him to throw the gun out and come out with his hands up, or I'd throw in a can of tear gas.

The woman of the house started to scream and kick, and at the same time the subject in the box was hollering out that we shouldn't shoot because he was stuck in there.

The lid of the box slowly opened and the gun fell out to the floor. There had been about six pistols and a couple of shotguns piled in the chest. It would have made one hell of a coffin if he hadn't given himself up.

The man that we dragged out of the window box was the woman's brother, and now we had enough to arrest both of them. She was arrested for concealing stolen property and disorderly conduct—fighting—and him for pointing and aiming a weapon.

We confiscated about two thousand dollars worth of property from the house, and by the time we took it all downtown it was seven in the morning. We questioned the guy for about two hours and he continued to maintain his innocence of any knowledge of robberies or burglaries. We must have finally hit a soft spot when we began to talk about how involved his sister was, and the fact that she could be facing ten years in jail. He said if we promised to give her a break and not charge her, he would tell us the whole story. We told him that we would talk to the District Attorney and see to it that she got a break. We then turned the questioning over to the late shift Detectives so that Bob and I could go home, shower and shave and return to take him to court.

We got back to the bureau about ten o'clock a.m. and the day Hold-up Squad, along with the boss that had chewed me out a few months ago, were excited as hell. The boss saw me in the hall and said with a smile, "You S.O.B., you did it again, eh?" I didn't know exactly how to take that, but when I went back into the interrogation room, the late shift Coppers told Bob and I that he not only kicked into the burglary but also to being the driver of the getaway car in about twelve hold-ups. He also put down about six other guys who were well known hold-up men in the city.

We took him to court and spent the entire day in the District Attorney's office getting affidavits from the suspect implicating his accomplices. We finally got him into court for his initial appearance and bail was set at twenty-five thousand dollars. His sister was charged with a misdemeanor and was released without bail.

Once again we were heroes for a couple of days. That's about as long as it lasts—either a couple of days or the first time you screw up, whichever comes first. There are just too many Coppers making too many good pinches for any one person to stay at the top of the pack—that, along with the fact that it was so easy to get into trouble and also the fact that the Department was so fast in finding fault.

I think back now to how things have changed. We were the proud recipients then of what some people called a union, and they were just starting to sprout their wings and try and show the established Department and city that they were no longer going to get away with harassing the poor Coppers. Well, like anything else that's new, the union had many faults.

One of the biggest mistakes they made at the beginning was to challenge the Department trial board, which had been more commonly referred to as a Kangaroo Court.

I went along with them in some aspects but the first thing they did was challenge the penalty system.

In the past, if the violation of Department rules was not too great or if it was the offenders first time before the trial board, the penalty was usually to work a few regular off days. It was only in the case of the more severe offenses that the Copper was suspended.

The union said that it was unethical and unconstitutional for the Department to take away off days so from that time to the present they no longer go along with that method of punishment. Now, for even the smallest infraction, the offender is punished by suspension. What does this mean? Well, I've seen uniform Coppers get busted for smoking in a Squad or reading a newspaper in the car, or getting drunk off duty and wind up being suspended for ten days. (These rules may have changed since the date of this writing.)

When wages were somewhere around fifty dollars a day, that fine of anywhere from five hundred to a thousand dollars for violations that ordinary citizens not only wouldn't be charged with, but, in the case of being drunk, were fined ten dollars, in my opinion wasn't equitable—but more on the union later.

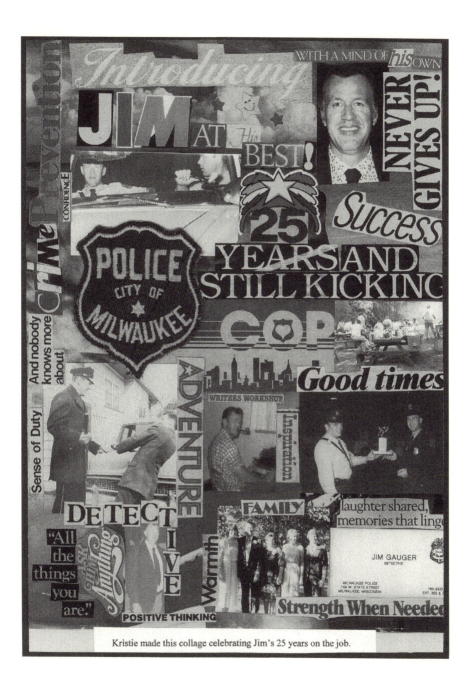

Kristie made this collage celebrating Jim's 25 years on the job.

25. More Informers

Ernie, Dick and I had been together for about ten months and we had a very good relationship both on and off duty. We were assigned to an area that I was extremely familiar with and that, along with the fact that they were fantastic Coppers, led us to an unusual amount of arrests. We developed a good supply of informers and used them constantly.

One that we developed by giving him a break on a misdemeanor charge was a very intelligent individual. In fact, he was a registered pharmacist. His only trouble was that he took more of the pills than he sold, and for that reason he not only got in trouble with the law, but was also nicknamed "the pill man."

Well, this "pill man" would call us about once every week or two and would say, "Hey man, I just delivered a prescription to such and such an address and saw something in there that may interest you." What he actually was telling us was that he had sold some drugs to someone and they had ripped him off. So the stuff he said we would be interested in would either wind up to be drugs or stolen property that either he had seen or was offered to him in payment for the drugs. In any event he would always come down to the bureau when asked and would always swear to a search warrant.

I think back now and I do believe the best informers I had at that time were a gal and guy. I came in contact with him first when he was arrested for trying to cash a forged and stolen check. I was assigned to question him and he readily admitted trying to cash the check and also did not hesitate in telling me where he got the check from. He was a small time thief and had been arrested prior to this for mainly traffic violations and a few misdemeanor thefts. He never served any time in the State Prison and the mere thought of being charged with a felony put the poor guy into a cold sweat. He was obviously the perfect person to extract information from, but I hardly suspected that he would be providing us with such knowledgeable enlightenments for the next two years.

Dick and I started off by telling him we would talk to the District Attorney and see if he couldn't take into consideration the information he had for us and maybe get him out on his own recognizance.

The perfect position to get an informer in is to have him charged with a felony, get him out on bail and then have his case adjourned several times, each time extracting some other tidbits from him. Finally, if the information was extremely good, get the case either dismissed or reduced to a misdemeanor.

Anyhow, this particular informer, who I'll call Dan, said he had just seen a large amount of checks on that very same day and was given the particular check he was caught with, by an unknown black male, who wanted fifty percent of what Dan got for the check. He said it was already dated and the complete face was made out. He further stated that he was also supplied with the necessary pieces of false identification to go along with the payees name on the check.

Dick and I took him to a Judge who heard his testimony and issued a search warrant for the residence that he described and pointed out to us. Dan was really a funny little guy—small in stature with pitch black skin. He always wore a large pair of sunglasses and a funny looking little hat. Whenever we had him in the back seat of the Squad, either for information or to point out a particular house, he would always slide way down in the seat so as not to be seen. Several times I would look in the back seat to talk to him and think for a moment that he either had fallen through the floor board or slid between the seat cushions. We had many a good laugh with this guy.

Getting back to the first search warrant he provided us with. We executed the warrant with a lieutenant and several uniform cars. There were no answers to the knock on the door so we had to break it in, and once in we were confronted by several adult males and females. I read the warrant to a female who claimed to rent the home while Dick started the search of the residence. He immediately called me into the living room where he found a bunch of the checks that Dan tried to pass. He also found a check writer and the typewriter used to fill out the checks. In fact, one of the checks was still in the typewriter.

We had left the lieutenant in the living room talking to the woman of the house who was seated on a large cushioned chair, when suddenly we heard the lieutenant holler, "Don't do it lady; don't do it!" I ran back in the living room and much to my surprise found the lieutenant pulling on a small knife that the woman had suddenly plunged into her stomach. We got the knife away from her and had her conveyed to a hospital. The wound was diagnosed as being very minor and she would be released in time for court the next day.

For the longest time after the incident we kept asking the lieutenant what teed him off so much that he tried to stab the poor gal. I kept telling him that I couldn't tell whether he was pushing the knife in or pulling it out!

After the knife incident I saw Dick come walking through the dining room carrying a white pillow case that was full to the brim with something. He turned it over on the living room floor and out fell more checks than I figure my wife could write in a lifetime.

Once we had arrested all the adults in the home on a variety of charges stemming either from the checks or their being wanted, we took the pillow case to the bureau and started to count and list the various types of checks and identifications. I believe at that time we counted more than seven thousand checks, three hundred some odd identifications that varied anywhere from

Master Charge cards to Social Security cards. We also had another typewriter and check writer.

It took us several days before we had all the checks listed and where they were stolen from. A good many of them were still in the original boxes and upon checking with the printing company, we realized that they were stolen right off the loading dock.

The sad thing about recovering all those checks was that all the District Attorney's office would issue was misdemeanor charges of receiving stolen property against all the parties involved, because the total value of the blank checks was less than a hundred dollars. However, I must say we put a pretty good dent in their operation for awhile.

We met our informer that night and thanked him for the information. We told him that the District Attorney would undoubtedly give him a break on his charges if he came up with one more productive search warrant.

It wasn't a week later that we got a call from Dan (our informer) and he stated that he not only knew where some checks were, but that they also printed fake driver's licenses in the same house. We hit that house the same night with another search warrant prompted by Dan. We received a large amount of checks, but more important we recovered sheets of State Seals that are used as a background on driver's licenses.

Word had apparently gotten out that we were going to hit the place because it was obvious that a large machine had been moved from the place, and some neighbors stated that a U-haul truck had been there most of the day.

This appeared to be a large operation and the one subject we arrested was not only demanding a lawyer, but the one that showed up was again one of the top criminal lawyers in the city. He was very polite and very congenial, but at the same time very demanding that his client not be questioned in any way. Once again the District Attorney's office issued only misdemeanor charges and the subject in question was on the street the same day. I lost further contact with that particular case, but I believe that the whole operation was later squashed by state agents.

Anyhow, our little informer had once again come through and we did get his case reduced to a misdemeanor with the disposition being two years probation. We later told him that any further information he had would not only be appreciated by us, but we would also see if we couldn't get him a few bucks to boot. We said this knowing full well that any money we gave him would have to come out of our own pocket. In fact, Dick, Ernie and I used to keep a little kitty around of about fifty bucks just to give to informers if necessary, although they never received more than five or ten bucks at a time.

Speaking of paying informers, that's how I lost Dan. It was a couple years later that the F.B.I. was looking for a particular party that I felt Dan knew. When I showed Dan a picture, he identified the subject and stated that he knew where he probably would be. I met several F.B.I. agents in the hall of the bureau and they asked me if they could talk to my informer. I arranged a meeting and before my introduction even got out of my mouth, one of the agents was handing Dan a hundred dollar bill. He told him there was more where that came from. I never saw Dan after that.

We always figured that Dan was never the real brains behind all the information that he had, because every time we pushed him a little bit, he would always say wait a minute and then make a phone call. We finally got him to take us to his source of information and it turned out to be his girlfriend.

I'll call his girlfriend Sharon and describe her as a black female about twenty-eight years old and fairly attractive. She dressed extremely sharp and lived in an immaculate home in the inner city with her four-year-old son. We also learned that she was on probation for forgery and definitely faced jail the next time she was caught, which was only a few months after we met Dan.

If we thought Dan had a lot of information, it was nothing compared to Sharon. She was involved with a group of men and women that had a corner on forgeries, theft, prostitution—you name it, they had it.

It was absolutely nothing for the gals in the group to walk into an open door of a business place and go right up to a desk, open the register, or safe and remove practically anything they could carry. Those gals were tall, extremely attractive, dressed to kill and had a line that could con most anybody. They would simply walk into a jewelry store, sit at the counter and have the clerk show them any amount of rings of any price until they found one that looked similar to the fake ones they had in their pockets. While one would distract the clerk by either showing a leg, or talking small talk, they would make the switch and then nonchalantly walk right out of the place.

In the majority of the cases the switch was never noticed until several hours later and by that time the descriptions were vague. In each case they were described as tall black females, attractively dressed and wearing large sunglasses.

We later learned from Sharon that it was her job to drive these women around, and after looking through numerous complaints, the description of Sharon's car came up on many of them.

We arrested many of the people she named on a variety of charges—many times just so that we could get a picture of them and a handwriting sample. The writing, of course, was always disguised. We showed their pictures around on numerous complaints and actually had a portfolio on their activity. In fact, in the next year we must have linked that whole group with up to a half million dollars in a variety of thefts and forgeries.

Several of the men in the same group were finally convicted and sent to prison—mostly for parole revocations or getting caught by other jurisdictions—and having our cases read in. The majority of the women involved never served more than a day in jail. They had the best lawyers and, in fact, one of their lawyers I was told by Sharon, took his fee out in trade and is presently a Judge.

Sharon would go out during the day with several of the women, take them to stores to cash checks and then when she got home she would call me and tell me what she had done. We would then go back to all the stores, show pictures, get identifications and then instruct the managers to send the checks through the bank as we had to have a complainant.

Would you believe that in a great number of cases the stores refused to prosecute because they said it took too much of their time to testify in court and they found it more profitable to absorb the loss? The sad part is, that loss falls right back on the consumer. Many Police Departments, ours included, paid little attention to forgeries because the F.B.I. does not include them in a special category as they do violent crimes such as armed robberies or burglaries.

During the times we had Dan and Sharon as informers we did a great deal of work on forgeries and found that in most every case they led to burglaries, robberies, drugs and most any other crime you could think of. Our Department wouldn't start a check Squad but would merely tell us to let the checks go and work on burglaries, because the clearance rate was down. Like I said before, it's all just a big game of numbers.

I can't recall all the search warrants Dan and Sharon gave us, but one of the best arrests they supplied us with was a white woman, about thirty years old. Not only was our city looking for her, but several other counties in the state as well as several other states were also looking for her. When we found out she was in the group with Sharon, we immediately made it known that we really wanted her. Sharon went so far as to tell us when and where she would be with her, at what time and what kind of check this gal would be cashing.

We planted on the store for several hours after which I gave Sharon a call at home and she wondered where we were. I apparently had missed her car, and when checking with the manager of the store, sure enough, she had been there and had cashed the check that Sharon said she would. I told Sharon that we no longer wanted to catch her in the act of cashing a check but merely wanted her, right now.

Sharon provided us with an address which was just two doors from her own house and said that she was definitely in there right now. We hit the house without a search warrant and after being met by a black male at the door, who we had to throw in for disorderly conduct, we conducted a search of the two-story home with negative results. I then went back to Sharon's home, two houses away, and told her the girl just wasn't there. Sharon said that she definitely didn't leave and she was sure she was there.

We went back to the house and sure enough, we found a loose panel in the ceiling of the second floor and when pushing on it we could tell that either something soft was lying across it or someone was sitting on it. Somebody said, "Step back so I can blow a hole through there"—at the same time we heard scrambling and a woman's voice pleading for us not to shoot. As attractive and sharp looking as Sharon was, that's how directly opposite this white gal was. She was what one may describe as a dirty, filthy white gal that was a junky, pusher, hooker and whatever else there was.

When we finally got her out of her cubby hole, we took her to the bureau where she was identified on many complaints for forgery and thefts. She was wanted by any number of jurisdictions and after spending several months in jail and never saying a word, she was sentenced to a total of twenty years in the State Prison for women.

Sharon came through once again. It was now that we told her that we wanted to conduct a really big investigation and with all the knowledge that she had, we felt we could start a John Doe Investigation. A John Doe is just a matter of getting a DA to find a Judge that will find probable cause to open an investigation not open to the public. The DA can then subpoena any number of people and put them under oath and try and extract information. Once the information is extracted from the witness, the DA can use the information to charge certain people.

We sat down with Sharon for several hours and went over piles and piles of complaints with her naming all the actors involved—including her. It was getting late in the evening and we took her home with the understanding that we would meet her the next day to complete our investigation. She indicated at that time she would furnish us with several names of really big dealers in the city.

The next day I called her and after receiving no answer, we went to our usual meeting place, and after she failed to show up we went to her home and found it vacant. No furniture, no Sharon, no nothing. She completely disappeared and I have never seen her to this day.

We got inquiries from all over the United States regarding her, but she did one of the best Houdini acts I have ever seen. Either that or she was buried somewhere. Whatever her fate, and no matter what a rotten gal she was, we still owe her because she cleared a hell of a lot of crime for us.

I'll never forget one gal that Sharon was involved with. Talk about a pro! This woman used to teach boosting (stealing)—at least that's what I was told.

Dick and I were sent to a suburb to talk to her after she had been arrested and found to be carrying checks that were stolen in our city. She was a black woman about forty-five years old that had a record which included some eighty convictions. Most of her convictions were for shoplifting and drug offenses.

This woman was congenial and cooperative and all she wanted to do was get out of jail so she wouldn't miss her morning fix. We had quite a talk and during our conversation she told us she had a one hundred dollar a day heroin habit. That means that she had to be shooting up at least two or three times a day, paying a street value of one hundred dollars a day for the stuff.

I couldn't help but sound amazed at what she said. I told her that I thought she was full of shit if she was trying to make me believe that she could support such a habit. "It's simple," she said. "All I have to do is boost enough merchandise to cover it, and that's no problem." She went on to say that she had to shoplift three times the amount she needed because her fence would give her one third of the ticket price of the articles that she stole.

"In other words," I said, "You have to boost three hundred dollars worth of articles a day?"

"Either that," she continued, "or build up a reserve in case I have a couple of bad days or in case I get sick from some bad junk and can't get out of bed."

The more I talked to her the more I realized she must have been telling at least half truths, because I most certainly didn't have enough to bust her and we were talking to each other just merely on a conversational basis.

She went on to say that the best items for her to steal were pant suits and other expensive clothing that weren't too bulky. She also said that sheets and pillow cases brought a very good price. I had noticed on a table next to us there were two double sets of sheets and several pillow cases. All these items were still in cellophane and had the price tags on them. I motioned to them and asked her if that's how she was caught and she indicated it was.

I then asked her how the hell she got out of the store with all that junk. Then without hesitation, she got up from the table and pulled her skirt, which was below her knees, away from her waist and showed me her boosting skirt. The skirt is nothing more than a large sack, sewn to a pair of shorts. All the shoplifter has to do is stand by a counter and just keep filling up her skirt with any items she can grab. "What about the sheets?" I asked. "These things must measure at least four inches by eight inches by eight inches and weigh several pounds." With this she grabbed the two packages of sheets and before I could blink an eye she shoved the two packages up between her legs, never bothering with the booster skirt and then walked back and forth across the room several times and no one in the world would have known that she had stolen merchandise between her legs. "Just like that and out the store I go."

By now I must have had about thirteen years on the job (which would make it the early 70's) and this was a new one on me. But that's what made this job so great. How many other places can you go and work and be given a lesson in the finer art of shoplifting by a real professional—and all for free!

The professional booster, rarely, if ever, causes any bodily harm, and when caught don't usually cause too much disturbance after the initial biting and scratching during the arrest. The only person they hurt are you and I, the consumer, because the loss to the store is made-up by a price increase.

I read somewhere that the total loss in the United States in a year due to shoplifting and internal thefts was somewhere over a billion dollars. According to the National Association for Shoplifting Prevention, in 2006, more than $13 billion worth of goods are stolen from retailers each year. Now that's a lot of sheets and pillow cases!

But the type of theft that usually upset me the most was the pigeon drop. These types of people usually prey on the elderly citizens that have a few dollars in the bank, and feel they can suddenly make a few thousand dollars tax free to supplement their Social Security Income or meager pension that many times has been eaten up by inflation. Add to this the fact that very few of us can pass up a good deal, no matter even if it sounds a little shady, and you have the ideal prospect for the con man or woman.

There must be good money in such a scheme because there are actually teams of men and women that travel across the United States at least once a year stopping only long enough to put their idea into operation and then travel on before the local authorities catch up with them. One would also be surprised at how many of their victims are actually too embarrassed to even file a complaint.

The most widely used pigeon drop that I know of is the one where a male calls by phone to some unsuspecting elderly person that they have followed home from a specific bank on a previous day. The caller states that the bank has caught one of their tellers making illegal withdrawals from the bank, and the illegal withdrawals have been made from the projected victim's account.

The man then asks them to cooperate with the bank official and the F.B.I. and come to the bank and draw out a specific amount of money. They also tell the unsuspecting victim that security people from the bank will be watching them, and that the teller will undoubtedly try and talk them out of making the withdrawal.

They also say that they should insist on getting cash. They tell them that after the withdrawal has been made they should either go back home or in some instances they meet several blocks from the bank. In either case the victim is then instructed to give the cash to the men that the caller states are sent from the bank and are also agents.

Once the above transaction has been accomplished the unsuspecting victim usually stands there with a worthless receipt given to them by the con men. It usually doesn't register that they have been taken for at least several hours which gives the con men a chance to get out of the city.

I found in one instance that the entire telephone transaction took place just one block from the victim's home, and that the confidence man (or "con man) never even left the telephone booth until the subject had returned with the money.

In several instances we traced the actors back to the central library where city directories are available. They apparently would follow some old person home from a particular bank, and in some instances they would get a look at his passbook as it was being handled in the bank. They would then go to the library, get his phone number, occupation and spouses name and would be well on their way.

One that I handled had a little different twist. It went something like this: An elderly woman about seventy years old was on her way to church when a car pulled up next to her. A middle-aged white female asked her if she knew the way to the Social Security building. The old woman said no and the occupant of the auto held an envelope in her hand and stated that she had just found the envelope on the street and didn't know what to do with it. The envelope was sealed and the purported victim asked why she hadn't opened it as maybe the owner's name was inside.

With that the woman opened the envelope and showed a large amount of bills to the elderly woman—some of which she stated were thousand dollar bills. Also inside the envelope was a note that read "Dear brother, here is the money we won from horse racing. Give some to mother. Don't try and contact me because I'm going to heaven," and it was signed, "your loving brother."

The elderly woman then told the woman in the car that as long as there was no name on the envelope the money was hers to keep—at which time the con was well into its making. It was at this time the woman in the auto answered by saying that all three of them, the two in the auto and the old woman could split the money. But she said before they do that the elderly woman would have to show her good faith by putting up fifteen hundred dollars. Then they would all go to an attorney that she knew, and he would split it up evenly.

With the full consent of the victim they all drove to her bank where she attempted to draw out fifteen hundred dollars in cash from her savings account. The bank employees tried to talk her out of it, but she insisted and they finally gave her a certified check for fifteen hundred dollars. This apparently posed no problem to the two con women as they took the elderly woman to another bank and told her to cash the check and open a savings account for five hundred dollars. Once she had done this she was instructed to place the thousand dollars along with her diamond rings in a brown envelope. This was then given to one of the women who sealed it and must have then made the switch.

The three then went to a restaurant where the old woman was told to stay while the other two would go upstairs to see their attorney. After waiting an hour the elderly woman opened the envelope and found nothing but several scraps of paper and two dime store rings.

By the time she got home and told her husband what had happened several hours had passed and the description of the two white females that the elderly woman gave was so scant that it fit half the population. As ridiculous as it sounds, it apparently still is executed several times a day throughout the United States.

26. Union Negotiations and The Blue Flu

About this time came one of the more difficult times in my Police career. As I mentioned before, the Police union had gotten much stronger and we had been working without a contract for several months. The union talked about everybody calling in sick, or what was more commonly referred to as the "Blue Flu." Talk about it had been strong in the past few weeks and a general meeting was held where a hand vote was taken and it was agreed upon to put the sick call into effect if the city refused to bargain in good faith.

I had never been involved in any type of contract negotiations and was completely unfamiliar with who was right and who was wrong. At that time I was still very much interested in the type of duty I had and in fact was very satisfied. Not saying that there apparently weren't many wrongs that the city fathers and Police administration in general were laying on us. But the general feeling of all the Acting Detectives was that we were only assigned to the bureau in an acting status and we could be sent back into uniform at the whim of the Chief.

I believe it was on a Friday or Saturday night that something touched off the uniform men and they started going home sick on our shift, and the late shift started calling in sick.

The next day we were instructed to work from eight at night until eight in the morning and the day shift would cover the other twelve hours. We were still completely undecided about what to do. At that time I blamed the Chief, Mayor, Aldermen, Union and General Administration for the predicament they had placed us in. Even to this day I can't visualize how grown men cannot sit down and discuss things in an ordinary and business-like manner without causing disruption and destruction.

A million thoughts were going through my mind. Was it my duty to go to work and uphold the laws and ordinances that I was sworn to uphold? Was it my duty to follow my fellow Officers in their strike against what many felt, with good cause and reason were archaic demands and rules of the Department? Did I owe it to myself to protect the position that I had worked so hard for?

Nobody had the answers. Ernie and I were both acting men and Dick was a made Detective. None of us knew what to do.

Eight o'clock in the morning of our first twelve hour shift we held a general meeting in the back room of the Bureau and it was decided at that time we would join the uniform men and call in sick. I went home somewhat relieved that a final decision had been made. Apparently after I left the assembly, the Chief of Police came in and gave a long talk on how the bureau was the main stay of the Department and that we shouldn't let him down at a time like this. He also apparently went on to say that if we stuck with him through this ordeal, he would never forget us. These words later proved to be nothing more than a troubled man's last pleading stand, for in the years, to come he had indeed forsaken many that stood by him. But that is really neither here nor there. I also lost the faith, ever so small, that I did have in the union and to this day think it is filled only with hypocritical men bent on fulfilling only their own political and financial fantasies.

Anyhow, we all went back to work with the exception of three black Acting Detectives who I give a great deal of credit to for standing by their convictions. But, I also feel that they had a lot less to lose than me, merely because I don't think the Department would have sent them back into uniform.

Even to this day I feel somewhat guilty about going in to work and I still have no idea who was right or wrong. The union hasn't proven anything to me as being leaders and neither has the administration.

I don't recall how long the Blue Flu lasted, but I think it was about six or seven days. My first day at work after the Blue Flu made me realize that all my fears of reprisals and terrible hard feelings between uniform and plain clothes were all coming to pass.

My first taste was when we all walked down to the garage to get our Squads and I saw a uniform man on station security that I hadn't seen for a long time. I walked up to him, put out my hand and announced my greeting—he responded by turning his back and walked away.

That small incident was nothing compared to the sometimes drastic reactions we received—especially from the outlying Squads who naturally are not as busy as the inner city Squads and whose occupants had a good deal of time on their hands to discuss and vent their frustrations.

The Blue Flu did not accomplish a great deal, mainly because of the tremendous cooperation and response from the citizens. There was practically no crime of any significance that occurred during that period.

The bad feelings between uniform and plain clothes lasted for several years. Many longtime friendships between Coppers and their families were because of the sick call. I felt very fortunate when I received a call from Dave and Warren, who were still in uniform, and they both wanted to tell me that there were no hard feelings between us. They agreed that I had been in a very tough situation.

At about this time our Department put into effect a new system for the bureau. It was the use of pneumatic machines. These were tape recorders that were hooked up through the phone system and we would call in all our reports and have a secretary transcribe and type them for us. Up until that time we typed our own reports. It saved a great deal of time and bares little mentioning except that I recall the first time I tried to use it.

We had been given a brochure of about four pages that were full of instructions on how to use the new operation. I really hadn't read all the instructions. After Dick and I handled a run of the mill burglary and were headed back to another spot, Dick pulled up to a telephone booth and said there was no time like the present to learn how to call in a report.

There I was in a small, half-lit phone booth, struggling with my memo book, the instructions, and still trying to hang onto the phone. Besides that it was raining outside, was very stuffy in the booth and when I dialed the number and heard a beep, which indicated I should start, I was almost panic stricken. I must have been on the phone for half an hour and when I returned to the Squad I was completely drained.

The next day I asked the girl who typed the report how I had done and she said with a smile that she had been trying to get a hold of me the night before to tell me that all she got out of the machine was my name. She said I waited so long to say anything else that the machine shut off and I was apparently talking to myself. Nice shot, eh? Once I got used to the new machines they worked great and saved me a lot of time.

27. A Made Detective

I can't begin to realize how long it's been since I started to write these words of wisdom or recollections or memories or whatever you might call them. It apparently started when I had about eight years on the job and was riding an ambulance. Fourteen more years have passed and I have finally reached a plateau which I always thought to be impossible and yet I realize that this is one of the finest jobs on the Department. I am now a day shift Detective. It is now 1980 and I have been a day shift Detective since July of 1978.

How meaningless that may sound, but it was a very big event for my family, and then I think back to all the thousands of experiences I've had in the past twenty-two years on the third and second shift.

I haven't written anything for the past six or seven years and every time something of interest would come up, which was practically every day, I would have the intention of putting it on paper, but would subsequently either forget to do it or not find the time.

Speaking of time, my beautiful family is really getting big. Karen is twenty and working full time and just one of the most fantastic kids imaginable. Kristie is a freshman in college and also a tremendous kid. Jeff is seventeen and just one of the most beautiful people one could ever meet. It was he that got me started writing again because he read my book so far and said he had enjoyed it. Naturally, a child would enjoy hearing about his father's exploits and that was and is the main reason for my writings.

I might also mention at this time that life with a Policeman has also become more bearable for Marlene. Working days after twenty-one and-a-half-years of nights has made our life almost normal. Renewing our friendships with people we haven't seen for years, enjoying the evening hours together and living the life with our family that has escaped us for so many years because of my job. Being days, I now have every other weekend off. While on nights, my weekends off were every three months. And still, in twenty-one and-a-half-years she not only has raised a family that anyone would be proud of, she has never once complained of my profession.

Getting back to recollections from my memo book—the date must have been about July of 1971, and I was still partners with Ernie and Dick. It was a warm summer night and Ernie and I had just finished handling two minor burglaries when our Squad, along with two other Detective Squads and a lieutenant, were told to call our main desk. We immediately figured it to be a murder because these types of crimes are usually kept from the press which monitors our calls on the radio. This would give us a chance to get involved in the situation and have the right answers and the proper identification of the victim to give to the press by the time they got to the scene.

Well, this call was exactly what we figured. We were told that a young girl's body had been found way out in a field by someone running his dogs. We were also told she had been bound, gagged and stabbed numerous times. I later learned from the count of the wounds she had been stabbed forty-nine times.

The body was in a very remote and desolate area. The young girl had apparently taken a short cut from her girlfriend's home, and met her tragic death by running into some mental degenerate that not only mutilated her but also performed all sorts of sexual fantasies with her.

The next several hours were devoted strictly to the scene which was an area covered by gullies, heavy underbrush and millions of bugs. To top it off, it started to rain. In fact, I even got my picture in the local paper on my hands and knees under a tarp that was being held by uniform men while Ernie and I tried to photograph, measure, and recover a foot print found at the scene that may have come from the actor involved.

Most people have no conception of how involved a homicide can be. Television has portrayed it as the Detectives coming to the scene, and calling for all kinds of help in doing the laborious task of collecting evidence. In reality the collecting of evidence usually falls on the hands of the original investigating Detectives. I believe homicides are the most interesting and fascinating cases that any Officer or Detective can ever become involved in. Once the shock of the original gruesome scene passes through your mind and you come to the realization that the victim no longer is suffering, the challenge of finding the twisted degenerate mind that caused this act is almost overwhelming. In this particular case hundreds of man hours were spent, but to this day the case is still unsolved.

Several months later a man was brought to trial for the attempted murder of a young girl in which she was abducted from a shopping center, pulled into a van, bound and gagged and stabbed numerous times. By playing dead she had actually been dumped from the car by her assailant and she later recovered. She identified her attacker from photographs and he was convicted of her assault and sentenced to prison. He was also questioned at length about the murder of the young girl who was stabbed forty-nine times, because he answered the description of someone that was seen loitering at the scene and his van also matched one seen in a parkway near the scene. He refused to take a polygraph exam and he was never tried for the murder of the young girl in the field.

The last I knew he was awaiting a new trial as his original conviction was overturned by the Supreme Court because of a technical error in the trial. Who knows, he may even be walking the streets again one of these days, commit another violent crime and become the crusade of some politician in that he never should have been released. The current laws concerning these deviates should be changed. Sound familiar? Read it in any newspaper at least once a month.

Homicides most certainly aren't the only types of deaths I have investigated, although they are the most interesting. In fact, it was only a month later that Dick and I were sent to a park that was just a few blocks from my house. We were sent there to investigate a body found on a park picnic table. By the time we got there several hundred people had already gathered. The area had been roped off by the uniform Officers and we had to walk several yards through a secluded area. While walking, I could tell we were getting close to the scene not only because of the stench, but by the pale faces of the uniform men that were coming from the area.

I found, after my first few death investigations, that when the death occurred a few days earlier, it doesn't do any good to hold your breath because sooner or later you have to take a deep breath and then the stench is only worse. I found the best way to beat it was just to try and breathe normally and after a few minutes the stench would either get too much for you and you would throw up, or you could actually get used to it. Thank heavens the latter was the case here.

What we found was the body of a young white male who apparently rode his ten speed bike to this particular area for a particular purpose—that purpose was to take his own life. He had carefully placed his bike near the bench and then had removed a knife that he apparently had brought with him and slashed both his wrists so deep that even if he had been found within ten minutes he would not have been able to be saved.

This in itself was not the most gruesome part of the scene, but what was, were the eye sockets and other body cavities that were filled with maggots. The maggots were brought on by the warm weather and the fact that he had been there for several days.

As it turned out, he was seventeen years old with a previous mental problem and life itself apparently was more than he could cope with. His whole life received about twelve lines on page six of the next evening's newspaper—very tragic and very, very sad.

In my memo book I just read through sixty some burglaries that I took and most certainly something of interest happened along the way but nothing outstanding that I can recall.

Regarding burglaries, I do remember testifying in court one day and having to come up with some figures to qualify me as an expert. Looking through my memo books I came up with figures that showed I investigated better than three hundred burglaries a year. That doesn't include all the hundreds of other investigations, so you can see that my life has never ever been boring or run of the mill. In fact, I'm still living, to this day, that dream I mentioned at the beginning of this book of dealing with rich men, poor men, beggar and thieves, and many times it still is a fantasy to me.

The year was still 1972 and a notice came out that the Detective exam would be coming up in the next few months. I had been at the bureau for about three years and fell short of taking the last exam by less than a month. This was my and Ernie's first try at the exam.

We decided to study together and sent for numerous books that dealt with Police promotional exams and spent every free hour for the next two months going over these books and any other material we could get our hands on. We tried to get our off days together and when we worked together we would study constantly until we got a hitch. We also asked for various plant jobs that were around.

These plant jobs covered the Chief, Mayor, one Judge and a Copper's house that had been fire bombed. The plants started right after the riots of 1967, and continued around the clock. Whether they were qualified or not, it was one of those jobs that you did, and at that particular time they worked out quite well for studying.

Speaking of those plant jobs, I wonder how my neighbors would feel about having a Squad car parked in front of their house twenty-four hours a day. Some, in fact most, people were very considerate and took the whole situation in stride and many times brought out coffee and cake. To some we were definitely an inconvenience, and they took little time in making their feelings known.

I recall one of my first days at the Mayor's plant job. It was a very warm summer evening and I had the passenger's door open for more of a breeze and was watching the Mayor's house across the street when I suddenly began getting wet. It took me a few seconds to realize that the sun was out and it wasn't raining. The neighbor had come out and put a sprinkler a few feet from my Squad and turned it on high. What a turkey!

Anyhow, getting back to studying for the exam; Ernie and I studied so much over the next several months that my mind was completely bogged down with statistics and facts. We even bought a book on how to prepare ourselves for taking the exam—down to how many hours of sleep we needed the night before to what we should eat the morning of the test.

The same book stated that if I was really prepared I should walk into the exam with confidence and the first thing I should do is page through the whole exam. They said that I would immediately recognize questions in the exam I was familiar with and this would put my mind at ease.

Well, let me tell you that I paged through the fifteen pages of the exam and never recognized a single question. I was ready to say the hell with it and walk out. I think the only thing that kept me in the room was the shaking heads of the rest of the Coppers that must have felt the same way.

Several weeks later Ernie and I were notified that we had passed the exam and in the next few weeks would have to appear before the Fire and Police Commission for an oral interview.

Ernie and I had already come up with the idea that if we were going to school, we could get a better mark from the Commission, because this was the start of the period in time when education supposedly meant everything and on the job training had little effect. We signed up for a course at one of the local universities and attended classes once a week. Our whole theory was ruined by the first Copper in the oral exam, because when they asked him about his educational background, he blurted out that he and several others had signed up for school, because that's what we heard they wanted to hear. As of this date, Ernie and I have proudly earned two university credits.

Kind of an interesting series of events occurred about this time. Ernie and I were sent to a hotel in the downtown area by our Inspector of Detectives. He said that a very influential head of a union insurance program had lost some property and we should handle the whole thing very diplomatically. The property that the elderly gentleman apparently lost was a gun, which he carried in his brief case. When we met the gentleman he was extremely nice to us and we immediately took note of the stares from the heads of our union, who were at the same hotel, when this man took us into the bar and ordered dinner and drinks for us.

Actually, this wasn't necessary because the man was really a nice guy and we would have done all we could for him anyway. As luck would have it we hit it right; and, after rattling the cage of one of the hotel porters, the gun mysteriously returned to the owner the next day.

Let me tell you, that grand gentleman was totally amazed at the fast action we gave him. He not only bought dinner and drinks again, but his last statement to us was that if he could ever do us a favor we need only ask. This didn't immediately impress us because many people make rash statements like that and after a few days they forget who you are. In this case, Ernie and I thought about it for a few days and after having passed that exam, along with seventy-five other guys, we thought we should give him a try.

We went to his office and the minute his secretary told him who was there to see him, he immediately came out, grabbed our hands and ushered us in. He was the most gregarious type person I had met in a long time. When he asked what he could do for us we explained as tactfully as we could what our position was and what he thought about it. There wasn't the slightest hesitation when he told us that he is a personal friend of one of the commissioners and that we should not concern ourselves because we were "in."

Ernie and I took the whole thing with a grain of salt. In fact, my appearance in the commissioner's office for my oral interview took less than three minutes, during which time I thought the man asking the questions was the friend of our friend, when in fact his friend was the guy saying nothing. For those three minutes I got a mark of 78.5.

Bob went in after me, stayed for fifteen minutes and got a 79. Maybe if I would have stayed there for an hour I could have gotten an 82!—because they most certainly could not get a complete impression of me or my abilities in that three minutes.

Anyway, a couple of weeks passed and we heard that in a couple days the results of the exam would come out and we would find out our position on the promotional list. We felt we had to get in the top fifteen to stand a chance of getting made a Detective. The list only lasted for two years and at the end of the two years if your number was not called, they destroyed the list and started all over again. This meant we would have to take the Detective's test again.

We decided to see our new friend one more time and again were met with the same cordiality. The man told us that we had nothing to worry about and that one of us would be number twelve and the other thirteen. You can imagine how we felt because we had never dealt in anything like this before and even though one always has suspicions of political activity in the results of anything public, we actually, at this time, thought the guy was full of crap and just trying to humor us.

You can imagine my thoughts when I called the Department on the day the results came out. I nervously asked a Captain to open my envelope and when he said I was number thirteen I told Marlene and she immediately broke out in tears. The pressure on her must have been tremendous.

Now my wheels really started to turn. I really wondered about the political machine. I couldn't wait to find out where Ernie placed. I called him and he said nineteen and then my mind went blank. If he would have been number twelve there would have been no doubt, but now we didn't know. We probably will never know because we've never gone back to the elderly man, and the commissioner has since left the board. As it turns out, it's one of those stories I can tell and simply leave it to conjecture. I suppose it really didn't make that much of a difference because within a year we were both made Detectives. What a fantastic feeling. Many people will accomplish a great deal more, but to me, this was the moment of a lifetime.

28. Coppers Down

It was still 1972 and Dick went off the car. We got a guy that had just been transferred from the Vice Squad. He had spent the last five years running the gambling Squad and was one of the highest paid Detectives on the Department because of his tremendous amount of overtime. I had worked with him briefly in uniform but other than that, really never had much contact with him except for a couple of search warrants while in uniform. He was one of the youngest Acting Detectives to go to the Vice Squad because of his constant drive to make arrests and go to court. He told Ernie and me that he knew nothing about investigating burglaries, and that we should have patience with him for awhile. His name was Carl, and not only did he learn fast, but he knew a million people, mostly black, mostly from the inner city and most were indebted to him for one reason or another. This guy had a hundred informers if he had one, and he knew every after-hours joint in the city.

The happenings of one night will hopefully portray the full feeling and anguish that went into that one night. We not only made use of one of Carl's informants but the events also brought back vivid memories of my days on the roving paddy wagon.

It was a night like many before; a cool misty Wednesday night in February. The time was somewhere close to 10:00 p.m. Carl and I had just left an after-hours joint where we had shot the breeze with one of our informers and were heading down farther into the inner city area just to look around and, more or less, see what was happening. We both saw some action at the same time. Two uniformed men had two black men up against the wall of a building and both Coppers had their shotguns out. Carl, my partner, wheeled around and I jumped out of the Squad and at the same time asking the Coppers if they needed any help. It was fairly obvious that they had the immediate situation under control.

Then they hit me with a statement that tore into my stomach, "How are the Coppers?"

"What Coppers? What're you talking about?"

"Two Coppers just got shot about four blocks from here."

"My God! You're kidding! How bad are they?"

"Both got shot in the head and it looks bad, they're giving out a description of the guys and they say they're wanted for murder."

We jumped into the Squad and raced down the street. Nothing was said between us, but the feeling must have been mutual. Let's hope and pray they're not dead. I've had this feeling for the past several weeks, all that's happening in the United States and all the tensions, something like this had to happen.

A million things went through my mind—the least not being giving my wife a call because I knew she would be watching television and I knew they would break in with the information that two Coppers had been shot—no names, nothing more and the words would send fear, shock and anguish into hundreds of hearts of wives, mothers, brothers and sisters of Officers.

The thoughts left me as they banged us on the radio and told us to report to the shooting scene. On the way it brought flashes back to me of the year of the riots. Coppers all over the streets stopping cars and pedestrians—all having shotguns or revolvers in their hands. The radio was going wild with different Coppers asking for more information and if there was any better description of the actors.

It only took us a few minutes to arrive at the scene and the first thing I saw sent a chill up my spine. A roving wagon, one like I had spent so much time on, was parked at a curious angle in the street with two Cadillac's in front of it. The rear doors were open and I had been down at the bureau long enough to have a good idea what was transpiring before anything was said.

We approached the back of the wagon where we saw several of our bosses. The scene on the damp black asphalt street was sickening. Blood, chalk marks in the form of two bodies head to head, directions, dates and times. I had investigated many shootings by this time and the grizzly evidence was all there in front of us.

Our boss was telling us he wanted a systematic search of every house and yard in the area. While he was giving us and several other teams the instructions, my eyes kept returning to the open wagon doors with the light on inside. I recalled so vividly being in the same position many times before. It kept flashing through my mind. The hundreds of people I had put in the back of the same kind of wagon, the many that had fought with us. The many times I had been knocked to the ground and wrestled in the gutter. All these images kept flashing in my mind as if they happened just yesterday.

The boss gave us a brief description of what had happened, to the best of his knowledge. At about five minutes after ten the Squad had radioed for help and had given its location. Within one minute, two plain clothes cars arrived at the scene and found both Officers lying in the street directly behind the wagon. One of them was obviously dead; the color was already leaving his face as the blood poured from a hole in the back of his head. The other Officer gasped several times, blinked his eyes once or twice and then his head and body relaxed. He was also dead. That's all the information he had at this time, except that one man had been arrested and he was wearing one of the dead Officer's handcuffs on one wrist.

We took two uniformed Officers with us and started our house to house search. We made it only as far as the first corner house and there I interviewed a young white woman who lived in the upper flat. She was hysterical and after getting a brief description of what she saw we left, realizing that she had just come home and could give us no useful information.

By this time Carl had already found one of the numerous reluctant witnesses. He lived in the lower flat and his living room window looked directly out onto the street where the shooting took place. It was obvious that he knew something, but as was the custom in the inner city area, he didn't want to tell us anything. He was a young black male about 21 years old and we talked and talked. His eyes kept flashing towards the other members of the house who stared at him. If their thoughts could be read, I'm sure they would say, "You tell that white bastard anything and we'll cut your heart out."

After reaching an impasse with him we told him that we were going to take him downtown and talk to him. He had the choice of coming with us voluntarily or going by force; we didn't much care either way. We felt sure that if we could get him away from the present environment he would loosen up.

Once downtown the young man talked more freely and even though he didn't have that much to offer as far as a witness goes, he did hear the shooting and when he looked out his window he saw an unknown figure running down the street and the bodies of the two Officers lying at the back of the wagon. He also told us that he was from down south and was staying with his sister's husband's relatives and they had told him not to talk to the man (us) or they would throw him out on the street. We took a statement from him and took him back home.

About an hour had expired now and by the time we got back to the scene all the preliminaries were done. Photos taken, measurements by the City Engineer, evidence gathered, and the scene roped off and the Squad and two Cadillac's were being towed away as evidence. A gun had also been found in a yard across the street from the shooting, but it apparently had nothing to do with the case and had been thrown away by one of the reluctant witnesses as a Copper approached him.

By this time no real witness had been found and the word had gone out to throw in anybody who they thought might either be involved or was a witness. Later on, this procedure was called "undo harassment" but at the time it was the only way to operate. Since several men had been arrested we were told to go downtown and help with the questioning.

As we got downtown and walked through a waiting room, I saw and recognized an attorney that I had numerous previous dealings with and thought was a fairly square guy who wouldn't give me the fast shuffle. How wrong I was. This perverted little individual had brought in to be questioned an eye witness to the whole shooting, but before she was turned over to the

Detectives, he told her not to say anything—only to give her name, address and date of birth. This was another example of the fantastic cooperation between us and the members of the Bar. Not only did he tell her not to cooperate, but several days later his firm was representing several others involved and was the first law firm to claim that brutality was used when questioning their clients. After they got the publicity that they were apparently after, they dropped their clients because they couldn't come up with a retainer fee. To me it just didn't make sense. Talk about ethics!

Carl and I went back into the interrogation rooms. They were filled with prisoners, uniform men and Detectives. I'd never seen emotions running so high—grown men, plain clothes and uniformed men with years on the job, tears streaming down their faces. The prisoners were being talked to, some forcefully, some gently, but it was all the same. No one knew anything and no one saw anything. It was obvious they were all lying, but the truth would be slow coming.

Interrogating a prisoner is always slow and methodical. It's impossible to think that a man will confess to a crime, especially a crime of violence, by just preying on his conscious and saying "please confess." In many cases it takes hours upon endless hours of talk and repetition.

The woman witness that had been advised by her attorney to say nothing had to be released. What a mockery of justice. The attorney and the woman were told to leave the building. The attorney was told to never expect any cooperation from our Department again.

The questioning went on and on for several hours. The man with the handcuffs on was changing his stories as fast as a new one would come to his mind. He stuck basically to the fact that he was stopped by the Squad for something that he didn't know what and that for no reason the Officers put a handcuff on him and started to beat him. He also stated that when they were putting him in the back of the wagon some unknown black male came up and shot both of the Officers. He said he didn't know who he was and that he fled the scene because he was scared. By now it was almost two in the morning and we were still no closer to the truth.

I had called Marlene earlier and asked her if she had watched television. She said yes and asked the Officers were. I told her both were dead and I could hear the pain in her voice as she said, "I'm sorry." I told her I'd be late getting home and she knew that this would be another time that my job would keep me away all night.

The whole questioning was going bad and we weren't getting the right answers when suddenly Carl got a phone call. It was one of his informers from his Vice Squad days. I was sitting across from Carl as he was talking on the phone and I could tell by his face that it was something good. He hung up, told me who it was and said that the informer had given him the name of the guy that did the shooting and that the weapon used was either in the hallway of a house across the street from the scene or in the back yard. The informer further stated that he couldn't talk anymore and that if we wanted more information we would have to come and get him. This meant that we would have to go to the house where he was shacking with his girlfriend, arrest him and drag him out of the house. All this was done to cover the fact that he was giving us information.

Naturally, this information wasn't free. It would cost us nothing monetarily wise, but in the last few months there had been enough good evidence gathered on him by the Vice Squad so that he was now facing a maximum of sixty-five years. What he was actually doing was just trying to save his own tail, which is what any good informer tries to do.

At this point we didn't care what his motive was, and after we arrested him in his girlfriend's house and got him in the Squad car, we told him that he could be sure that we'd see that he got some sort of consideration if the information that he had given us was good. He said it was and then he slid it on us.

The story he gave was amazing. He said that he saw a girl he knew walking down the street. He stopped and gave her a ride and she told him that she had just come from a Police station and that she had seen two Coppers get shot. (This turned out to be the young girl that had been thrown out of the station with her attorney.) The story she told him was that she was in her front room with several of her friends when they heard sirens and saw flashing red lights outside. A group of them went to the front porch and saw two Policemen fighting with another man and all three fell to the ground. Suddenly one of the men in the group she was standing with bolted from the porch and ran towards the three figures on the ground. When he got to the three he pulled a gun from his pocket and started to fire. He then ran back into the house where she was and the whole group followed him in. He then laid the gun on the kitchen table, took off his coat, which had blood on it, and shoved it under a chair. She stated that she then grabbed the gun, took it into the rear hallway and threw it away.

Right after this the Police came into the house, arrested three or four black males that were there, but didn't take the man that did the shooting because he had crawled in bed and pretended that he was asleep.

Amazing, absolutely amazing! He told the story several times in front of another group of Detectives and the bosses. I could tell that some believed him and some didn't. The story just seemed too wild and disconnected.

We questioned him for about a half hour and from his answers Carl and I felt he either had definitely talked to the girl or that he was a witness himself. Some of the information and facts could only have come from an eye witness. I kept thinking back to the attorney and thought that dirty rotten little bastard. If only we had that girl here now we could probably get at the truth. The informer told us that the girl was scared and that if we faced her with the information that we now had, he was sure she would break.

We had him go over his story two or three more times and then locked him in an interrogation room away from everyone else and told him that we'd keep him for a couple of hours and then release him. This was done to protect his identification and after his release he could give his girlfriend any story he wanted.

By this time it was all too evident that not only was the murder weapon important to the case, but it was a crucial piece of evidence. We also learned that the name our informer gave as being the murderer had come up in conversation with some of the reluctant witnesses. He had been picked up and was being questioned. Naturally he would say nothing.

We learned from some of the first investigating Officers that the house in question was indeed entered right after the shooting, several black males were arrested and there was an unknown black male sleeping in bed and he had been left there.

Armed with the information that we got from the informer we got hold of the District Attorney and a Judge. The Judge issued a search warrant for the house in question and named the objects being searched for as the gun and bloody jacket.

We searched the house with half a dozen other Detectives and even though there was enough junk and garbage in the rat infested house to fill ten garbage trucks the information we had from our informer was exact.

One Detective found a 32 caliber automatic in the rear hallway under a pile of clothes. The clip was in it but it was empty of the nine shots it apparently could hold. A closer look at the gun made my stomach turn. It appeared that there were also particles of flesh on the barrel. The full truth may never be known, but after questioning all night by the Detectives and further questioning the next day by the District Attorney's office, enough statements were obtained (our reluctant witness included) that the suspect was charged with two counts of first degree murder. He apparently had actually executed the two Policemen by placing the gun to their heads while they were on the ground and in cold blood began to fire.

At this time, only God knows what the outcome would be in the months to come, after the trial. The only thing that is known for sure now is that a wife lost her husband and a mother lost her son; gunned down like animals in that perpetual jungle of humanity. The cries will be heard for weeks and the complaints of brutality to the witnesses will probably last for months, but as far as I am concerned they will fall on my deaf ears, because I know the truth.

Since it takes me so long to write, the trial of the two murdered Policemen has now been over for several months. The suspect was found guilty on both counts of first degree murder and was sentenced to two consecutive terms of life in the State Prison. I should also add that several witnesses were charged with perjury and obstructing justice and they also received sentences.

The trial itself lasted several weeks and during one of those days the original investigating Detectives, who were also the first ones on the scene, testified. These supposedly hard, cold, uncompassionate men actually broke down on the witness stand when they had to recall the two slain Officers dying in their arms. The actors will eventually get another chance in life; the Officers will not.

29. Gin Mills and Struggles

I met more thieves, crooks, gamblers, pimps, prostitutes and tavern keepers in the next few months than I ever figured existed. Carl was one ball of fire and never sat still for more than a minute. He smoked at least three packs a day and put Ernie and I to shame at the bar. The combination that the three of us made worked fantastic for not only ourselves, but for the Department also.

We came up with more arrests, search warrants and activity than one could possibly imagine. In fact, to this day, even though we have other assignments, the three of us are still the closest of friends.

The three of us made a funny combination. Carl not only ran the gambling Squad, but was quite a good gambler himself. Ernie never bet more than a dollar on a football pool in his life, and I was somewhere in between—closer to Ernie's state as a gambler than Carl. And yet when we worked together the most money that ever exchanged hands between us was the quarter for the pool table.

We all became quite proficient on the pool table, which was a tremendous tool we used in the black taverns. We obtained a lot of very good information from informers while in these taverns.

I think I may have mentioned it before, but if I didn't, the fact still remains that I would rather work in the black community than in the trashy white section or the hippy section of the city. I found that a black person will never hold a grudge. You could battle him and arrest him one night and, if you treated him fair and he had it coming, he'd be the first one to buy you a drink the next day, whereas in the hippy part of the city we were hated forever.

I can remember having outside jurisdictions come into our city and be looking for someone. If the suspect was in our area we would get assigned with them to help them out. Once we took them into the inner city and started hitting our places for information as to the whereabouts of their fugitive, the guest Coppers would always be amazed. We usually took the guest Cops out and got them a couple of drinks to loosen them up to get their courage up, and then we would start. I know for a fact that in several cases this was the most exciting time of their careers.

Carl, I and usually two of our visitors would walk into one of our gin mills and Carl would proceed to walk up to the first pool table, shove all the balls in the pockets, put his quarter in and announce we had the table. This would usually blow our friends minds. It was something straight out of the TV shows. Then we'd grab our informer, man handle him outside, slip him a couple of bucks and get the information we needed. We needed to make it look good for the other tavern patrons so they wouldn't suspect that the informer was an informer. Apparently, that is why we usually had to have a couple of drinks first, because I sure as hell wouldn't do that sober.

All in all we had a lot of respect in that area, because the next day we weren't afraid to walk right back in the same place and buy the house a drink—usually making sure the bartender didn't take more than three or four dollars.

I also recall using other outside authorities, one being the State Agent for the regulation of Alcohol and Tobacco. These guys had more power than I realized. They had the right to go into any tavern and search the entire area that was covered under their particular license; this usually included the back storage rooms and basement. We met one of these agents in court one day and bought him a cup of coffee.

He seemed like a neat little guy—no more than five feet five and a hundred-twenty pounds. He was a real true Cop lover. He said he covered about five or six counties in our state and that unless he got a complaint it was not unusual for him to never get to check all the taverns in his particular area. That being understandable because we had fourteen hundred in our city alone. As we talked he said if we ever needed his help we should never hesitate to call him—twenty-four hours a day.

It wasn't two weeks later that we had a burglary at a liquor store and a witness got a license number of a truck seen leaving the scene. It also wasn't a couple hours later that we got an anonymous call that told us that the stolen liquor was in the basement storage locker of a tavern in the heart of the inner city. We went down to the tavern and found the truck, but we had no authority to search the tavern so we gave our little State Agent a call.

He was at the front door of that gin mill within the next hour and announced in a very authoritative voice, "Follow me." I suppose the fact that we had the backing of two or three men from the Tactical Squad had something to do with it.

Our little friend strode right through a wall of junkies and run of the mill degenerates, stepped right behind the bar and flashed his badge and identification that was three times the size of mine. And he then announced that he was a State Agent and was about to check out the tavern. He sure as hell knew what he was doing because he started by checking the liquor bottles behind the bar for refills. He did this to cover his real reason for being there. He then announced to the owner that he wanted to check his invoices and stock in the basement.

We followed him down the stairs and after first checking the obvious he asked the owner to open a locked door. The owner naturally said he did not have a key. He found the key very conveniently when the Agent told me to take if off the hinges. Not the least bit to our surprise we found the whole load of stolen liquor in that locked room. We photographed it, recovered it and returned it to a pleased owner.

We then ordered the tavern keeper to come into the District Attorney's office the next day for possible charges. Before the night passed we received enough information from the tavern keeper to keep the Vice Squad busy with a few busts—mostly for narcotics violations.

We didn't press charges the next day but held them over his head for a few weeks until he gave us a little more information. In fact, he wound up to be one of our better informants for the next few months. This made everybody happy. The agent got to swing a little weight around and we accomplished what we set out to do.

All my cases with Carl weren't that easy. This guy was, and is to this day, a workaholic. Everything he did or does is 100 miles an hour. No matter if it's working, drinking, gambling or family life. Needless to say, he was one of the greatest partners I ever had. In fact, it was only a few months later that I was to find out if he could really handle himself. By this time it was the spring of 1973 and I was thirty-seven years old and not particularly thrilled about getting my ass kicked. Sure enough, Carl was still so gung-ho that he had to stick his nose into a group of people that were milling on the street and pouring out of a gin mill. They apparently were looking at several cars that had been involved in an accident. Carl said, "Let's see what's happening," and before I could say mind your own business, he was out of the Squad announcing that he was an Officer and asking if anybody was hurt.

Unknown to us, four young guys high on pot had hit about four or five cars and had finally come to a stop. The trouble was that the tavern people weren't that friendly to Coppers and neither was the crowd. By the time I got out of the car, after calling for a Squad to investigate the accident, I was shocked to see Carl and one of the youths really going to it. It was obvious that Carl wasn't losing so I went to the car and caught a glimpse of one of the other youths reaching on the floor in the back seat. I thought he was going to come up with a weapon, even though later it turned out that he was trying to get rid of his stash of weed, so I pulled him from the car and immediately felt his friend on my back.

Once again, there I was, past the age of really wanting to get involved in this bullshit, rolling in the gutter with Carl and these three young toughs. To make a long story short, I found that Carl was perfectly capable of handling himself and after one of the good citizens in the crowd did call for help, the fight was over. Total loss to ourselves: one watch, two pair of pants and my nice new tie.

I guess we didn't do that bad because one of our young friends wound up in the hospital to get a few stitches and, the next day in court after Carl and I had a chance to clean up, we most certainly looked like we came out on top. Talk about adding insult to injury! After several adjournments the three tried their case in front of a female Judge who stated that she had known Carl and me for years, and that we did not have the reputation of getting into fights. She fined them all a substantial amount and ordered them to pay each of us forty-five dollars to cover the damage to our clothes. The forty-five dollars was to be paid immediately. We went out into the hall with the three young people and their attorney, who by the way we were also close to, and we held out our hands while they each dropped in their allotted amount until we each had forty-five dollars. In fact, I recall the one fellow placed a ten in my hand that fell out and I couldn't believe the look on his face when his attorney told him to pick it up and place it back in my hand.

This whole thing must have been too hard for one of these young fellows to handle, because we heard from his lawyer some months later that the kid shaved off his beard, cleaned up his act and was studying to be a Priest.

That wasn't the only time Carl got me into a scrape. It wasn't more than a few months later we investigated a burglary of an elderly couple's house in which, among other things, a grey metal box with personal papers was taken. To make another long story short the kid that burglarized the house apparently left the box laying outside and his mother's boyfriend found it. He, in turn, called the people and wanted a reward. They in turn called us and we waited for the individual. We talked to him briefly in the house and then conned him into coming to the station with us. When we got to the front of the station he decided he wasn't going in.

We each grabbed an arm and suddenly felt our feet leaving the ground. This guy was a monster. I think if he really wanted to he could have torn our heads off. Meanwhile, a Good Samaritan Copper that was standing station security decided to get into the act and started to beat this guy over the head with his night stick. All that did was piss the guy off and after the Copper realized he wasn't doing any good, he left the scene never to be heard from or seen again.

We finally got the guy handcuffed, into the station, booked and conveyed to our headquarters downtown, but not before he made an official complaint to that station's Commanding Officer about us beating him on his head. Well, we couldn't tell the boss about the Copper with the stick, so we had to deny the whole thing.

The next day the man was charged with resisting arrest and after several adjournments his case finally came up. The District Attorney that was handling the case was brand new. In fact, I recognized him as being a former star player for our state university basketball team and I also remember him from playing on one of the inner city playgrounds during the summer. At first he wasn't the most pleasant fellow in the world, but after we got to know each other a little better, it was obvious that his unfriendly attitude merely came about because this wasn't the easiest or the most prestigious case to try.

It was just a simple case of resisting arrest and it was the defendant's word against ours. It's funny how we could pick the Judges, but I imagine after spending day after day and week after week in court, one's reputation passes on—both good and bad. This Judge, for instance, was not a complete lover of Police and we had a good chance of losing this case. This really didn't matter that much to us, but we felt sorry for the new District Attorney.

Both Carl and I testified and if the case would have ended there we probably would have won, and a good defense lawyer with a client playing with a full deck most certainly would have beaten us. Well, the lawyer was good, but the guy he was defending was a nut, so we told the District Attorney to just let the defendant ramble on and we felt sure he'd talk himself into jail. Sure enough, he got himself wound up on the stand and the first time the liberal Judge told him to wait for the question to be asked before he said anything, he told the Judge to go to hell and mind his own business.

For that he got thirty days in the House of Correction and a money fine. Not too bad for a shaky case and one tried by a new District Attorney. In fact, he was one of the few black District Attorneys in the office and until the time he left for better things, it was not unusual for us to seek him out when we were getting a warrant. Naturally, his first trial would always come up and a few laughs were exchanged.

30. District Attorneys and Judges

Throughout the years I've become acquainted with a good many attorneys and Assistant District Attorneys and Judges and just like any other profession some are good and some are bad and some are indifferent.

Just as good defense attorneys shop around for the best Judge to try his case, so a good Copper will try and pick his favorite District Attorney. This was not always possible, but when you've spent as much time in court as I have, I sometimes was able to pick and choose.

Just as a good attorney will always at least listen to his client, a good District Attorney will always listen to the arresting Officer and many times take his advice. I remember Carl and I had led a young District Attorney through his first jury trial and conviction and at that time he said he'd never forget us. He later on not only became a first assistant D.A. but also a criminal Judge and later on, the Chief Judge. And to this day when I see him at a party or retirement, he always brings up his first trial and how we helped him through it.

One trial that comes to mind about that time was what Carl and I call the "purple panty caper." It started out as a burglary of a lower flat in a rundown four family unit. The complainant suspected the lower tenant and not only did we lift his fingerprints inside the apartment that was burglarized, we also got a search warrant for his apartment and found a pair of the complainant's purple panties by his bed.

Several months later the case came to trial and not only did we have a good case and an excellent District Attorney trying the case, but the defendant was indigent and wound up with one of the most pathetic trial lawyers in the county. This one we had knocked, so I thought.

The jury was picked and the District Attorney seemed somewhat concerned about several members of the jury. Apparently, the District Attorneys have their own grape vine and they send names to each other with the results of their various jury trials and their respective opinions of the jurists. Well, apparently our whole jury was made up of a liberal bunch of do-gooders that had come back with several not guilty verdicts. The handwriting was on the wall when the jury filed into their respective seats for the start of the trial and one middle aged gentleman smiled and waved at our defendant. About that time we should have thrown in the towel because even with our fingerprints and purple panties, the jury still found the guy not guilty. The District Attorney was really upset with losing that case especially losing to that incompetent attorney. Naturally, we never let him forget it!

I must say that at times it's difficult to remember specific instances, even though I'm looking through my memo book. Hardly ever a day went by that something didn't happen that I could write about, but in all fairness to myself and whoever may read these words, I will try to keep these stories up-to-date.

I just paged through my memo book from 1974, and recall without much excitement about arresting a Mexican and two white males for criminal damage to property. I suppose the whole incident doesn't deserve more than a few lines, but at the time it was a big case and drew quite a bit of print in the local newspapers.

Ernie and I were sent out to the Waukesha jail to talk to a Mexican who had been arrested for shooting out several windows in business places in their city. We talked to him for about two hours and then brought him back to our city. It seems that he, along with his girlfriend and her two brothers—one being a juvenile—had gone out on several evenings in the past few months and, using wrist rockets and sling shots along with BB guns, had shot out windows at random in homes and business places in our city and surrounding jurisdictions.

Well, I had not been fully aware of the extent of damage that had been occurring in our jurisdiction, because most of the complaints were handled by the uniform men. It was not until I started to pull some of the complaints that I fully realized the magnitude of their actions. The total property damage done by these young people had reached just above a half million dollars. It appeared that they would pick one main street or one side street and shoot holes in every store or home in that area. In fact, one home was fired on and a Police Officer lived there. The missile that they used hit the refrigerator just as he was opening it up to get a beer. That was almost enough to turn him into a tee-totaler!

After numerous court appearances and meetings with the District Attorney's office it turned out that the only one to confess to all of these crimes was the original Mexican. The girl was protected by him and her two brothers—the one being a juvenile would not make any statements. In fact, their father almost threw us out of the house even though we were able to recover several missiles and their propellants in their homes.

To make a short story even shorter, the Mexican got five years in jail. The two brothers received nothing because the District Attorney wouldn't charge them merely on the information from the Mexican, and so the only people that were really out were the complainants and their insurance companies. So you see, even as far back as 1974, the judicial system was making fools of the very people that supported it.

It's very hard for a layman to believe and understand when an Officer tells them that as fast as the thieves and crooks that prey on them are arrested, the system frees these very same culprits. And yet I sit daily during the morning line-ups, when the previous night pillagers and marauders are paraded in front of myself and fellow Detectives, and find it not unusual to hear that one or two have been arrested not less than ten or eleven times for burglary as a juvenile. Now that they have been adults for a few years, they've been arrested for burglary once or twice, and have never seen the inside of an institution.

When speaking of line-ups, I'm referring to the daily morning practice of bringing in the previous nights arrestees for major crimes and parading them in front of the working Detectives. It's a good practice and makes those working aware of the latest crimes and who's responsible. The line-up is held in the Detective assembly which is a room I would say covers about 2000 square feet and has row upon row of grey metal desks with a stage to the front. Prior to roll call, these individuals are brought on the stage five at a time. They are asked their names and what they have been arrested for. The responses vary from "kiss my ass" to being very informative.

I remember one genius who had been arrested for armed robbery and who had denied any part in the robbery. While on the stage the Lieutenant in charge was describing the crime and was reciting what the actor in the robbery said. "Give me all your money or I'll blow your head off."

To which the subject on the stage replied, "I never said that I would blow her head off." This brought a laugh from the audience and an immediate response from the Hold-up Squad.

I remember another time when Carl and I were in the audience and the subject on the stage who had been arrested for murder and robbery started to sway back forth and suddenly jumped from the stage and started to run on top of the desks toward the back exit. Not only was everyone somewhat shocked, but so was he after he got across about eight desks when someone grabbed his ankle and he flew head first toward Carl, who greeted him with a sap to the head. Needless to say that ended the episode.

Typical logic for some of our social workers came to my attention just in the past week when a member of our famous city motorcycle gang was arrested during a search warrant and found to be in possession of a variety of guns. He was on parole from our State Prison, and naturally possession of fire arms was illegal. Not only was he armed, but he lived above the clubhouse of this gang, disregarding the direct order from the court regarding his parole which indicated that he should have no contact with his former club members.

When his parole Officer, a woman, was asked about this she stated that he had promised her that he would have no contact with anyone else in the building. She further stated that he seemed like such a nice young man that she felt compelled to believe him.

My personal belief is that she was scared to death of this lovely fellow and felt obligated for her own welfare to bend over backward for him.

31. And More Informers, Cases, Partners and Family

I know that in the past I have talked about the importance of informers. As I read through the pages of my memo books, I constantly see how they played not only an influential part in my life, but also how it made certain aspects interesting and humorous.

I remember getting a call from one of my best taverns—in fact, throughout the years it remained one of my best sources of information. The caller asked if I was looking for a certain individual and after checking with the local and state agencies I called him back and said we had nothing. He said he was sure that the individual he was talking about had just escaped from a prison farm and was sitting next to him at the bar.

I checked further and still found nothing. It was several hours later that an urgent message came across the teletype indicating that this subject had escaped from a minimum security prison up state and had taken the Prison Director's auto. Apparently, the local community got mixed up in their teletypes and by forgetting to press a button, they were sending the message just to themselves. I called my informer back and he told me that the guy had just walked out, but that he would be back in a couple of hours.

Now a little something has to be said about informers, and I mentioned it before when I explained about the informer the F.B.I. had bought from under my nose. I was determined it would never happen again, so my informers and my partners' informers remained strictly confidential to the point where I would rather blow a good case, than either burn my informant or turn him over to another Copper.

I should also mention that some bosses did not always go strictly according to the rules. When I say my informer called and the wrong boss answered, this means the informer said he had good information for me about an escapee, but this particular boss sent one of his hand-picked Detectives to meet him instead of me.

Needless to say, my informants had been well coached and when these two fair haired individuals walked into the tavern and asked if anyone had called, not only did they get the cold shoulder, but my man told me later that they were actually sitting next to the escapee in question and that he had offered to buy them a beer.

My squealer had to wait until I got off work and got my last mark. It was at this time I found out he left word that I should call him. When I got a hold of him he asked what kind of B.S. was going on down there, and if I wanted the guy he was at the gin mill.

I grabbed two Detectives from the next shift and we plowed through the tavern door like gang busters and not only got our escapee, but he had a stash of cocaine on him, and he was armed.

The next day a comment was made at roll call about the good bust, but it was made by one of the bosses on my side.

It was only about two weeks later that some old time burglar used one of the oldest tricks in the book. He tied a bunch of bed sheets together and lowered himself from a window out of our own County Jail. Well, you can imagine what kind of print that got! The local sheriff's Department was crawling the walls and combing every nook and cranny in the city and surrounding county to find the escapee. Sure enough, it wasn't but a day or two that I got a call from my snitch—who for the sake of easier reading I'll give the name of Roy.

Well Roy, it seems, not only was my informer, but he was also the most trusted amongst the local hoods. In fact, the old ingenious escapee was, at the time of the call, hiding out in Roy's own home.

Apparently the old timer either ran out of money or was getting under Roy's skin after a couple of days, so Roy dropped a dime on him and made arrangements that I would nail him someplace on the street after he left the house. The only catch was the fact that the escapee never left Roy's house, because the bed sheets had torn during his escape and he broke his leg. Roy finally threw caution to the wind and agreed that I could make the bust right in his house. The signal was all set and the house was surrounded by about two or three bureau cars and a couple of Tac Squads.

Roy had said that he would turn on the porch light and put a pail out on the front porch when the old guy was sacked out on the front room couch. When he put the pail out we should come pounding through the front door and make it look good. The whole thing went down as planned and three of us went through the front door—one grabbed Roy and threw him up against the wall and when he turned around, the Copper thought he was going to take a swing so he knocked him on his ass.

The second Copper was me, and I went running for the couch and held my gun on the poor guy that was lying there and it wasn't until I saw his eyes grow big as silver dollars that I realized that he was just one of the local pickles. The third Copper grabbed the right guy and not only met no resistance, the old guy said he was getting fed up with Roy's B.S. and housekeeping and was ready to give himself up anyway.

Word got out that in the last three months I had arrested three people that had escaped from various institutions. A few days later I received word that one of the local snakes wanted to talk to me. I met him in a corner of a particular bar, and he announced that a few guys had gotten together and scrounged up five hundred dollars that was mine if I would tell who my snitch was. In fact, he said even Roy was going to throw in two hundred.

Not only didn't I take that money, I can honestly say I never took one thin dime as long as I've been on the job. Coffee, a meal, a drink, or a cigar, yes—that was different—that's in friendship, not for selling my soul.

Gee, here it was summer again and I was sent to one of those tragedies that take all the glory and joy out of this job. It happened in the same park that the guy slit his wrists, but this time a shop picnic turned into a nightmare when a little girl, the same age at the time as one of my own, climbed up on the edge of a portable bar and pulled it over on her. It crushed her skull in one blow.

Absolutely tragic, and yet I suppose tragedies and painful disasters are a constant part of this job. I've seen death in so many ways: shootings, stabbings, hangings, accidents, mutilations, overdoses, and any other possible means. Yet, this is all part of life itself. I would imagine it's just that Cops see so much more of life than the average person.

I recall one particular shooting; it took place at a filling station. The attendant was just some young drifter about twenty-two-years-old. He was traveling across the country and paying his way with odd jobs. Little did he realize that he would fall prey to some degenerate mind, because not only was he the victim of a fifty dollar robbery, the actor took him in the back room and blew three quarters of his head off with a twelve gauge shotgun. I recall it was a twelve gauge, because we not only found the spent shell, but it was my unpleasant task to sift through the blood and matter with a snow scrapper looking for pellets and other evidence. That's enough to make even the best Copper's stomach give a little twinge.

It was right about this time that Ernie fell from the graces of the bosses and was taken off the Squad. In fact, it was at the same time Carl went days. The three of us had not only been partners, but our families had grown up together. Hardly a week went by that we didn't get together. As I said before, partners are like brothers because you spend so much time together. After Ernie and Carl left, I got Bob back as a partner. Bob had been sent to the bureau about a year after me, and having him assigned to the car with me brought back a lot of memories.

As I mentioned before, Bob, Dave and I had become good friends—not only at work, but also our families had become close. If I was to exemplify the character of Bob, I would have to say that he came from a conservative family whose father was also a Police Officer. There was quite an age difference between his father and himself, so that he was still quite young when his father retired and moved to a farm in a small community outside of Milwaukee County. It was in this small community that Bob grew up. He eventually left for the service, came home and married his high school sweetheart. He subsequently moved to Milwaukee and became a Police Officer. Up until the time he and I worked plain clothes together, he was probably one of the straightest guys I knew. Strictly a family man—absolutely no messing around.

It seems that working special was more than he, and I might say many men before him, could handle. Sixty, seventy, eighty hour weeks with every night topped off in some gin mill. And, if you had the least bit of a problem at home, there were a dozen gals in those taverns that were eager to listen to the problems of some sharp looking Copper with a few bucks in his pocket. They could either listen at the bar or at their place.

It seems that Bob got caught up in one of these situations and wound up with a girlfriend. I still, to this day, blame his background because this whole episode of being in plain clothes changed him completely. It wasn't a matter of but a few months after he came to the bureau that he left his wife and family. After going back a few times, he left them for good. His wife called on Dave and me for help. It made for a very strange partnership, where I would be spending the day with Dave and Bob's wife, taking her for different counseling sessions, and then working with Bob in the evening hours knowing full well that he knew what was going on. This lasted for a year, in which his whole family life turned into a tragedy.

During one of his brief stays at home, his ten-year-old son came home from school during the week and complained of a stomachache. Within four days he died of massive stomach cancer and it was Dave's and my duty to serve as pall bearers. It seemed that this brought Bob back to his senses for a short period of time, but that was as long as it lasted and he was out again. He never really seemed the same and it wasn't but a few months later that Ernie and I got back on the Squad together. It was only a few months after that when Bob was standing in the hall of a local university he was attending, and he suddenly fell over with a massive heart attack and died.

It seemed that all the problems of the world were on his shoulders and he just could not bear up under the load. Just one year after putting his young son to rest, Dave and I carried Bob to his resting place next to his son. He was thirty-eight years old.

I wonder how many thousand Coppers die from the pressure of this job and yet only recently have some of the more progressive Departments recognized that some of the social diseases such as alcoholism and mental breakdowns are a direct result of the job. I have always made it a practice to try and leave the problems of my job where they belong—at work. I know that many times Marlene must have felt the pressures that I was under, but each time she would take the time and care to help me and she never burdened me with the problems of raising a family that she must have been under.

During this time, one of Carl's, Ernie's and my better informers died. He just went to bed one night and didn't wake up. The Medical Examiner decided to check several of his organs and blood to determine if there was any foul play because he was implicated in one of the recent underworld drug related murders. The M.E. determined that he died of natural causes.

This guy was one of the baddest (if that's a word) guys I ever met in my life. He was a thief, drug dealer, forger, and would do absolutely anything else for a fast buck. They say he was so bad that he's still standing at the pearly gates and God won't let him in because he won't give his name. This guy spent almost twelve years in State Prisons and it took us almost a year before he would even talk to us. In fact, if I told his cohorts that he informed on them (which I would never do) they would say I was full of shit. Everyone has their price, and sometimes to him it was just a friendly word from someone on the other side.

32. Con Games

There's a new con game that I had to investigate. At least it was new to me. It probably has been around a long time, I just never heard of it. I received a communication from the Los Angeles Police Department inquiring about the legitimacy of a magazine called the Law Enforcer. It seems that several business places in that community had been contacted by someone in our city soliciting advertisement in that magazine. The name of the game was "screw the unsuspecting public" and it worked like this: very simply, several ingenious men would set up an office and hire a few girls to go through telephone directories for any state except ours. They would then mail them a nominal bill for advertising that said they had placed for in some fictitious magazine—usually with some law and order wording. Not only was there no advertising, but there wasn't even a magazine.

These individuals made the bill small enough so that the companies involved simply either sent the money or threw the bill away. Hardly any of them took the time to complain, and if the Better Business Bureau or Consumers Fraud Division got enough complaints to become interested, these characters just found another office and started a new business under another name. Not bad for a part-time scheme! It was well established when I found it involved hundreds of thousands of dollars. When I went to the District Attorney's office to make some inquiries they weren't the least bit interested because they felt they could not prove venue. In other words, they could not prove that the crime was committed within their jurisdiction.

Speaking of the District Attorney's office, several years ago (in the early 1970's) they made the practice that they would not even consider issuing warrants against someone that was merely implicated by a co-conspirator. In other words, if someone was arrested and through interrogation he implicated someone else, the District Attorney's office would not prosecute the other party without other evidence. For example, the other day I investigated a burglary and to make a long story short, the victim had been picked up on the street by two individuals who gave him a ride to a gas station. While at the station they caused a disturbance and the Police were called. Well, the Police took down all three names and told all three that they were too drunk to drive, so the three parked the car and went to the victim's home where they had a few drinks from a bottle that they purchased on the way.

After a few hours, all three left in a drunken condition with the victim going to a gin mill and the other two going back to their car with their partially filled bottle. The complainant had a few drinks, went home and fell asleep on the couch. When he woke up in the morning he found his television, stereo and other furniture missing and his bedroom window smashed in.

When I got there he told the whole story and also told me that the bottle that his two friends had taken with them was now on his kitchen table. Not only that, but when I dusted for prints on the bedroom window I got four beautiful latent lifts off a piece of broken glass. These prints were checked against the names off the reports that the Officers had filed the previous night—and sure enough, they matched one of the individuals.

I gave this information to the next shift and both the individuals were picked up. The one who left his prints confessed and turned over the property he had and also implicated the other actor. The second man admitted to everything except going back and burglarizing the home. So all this evidence was presented to the District Attorney's office and naturally they issued against the individual with the prints, but a warrant was refused against the other guy even though he was implicated by his partner. The auto used by the individuals was listed to the second guy; the Police placed him within a few blocks of the burglary and his mother gave an alibi that proved to be false.

When I questioned the Assistant District Attorney that refused the warrant he said, "Hey Jim, why should the taxpayers have to pay for a trial that we have a good chance of losing? Let the guy go and you'll catch him again. Besides, you know our policy on co-conspirators."

It seems that any of your small counties would relish that type of case because they probably only have a few a month. The trouble is, with a large metropolis like ours, they can't or won't take the time on a case such as this that doesn't involve a violent crime. They would much rather deal in statistics that shows what a tremendous job they are doing as far as convictions are concerned.

The District Attorney was right, he will get caught again and probably it will be a better case and they will get a conviction—but what about the new victim?

33. A Most Interesting Case

Every Copper sometime in his career experiences the most interesting case that he has ever been involved in. It happened to me in the early part of 1975, and because of that particular case it was possible for Ernie and me to get back together on the Squad.

To give a little background on the crime, let me say that it was not the most unusual homicide of the decade, but circumstances that surrounded the whole case were fascinating.

It seems that there was a tavern in the city that had been under the same ownership for at least forty years. First by a young couple who had bought it during the depression and ran it together for some thirty years, then as old age had taken its toll and the husband died of a heart attack, the elderly widow had tried to run it by herself. The pictures on the walls reminisced of days gone by when the tavern was filled with fun loving people and the young couple stood proudly behind the bar. Since her husband died, the poor elderly lady had fallen on bad times and because the neighborhood had changed drastically, the tavern itself had become more or less a hangout for vagrants in the area. The building itself was probably built around the turn of the century and must have been at that time a quiet and exquisite meeting place. But now the years had taken their toll and the building was in bad need of repairs.

The first floor held the tavern proper and through a drape covered opening at the end of the room was a small living quarters consisting of just the bare essentials—old stove, refrigerator and a torn up couch that the elderly woman used as a bed.

She apparently had become somewhat senile in the past several years and had run her business in a disorganized fashion. In fact, the tavern did not have a license for the past four months and her relatives were in the process of putting her in a nursing home, but such was not to be her fate.

On a chilly day in October of 1974 two young twenty-year-old men went to the tavern for what they later said was to help the elderly lady out, but they probably went there for a free drink or a handout. They walked through an unlocked rear door leading to the sparse living quarters and found the elderly lady lying on the couch on her back with her legs tied together with a piece of white cloth and a white cloth tied tightly around her neck. Her face was swollen with her eyes shut and her nose at an angle that indicated it must have been smashed against her face. Her clothing was disarranged and was saturated with blood as was the pillow that was under her head. She was obviously dead, and had taken a tremendous beating.

The young men called the Police and after all the preliminary work was done the body was conveyed to the Medical Examiner's office where he removed her three sweaters and two men's pair of pants. They found that she had suffered a large laceration to her head caused by a blunt instrument, a broken rib cage possibly caused by stomping on her chest, a fractured nose, fractured jaw, fractured collar bone, and numerous contusions and abrasions over her entire body. The cause of death was from several internal injuries and massive hemorrhaging as a result of numerous blows to her entire body by a blunt instrument that had been used with great force.

Investigation at the scene showed that someone had cut the screen on the outer rear door, unlocked it and case knifed the inner door. The elderly lady must have been awakened by the intruders and must have put up a hell of a fight because the entire rear room, along with a portion of the bar room, was covered with blood and there were blood streaks on the door leading to the second floor. The fact that there was blood streaks leading to the second floor indicated either that she tried to escape or the actors intended to go to the second floor but changed their minds. After all that was done, they tried to cover their crime by pouring gas on the floor and setting the whole place on fire. The fire apparently didn't get ignited right and the fire extinguished itself before it could do any real damage.

The best suspects at the time seemed to be the twenty-year-olds that found the body, because after several hours of interrogation several inconsistencies were found in their stories. However, two polygraph exams positively eliminated the two suspects.

This horrendous crime only caught about a dozen lines in the newspaper and a twenty second shot on TV. I suppose that's all it deserved in a city that already had eighty some homicides that year. In the next several weeks, at least three or four good suspects turned up. Each one was questioned extensively and after their alibis were checked, they were all released.

It was almost a month to the day of the crime that a woman came to the Detective Bureau and told the Detectives assigned to the case that her boyfriend had told her that he killed the old lady in the tavern. These things happen every so often when a boyfriend and girlfriend get in a hassle, especially in that section of the city. But in this case, her male companion turned out to be a Native American Indian whose record showed he had several arrests for burglary, battery, drunk and he also had a violent temper. He had several arrests for disorderly fighting and resisting arrest. To top that off, we learned that he lived upstairs in the tavern for about a month and paid the elderly lady $12.50 per week for rent.

The girlfriend telling the story was not the most chaste of character, but she swore to an affidavit that he told her he robbed the old lady and then killed her when she made a fuss. The girlfriend even passed a polygraph test on the statements she made. And in fact, the Coppers assigned to the case even came up with another witness that said the Indian had told him he had to get out of town because he killed an old lady.

Everything started to fit in place and after searching for the Indian for a few days he was brought in for questioning and agreed to take a polygraph exam. The test was given, but because of his extremely low intelligence, the examiner found him to be an unfit candidate for the polygraph test. However, the examiner did state that the Indian was very deceptive when questioned about the murder. The suspect was held overnight but had to be released the next day. He was ordered to come in another day to try another polygraph exam, but by this time he had gotten himself a lawyer who advised him not to take it.

The investigating Detectives did a good job, got more evidence against the Indian and tore apart his alibi witness. Several days later the District Attorney's office issued a warrant for first degree murder against the Indian. By this time, he had fled the state and was picked up in Chicago where, for a short period of time, he fought extradition.

He was finally brought back to this state and after a preliminary hearing was bound over to Circuit Court with his jury trial being set for May of 1975.

While all this was going on, Ernie and I were assigned to different cars and involved in our own variety of offenses. This is why we paid very little attention to that particular homicide. Besides that, because it occurred in another district, we were not assigned to the murder, along with the fact that it was cleared by an arrest, and there were several other unsolved homicides by this time.

It was, I believe, the later part of April when Ernie came up to me and said that some gal that we both knew approached him in one of our local gin mills and said that she had a girlfriend—that we also both knew—that had something on her mind that was really bothering her. In fact, she had some information about some old lady that had been beaten to death.

Ernie and I spent the next few days going through some of the old unsolved homicides but couldn't come up with anything. By now we were hearing the same story from other sources—this gal was really starting to crack up. Her husband, who we also knew, had been sent to prison for burglary and she had become a lush.

More and more information came to us from the informers we had in the tavern, including the one that just died. In fact, the only conclusion we could come to was that they were talking about the elderly lady in the tavern. We pulled that report before but had put it back when we saw it was cleared by an arrest. We even talked to the Coppers that handled the investigation and they said it was a good case and it was ready for trial. I later talked to the Indian's attorney and he was trying to get his client to plead guilty to a lesser charge because he thought the state had a very substantial case.

Ernie and I talked it over with a few of the bosses and they said we had no choice but to get the woman in and see what she had to say. Ernie and I both felt that there was more to it than that because we knew that if we brought her in and she asked for an attorney we had absolutely nothing at all. In fact, I wasn't that sure we had anything anyhow. But Ernie wouldn't let it lie still. He said we had to bring her in and find out what happened.

So, almost seven months after the homicide and two weeks before the Indian's trial, Ernie and I went to the woman's upper flat and pounded on the door. After a few minutes and no response we were ready to walk back out, when we heard her voice on the inside asking who was there. We told her Ernie and Jim and she asked what we wanted. By this time my heart was in my stomach and as we opened the door to the darkened flat we could see that she must have been going through hell. She was sober at this time but it looked like she hadn't eaten in days.

She was living in a second floor filthy rat trap with her two children. We could tell that what she was keeping in her mind was more than she could possibly bear, and she was one of the toughest gals I had ever met in my entire life—up to that point. We both knew that our first words and first impressions were critical and it appeared all three of us were struggling with our individual thoughts.

Ernie and I started it out straight and direct. "Joan, we have to talk to you about the old lady that was killed. We know you have something that's been eating you up inside for a long time and we want you to get it off your mind." She hesitated a long time and just by the expression on her face we knew we were on the right track. She never spoke and I continued, "You know we found fingerprints on the bloody doorway and we want you to come downtown and talk the whole thing over with us."

Her first words then came "What about the kids? I'll have to take them some place—who told you about this? Somebody's telling a G.D. lie!" She was falling apart. "Will you guys take me by my girlfriend so I can drop the kids off?" Right then I would have taken the kids anywhere she wanted us to because we knew we were close. We assured her that was no problem and even helped her gather a few things for the kids to take along.

All the way to her girlfriend's house not a thing was said about the crime, only small talk. I knew that both Ernie and I were trying to get our minds straight as to how we were going to start an interrogation. We both knew we had set the original pace by talking about prints in the blood smears even though that was a false statement, but from her reaction we knew she was worried about it. What was even more amazing was that the girlfriend she left her two kids with was the same one that had contacted Ernie and me with the original information.

We got Joan downtown and all three of us entered a small space. An eight foot by eight foot interrogation room, bare of windows, with the only interior decoration being three chairs, a table and a few non-descript phrases left on the walls by previous clientele.

The stage was set. "Joan, just to protect all our interests, I want to explain your rights to you." I went through the Miranda constitutional rights warning quickly and got a few brief nods assuring me that she understood, but didn't really care. She should have, because with her record she must have heard them a dozen times before and judging from her character she must have given previous Coppers a pretty rough time. But this time she was completely broken.

What a stumbling block those Miranda Constitutional Rights have been and how many countless guilty persons have gone free because of them. I know the saying—may a thousand guilty go free rather than one innocent man go to jail. But really, that's about it. Does that really make sense or is it just another phrase to justify a liberal way of thinking? The fact remains that in twenty-five years of Police work I myself have never experienced an innocent man going to jail, but have rather seen many guilty men go free. In fact, this case is just one of those because if Joan would have exercised her rights and not confessed, that poor old Indian would probably have been locked up for a long time.

Anyway, so much for that! I continued, "Joan, a lot of people have been talking about that old lady that was murdered and they all say you know something about it that's been really tearing you up, so we checked the murder file and found some fingerprints on a bloody doorway."

"They can't be mine; I wasn't even in the G.D. room."

That was it. We knew we had her.

"It's Ken, that S.O.B. I told him I didn't want to go along but he made me. He said he'd kick my ass if I didn't. I was scared. He beats the hell out of me all the time so I was scared. We were drunk out of our minds."

The tears were flowing now, she was almost hysterical. "Tell the whole story Joan; tell us everything so we can help you out. If he forced you to help him we can tell it all to the District Attorney. Let's start from the beginning, tell us just the way it happened—don't leave anything out."

"That rotten S.O.B. was drunk and mean. When he was sober he was fine, but when he was drunk he was an animal."

We knew her boyfriend Ken from prior dealings but always thought he was just a petty thief, con man, and a Cop hater. Until she told us, we didn't even know he had been sent to the State Prison for five years for burglary a few months ago. It was important that we get a statement from her. The first statement, even though a lot of the facts that incriminate the person telling the story are left out, gives the investigator something to go on, something that can be picked apart, added to, subtracted from and finally and hopefully come out with as close to possible, the truth.

This is Joan's first statement, signed and given probably within half an hour after we had her in the room and possibly one of the fastest murder confessions I've gotten until I was assigned to homicides, which is a whole separate world.

"On October 16, 1975, at approximately 10:30 p.m. while Johnny Carson was on television, Ken came into the house drunk and told me to get dressed because we were going by the old lady, meaning Verona. I got dressed, got into his car and went to Verona's tavern, arriving about 11:00 or 11:30 p.m. We went to the rear door and after Ken knocked a couple of times he just kicked the door in, snapping the lock off. We went in and it was pitch black. Ken had a flashlight that he used. Verona must have heard the door breaking and asked who was there. We didn't say anything—I was scared. I didn't know what was going through Ken's mind. I thought we came over for a few drinks. I stayed in the kitchen and Ken went into the living room right off the kitchen. I could hear him say something about money and Verona asking him what he wanted and that he should get out.

"Then I could hear rustling of clothes and Verona saying for him to leave her alone. I could see the light moving back and forth on the wall and knew that Ken was probably hitting the poor old lady. She kept pleading, 'Don't hit me, don't hit me, please leave me alone.' I kept yelling at Ken, are you nuts? Are you Crazy? Leave the poor old lady alone."

"Then he yelled for me to get my ass in there and help put the old lady on the couch. I went into the living room and grabbed Verona by the ankles, there was a little light coming in the window from the street lights, I was going crazy, screaming and sobbing, and the dirty bastard kept telling me to shut up.

"I knew Verona was still alive because I could hear her breathing and moaning. I said to him, why the hell did you have to keep hitting her? What the hell's wrong with you? I said, I'm calling an ambulance. Ken just kept telling me to shut up. Then he told me to go through her purse. I did, but didn't take anything. While I was looking through her purse and a desk drawer, Ken grabbed me and said the old lady was dying. I went hysterical. I could feel blood on the floor and on my shoes and I could still hear her moaning. I told Ken I was getting out of there and he grabbed me and said not to fall apart on him now and I said what did he expect?

"I walked out the kitchen door and Ken followed me, carrying a cardboard box with half pints of booze. From the time he kicked in the door until the time we left was only about ten minutes.

"We left the tavern and went to another tavern where Ken sold the half pints. Ken then said that he was going to get some gas and burn everything down. We bought gas and went back to the tavern. I didn't see him go in the rear door but when he came back to the car the gas can was empty.

"After that we went home and Ken passed out, but first kept telling me that if he went to jail, so would I—for the rest of my life."

That was it! That was her statement. She signed it with beautiful handwriting. I suppose that doesn't mean a thing but it again showed me that Joan was a fairly intelligent person, which I suppose also doesn't mean a thing.

Ernie and I knew that she left a lot out of her story but both felt that we had enough for the time being. We told our boss and everybody got excited. Up to this time I don't think anybody believed us. Even to this day when I've been in on dozens of murder confessions, the thrill is beyond description.

It was now about midnight and our boss said that we should go up to the State Prison right then and talk to Ken. Neither Ernie nor I agreed because we had a lot of evidence that we wanted to try and get from Joan's home, but he was the boss so Ernie stayed behind to get the evidence and I and another Detective went to the State Prison.

By the time we got there it was 2:00 a.m. and by the time we got to see Ken it was almost 3:00 a.m. Ken and I passed a few off-hand remarks and then I advised him of his rights and told him why we were there. He said, "You got to be shitting me, that crazy broad's lying. Sure I knew Verona. Joan and I were there many times. I used to help the old lady out. The first I knew she was murdered was the day after on TV." He also said he and Joan were married a couple of months ago in another county by a Justice of the Peace. I thought this would be valuable later because if the marriage was invalid, Joan's statements would be more credible and less open to challenge as being privileged between husband and wife, which, in fact, caused no trouble at the trial.

Ken then told us that he beat Joan on many occasions but that the dirty bitch deserved it and that if we didn't have anything more to say he was going back to bed. What a cold S.O.B. Here I thought he was just a Mickey Mouse thief and not only was he involved in the Verona murder, but we later were contacted by Detectives from Illinois who stated they had information that he may have been involved in the murder of Senator Charles Percy's daughter, but they couldn't prove it and that case remains unsolved to this day.

I told the warden what we had and he said he would put Ken in isolation until he heard from our District Attorney. He also asked me if I was sure Ken was involved because he was not only a trusted prisoner but he had complete access to the entire prison.

By the time we got back to the city Ernie had made arrangements with the city sanitation crew to clean out a sewer. Apparently, Joan had thrown her bloody cloths down there after they left the tavern. We later recovered her bloody jacket and shoes.

Ernie had also gotten a search warrant for Joan's house and there we recovered Ken's jacket still in a cleaning wrapper but with obvious small specks of blood still visible. He also found the flashlight that they used to beat the poor old lady and this not only had visible blood spots, but was dented from the blows.

We went home for a few hours sleep and were back in the District Attorney's office early the next morning. The news media was already there, not because of Joan, but because the Indian was in the County Jail awaiting trial for something he didn't do and this was real news.

It took about three days for the Indian's release and his release included getting a few minor charges dismissed, mainly because of his having been incarcerated for several months. I still believe to this day that the Indian, in all probability, went to the tavern between the time Ken and Joan left the first time for the gas and then came back. I think he actually found Verona tied up and in fact may have taken a few things, but being in such a drunken condition he probably didn't even know what he was doing. And when he told his girlfriend that he had killed the old lady and then flunked the polygraph, he really believed he killed her.

Now started the most important and often the most difficult part of any investigation; proving the case. This District Attorney we had was very methodical, thorough, and very qualified and said that if we didn't get a statement from Ken we had problems with first degree murder because all we had was Joan's statement and she said she didn't actually see Ken hit Verona.

Ernie and I took Joan into a side room at the District Attorney's office and it wasn't but a few minutes later that she now recollected a few other details. This is what I mean about people leaving out part of a story in their original statement, usually trying to downplay their participation.

Joan now recalled that when she picked up Verona's feet, the old lady started to moan so Ken stomped on her chest and after the stomping, Verona just made a gurgling noise. She also stated that a few days later her and Ken were talking about Verona and he said "You know the old lady only had one tit."

This was a fantastic statement because Verona did in fact have a mastectomy and the statement showed that Ken must have searched her body for money or possibly something else—who knows what goes through a demented mind. Joan also added that while she visited Ken in jail in another community he told her to make sure she got his coat dry cleaned and that she shouldn't worry because Verona was just an old broad and so there was no great loss.

We took Joan back into the District Attorney's office and he was pleased with the additional information but still wanted more participation and observations out of Joan rather than base the whole case on a statement made to her by Ken.

We knew Joan was more involved than she was saying but it was really hard pulling it out of her. By now we hadn't had much sleep for a few days and we decided to take a lunch break. This District Attorney was going to call Ken at the State Prison on a conference call line with our boss on the other end of the line, so Ernie and I took Joan to a local Burger King and there, while eating a hamburger, Joan broke down and told the whole story. I still have my original memo book with a splotch of ketchup on her final statement.

She said that after Ken broke in the door they both went into the kitchen and Ken shined the light in Verona's face and said "This is the Police: we're investigating. Where do you have your money? Verona didn't respond so Ken back handed her with the flashlight in the face, knocking her to the floor."

Joan said that's when she left the room and a few minutes later Ken said "Get your ass in here and give me a hand." Joan said she pleaded with him to leave her alone but he insisted that she help him tie-up Verona. She said she was scared and hysterical and tore up a pillow case and tied Verona's hands and feet and that was when Ken stomped on her chest. To this day I still wonder who actually did the stomping.

She went on to relate that they went and got some gasoline, came back and splashed it around in the tavern and then trailed it out the back door back toward the alley. She said she saw Ken throw a match and saw the trail of fire go in the back door.

Now it was finally finished. We felt we now had a good case. The District Attorney was pleased with the new statement and when we talked to Ken that afternoon on the conference call he didn't actually admit to the murder but he did admit that he was there and did admit hitting Verona a few times.

That was it! The case was over for all practical purposes. The next few days Ernie and I finished a few details that the District Attorney wanted done. In fact, we videotaped Joan's statement. This was the first time videotaping a statement was done in Milwaukee and I believe the last, because the operator of the video machine quit.

We then took Joan back to the scene to reconstruct the crime and there was no doubt in anyone's mind that she knew exactly what happened. Ken was charged with first degree murder and arson, and after a four day jury trial he got life plus 20 years consecutive.

Joan was charged with party to a crime and because of her cooperation she received probation with a few days in the House of Correction. It seemed like a small price to pay for such a brutal act, but without her we would have had nothing.

Ernie and I were heroes for about two days and we both thought we should have been made honorable Indians, but the hero status lasted only as long as it took for another team to make a good arrest and then it's all part of the past.

Joan would call every once in awhile, usually when one of her kids got in trouble. I wonder why they got in trouble with such a fantastic mother image! I also heard from her when one of her boyfriends beat her up.

Up until the time I got assigned to the Homicide Squad, which were the most fascinating times of my career, that case was the most interesting I had worked on.

34. Dayshift

Let's see now, where was I? Oh, yes! It was mid 1975 and the Department finally broke up Ernie and me for good. It had been a fantastic association and we're all still good friends to this day.

Carl had gone days and I went through a variety of partners, all good, but none like Ernie and Carl. A good partner is like a brother. We tried to convince Carl to stay nights and wait for us to go days, but we couldn't. Actually, it took me another two years to go days and it took Ernie another four years.

I think what I'm going to have to do is skip over the next few years and if, in fact, any of my former partners that I omit ever get a chance to read this, I'll have to apologize. I'll pick out the good happenings that I can remember until I went days in 1978, and then try and get more detailed again.

Well, here it is, I'm sixty-two years old, have been retired from the Police Department for seven and-a-half years and have been employed as an insurance investigator for all that time. I have been blessed with nine grandchildren and this May will be celebrating forty years married to Marlene and I still haven't finished the doggone book. I have a stack of notes and a thousand memories and I'm determined to get it done.

One last story going back to 1977 with Ernie that I have notes on and I think was kind of interesting. We were sitting at the corner of the bar at the Cobra Club shooting the breeze with Billy, the owner, when we heard a commotion by the rear pool table. Billy asked us to throw out a couple trouble makers. We approached the guys and apparently caught them by surprise, because they all had identifications that matched their description and apparently gave their right addresses. This was unusual in this part of town. We checked them out and none were wanted so we just escorted them out of the bar and went back to our conversation with Billy.

Well, two days later a different Detective Squad was sent to the Cobra Club for a fire bombing and found that someone had thrown a fire bomb through the window and it landed and exploded on the bar right where Ernie and I had been sitting previously. It burned a few of the patrons, one severely, and they all tried to get out the back door but it was locked. Fortunately everyone got out alive and when the Squad got there Billy said someone had looked out the window and saw one of the guys Ernie and I had thrown out running down the street.

The Detectives called for Ernie and I and we had to go downtown to get my memo book from that night with the guys' names and addresses. We then got a 700 Squad and went to the house address I wrote in my memo book from checking the I.D.s a couple days earlier. Ernie and a couple Coppers went to the rear of the house and I and another Copper went to the front. Well, they must have seen us coming up the porch, because by the time I looked in the front door window I saw the guy running towards the back of the house. We smashed the door open and by the time the guy was at the rear kitchen door I was all over him. I knocked him to the floor and the other Copper was handcuffing him and, believe it or not, the guy's clothes were full of gas. He was a real asshole and fought and screamed and cussed and the more trouble he caused the more people got involved, and by the time it was all over four other people went to jail.

The next day we took his picture around and found a clerk at a gas station down the block from the tavern that remembered selling him gas. The District Attorney issued arson, attempted murder and four counts of endangering safety—and the guy got ten years.

Talk about a strange world; twenty-three years later I was sitting in court to testify in an insurance related case and this same guy was called as a defendant in another case. I didn't recognize him right away but I did recognize the unusual name, and once he walked in front of me I knew it was the same guy.

It sure pays to be in the right place. This way Ernie and I were heroes again and if we had been sitting at the bar when he threw the fire bomb we would not only have been burned, but we probably would have been fired.

I think that was the year that I was second in the Bureau in overtime. I never wanted to be first because that name always got in the paper and the bosses always got on the guy and cut his hours. Second was good enough for me and the money sure helped at home. I think that year I made twenty-one thousand dollars and that included probably fifteen hundred hours in overtime, so you can imagine what our base salary was.

I don't know if I ever mentioned anything about plant jobs that went on every night. These were still left over from the days of the riots in 1967, and involved early and late shift plants at the Chief's house, Mayor's house, several Judges and a couple of Detectives that had been threatened. At least one or two nights a week were spent sitting in a Squad—one in front of the house and one behind—for the entire eight hours. Those were the longest nights of my career and a thousand stories came out of those plant jobs—most of which I couldn't tell and the rest nobody would believe anyway. But let me just say that nobody got killed, hurt, or fired during those plant jobs and I think I'll leave it at that.

My time finally came and I went days after twenty-one and-a-half years working nights. I owed it to my family, who stood by me all those years. Karen was nineteen and working full time, Kristie was seventeen and going into her senior year of high school and Jeff was fifteen and just about to enter high school. They all grew up with me nights and Marlene raising them, and she did a good job. Most Copper's families are usually separated or divorced and Carl's and Ernie's families were the exceptions, and all our kids were really close. In fact, we still get together with all the kids and now grandkids once a year and at the last count there were forty-three of us. We see each other at weddings and, sadly, at funerals.

I can recall the first few days I worked the day shift. After supper I would read the paper and do a few things around the house and then settle down for some TV and suddenly I realized that there was no room for me. Everyone had their spot and I wound up on the floor. I had to knock down two walls and add on more square feet in the family room just so I could get my own chair!

I found that working the day shift was a completely different job, and a completely different way of life. It was more relaxed, less violent crimes, older and more established partners and a huge cut in overtime. For the next few years I was assigned with Jerry, who was a very devoted family man, and a much underrated Copper. We had some good years together, cleared some crime, sent some bad guys to jail and generally kept a work good pace.

35. The Bembenek Case

Up until that time, the only specialized Squads were the Robbery Squad and the forgery Squad. Most other crimes, including homicides, were handled by the Detective Squad that covered that particular district or geographical area; or they would assign a specific lieutenant to the case and he would pick several Detectives to handle the case with him.

One of these murders came up on my off day in May of 1981. I didn't realize it at the time, but it would have a big impact on my career and I would spend hundreds of hours and travel thousands of miles working the case. Furthermore, this case still made news even after I retired.

It was the Christine Schultz homicide. Christine Schultz was the estranged wife of Alfred Schultz, who was a Milwaukee Detective. Alfred was now married to Lawrencia Bembenek who also had been a Police Officer but had been fired during her probationary year for getting caught passing a joint during a rock concert. I really never had much contact with either one of them. I met Fred maybe once or twice and never had much more than a brief conversation with Laurie. The fact that their life styles were completely different than mine, and the fact that we worked different shifts also played a part.

The only thing I have in my memo book is that I came to work on May 30th and was assigned, along with many others, to the homicide. I also noted that the victim had two children, ages seven and eleven, which were also Fred's kids. Christine was shot with either a 38 or 357 caliber gun in the upper right back. The bullet ricocheted off her collar bone, and traveled through her heart, lodging in her chest. I noted that the suspect was a white male, five-foot-eight-inches tall, heavy build with a six-inch pony tail, green jogging suit and wore a ski mask. I also recall that Fred was working the night of the murder with Mike, and that they were at a District Stations doing reports when he was notified of the shooting of his ex-wife.

Fred and Mike went to the victim's house, and after a short period of time they were sent to notify Laurie. Mike was responsible for checking Fred's off-duty gun. They apparently did go to the Schultz's apartment and supposedly woke Laurie. Mike checked Fred's gun and later wrote a report that he didn't think it had been fired, but noticed dust on the cylinder. Mike did not write down the serial number of Fred's gun—big mistake!

The next few weeks I spent a good deal of time interviewing neighbors, friends and relatives of Fred, Laurie, and Christine—including Christine's lawyer who said she had come to him for the divorce, and said Fred had threatened to kill her and that she was afraid of him.

The Department had Fred working days, and on the 18th of June 1981, a lieutenant named Karl, who was in charge of the murder investigation, sent Fred and I to the murder scene just to check the whole house over to find out if Fred could notice anything out of the ordinary. Fred had already taken a polygraph test and passed. Laurie had refused to take a polygraph and because of that and other inconsistencies in their stories, Laurie had become a prime suspect.

We spent several hours in the home of the murder without finding anything unusual, when Karl told me we should settle one thing once and for all. I should take Fred's off-duty gun and his service revolver to the crime lab and have them checked against the slug recovered from Christine's body. Fred heard the whole conversation, and as I recall, didn't make anything of it. He said we would have to go to Laurie's parent's house where they were staying to pick up his off-duty gun.

We went to the house and Fred went in and came out and gave me a 38 Smith and Wesson snub nose revolver in a black holster. I placed it in my brief case. He then said that Laurie wasn't home; she was probably jogging and we should look for her. We found her a block away. I pulled into an alleyway and Fred immediately jumped out and ran to Laurie and they talked for a few minutes. I'm sure that he told her what we were going to do, and then he came back to the car and said we should stop back at the house and I could meet Laurie.

Back at the house the conversation was mainly about Laurie's modeling career. She showed me a portfolio that she had prepared and, at that point, Fred asked if I wanted a beer. That was my famous beer—and I almost took a rap for that one beer. The rest of the conversation was mostly Laurie talking, and like I explained to Marlene when I got home, I'm not a prude, but Laurie had the filthiest mouth I had ever heard from a woman. Each time she would come out with one of her expletives, Fred would hit my arm and say, "Isn't she great? Now you know why I love her!"

As we left the residence she made one last comment that I later testified to, "Why would I kill that broad? Then I'd have to take care of those rug rats."

Well, we went to the crime lab with both the guns, and I inventoried and took down their serial numbers and gave them to Monty, the fire arms examiner, and we went to a waiting room for what seemed to be an extraordinarily long time. Finally, Monty came out and said to me that he wanted to see me alone. He took me out of the room and said he had found blood on the end of Fred's service revolver and also blood in his holster. Let me tell you, my heart started to pump and I realized that he and I were both Detectives, so I called my boss Karl; and, he and his partner—also a lieutenant—came out to the lab. They talked to Fred for a while and then to Monty, who said he needed a certain brand of bullet for testing because it was that kind of bullet that was used to kill Christine. He said this brand of bullet was somewhat rare and he didn't have any in his vast collection. Fred said that he had some at Christine's house, so we went and got them and brought them to Monty. It turned out later that Fred's off duty gun was determined to be the murder weapon.

I'll never forget the ride back to the building after the crime lab. I was driving the Squad with Fred as a passenger and with Karl and his partner in a Squad in front of us. Naturally, Fred didn't have a gun because it was at the crime lab. Then he suddenly started to wail and moan and pound his fist and head on the dash board. I reached over and got a grip on his suit coat because I thought he was going to take a header out the Squad. To this day, I really feel that at that moment, he realized Laurie killed his ex-wife.

Little did I know that the Christine Schultz case would occupy a good deal of my time from that date until I retired some nine years later. Bembeneck had been a good suspect right after the murder when Fred passed a polygraph exam and Laurie refused to take one.

Most of 1981 was spent on the Schultz murder when time permitted and, several weeks after the gun incident, Laurie was charged with first degree murder. At the time of the autopsy a fiber was found on Christine's leg and several human hairs were found on the scarf that gagged her mouth. A wig was found by a plumber that was pulled from a clogged drain in the apartment that Laurie and Fred shared with the fiber found on Christine's leg matching the wig. When Laurie was arrested at Marquette University where she worked as a security guard, a hair brush was found in her locker and hair from that brush matched a hair taken from the scarf gag.

These things, along with other circumstantial evidence, were what the State had for their case. Laurie subsequently hired a famous lawyer out of Madison, and after the preliminary was held, she was bound over for trial. She then posted bail and the trial was set for the first part of 1982.

The Homicide Squad

36. The Homicide Squad

About a month before the Bembeneck trial was to start I came to work and Karl, the lieutenant, said I along with six other Detectives were assigned to a new Homicide Squad that would be in place for several months during January, February and March of 1982. He stated that when vacations started we would go back to our old Squad. It seemed like a nice variation for a few months and sounded interesting. Little did I know that it would change my whole life. A whole new career! Trips all over the United States, exposure to the media, fantastic cases, top District Attorneys, and unlimited overtime.

The emotional pressures of working every day on Homicides was beyond description. The highs and the lows that I must have brought home every night really never struck me until I retired and Marlene told me how it affected the entire family. I suppose thinking it over, it must have been as dramatic an experience for my entire family as it was for me. Hours would run into days, into weeks, into months and many times we would go home—just because that was the thing to do but I could hardly wait to get back to work. Let me describe as best I can what the Squad was all about and a little bit about the original group.

The original objective was to pull out old homicides that had been put aside for any number of reasons: lack of evidence, lack of man power to investigate, or sometimes the case would just turn cold. The way homicides had been worked on in the past and who they were assigned to was more or less by Squad district. In other words, if a murder happened in the Squad district that you were working that particular shift, either your Squad or the Robbery Squad usually got assigned. And if you and your partner happened to be relieving on that Squad that particular night, you would generally work it for a few days and if nothing developed and it wasn't a high profile case, it just simply got set aside.

The way the Homicide Squad was set-up was we would meet every morning and take an old case and sit around a large wooden table in what then became the Homicide Room. We would take turns reading the entire file from front to back. Each Detective would take notes and when the file had been completely read we would each bring out our individual points and one Detective would list all the points and then we would sit and hash over the whole file.

What became apparent, right from the start, was that each Detective had strong opinions and even stronger work ethics. I don't know how Karl picked us all out, but it was quite a group. It also became apparent that many cases were abandoned for some unknown reason, when they actually were very close to being solved. I remember the criticisms made after reading five or six hundred pages; the answers were there but never developed.

I also remember saying that we shouldn't be too critical because the same thing may happen to us in years to come when our work may be scrutinized. And, yes, that did come to pass. But let me describe the original members of the Squad. The unit was headed by Lieutenant Karl, a full-blooded Italian that had risen through the ranks and had spent a good deal of time in internal affairs before coming to the bureau. He was sharp, fair, and above all, knew how to handle our distinct personalities.

There was myself and another Jim, who was a fairly new Detective and was low key but had a lot to add to the unit. Pat was one that had been picked by Karl because of his vast crop of informants. The guy was an outstanding Detective that really didn't want to work the day shift because it cramped his style. For the next five months he and I were partners and I learned a great deal from him.

Then there was Tom. He would wind up being my partner for many years until he died at age forty-nine. He was a legend in his own right. His dad was an Inspector of Detectives that had retired and his brother was a uniform Cop. Tom was divorced for many years and he had raised his four children. Our life styles were like night and day, but he was an unbelievable Cop.

There was also Rosie, whose first name was Roosevelt, but everyone called him Rosie. He was the only African-American on the Squad. Rosie was raised in Milwaukee and was a star athlete from one of the local high schools. He always described growing up in the inner city of Milwaukee. He said that all his friends either became Cops, lawyers, or went to jail. He had a large build, a large ego and was extremely intimidating. He had this zeal and determination for solving murders and he was good at it. He was also controversial and didn't particularly care what anyone thought of him or his tactics. Off the job, he was the perfect gentleman, and Marlene and my kids thought nothing but the best of him.

Then there was Ray. We thought he was picked because he was related by marriage to the Chief, but in fact he was a good steady Copper who wound up heading the Homicide Squad in future years.

Last but not least was Mike—a very large domineering man who was a Vietnam veteran and bomb and explosives expert. I knew him as a uniform man when Ernie, Carl and I were together and he also was a good Copper who added a lot of expertise to the Squad.

That was it—that was the Homicide Squad of the Milwaukee Police Department for the next five months. During that time we handled a number of interesting homicides and I'll mention just a few, because over the next years I was involved in over eight hundred homicide investigations in one way or another.

I remember one of the first cases involved Edna and Jason, which was a particularly brutal murder. Edna was twenty-eight-years-old and lived in a second floor apartment in the inner city with her two sons; Jason was four years old and there was also a baby. They had not been seen or heard from for several days and were discovered by a downstairs neighbor.

Edna was stabbed numerous times with a screw driver that was left in her neck, and Jason was stabbed once in the back, once in the shoulder, and twice through his skull. The baby was still in the crib and appeared unharmed even after having been there for several days, with what we thought had been without food or water.

As it turned out, the neighbor guys downstairs had apparently discovered the bodies right after the murders, but spent a few days stepping over the bodies to ransack and remove most of her property. Besides that, the father of the baby apparently also discovered the bodies and spent a few days coming back and feeding the baby while the two bodies were left to rot.

Neither the neighbors nor the father were ever charged with anything and before we could arrest the cousin of the victim, who was our prime suspect, he was killed in a shoot out. I think the case is either still open or in later years someone made it an exceptional clearance.

This brings another thought to mind. I remember how our clearance rate on homicides would vary between eighty and ninety percent and how both the Department and our Homicide Squad were proud of those statistics. And as the years went by and I accepted these figures, I realized that meant ten to twenty percent of the years' murderers were still on the street, and I wondered how the families of the victims must have felt.

I also remember when the TV series *NYPD Blue* and several other homicide shows started. They would have a dry-erase board that they kept track of the homicides and who was assigned. We also had such a board and every New Years Day, we all worked—it was time-and-a-half and we would come in and wipe the board clear to start the New Year clean. That didn't mean that the old homicides were left alone, but they sure were put on the back burner.

Anyhow, at the same time we were investigating the Edna and Jason homicides, I was in court practically every day on an old case, and also preparing for the Bembenek trial that was supposed to start in a few days.

At the same time, we got assigned a new homicide that involved a son killing his mother, and that took several days because he fled after the killing and was subsequently brought in by his lawyer. I recall this one specifically because when I questioned him about the murder, I also advised him of his rights and the fact that he had an attorney, and in fact the attorney brought him in. I specifically asked him what his attorney said, and the subject said his attorney told him to tell me anything I wanted to know. So this resulted in a complete confession and subsequent conviction for first degree murder. There weren't too many lawyers like that around.

Looking back in my memo book, I remember that just prior to the Bembenek trial we had a double murder of a big time drug dealer and his girlfriend. They were both found shot to death in their residence, one in the back hall and one in the kitchen. It appeared that the dealer answered the rear door and was killed immediately, and then the actors went to the kitchen and shot his girlfriend. This case lasted months on end and involved some of the big time drug dealers in the city. Names like "Coons," "Chicago Al," "YC," "June Bug," "JB" and a host of others. Pat was my partner at that time and he knew every scum bag, dope peddling dealer, and after-hours joint in the city and we visited them all. This was another one of those murders where everyone knew who did it, but no one would come forward. The case just dragged on and on for years.

In fact, several years later when Tom and I were partners, we spent a week in Iowa interviewing people and recovering clothing and other evidence from that same case. Ironically, after I retired, Mar and I were watching some exposé TV show like *Hard Copy* or something else, and they were talking to some people and they referred to this same murder and how the Police never followed-up on information, which included interviewing witnesses in Iowa.

I wasn't paying that much attention to the show, but Mar said, "Didn't you and Tom spend a lot of time in Iowa on that case and bring back a lot of evidence?" I then started to pay more attention and realized they were talking about the double murder. Their facts were totally wrong. Throughout the years I found a great deal of misinformation in the media. Can you believe that?

Two days before the Bembenek trial started, we had an unusual murder. Three guys got together to do their drug thing, and one thing lead to another, and two of the guys strangled the third. This in itself wasn't that unusual, but when they shoved the body under a bed and called their friends over to show it off, and then threw the body out the second floor window but couldn't get it into a car because rigor mortis had started to set in—that's what made it unusual.

That murder was cleared in a day because it was the talk of the neighborhood. When we took the confessions, there was no remorse, only regrets that they had showed off the body and bragged about it.

I think it was the same day we took the two subjects to the D.A. who issued first degree murder and robbery on both of them, that the Bembenek trial started and the jury was picked.

37. The Bembeneck Trial

This was a trial that had gained national attention and the media stormed the courtroom. There were 144 seats in the courtroom and every day the hallways were packed with spectators waiting to get in. Marlene and her girlfriend spent a few days there and somehow they were able to get seats.

The trial started in the Circuit Court of Milwaukee and the presiding Judge was a former Assistant District Attorney, who was well respected by both sides. He was a no nonsense Judge that had complete control of the courtroom at all times.

The prosecutor could only be described as a very low-key individual of fairly large stature with a full beard. He had been assigned to the Bembenek case and had done his homework. He was well prepared, as were his witnesses.

The Defense Attorney could not have been more opposite. He was an attorney out of the state capitol area that dressed to the hilt, and matched his flamboyant demeanor with a large amount of jewelry and theatrics.

The jury consisted of seven women and five men with two alternates. The only charge was first degree murder with the penalty being life with parole eligibility in eleven years and three months. I still say to this day that the Defense Attorney misjudged the people of Milwaukee, and especially the jury.

I testified the seventh day of the trial, and only for about an hour and a half. My whole testimony was about the gun and my conversation with Bembenek and Schultz, and the results of our trip to the crime lab. Her lawyer tried to make an issue out of the fact that at the crime lab, I had taken the time to record the serial numbers of the guns. He did this to cast doubt on the Detective that first went to the house with Freddie, the night of the murder and found the gun, and said it had not been fired, but failed to take down the serial number. I was just about to step down from the stand when the defense attorney said in a casual manor, "Oh, by the way Detective, isn't it a fact that while you were at the Bembenek residence and on duty that you had several beers?"

Well, I wasn't really surprised that he asked the question and I sure as hell wasn't going to correct him and say it was only one beer, so I just said, "Yes."

He said, "Thank you and no further questions."

I thought the testimony went well and the beer subject would not be an issue and so did Marlene. But the next day Pat and I were on our way to the Federal prison in Minnesota to conduct an interview. I was driving and Pat was reading the latest Bembenek news when he casually said. "Uh-oh;

I think you're in a little bit of trouble." The news media made an issue of the beer and by the time we got back several days later, the shit had hit the proverbial fan. The Chief at that time thought the whole thing was kind of amusing, the Inspector of Police wanted me charged, and the head of the Bureau quit talking to me for the next several weeks until the whole thing was dropped. I had to write a "Matter Of" in which I indicated that the only reason I took a beer was to relax a tense situation and gain the confidence of the people I was with.

Actually, having a drink on duty in those days was not that unusual. When I told Mar that I may take a rap for the beer, all she said was that if I do get charged, I should just take the time off and not complain because of all the things my partners and I did throughout the years and never got caught—nothing illegal mind you—just goofing around. She always was a smart lady.

The case itself was circumstantial and yet fairly simple. Bembenek did not have an alibi for the night of the murder. The gun that was used was the off-duty gun of her husband's and was in her residence the night of the murder. The actor was masked and had either a wig or a pony tail, and a wig was later recovered from the drain of the bathroom where Bembenek and Schultz lived. Also, a fiber found on the victim's leg was consistent with the wig, and a hair found on the gag of the victim matched a hair taken off a hairbrush belonging to Bembenek at the time of her arrest.

There were a multitude of other issues for both the prosecution and the defense, but that was the basics of the case and what the jury later said they concentrated on. The trial lasted two weeks and between the press and writers and spectators, they left the courtroom and hallways in shambles every night.

After four days of deliberation and several requests to view evidence and have testimony read back, many felt that the jury would come back hung. On the fifth day the jury came back with a guilty verdict and Bembenek was immediately sentenced to life in prison, and was taken there that same afternoon.

Everyone in the courtroom seemed stunned that it was finally over. Bembenek stayed very composed as the verdict was read and the sentence pronounced. Schultz broke down and sobbed on his father's shoulders and Bembenek's mother, father and sister were in tears. Several members of the jury were interviewed after the trial and those that would talk said the deciding factor was the gun, and how they felt Bembenek was the only one to have access to it, and without the gun there was no case. They also said that the first vote upon selecting a Foreman was six guilty, with five of those six being women and six unsure. The subsequent verdict was unanimous, as it had to be, and throughout the years to my knowledge none of the jurors have ever changed their mind.

After the trial ended and I got back in good graces with the bosses—after my little drinking episode with the Schultz's—I thought that would end my involvement in the Bembenek case. Little did I know at the time that the case would follow me for the rest of my career.

And even now, having been retired for fifteen years, Bembenek is still in the news trying to have her conviction overturned.

38. Solving the Unsolved ... and More

So it was back to pulling unsolved murders and reading the files from beginning to end. One day someone had pulled a file while I was out of the room, and when I went back in, I didn't hear the victims name or the address. What we would ordinarily do was read the face sheet of the complaint, which included the victim's name, date and time of the offense, Squads sent, cause of death and so on. It wasn't until we started to get into the evidence portion of the file, and where the body was found, that I suddenly realized I knew the victim—at least I had met him before.

He was an elderly gentleman in his late seventies that lived in the heart of the inner city. I recalled to the other guys that about a year ago I had investigated a burglary at his house and found the home secured like a fortress. All the basement windows were barred, the first floor windows had heavy mesh wire and all the doors were dead bolted with several locks. The actors used bodily force on the rear door and just took some small items, causing more damage than anything else. What I found interesting at the time was the old-timer had thousands of dollars in tools in the basement. He was an avid wood worker and a real true craftsman from the old country. He took great pride in showing me all the fancy cabinets and wooden figurines and plates that he had made. You could see this had been his whole life. He and his wife had lived there for forty-five years and she had died several years earlier.

His family had been trying to get him to move out, but this was his homestead. The poor old guy was found behind his car in the garage with the door open. According to the autopsy he had been beaten to death with a two-by-four that was still at the scene. He was beaten so hard that wood slivers were embedded in his head. His body was also bruised and his eyes swollen with black and blue bruises from the savage beating.

This one really bothered me and all of us took an interest in it. The file was fairly thin and was probably one of those that were handled by several Detectives and uniform personnel that lost track of the case after several days, either by lack of interest, or being assigned to another area or whatever. I say this because four of us went out and started talking to the neighbors and it was just like, "What took you so long to get here?"

In the first block we had three people that had first names of several people involved. By the time we went back to the Bureau that night we had three in custody, and by the time we went home we had confessions.

It seems the old guy just went to open his garage door and a few punks asked him for money. When he said he didn't have any—which he didn't—according to the statements, they beat him to death with the two-by-four and then kicked and stomped him until he quit breathing. Then they went to the playground, shot some craps and bragged about killing the old white guy.

It was about that time in my career when I took my first of many extended trips around the country. Pat and I flew to Virginia to interview someone in the Federal Penitentiary. The per diem paid by the D.A.'s office at that time was forty-nine dollars a day plus hotel and miscellaneous expenses.

I could write a book just on my trips and the expense money. But on this particular trip we took a side trip to Hilton Head and had lunch on the veranda. We watched the people that could afford to be there, tee off and putt on beautiful greens. Reality set in when we got the bill and we had spent our entire allotment of meal money for two days in one sitting! But the trip was good and made me realize that this Homicide Squad was a pretty good deal.

When we got back, it was time to end the Homicide Squad for the summer, and we all got ready to go back to our own shifts and Squads. I was hoping that the next fall I would be chosen for another couple months of Homicide investigations.

The next day, when we all came to work, Karl announced that the Homicide Squad was going to be made permanent with four Detectives and himself. That's how Tom and I became partners for the next eight years, and Rosie and Ray ended up working together. Ray became the book man and record keeper for most of the time, and Rosie either worked by himself or rode along with Tom and me.

I think I mentioned it before, but it needs repeating that Tom and I had absolutely nothing in common as far as our personal lives, but we made a good team until his untimely death eight years later. All four of us were strong willed and opinionated, but rarely clashed for more than a short period of time. I have to give credit to our boss Karl for keeping us in line, which had to be almost a full-time job in itself.

We spent endless hours reading reports, going to court and the D.A.'s office on almost a daily basis, and interviewing hundreds of witnesses and neighbors. We thought we were really making a difference in the number of homicides committed during our first full year, because they dropped off rapidly. But reality set in the following years, and I came to realize that all the laws and other methods of prevention can never stop a homicide. Take away the guns and knives and other weapons and people will still find a way to kill another human being. In fact, many of the methods were really bizarre.

Sometimes it takes months or years for partners to get comfortable with each other during interviews and interrogations. You try and not interrupt during the questioning, but it becomes hard when you feel the right question is not being asked. You have to trust your partner that he knows which way to do the questioning and always give your partner a chance to get his two words in.

Tom and I had a good feel for each other, and several weeks after we started to work together we took our first really good confession together. Now, normally a confession is not all that hard if you have witnesses or good physical evidence, but some can be really tough, especially when you know you have the right person and you just can't get the truth out.

This particular investigation started when two old ladies were cutting their grass in front of their houses. They noticed a foul smell coming from the trunk of the vehicle that had been parked in front of their house for several days. They called the Squad and before the car was towed, they pried open the trunk, and sure enough—there wrapped in a rug and bound with rope was the remains of Pitacio. He had been beaten to death about a week earlier and was really ripe. The cause of death was a skull fracture caused by a blunt object, and also defensive blows to his arms and sides.

We started out by picking up his girlfriend and several other friends who gave us the name of Wally, and where to find him. We picked up Wally and just by his actions and demeanor, thought we might have the right guy. We advised him of his rights, gave him a sandwich and cup of coffee and spent the next five or six hours going over every aspect of his life for the past two weeks. By the time we were done we knew we had the right guy, but he just wouldn't kick in.

We were just about to give up and take him back to the holding room when, as we were walking out the door and just about had it closed, one of us gave it one last shot and said, "That's your last chance for any type of self-defense. We're going to the D.A. and looking for first degree murder."

The door was just about closed when Wally said, "What can I get if it was self-defense?" and we knew we had him.

He then gave a full confession and told us that he and Pitacio argued over money that Pitacio owed him for car work, so he picked up a metal bar and beat Pitacio over the head until he was dead. This all happened in Pitacio's house and before leaving with a couple of TV's, Wally used a mop to clean up the blood from the floor and then took a rug from the bedroom and wrapped Pitacio in it. Then he cut up some rope, tied Pitacio in the rug and dragged him out and put him in the trunk of Pitacio's car.

By now it was midnight and we took Wally back to his cell, wrote reports till three, went home and started again at seven in the morning. We got Wally out of the cell and took him to Pitacio's house where Wally pointed out the mop, bucket of water, TV stand, piece of rope and the knife he used to cut the rope. We recovered all this evidence and then recovered a TV from his girlfriend's house and another one from his house, and just prior to taking him back to jail he showed us the garbage can where he threw the lead pipe.

After dropping him off we went back and searched all the garbage cans in the area and then, at the request of the assistant D.A., got a search warrant for the city dump fill sight to try and find the pipe. We went to the sight and told the manager what we were looking for and he gave us a strange look. He pointed to a pile of trash and dirt that conservatively measured a hundred yards long and wide by about fifty feet high. We just got back in the Squad and returned the search warrant. Wally pled to second-degree murder and got about twenty-five years, and in all probability is either dead, in prison for something else or back on the street.

It's amazing how busy we were. Every day we would spend at least a little time reading reports on every homicide, cleared or open. And these were just the murders; the attempts were probably ten to one.

Like I said earlier, I'm just going to write about the most interesting cases. Throughout the years, I went through my memo books and made endless notes, and now going back over the books, they bring back a lot of memories.

I recall several Detectives coming from Detroit to look for a murder suspect. We talked over lunch and they said they had over five hundred homicides at that time of year; we had only about eighty. I pointed out to them that they had a Homicide Squad of two-hundred-fifty, while we still had only four and Karl as our Lieutenant.

I also recall that it was about this time that we had a particularly gruesome case in which a drug dealer was taken to a vacant home, bound from the top of his head to his ankles in clear tape and then shot in the head. Tom and I had the autopsy and brought back what we called the death mask and laid it on the big oak table in the homicide room prior to inventorying it. Well, someone suggested ordering out for chili and as we sat around the bloody mask eating our chili, we suddenly became aware that maybe we were getting a little callous. That one remained unsolved along with another drug murder that we were sure we knew the right guy, but could never prove it. We had him in numerous times, but he always had his high price lawyer with him.

Lots of people get away with murder. Like the young man who was coming home from work and stopped for a six pack of beer. On the way home, four males tried to grab the beer and when he resisted, one of them shot him right threw the can of beer, into his chest and killing him on the spot. One of the four was picked up and gave Tom and me a full confession and named the other three, including his brother. He said after the shooting they ran down the alley, and then came back when they saw all the red lights and watched the Police conduct their investigation. We subsequently picked up all four and they all gave different alibis and locations where they were. The case fell apart when the first subject changed his whole story. His mother testified that he was home all night and had a mental problem, and had lied numerous times in the past.

When we couldn't put the case together, the charges were dismissed and I believe the case remains open to this date, mainly because we had the right guys, but couldn't prove it. I hate to say it, but the murder was not a high priority that generated a lot of publicity.

One thing I do remember about the four individuals was that one became an assistant manager at a Burger King we frequented. One went to jail for an armed robbery and attempted murder and one we arrested for the murder of an old lady several years later. (I'll refer to her as "Betty" and I'll write about that case later because it was really interesting.) The fourth individual, who was the original informant, wound up in a mental institution for the criminally insane.

On one of the following days, we were sent to a possible homicide in a flop house on the south side. The victim was found in his bathroom with his pants around his ankles and a belt around his neck, slumped to the floor and wedged between the toilet and tub. The doors and windows were all locked from the inside and there was no forced entry. We immediately started looking for roommates and questioned all the other residents of this deplorably filthy, run down, so-called apartment, and found nothing.

We were just getting prepared for a long investigation when we got a call from the Medical Examiner that the individual had died of natural causes, with contributing causes being scleroses of the liver and extreme heart disease.

Putting the whole thing together, we decided that the subject was in the bathroom getting dressed and had put the belt around his neck while he put on his pants when he had a heart attack, fell to the floor and as he fell the belt wrapped around his neck. About ten hours of work and thirty pages of reports, and all we had was a sudden death.

Another unsolved murder involved Angie, a five-foot-six-inch, one-hundred-fiftyfive-pound black dancer and hooker that had a lengthy record, but didn't deserve to die in a backyard with a forty-pound block of concrete covering her head that buried it six inches in the ground. Evidence showed that the murder was probably committed by one of her many boyfriends and her body was found in the backyard where one of them used to live. About a year later another black female hooker was also found at a construction site when they were clearing the area for a new store. Her body was completely decomposed and identification had to be made through her teeth. She was killed by the same boyfriend and he got away with both murders.

Tom and I worked on those two murders off and on for about two years. We questioned, followed and harassed one of the boyfriends until he filed a complaint with the Department, D.A.'s office and anyone else that would listen. I carried his picture in my book until the day I retired and know to this day that there were no witnesses to the murders and no physical evidence to convict him, but as sure as their bodies are in the ground, he put them there. What's even more troubling on those cases is that his white girlfriend, who was a nurse, knew all about the murders but was too scared to talk. We promised her practically anything but all she would do was stare at the ground until she would sob uncontrollably, get her composure and then tell us to leave. Now that I look back through my memo books, it's amazing how many murders went unsolved. Apparently it's not like *NYPD Blue* after all.

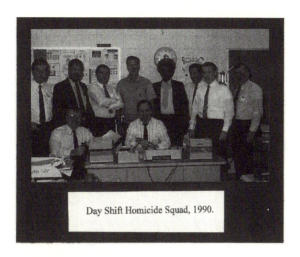

Day Shift Homicide Squad, 1990.

Keeping track of the yearly homicide total with Elvira.

On the job in the 1980's.

39. Fresh Murders

By now it was the summer of 1983, and Summerfest—Milwaukee's ten-day long festival of music and food held on the lakefront—had just ended the night before with a banner year. I came to work Monday morning with a ton of reports waiting to be done from the weekend. I barely got punched in and got my cup of coffee when Karl came to the back room and said, "Well, we got three new ones."

The first one was a shooting with the suspect named and the late shift was out looking for him. The second was a stabbing in which the suspect wasn't named, but they had an Illinois license plate and a good description of three people in the car along with several children. This one also appeared cut and dry. I volunteered for either one, but Karl just laughed and said, "Get your ass down to the Summerfest grounds and meet the late shift Detectives."

There on the ground lay Debbie, a windbreaker tied around her waist with her blouse open, bra cut and stab wounds to both breasts. Her slacks were also cut open and part of her body was cut away, probably when the actor sliced her pants. The autopsy would later show that the cut to the body was probably post mortem and she was sexually assaulted after death.

The late shift Coppers had a suspect in custody, but it turned out he was just some drunken student from the local university that happened to fall asleep under the overpass about thirty feet from where Debbie was found. He didn't see or hear anything and after a check with his buddies and a line-up with potential witnesses, he was let go.

Debbie was a 29-year-old divorcee with two children that were staying with their father for the summer. She worked in a factory and lived with her boyfriend for the past two years. She was born and raised in northern Wisconsin and came to Summerfest with her mother, her mother's boyfriend, her sister and her sister's husband. After Summerfest closed they went to a bar a few blocks away and her relatives left her at the bar before closing time. She was with a white male truck driver named Don from Texas, who had a southern accent. That's it.

My memo book says in the next few days we must have interviewed forty people and after all that time we still had nothing more than a white male named Don with a southern accent. Tom and I sent teletypes all over the Midwest and received a ton of calls. We traveled throughout Illinois, Indiana, Michigan, Iowa and most of Wisconsin and showed the witnesses a ton of pictures of the victim, but still all we had was a white male truck driver named Don with a southern accent. I remember a couple of years later we received information about a driver that was in Milwaukee about the time of Debbie's murder; in fact his name was Don and he had a slight accent.

We again showed his photo to all the witnesses and even drove to northern Wisconsin to show the photos to Debbie's relatives, but by now all their memories were foggy and we came up with the same negative results.

I suppose you wonder why so many murders go unsolved. Well so did I, but the fact remains that there were just not enough hours in the day or days in the week and when the investigation got cold, it took a back burner to the new cases.

Carrie Ann was a little nine-year-old girl who lived on the south side with her mother—who was divorced from her father—and her older brother. She apparently was a nice little girl who got in the normal trouble for a nine-year-old, and didn't live in the most flourishing of neighborhoods. In this day and age she probably would have been the perfect child. Well, on March 16, 1982, she was sent home from school for some minor disturbance. Since she only lived a block from school, I'm sure the teacher had no real concerns about her arriving home safely. She never got home.

The Police were called and because of her age, and the fact she had never been missing before, an all out search was put under way. After several weeks of searching by the uniform Police and the Youth Aid Bureau, and several supposed sightings by her friends and neighborhood kids, the search was then assigned to one youth aid team.

On September 4, 1983, the day before my birthday, Tom and I were sent to a grisly sight. Carrie was not missing anymore; she had probably died the day she was sent home from school.

Her mother had the rear porch torn down at their home and the carpenter was digging footings, when he came upon a pile of bones lying under the porch and covered with about a foot of dirt. By the time we got there it was obvious that the carpenter had taken several shovels full of dirt and bones, before he realized what he had found. Tom and I started to dig around the bones and clothing with our hands and small tools, and then waited for the Medical Examiner. The excavation of the remains and the collection of the clothing, bones and dirt samples took at least ten hours. It was tedious work in that we didn't want to destroy any possible evidence.

We made it a homicide because she most certainly didn't bury herself, and because all that was left were bones, no cause of death could be made with any certainty. At that time, Milwaukee County had one of the most inept assistant Medical Examiner's possible, which I'll address later. Some of the damage to the bones was first thought to be from a blunt object, but was later determined to be from the carpenters shovel. The news media went wild and started to accuse everyone from the family, to the school officials, to the Police Department.

Now the Homicide Squad had the investigation and we started by reading all the missing reports filed by the Youth Aid Bureau. Carrie's teacher had sent her home for walking in the school halls without permission. But prior to that, she was taken to the principal's office, and prior to her being sent home, her mother was notified. And several hours after she failed to show up at home, her mother called the school and the Police were notified.

Reading more of the reports showed why the investigation had taken so long. Several of her friends and her stepbrother and sister, had insisted that they had seen her on several occasions and that she didn't want to go home, and was running away. When, in fact, she was buried under the porch the day after she came home. That's just an indication of how investigations can get so screwed up by witnesses, that subsequently no charges are filed.

In this case, after reading all the reports, which were several hundred pages, we started by going to the funeral parlor and the cemetery. At the cemetery one young man was so distraught that he started to sob uncontrollably, and kept raising his arms and looking to the sky.

The next day Tom and I were at his door. We had him downtown for several hours and arrested him on some minor warrants, but we just couldn't get a good statement from him even though we knew he either had something to do with the burying of the body or knew what happened.

We spent endless days talking to all her friends, teachers, relatives, neighbors and anyone else that might have information. It all led back to her house, her stepbrother and his friends. It also involved alcohol, drugs and possibly a sexual encounter by a relative. It was almost two years later that we got somewhat of a break when the original sobbing juvenile was picked up for something else. Tom and I had another chance to talk to him and he gave us a statement.

He said that after Carrie came home from school, her stepbrother and his friends were having a party in the basement that involved drinking and drugs. Carrie had gotten high and went to the rear porch for some fresh air. The guy continued to say that he was with her on the back porch when she suddenly fell off the railing onto the ground and didn't move. He thought she was drunk and passed out, so he put her under the porch so she could sleep it off. He then said that the next day her stepbrother and his friends found that she was dead so they buried her.

The story was incredible and yet credible because of all the statements we had gotten in the past. We went to the D.A. with everything we had; the D.A. questioned all the parties that may have been involved, even sending me to Tucson, Arizona to find the subject, Jake, who supposedly was involved. Most of the witnesses confirmed that there had been a party, and that Carrie was there, but that's where all the information changed because no one really wanted to get involved.

Bottom line was that we didn't have a cause of death, so it really wasn't a homicide and by now our witness had gotten a lawyer, and changed his story several times. The D.A. felt rather than just pursuing a charge of concealing a death, we should keep the case open and wait for further information.

Even in tragedies people lie and lie and lie. I wonder what goes through their minds for the rest of their lives. Do they go to Church or confession? All these witnesses were young. What do they tell their children in later years, or their spouses? Apparently, life goes on and the tragedy remains with the family.

I mentioned before that we went to the funeral and cemetery. That may seem strange, but we made a habit of it. In fact, we always asked for the registry at the funeral home, made a copy of it and kept it in the homicide file. I don't know that we ever used the information in an actual case, but it was just one of those areas we always covered.

Homicide Cops are a strange breed. They work on whims and intuitions and all sorts of strange hunches, and they're all opinionated.

The strangest funeral I covered was when a big-time gambler got murdered down south and he was buried up here. Guards from Waupun Prison were bringing his brother down for the funeral and were not allowed to carry weapons, so a couple of us were assigned to sit through the funeral just in case something happened. After several hours of watching people go up to the casket and several of the mourners actually climb on top of the body and wail and sob, it was finally over. We were just about to leave when the funeral director stopped us and said he wanted to file a theft report, because several pieces of expensive jewelry were missing from the deceased's fingers. I know it wasn't the guy we were watching; he was handcuffed.

After we had a couple slow days, we were then contacted by out-of-town Detectives who had a strange search warrant that they wanted help executing. They had a murder in their county in which the victim was found off the roadway in a secluded area and all they found was his torso. His head, arms and legs had been cut off almost surgically and all the blood was drained out. They had been working on it for several weeks and had enlisted an archeologist from the state university to help with the identification. The Coppers said they were surprised when they finally got an I.D. at how close the professor had come to his age and other features that need no mentioning.

When they did get an I.D., they found that the victim was a twenty-two-year-old gay man who was last seen leaving a gay bar in our city. In fact, they had an informant whom had sworn to the search warrant that the weapon used to kill the young man had been buried in the parking lot behind the bar. Another first! We went to the bar and sure enough, the parking lot was gravel. The search warrant was read to the owner, and you should have seen his eyes when big pieces of machinery pulled into the alley.

About four hours later the Detectives told the owner that they didn't find anything and that he should contact the city regarding filling the holes they left. I don't know if that murder was ever cleared or the holes filled.

I remember doing some work on another homosexual murder in which the victim was found burned to death on the bed in his apartment. The cause of death was blunt force trauma to his head. The autopsy showed he had carbon in his lungs so he must have been alive when his bed was torched. The scene and investigation was handled by some other guys and we just read all the reports, which we usually did when things were a little slow.

One of the reports indicated that there were several checks missing from the victim and one of the checks had been cashed at a local bank. I went to the bank and talked to the manager, and he gave me the films for that day. Sure enough, there was a picture of the check casher. The photo was blurred and grainy, and an I.D. from the photo was almost impossible.

I was telling Ernie about it and he said he had read an article about some computer enhancing machine that the University of Wisconsin had and thought they might be able to help out. I talked to Karl and he said to give it a try so I went to the university and spent the whole day with the university Police. They showed me the campus and took me to their Science and Industry building. I was introduced to several professors and students that took the photo into their lab. They showed me how they enhance all the small dots that made up the picture and how they could clean up each dot.

The finished product was less than I expected, but was definitely more than I had before. They said they could blow the picture up to most any size, but the bigger it got the more distorted the facial features became. I took the picture back and gave copies to several Squads and sure enough, one of the Detectives hit the right house and an old lady looked at the picture and asked, "What are you looking for my son for?" That had to be pure dumb luck, because I don't think anyone but a mother could have recognized that picture. Her son was subsequently picked up, confessed to the murder, and got life in prison.

40. The Polygraph Test

Many people ask me about polygraph exams and what kind of faith I have in them. First of all, let me say that throughout my career and mostly during homicide investigations, the actual test or the threat of a test is a great investigative tool. Would I ever take a test? Absolutely not. Let me give you an example.

All the while I was on the job and even before that, every time I would travel on Lisbon Avenue, and especially in the days when there might be a gasoline price war, there was a small station on the corner that always had the cheapest gas. It had been there forever and was owned by the same guy for many, many years. The guy lived in an apartment just a block away and he had, I believe, seven children from several marriages and none of the kids got along with the father or each other.

One day the old guy was found beaten to death outside his apartment building, but Tom and I didn't get the case for several days. The old man had two young brothers working for him and they immediately became prime suspects, if for no other reason, than the old guy was kind of an asshole and probably treated the brothers consistent with his nature. They were immediately brought in, questioned and agreed to take polygraph exams that they passed with flying colors.

With this information and knowing the relationship with their father, we immediately concentrated on the sons. We had them all in and questioned them at great length and even though several of them admitted hating the old man's guts, they all denied the murder and robbery and all had good alibi's. All refused to take polygraph exams.

We worked on that case for the next several weeks in between several other homicides, including two baby deaths by parents and several trips for interviews and showing photos on the Summerfest murder.

We talked again with all the neighbors in the apartment buildings around where the old guy died and then hit all the business places in the area. It still seemed like it had to be someone he knew. We came to work one morning and were told that some young punk had been picked up for a burglary. This punk said if he got a break, he would tell who killed the old man.

We promised him all kinds of crap and sure enough, he said the two brothers had told him all about how they beat and robbed their boss and beat the polygraph test. We immediately picked them both up and it didn't take but a couple hours and we had two full signed confessions. In fact, the one kid said that after he took the polygraph and the Detective came back into the room, he was just about to confess when the examiner told him that he and his brother passed and they were going to be released—so much for polygraphs.

Several years later the Homicide Squad was expanded and Don went to a polygraph school. We brought out the old tapes from the murder and he looked at them and said that there was no doubt the kids were lying their asses off on their exams, but the examiner read the results wrong. There are apparently different polygraph schools that teach different techniques to reading the results.

Did you know that many of the really good criminal lawyer's give their clients a polygraph test but never divulge the results?

41. Serial Killers

I see in my memo book that this was about the time that Tom and I arrested William and Jacob. William had written the *Thirteenth Juror*, about his views on the Bembenek case and Jacob was a little slime ball that aggravated everyone involved in the Bembenek case including the prosecution, defense and the Bembenek family.

I think once I'm done with this whole book I might spend some time on the Christine Schultz homicide, but trying to fit it in between all the other interesting cases I've had, it would take forever. Anyhow, William and Jacob were just cogs in that whole investigation and were mainly looking for publicity. Jacob had tried to intimidate one of the original investigating Detectives and William was arrested just for being with him. Like I say, that case followed me for the rest of my career.

Sometime in late 1983, a Captain came up to the Homicide room with a small article about how two drifters were in jail, one in Texas and the other in Florida, and that they had been implicated in numerous homicides throughout the United States. They were Henry Lee Lucas and Ottis Elwood Toole. He suggested that Tom and I make some inquiries and get information on them to determine if they had any connections to the Midwest.

We made our first call to a Texas Ranger that was in charge of part of the investigation, and in fact, one of the subjects was incarcerated in his County Jail. He also told us that several different jurisdictions were trying to get a seminar formed to pool knowledge from law-enforcement officials from around the United States and Canada. This really piqued our interest when he started talking about a seminar that was planned to be held in one of the southern states, especially seeing that it was the middle of winter in Wisconsin.

We ran the idea past the Assistant D.A. that was in charge of trips, and he immediately said there was no way he was sending us without some evidence that the drifters had been through Wisconsin and we could link them with possibly one of our unsolved murders. This became a challenge that was right up Ray's alley. He did some research and put together a loose leaf binder with about thirty-six unsolved murders that included the scene, photo, cause of death, and any unusual circumstances. The book was a work of art and we took it right over to the D.A. and he again turned us down.

The next step was that we sent to Detectives in Texas, Florida and Louisiana descriptions of several of the homicides and they agreed that there was a good possibility their guys may have been involved. They also said that one of the drifters was from Michigan and had served time for killing his mother there, and was known to have traveled through Wisconsin.

Then we got a lucky break. A Detective from Menomonee Falls—a Milwaukee suburb—had gotten a chance to interview Lucas in Texas. Lucas told him that he and Toole had traveled through Wisconsin and in all probability, had killed maybe as many as twelve women throughout the state.

This was all we needed—that information, along with a little help from the local press who now found interest in these serial killers. We went to the D.A. again and even though he thought we were pulling a con job, he gave us the okay to attend the seminar.

On January 17, 1984, Tom and I flew down to Monroe, Louisiana, registered at a very nice hotel and the next morning attended the seminar. When I walked into the meeting room I could hardly believe it. There in the room, along with about ten members of the press, was the Mayor and Police Chief of the city, one-hundred-seventy Detectives representing twenty states and sixty-three separate jurisdictions. The Detectives from the southern and western states had already interviewed the two drifters and the Detectives from Minnesota, Illinois, Ohio, Michigan and Wisconsin were making arrangements for interviews. After all the introductions, the press was asked to leave the room. We were all given packets with a background on our two subjects that had been described as possibly the worst serial killers the world had ever seen.

What I recall from noted in my memo books and from my memory, the first guy was Henry Lee Lucus. A white male born August 23, 1986—that made him one year younger than me. He stood five-feet-nine-inches, and one-hundred-fifty-pounds, with a glass eye. By the time of the seminar, numerous Detectives had questioned him and he had admitted to between one hundred and one hundred fifty murders throughout the States.

The second guy was identified as Ottis Elwood Toole, another white male born March 5, 1947, standing six-foot-one-inch, and two-hundred-pounds, who was described as a homosexual, transvestite, pyromaniac who practiced devil cult worship, cannibalism and had about a forty-eight I.Q. What a pair!

We spent three days going over volumes of information and listened to all the participants describe various murders throughout the United States that were still unsolved. Also described were the various methods of death that surprised even me. The Detectives from Texas said they had started a task force in October of 1983 and had cleared seventy-three homicides with either one, or both, of the subjects as participants and had an additional seventy-one that they believed one or both were involved in to some degree. They said they felt strong about the cases because Lucas had led them to the scenes, and in some cases described in detail where the bodies were found. The means of death—without being too descriptive—included sexual assaults and a wide variety of mutilations. They admitted to keeping parts of the bodies with them as they traveled across the States.

The one case that stands out in my mind was when three Detectives from Hollywood, Florida stood up and said, that no matter what anyone said, the murder of Adam Walsh was to be taken off any list as being cleared.

Adam Walsh, as you may recall, was the little six-year-old boy who disappeared in July, 1981 from a Sears store in Florida where he had been with his mother. His decapitated head was found later in a drainage canal 120 miles away. In fact, his father started the TV program *America's Most Wanted* as a tribute to his son. This show has been credited for clearing numerous crimes. Apparently, Toole had confessed to the Walsh murder but the Florida Detectives felt there was not enough evidence to link him to the crime.

Just as a point to connect and put that particular crime in perspective, when Tom and I interviewed Toole at a later date, he described how he had killed the Wash lad and what he had done with the body. Toole later recanted his confession, but after he had died while on death row in Florida, evidence was gained that implicated him in the Walsh murder. I believe the original Detectives were reprimanded for covering up some of the evidence so that they could continue working the case.

In 2008, the new Chief of Police in the Florida jurisdiction of the abduction announced the case solved and closed. He had a retired detective review the entire file and after a year's work, it was ruled that Toole, indeed, did kill young Adam Walsh.

We spent the next three days in the seminar listening to all the cases presented by the various jurisdictions, including the ones Tom and I brought down. All of the Detectives were very professional and were sincere in their efforts to clear the crimes in their jurisdiction if, in fact, they could prove it to their reasonable satisfaction. I know that everyone there took the confessions Lucas and Toole had given with a grain of salt. This was more evident after we talked to both of them, which I'll describe later.

The Texas Rangers and Louisiana Detectives had spent a great deal of time putting together a huge amount of information. They had traced both Lucas and Toole's individual travels from 1959—when Lucas was released from the Virginia State Penitentiary—to 1960 when he killed his mother in Tecumseh, Michigan; then all the way into 1983, when he was finally arrested in Texas and has been there since.

Toole was tracked from 1964, when he was seventeen-years-old until he was finally arrested in Jacksonville, Florida in 1983, and has been there since.

As I described before, the Detectives traveled to Texas from all over the United States. The thirty-six cases we brought down were great in comparison to some small jurisdictions that only had one murder in the last four or five years. Compare that and ours to Los Angeles, who sent down their top homicide Detective named "Jigsaw John" with fourteen-hundred unsolved murders.

This Jigsaw John was an interesting guy who carried a gold badge with the number one stamped in the middle. This badge was customarily given to the Detective with the most time and experience on the force. Several years prior to our meeting him, John was featured in a TV series appropriately named *Jigsaw John*. It apparently lasted part of one season and then was canceled. It seemed the cases were not compatible to TV, but they actually came from real cases.

The hospitality was great and one evening was spent cruising the Mississippi on an old steamboat with drinks and Cajun food galore. The seminar ended on Friday and I already had made arrangements with another D.A. to fly to Tucson to interview one of the suspects in the Carrie death. I couldn't leave Tom with all the reports, so Friday night we sat in the motel and a steak dinner, and called in a seventeen-page report detailing the results of the seminar.

It's interesting because I later used this same report for numerous talks that Tom and I gave at various Police Departments, local universities that offered criminal justice classes, and also to all the new Detectives in Milwaukee. Because of that, I lost most of those reports and this writing is done mainly from my notes.

Tom and I split up on Saturday and he flew back to Milwaukee. I went on to Tucson, found the guy I had to interview and then, because it was Super Bowl weekend, spent Sunday at a party that the Tucson Police Department threw. I also had checked into a Holiday Inn, showed my badge and got a government rate. I was told by the clerk that the only thing they had left was a suite with a big screen, TV and whirlpool!

I really started to like all the traveling and was making a fortune in overtime.

By the time I got back to work the next week, the press was starting to go wild about Lucas and Toole, and there was no doubt Tom and I would get a chance to talk to both of them.

We had to wait until the end of February to get scheduled to interview them, and the first one to become available was Toole. On February 18, 1984, Tom and I flew to Jacksonville, Florida and met the Detective in charge of interviewing Toole. This Detective was making a career of scheduling these interviews and I read several years later that he got in some sort of trouble with the Jacksonville Department with the way he handled the whole situation—including the interrogation of Toole.

When we arrived in Jacksonville the Detective put us up in a hotel, took us out for dinner and made arrangements for us to meet Toole the following Monday. He also gave us a background on Toole and indicated that this would, in all probability, be like no other interview or interrogation we had ever experienced.

All the preparation in the world would not have prepared us for Otis Elwood Toole. Tom and I were sitting in this small interrogation room in the Jacksonville Police Station with our cups of coffee and book full of the descriptions and photos of our unsolved homicides. When the door opened and the Detective came in with this character, the first thing that came to my mind was the movie *Deliverance*.

I recall how I used to feel when I'd go into a home and see cockroaches all over the walls and floor. How creepy I would feel. Well, this was no different. This guy knew all the ropes because we were probably the hundredth set of Detectives that had interviewed him. He immediately tried to take control—which we didn't allow—and which, in his warped mind, he seemed to appreciate. We already had been told what brand of cigarettes he smoked and once the introductions were done and the Jacksonville Detective left the room, we offered him a pack. Our interview that day consisted of that pack, and another pack-and-a-half, and between him and Tom, by the end of the day all I had to do was inhale the air to get the taste of tobacco into my lungs. I had a gigantic headache that only a good night's sleep cured.

We started out by getting background information on our friend Otis and found that he was born in Jacksonville, the youngest of nine children who were all dysfunctional as a result of an alcoholic father and mentally ill mother. Several of his siblings were in mental institutions and attempted suicides were a norm in their family. He was raised mainly by his mother and when she died he would lie down beside her grave. He said he felt the dirt and the dirt would become warm and start to move.

As a juvenile he ran away from home on numerous occasions, and several times would be picked up dressed as a girl. He was constantly insulted by other children and was referred to as a retard. His formal education was in special education classes. He dropped out of school after the seventh grade and was on his own since that time. He said he had been a homosexual all his life and even married twice, but didn't enjoy the female relationship marriage offered.

He said he was madly in love with Henry Lucas and kept a picture of Henry in his cell and in his pocket. He had numerous arrests in Florida for auto thefts, lewd and lascivious behavior, window peeping, cross dressing, male prostitution, burglary and just a whole litany of other offenses that included numerous arsons. In fact, he was in jail at the present time for killing his homosexual partner in a house, nailing the doors and windows shut, setting the house on fire and when the Fire Department arrived they found him sitting at the curb, watching the fire and masturbating.

During our interview that lasted several days he described all the methods he and Lucas used to kill people and because I want this book to be read by my children, grandchildren and great grandchildren, I won't go into the details. But they included mutilation, cannibalism, devil cults with marking the bodies, dismemberment, and overkill. He also said Lucas would have sex with the victims before and after death, and would take parts of the bodies along for gratification at a later time. He even said that they were stopped by a State Patrol when they had a body in the back seat of their car, but the Trooper never checked.

Then began the hardest and most intense interrogation that I had ever been involved in up to that time, but all this did was prepare us for Henry Lee Lucas. You have to take into consideration this man's mental capacity and state of mind. When they said he had an I.Q. in the fifties range, I think they were giving him more points than he deserved.

As I recall, it took us several hours just to get to know Ottis and have him get comfortable with us. Once that happened, we started out by talking about Milwaukee and what he knew about the city and how many times, if any, he had been there.

Immediately he said he and Lucas had been to Milwaukee several times on their way to Michigan to visit Lucas' relatives. So we pulled out a map of the United States and asked him to point out Wisconsin. He looked at it like a Chinese puzzle and didn't have the vaguest idea where Wisconsin, Michigan, Illinois or any other Midwest states were—in fact, he was lucky to point out Florida, where he was born and raised. It was obvious that he had a very limited mental capacity and enjoyed the notoriety that came from all the interviews.

Seeing that virtually hundreds of other investigators had interviewed him and he had admitted to any number of murders, I asked him if any of the murders affected him to the point where there might be a little remorse. He immediately said the only one that bothered him was the little Walsh boy, referring to Adam Walsh. I said I realized he had confessed to the kidnapping and slaying, but I told him that the Florida Detectives didn't believe him. He said, "I don't give a shit what they say. I snatched the kid from in front of a Sears store, kept him with me for a while and then killed him; cut off his head and threw it in a drainage ditch."

I then asked him if he had ever eaten any human flesh like investigators had indicated. I made the mistake of asking him that question while he was eating a barbecued chicken dinner we had bought for him. And while he's talking about filleting human flesh, barbecuing it and eating it, he's shoving the chicken in his mouth and smearing the grease all over his face. This was after about six or seven hours; Tom and I hadn't eaten and it probably was a good thing. This guy was so sick that I really believe he would admit to almost anything as long as you kept him supplied with food, cigarettes and some friendship.

We also noted that he made sure we realized he never killed any blacks, and after talking to the Florida Detectives we realized that a great amount of African-Americans were his cell mates and even as sick as he was, he feared for his life.

We went through all the homicides we brought with us, showing him pictures of live people, dead people, victims, suspects and a dozen homicide scenes that we already had cleared and arrested the suspects. We did this to see if he would confess to everything that was put in front of him.

We were now into our third day and really had no feelings on anything he said. We then showed him two or three pictures of an old lady standing on a corner somewhere in the central city of Milwaukee. The photo came from the homicide file and I think they were pictures taken from a photo album in her home to see what she looked like when she was alive. He grabbed the picture and said, "Yeah! I killed this old broad. I picked her up on a street corner and took her to a tavern in the area. It was a rundown place full of drunks and bums. We had a few drinks and she then took me to her apartment. It was on the second floor and down the street from a hospital. We had sex and then I strangled her with a telephone cord, shoved a bottle up her snatch and then set the place on fire."

Like I say, this was about the third day of putting up with his bullshit of trying to please us by looking at photos and scenes and with his limited mental capacity, trying to figure out the crime. The photo of the old woman was in fact a murder victim and the crime occurred about seven years prior to our interview. The file was still open and was a very low profile crime that really hadn't generated any press or publicity.

Tom and I gave each other a double take because the homicide file showed that the old lady was last seen on a street in the central city of Milwaukee and was also seen at a local bar frequented by drunks and vagrants. She was found early the next morning by the Fire Department. They put out an arson fire in her bedroom and found her lying on the bed, nude, with a wire cord around her neck and a plunger handle in her vagina. It was also noted that her apartment was three blocks away from a local hospital.

After being with Toole for the better part of a week we came back to Milwaukee with mixed emotions. The press was pounding at the door of both our boss and the D.A.'s office and all we could really relate to the D.A.

were the facts we had. The D.A. was Mike and he was really a good guy that later became a Judge. He was the one who was in charge of the money for trips and knew how important the trips and overtime were to us, but he also knew we wouldn't pull any crap on him or put him in the trick bag. We also knew that the probability of ever bringing Toole back to Milwaukee was remote at best even given the fact that the statement he gave seemed that he had some knowledge of the old lady's murder.

What was not in doubt was the fact that Tom and I would definitely have to interview Henry Lee Lucas.

We were only back a couple of days when things were back to normal. A couple of new murders, a week-long jury trial and contact with the Texas Rangers trying to setup a meeting with the now famous Henry Lee Lucas.

Prior to that trip I marked in my memo book that I should make note of how different it is now, than years ago, when arresting a suspected violent person on a warrant. When Dave and Bob and I were partners and even more recently when Ernie, Carl and I were partners, if you knew someone was in the house or had a reasonable belief he or she was in there, nothing was keeping you out. That was referred to as exigent circumstances.

But in these days everything was done by the current rules and maybe it was best for everyone involved, but it sure restricted how an aggressive Police Officer operated. I also remember by this time our great political leaders had placed the rights of the offender far ahead of those of the victims.

I had gotten a warrant for a murder suspect the week before and had gotten a call from a very reliable snitch as to where the subject was. Tom was off that day and operating according to the new policy, I contacted the Tactical Enforcement Squad and met with them a few blocks from the apartment where the suspect was supposedly hiding out. After relating all the facts to them I stood back and watched how this fine tuned group of Officers worked. And I say that with all respect. This was a truly professional operation.

They planned out their strategy that included a swift move to the apartment building and the placement of Officers at the corners outside. Four others then entered the rear hall of the apartment and proceeded up the back stairs to the only entrance. They all had full body armor, weapons that I had never seen before with laser scopes, a protective shield, bullhorn and a listening devise.

From the bottom of the steps, but within a view of the door, and with me bringing up the rear, the Sergeant in charge made his first announcement identifying himself and ordered the suspect to open the door and come out with his hands up. This was like in the movies. The only thing we heard was the locking of the door and another latch being put in place.

The Sergeant made another announcement and when receiving no response I figured they'd go charging through the door. But no, they told me to get in touch with the D.A.'s office and find out if a search warrant was necessary.

Seeing as they were now in charge of this whole operation, I contacted the issuing Assistant D.A. who got in touch with her boss. He made the decision that because we had established through neighbors by showing the suspect's picture, that he was seen the night before entering the apartment with his girlfriend and her children and no one had left since, that no search warrant was necessary and force could be used to enter.

With this authority the Squad leader made another announcement with the bullhorn that the door was going to be broken down and tear gas put into the apartment. With this announcement, a female voice said, "There are children in here and no one other than myself and I'm going to open the door."

The door opened and we all rushed in. The first thing that got my attention was that three little kids were watching TV and didn't have the vaguest concern about all these armed men plowing through their house. A different way of life and an incident in their life that will no doubt affect them in later years, and all the do-gooders and social workers will wonder why they have turned to a life of crime.

It took the Tac Squad about twenty minutes to secure the apartment room by room and it was obvious that under a pile of clothes in a back closet were either rats, cockroaches, some other animal or our suspect. Needless to say when a shotgun was poked into the pile, out came our friend. His girlfriend immediately denied knowing he was there.

The apartment was then searched for the murder weapon and all we found were more cockroaches and piles of dirty clothes. Come to think of it, I recall numerous searches of houses for suspects and the basement usually revealed a big pile of clothes, some still with the price tag attached, but always in a large pile. And usually under the pile were cockroaches, rats or other animals—or hiding humans, but always an unused washer and dryer.

I then took the suspect downtown and within two hours had a full signed confession. The whole operation took about fourteen hours, which wasn't bad for that type of operation. No one got hurt and I came to realize that the old days of kicking in the door and yelling, "Police!" with your hand guns drawn was a thing of the past.

During the first part of May 1984, Tom and I got word that the Texas authorities had granted us permission to come and interview Henry Lee Lucas. By this time the press was really hot on the subject and the Department got a lot of press. In fact, the Inspector of Detectives told them that we might be clearing a good deal of our unsolved murders after we talked to Lucas and Toole and compared notes. As it turned out this could not have been farther from the truth.

Tom and I flew into Williamsburg, Texas and immediately went to the Montague County Jail where the Texas Rangers were holding Lucas. The Rangers took good care of us; they set us up in a nice motel and wined and dined us. They told us to pick up a couple blank VCR tapes as we would be able to tape our interview of Lucas the next day. This was an added bonus because even if we didn't clear any homicides, we thought the tape could be used for training.

The next day was quite an experience. We brought along a couple of tapes and our book with all the unsolved homicides and were met by the Ranger in charge. He took us to a back room that contained a table, three chairs and a VCR camera set up on a tripod. Up to this point in my career I had questioned hundreds of suspects and witnesses, but this was the first time I was definitely not in charge.

The door opened and this little perverted one-eyed wimp came in with his cup of coffee, shook our hands and introduced himself like the celebrity he really thought he was. If this guy was the mass murderer everyone thought he was, then I was the Lone Ranger!

He immediately told Tom and me where to sit and asked if we had brought a blank tape. When I gave him the tape he put it in the camera and adjusted the lens so that it would focus directly on him sitting across from us. He then asked if we wanted a cup of coffee before we started and when we said yes, he left the room and a few minutes later returned with a tray with two cups of coffee including cream and sugar.

One of us then advised him of his rights, which in itself was a joke because he knew them better than we did. The next day and a half was spent interviewing this poor excuse for a human being. I say interview and not interrogate because he controlled the whole atmosphere.

We did a complete background on Lucas that went from his birth to the present. We then took turns going through all our homicides which included those that had been sent down previously, and to which he had been questioned about by the Texas Rangers. I had to give the guy credit as he picked up on everything we said. He even had us thinking for a while that he was actually involved in several murders in Wisconsin. He was shown a map of Wisconsin and picked out several communities that we later found to have unsolved murders that fit the profile of both Lucas and Toole. He also was very familiar with Milwaukee and mentioned several landmarks that would indicate he actually was in Milwaukee at some time of his life.

We came back to Milwaukee with a ton of notes and two full tapes of our interview. Both Tom and I were totally confused about his involvement with local murders and read our notes and viewed the tape for several days. We then presented all we had to Mike, the Assistant D.A., and let him mull over everything for awhile. Sometime during that time the press got a hold of the substance of our interview and made a big splash in the papers. For the next several days we had calls from all over Wisconsin and Lower Michigan. All we could tell them was to make arrangements to interview both Lucas and Toole and make their own determination.

We then met with the District Attorney himself and several assistants and the conclusion was that there was a good possibility one or both of our boastful friends may have been involved in crimes in Milwaukee, but without more definitive evidence there was no way we would be able to bring them back to Milwaukee for trials. Other agencies were still standing in line to question them. Toole was already on death row and Lucas had been sentenced to at least two life sentences and one death sentence.

We spent the next several months giving talks at our Police Academy and several other Police and Sheriff's Departments plus several local schools and then the whole situation was dropped. We kept in touch with the Texas and Florida authorities and it wasn't long before Lucas got religion through a local nun who got him an attorney. Lucas started recanting all his crimes, even the death of his mother, for which he had served time.

As of this writing I know Toole died in prison of some sort of liver disease, still maintaining that he killed Adam Walsh. Toole came within several hours of getting the electric chair, but it was stayed. I do know that many of the jurisdictions that had cleared homicides on the pair started to reopen their cases. As far as the tape that we used for several classes, it disappeared and I never saw it again. Probably some Copper has it at home on his shelf.

It was sometime in May of 1985, that the serial killer in Texas, Henry Lee Lucas, started to refute his many killings, because he finally realized that his death sentences just might be carried out. Having found religion, several clergy helped and some death sentence protesters, along with the American Civil Liberties Union—they were trying to get new trials.

42. A Quick Resolution Murder

When I write about the next murder I handled, I'll try and explain it just like I have it noted in my memo book.

On Thursday May 31, 1984, Tom and I were sent to a house on the lower east side of Milwaukee. Many years ago this area was heavily Italian. But in the sixties it was known as the hippie community and in the last few years, the neighborhood was again in the midst of change.

We were met at the door of this single family residence, which had to have been built around the turn of the century, by two uniform men and a female, who later was identified as a visiting nurse and the subject that found our homicide victim. The victim was a white female who would have been eighty-four-years-old in June, and was the widow of a former long time Milwaukee Alderman.

As was our custom, I handled the scene and Tom handled the interviews and called for any other help we needed. My book indicates that at 8:52 a.m. the body was discovered by the visiting nurse who found the front door closed, but unlocked. She in turn notified the uniform Police who, in turn, notified us. The Fire Department was also on the scene. We arrived at 9:30 a.m. and the Medical Examiner was called by Tom. He also requested a picture car and the Vice Squad. I noted that the front door was closed but unlocked, with the key in the lock; the rear door was closed and locked, and the screen on a rear bedroom window was cut and the inner window was raised. The rear inner door was locked with a dead bolt type lock and with the key in the lock.

My next entry was what I observed before anything was touched, moved or photographed other than things disturbed prior to my getting to the scene. I know because there was no entry in my memo book that the uniform Officers, Fire Department personnel and visiting nurse had touched or moved anything. It's never like you see on TV or the movies. Time is never of the essence. The victim was dead and I could take as much time as needed before the body or anything else was moved—which at times could take up to ten or twelve hours.

I described the scene in this way: two bedrooms, living room, dining room, kitchen, and rear hall leading to the upstairs attic. The victim was lying on her back with her head to the east and legs to the west. Her white T-shirt was pulled up over her breasts with her bra snapped, but up around her neck. She was wearing a tan long-sleeved shirt open in the front and pulled down on her right arm, and was nude from the waist down. She had a white gauze bandage on her right leg and a yellow gold ring on her left ring finger, a yellow gold ring on her right ring finger, a yellow gold watch on her left wrist and a gold necklace on her neck. Her legs were spread and she obviously had been sexually assaulted as there was dried blood in the vaginal area. Her blue slacks and underpants were lying three feet from her left leg and were turned inside out indicating they were pulled off. There were checks, bankbooks and a key pouch lying between her legs, and two brown shoes lying next to the couch; a purse was lying against her right foot. There were miscellaneous personal papers lying in an orderly manner on the couch as if the assailant looking through them had placed them there.

There was an open wallet lying on the floor by the shoes and two white boxes with pieces of jewelry lying on a couch by the front window, which had drawn shades.

There was an empty can of Pabst beer lying by the front window. By this time the Police photographer, the Medical Examiner and the evidence van had arrived. The photographer was instructed to take general pictures of the entire interior of the house and once he had completed that, he was instructed to take photos of every angle of the body.

The Medical Examiner and I then started to examine the body more closely and the following notations were made: abrasions on the face and forehead, and a pillow lying next to the head with blood marks consistent with those on her face indicating the pillow had been over her face. There was no evidence of stab or gunshot wounds and no obvious trauma that resulted from objects penetrating her body.

By this time, the evidence people had started to photograph and recover all the evidence Tom had pointed out to them, and the Vice Squad was recovering all the clothing. They also cut a large piece of the carpeting that contained stains and took the couch that the body was on. The body was then conveyed to the county morgue for an autopsy.

By now about six hours had expired and Tom had conducted all his necessary interviews and we began comparing notes. One of the interviews was of a couple from the Meals-on-Wheels program who indicated that they had delivered a meal about 12:15 p.m. the day before, and indicated they gave the meal to the lady at the back door. They didn't pay any attention to the way she was dressed. They did say however, that they saw a young black male loitering in the area and didn't get a good look at his face, but described the clothing he was wearing. They returned to the area about three hours later and the same male was across the street from our victim's house.

Now comes the irony of how some of these cases are cleared in a matter of hours by excellent Police work by the uniform division. We were on our way back downtown to start our reports and inventory all the evidence when a uniform Squad contacted us on the air. They said they had stopped a suspicious black male riding a bicycle, and when they patted him down for weapons, they asked what he had in his pockets and he pulled out several pieces of jewelry. A check also showed that the subject had just gotten out of prison and was on parole.

We instructed them to bring the subject to the Detective Bureau and then contacted the victim's relatives who came downtown and positively identified the jewelry as belonging to the victim.

By 11:30 that night we had a full signed confession, and the next day his fingerprints were found on the beer can. The suspect was a twenty-nine-year-old male who had just gotten out of prison for burglary and was on parole. He said he broke into the house for money, and when he was confronted by the victim he beat her, raped her and then suffocated her with the pillow. Having exerted himself committing the gruesome act, he then said he sat back and relaxed and had a can of beer.

All the bosses, the D.A.'s office and the press loved the quick resolution to the case and Tom and I were again heroes for a few hours. The next day the autopsy confirmed that the old lady had indeed been sexually assaulted, beaten and suffocated. The suspect was immediately charged with first-degree murder, first degree sexual assault, armed robbery, carrying a concealed weapon and habitual criminality. Had he been convicted on all the charges, he would have faced a maximum penalty of life in prison plus ninety years. He would not have been eligible for mandatory release for sixty years and not eligible for parole for thirty-five years. Those charges and figures all looked good when he was given a public defender and I testified to all the gruesome acts at his preliminary hearing. Even the family was consoled that everything possible had been done and the animal, as they called him, would never see another free day in his lifetime.

But that's not how the system works. Months later and several weeks before his trial, I was notified by the D.A.'s office that there had been a problem with the handling of the evidence. We had a Medical Examiner at that time, that as far as I was concerned was totally incapable of doing a good job, but she also had some strange tendencies. One in particular that I found quite offending was her habit of storing testicles from the cadavers in jars that she kept on a shelf in her office. When the press found out about this from an anonymous source, she was disciplined. In fact, several years later after she had been relieved of her duties under a lot of pressure, Tom and I found her in a sleeping bag on the steps of the Public Museum.

Well, back to the murder. The doctor, as she called herself and her diploma read, had failed to properly dry and store the vaginal samples taken from the victim, and when the crime lab finally received them they had grown moldy and were spoiled. And, because of the contamination, the crime lab could not link the suspect with the rape. Bob, the D.A. that handled most of our cases, explained it to me that a non-secretor is a person whose blood type cannot be gotten by his sperm or saliva. That meant that the defense could have argued that the victim had sexual intercourse with someone else at the time of the crime. As ridiculous as that sounds, the D.A. didn't want to take the chance with a jury trial and allowed the defendant to plead guilty to second degree murder and first degree sexual assault, which each carried twenty years. The family was furious and I don't blame them. They figured as long as he was pleading guilty to the sexual assault, that the D.A. could have tried him on that charge. I also don't blame the D.A. because I think at that time we were having trouble with juries, and had lost several good cases.

I can never believe juries; all they have to do is listen to the evidence provided by the prosecution and then how the defense attempts to refute that, and then make their decision. They always have to put in that human factor that allows these people to feel sorry for the defendant, and think they're doing the world a service by giving him or her more consideration than they deserve. But, that's the system and we have to live with it, good or bad.

Anyway, the family was allowed to express their anger and disappointment at the time of sentencing and the Judge did give him the maximum—two, twenty-year sentences to run consecutively. In fact, the forty years was consecutive to the time he was spending on his parole violation from his previous conviction.

The press gave the D.A.'s office and Medical Examiner so much heat that Tom and I spent the next several months, off and on, doing interviews with the crime lab and all the other parties involved. As a result, new drying machines were purchased and several other aspects of the Medical Examiner's office were upgraded. But, believe it or not, that same inept Medical Examiner stayed in her position until 1987.

43. A Familiar Face ... Dead

Weeks and months would expire and the need for the Homicide Squad became evermore a necessity. It was about this time that Kenny and Mack—two Detectives from the bomb Squad—were assigned to the Homicide Squad. They were two of the most thorough and capable Detectives I ever had the pleasure of working with. They were both African-Americans and had not only a great knowledge of the core area of Milwaukee, but were both well respected. I can't recall when we expanded to the early shift, but I do know that every homicide that occurred in the city of Milwaukee and occasionally the surrounding communities was reviewed by our shift. Usually it was just to keep track of what was happening in Milwaukee County and many times it was suburbs looking for assistance, because by this time we were recognized as one of the more knowledgeable units in the state of Wisconsin.

Not every minute of every day was spent on Homicides; we still had our occasional free time, but nothing like when I worked nights. We usually didn't miss the weekly Packer game on TV, but I also know that once an investigation started, it continued straight through. Many times just going home to get a few hours sleep was rejuvenating—never a deep sleep—because the work was so interesting that I could hardly wait to get back to it.

As far as I can recall there were only two times on the Homicide Squad that someone died that I knew personally. I went to many funerals, but usually just to observe the attendees and to pick up the visitation register.

On my first morning back after a ten-day vacation, we were sent to investigate a body in a garage. I think we probably knew it was a suicide when we were sent, and we didn't get a great deal of suicides, but if there were questionable circumstances, we got it.

There was no question that it was a suicide, but when we pulled up in front of the house, I saw a man I had been close to for a number of years but hadn't seen for at least a year and maybe more.

Al was crying and pacing back and forth. When I got out of the car he immediately came to me, hugged me and said, "Jim, its Butch!" Butch was his twentyseven-year-old son who I had not seen for several years, but had known him since he was about nine or ten years old. Al, his father, and I had become good friends through his business of selling pools. Marlene and I had bought one with a settlement from one of my many car accidents. We remained good friends until he encountered a vicious divorce, and combined that with a huge drinking problem.

Butch was really a nice kid that got caught up in his parent's problems and those, coupled with a bad relationship with a girl who had just broken up with him, was just too much for him.

When I went to the garage I found that he apparently had blocked the service door with a two-by-four and then shut the electricity off to the overhead door. He started his car and then placed a lawn chair in his favorite fishing boat, sat in it and died. The problem was that when he expired, he fell off the chair and became wedged between the boat and the wall. Also, because of being in that position for several days and the cause of death being carbon monoxide poisoning, the body was bloated and distorted. If I hadn't been told who it was, I never would have identified him.

Even though it was an obvious suicide and a note had been found, one of our bosses who could not accept the fact that every death was not a homicide, came to the scene. We had to conduct a full investigation.

After several days, a great deal of interviews, and much investigation, the death was ruled a suicide by the Medical Examiner and the body was released. The funeral was very sad; Marlene and I attended out of respect for Al and his family. Several years later I was notified that Al had died. When I went to that funeral, his family told me that he had never recovered from the loss of Butch.

There's so much sadness in this world and dealing with death every day can really wear on one's mind. That's why it was so important that I had such a stable family at home and strong religious ties, so I could keep everything in perspective.

44. Under, Undercover and a Snitch

I would imagine you have heard the saying about being in the right place at the right time. Well, Tom and I were in the right place and a Hold-up man happened to be in the wrong place.

Tom and I had a good friend who owned a garage in the heart of the core. He had been there for some thirty years and was a white male about my age who had been married for many years to a black female. He not only ran a garage in the inner city where the great majority of his customers were black, but he lived in the area and had an immaculate house and yard, and made sure all his neighbors had the same.

One summer day Tom and I and our friend were standing in front of his garage in our plain clothes that consisted of jeans, sport shirts and tennis shoes. That and the fact our Squad was Tom's 1972 maroon Pontiac convertible, no one would have guessed that we were the Police, which as it turned out was good and bad. Across the street was a filling station and our eyes were directed to this lovely young lady who was filling her tank, dressed in an extremely short mini-skirt.

We must have looked away for a minute and all of a sudden the air broke with the sound of a shot. Our eyes immediately focused on the young lady's car, which by this time was occupied by her and someone else and was rocking back and forth. A black male leaped from the car followed by the white female who was screaming, "I'm shot! I'm shot! I'm shot!"

From across the street we could see that her face was bleeding and her mini dress was now bright red with blood. I ran across the street and at the same time saw two black males running through the yards.

Everything happened fast and as I approached her I could see she was badly injured, but she was standing and still screaming. Tom already had called for an ambulance and other Squads. He gave our description and type of car we were in so there would be no mistakes, and he also gave a description of the two actors. He pulled up next to me and the woman kept yelling, "They shot me! They shot me! Get the bastards!"

She wasn't bleeding profusely and looked like she could handle herself until help arrived, so I jumped into Tom's car and away we went. We went up and down the streets and every once in a while we would catch a glimpse of one of the guys. Finally, I saw one of them run across a vacant field and into a yard. I told Tom to let me out and for him to go to the alley and I'd go to the front. Well, I ran about a block and a half and saw the guy peek around the corner of a house surrounded by a fence, and then he disappeared toward the back. I was pretty sure Tom was at the back so I jumped the fence and stood in the front yard with my gun out waiting for the guy to run back out towards me or to hear Tom yell or shoot or something.

Again to my surprise the guy didn't come running out, but the front door of the house opened and this big black guy with this gigantic German shepherd dog came on the porch. He took a look at this white guy standing in his yard dressed in jeans and tennis shoes with a gun in his hand, hair all messed up and breathing hard from the run and excitement.

The only words out of his mouth were, "Sic 'em" or something to that effect, but whatever he said was enough for the dog to come charging at me. I knew I wouldn't make the fence so I could either let the dog bite me, shoot him or hope by some strange fate that the dog wasn't as vicious as he looked.

I started yelling, "Police! Police!" Either the guy heard me and called the dog off or like Tom said, he was probably a Police dog and recognized me, but for whatever reason the dog stopped. This gave me a chance to jump the fence, and at the same time Tom was coming through the yard with our culprit in handcuffs.

After all the report writing and ribbing from everybody, the woman came back from the hospital and identified the suspect. He gave the name of the other guy involved and stated a full confession. It turned out that he jumped into the passenger seat of the woman's car and told her to drive. But, all she did was start to scream. He then grabbed her purse, which she wouldn't let go of, so he started to hit her in the head with the gun. The gun went off and struck the windshield. That's when we saw him get out of the car.

I asked him where the gun was and he said he threw it away when we were chasing him, because he thought we were just a couple of nuts in an old car that were gonna kick the shit out of him. Rather than getting his ass kicked, he got fifteen years.

This reminds me of a special snitch that Tom and I had. In fact, she was so good that at one time we convinced the Feds to come up with several thousand dollars so she could put a down payment on a house. I met her when I first got an anonymous call from a female that wanted to know what it was worth to clear a homicide that had been open for several days. I told her we could meet and talk things over.

We met her at a McDonald's and found her to be a black female in her early forties who was really street smart. She had grown up down south and came to Milwaukee as a child, graduated from high school and after several kids and a couple of bad relationships, had gotten a job driving a city bus.

Before we even discussed anything monetary, she told how she had been sitting in her mother's house a few evenings before with a bunch of other people, when this kid came flying through the front door and yells for everyone to hear, "I just hit this drunken S.O.B. with a stick and I think I killed him." With that he ran through the house and out the back door. She told us that she didn't know the kid personally, but had seen him in the neighborhood. She knew one of his relatives was in the house, and gave us her name and address.

We knew exactly which murder she was talking about. It seems that these two old drunks were just walking down the street and started to box a little like they always had, when this kid comes running up with a two by four and whales away at one of the drunks. After he had beat him to the ground he told the other drunk that he had saved him from an ass kicking and he wanted some money. Well, the other drunk was broke and hollering and screaming, so the kid ran away.

A half dozen kids had been picked up and put in a line up but the surviving drunk just couldn't make identification. The case was getting cold and it wasn't a real high priority case, but Tom and I went to the relative of the kid, and after playing on her conscience for a while she gave us a full statement. She told us what the kid said when he came in the house that night and also when he later on told her about the beating.

The next day Tom and I picked up the seventeen-year-old kid and got a confession in a few hours. He was charged as a juvenile and later waived to adult court where he subsequently pled guilty to homicide by reckless conduct.

This lady snitch, "Tasha," had no record and all she would ever say was that she was just doing her part—part of what, I never knew and didn't want to push it. She was so good that we called her one time because we were looking for a gun that was involved in a homicide, and we knew that the victim had some connection to her family. She told us that she had an idea who the killer was, but would have to do, "a little investigating on my own." When we told her that we were looking for the gun, she said she'd call us back later.

The shift hadn't ended when we got her call. She said the gun was at such an address and was in the front bedroom closet on the top shelf under a pile of clothes.

I asked, "How the hell do you know that?"

She responded, "I put it there."

We got a search warrant telling the Judge about this reliable, confidential informant that we couldn't produce for safety reasons and he gave us the warrant. Sure enough! Not only did we get the gun under the clothes on the top bedroom closet shelf, but we also got the shooter.

Even after I retired, I got a call from her and she said she missed Tom and me and she had some really good information, but needed some money. I referred her to the day shift Homicide Squad that found a few bucks for her and they got some good information. I wonder if she's still driving buses.

45. The Bite Mark Case

It was now the end of 1984 and Tom and I became involved in another really interesting case. It involved a little old white lady who I'll name 'Betty,' who lived in the heart of the inner city by herself in a lower flat. She was sixty-three-years-old, about five-feet-two-inches and two-hundred-fifty pounds; and I say this because the size of her made a difference. She was last seen alive in the early evening hours when a chartered bus left her off in front of her house after a day of bingo at a casino. The next morning a passerby saw Betty lying in a vacant lot two doors from her house.

Her slacks and under pants were pulled down around one ankle and her bra was pulled up around her neck. The entire upper portion of her body was covered with bites; not bug bites but human bites. The largest bites were on her huge breasts, but there were bites all the way down to her vaginal area. She must have suffered a long time because besides being suffocated, she also suffered from hypothermia from the extreme cold, which meant she was alive for most of the attack.

After we got briefed by the late shift on what they found, I attended the autopsy and because of the extensive bite mark evidence, a forensic odontologist was called in from a local university. His name was Dr. Harold and he was nationally recognized, but we made him even more famous. The doctor did molds and plaster casts of the bite marks and then the pathologist removed the breast and placed it in a solution in a bucket, which was then stored as evidence.

After the autopsy was performed and the cause of death was determined, I went back to the office. We started to lay out plans for interviewing all the neighbors, and questioning several people that were seen in the area. Surprisingly, among the people picked up were several of the same suspects we had in the murder of the guy walking down the street that was shot through the can of beer he was carrying. That case was where a guy by the name of Mark identified his brother and several others as being the shooters, but later changed his testimony and we lost the case. Naturally, these guys all had good alibis because they had time to get their stories straight, and so they all were released.

Tom and I had several court cases the next few days and by the time we got back into the Betty case, the results from the forensic odontologist had just come back. He provided us with photos of the bite marks from every conceivable angle, along with a detailed drawing. They showed that the actor that bit Betty had both a missing or broken front tooth, and a twisted tooth to the side of the missing tooth.

With this information we started to re-interview all the neighbors and questioned everyone that was arrested and had a missing tooth—never realizing how many people have missing teeth.

This went on for several days and we finally got to the block where Betty was found. There was a duplex right next to the vacant lot and I'm sure the occupants had been talked to several times, but Tom and I decided to try once more. Just by chance the upstairs occupants were home—a woman and her two twenty-year-old twin sons, both with the same first names, Luther John and Luther Michael. Tom and I talked to the mother, who indicated that she was home the night of the murder, but didn't see or hear anything. She went to bed early and thinks Michael came home about 3:00 a.m. with his girlfriend and didn't know what time John came home.

Tom took John and I took Michael and after we had talked to them for about an hour and had left the residence, we were standing on the sidewalk when Tom grabbed my arm and said, "We got him."

I said, "What the hell are you talking about?"

He said, "Come on, I'll show you."

With that we went back upstairs and said we had forgotten a few questions. Tom started to talk to John and told him something that must have amused him, and he started to laugh. There it was. The broken front tooth and the twisted tooth just like on the diagram and pictures. I could hardly believe my eyes. This was like something on TV!

We got back into the car and all I could say was, "I don't believe it, I just don't believe it." By the time we got back to the office, our boss Karl was there along with Rosie and Ray. We talked over what we thought we should do next. Arresting the kid was out of the question. Looking through the reports we found that he had been talked to at least three prior times and each time had an alibi that checked out. We decided to go to the D.A. and see what advice he had.

We told the D.A. the whole story and he called in an Assistant D.A. we knew personally. We had had several cases with him and really respected his decisions. In fact, he was in the process of getting ready to leave the D.A.'s office to teach at a university.

The first thing he did was to call Dr. Harold and asked him if he thought he could make an identification from the bite marks. The doctor said he was sure he could under the right conditions that included doing a full make-up of the suspect's mouth.

The D.A. said that he thought the best way to handle the case was to approach a Circuit Court Judge with the information we had and request a John Doe Investigation. The John Doe would allow us to subpoena witnesses,

Luther John in particular, and have the Judge order a complete exam of his mouth.

This was a particularly busy time. I was just starting another John Doe Investigation involving an old homicide with four suspects that couldn't get their stories straight, and kept blaming each other. Along with that case, the seventeen-year-old from the last murder was waived to adult court, and we had to prepare that case with another D.A. This was also the week that the crime lab results came back showing the conflict with the tainted blood. As I mentioned previously, the press were hounding us on that case, and somehow found out that we were starting a John Doe on the Betty murder.

We worked almost day and night for about two weeks (unbelievable overtime) and I filed lengthy reports regarding the tainted blood. This resulted in a meeting with several D.A.'s, several members of the crime lab, the Medical Examiner and his assistant, who was the strange lady who had done the autopsy, our boss, Tom and I.

The D.A.'s office said more was accomplished in our forty-five-minute meeting than was accomplished in the last fifteen years with regard to the Medical Examiner's office Besides setting a new standard operating procedure in the Medical Examiner's office regarding the preservation of evidence, we got the county to buy a drying machine so future blood samples would be dried properly.

I write about these cases and the endless hours spent on them, and I failed to mention that in between all these hours, I still had to keep a quality home life. And, that's where Marlene handled everything. She never once put any pressure on me like most other Copper's wives, and let me put all my energy into the job.

It was not unusual during these times to come home at 10 or 11 p.m., eat supper, catch up on what Marlene and the kids were doing, watch the news and go to bed. The problem was that the job was so interesting that many times I could hardly wait to get back to work. I know it was hard on Marlene and the kids, but none of them ever complained.

We not only served Luther John with a subpoena, but we brought him directly in front of the Judge who ordered the exam of his mouth to be done at that time. Luther John seemed a little stunned, but didn't object to anything. For the next three hours I couldn't believe what was happening. We took Luther John into a room next to the Judge's chambers and sat him on a wooden chair. In the room were Tom, I, Dr. Harold, the D.A., a crime lab photographer and a court appointed attorney for Luther John.

The photographer had a huge camera with a flat chrome plate in front of the lens. The doctor put Luther John's head back on a pillow and placed an apparatus in his mouth that opened his mouth the widest I had ever seen. The photographer then started taking pictures of his mouth by placing the plate in his mouth and photographing his teeth from just about every angle. All this time there was never a peep or movement out of Luther John.

When the photographing was done, the doctor heated up a large piece of wax, made it into a big clump, placed it in John's mouth and told him to bite down. I couldn't believe the cooperation from both Luther John and his attorney. Like I say, the whole process took about three hours and when we were done his attorney said we couldn't talk to Luther John, so we took him home, dropped him off and said we would see him sometime.

We heard nothing for almost a month to the day when we were called to the D.A.'s office and the Assistant D.A. told us that the doctor had made a positive identification of Luther John's teeth marks. He also said he would issue a first degree murder charge within a couple of days, and before informing Luther John's attorney, he wanted us to arrest him.

While we waited for the warrant to be issued on the Betty homicide, we were involved in another gang killing. This one was the result of a murder in 1983, where this victim of the murder was the suspect in a different murder, but we could never prove it. It's kind of funny how justice works sometimes in strange ways. If the guy would have confessed to the 1983 murder, he probably would be alive today and back on the street. Instead he took three twelve-gauge shotgun blasts—two to the back and one to the chest.

He was found next to his car in a strange garage. We got an anonymous tip and picked up an eighteen-year-old girl and her twenty-four-year-old brother, both gang members, who after denying their part in the shooting insisted on taking a polygraph exam that they flunked miserably. They in turn said they hadn't told the truth and gave the name of a third gang member. We picked him up and he also insisted on a polygraph exam (I don't know what prompted this, other than someone must have told them it was easy to beat) and after he also flunked the exam he finally confessed to the murder. He said the girl had lured the victim to the garage for sex and then all three guys took turns shooting him. This case took a year to go through the courts and the final disposition was that one person pled guilty to homicide by reckless conduct, and the other three who were going to testify against him, plead to some lesser charges. They were all back on the street by the time I retired in 1990.

In early January of 1985, Tom and I met with Dr. Harold and he showed us the plastic molds of Luther John's teeth along with the x-rays and overlays the doctor had developed. It showed positive proof that the bite marks on Betty's breast were from the mouth and teeth of Luther John. The doctor then dropped the bomb on us when he said he was very positive of his determination, but wanted the best forensic odontologist in the United States to confirm his findings.

We immediately went to the D.A. and told him. He said it wasn't a bad idea because if we locked in the best expert now, the defense would have to scratch around to find someone better. The doctor then said that the most renowned expert in the field of forensic odontology was also a State Senator in the state of Nevada and that his office was in Las Vegas. The D.A.'s office said they would pay for only one of us to take the evidence there to be examined.

Tom and I got together and I told Tom that he was more of a gambler and single, so he could take the trip. He immediately said no way and that we had to figure out a way for both of us to go. We then called Dr. Harold and told him our dilemma. He said there was more than enough evidence for both of us to carry, and that much of it was fragile and had to be hand carried. He told the D.A. that it was essential we both go.

Even though the D.A. thought we were pulling a fast one, he finally relented and said we could both go. He also said that in order for us to fly the cheapest way, we had to fly Fun Jet, which was a junket type flight, and that we would have to stay the required four nights and five days to get the cheaper rates. We couldn't believe it! We also knew that our boss's boss would read through the whole thing and make sure that only one of us went, so we didn't say anything until the day before the flight.

The boss was fit to be tied. He said he wanted to see the evidence that we were taking and if it didn't require both of us to carry it, one flight was being canceled.

Our flight was the next afternoon and we were all packed and ready to go when we went to the doctor's office to get all the evidence. He handed us a package of x-rays and a small suitcase with some plaster cast molds of John's teeth and the remnants of the victim's breast that had been preserved in a solution. Our boss would never buy that. So we did the next best thing that any good Detective would do. We went to Tom's house and filled a suitcase with books, locked it up and sealed it with tape.

Before we could leave for the airport, the boss called us into his office and said he wanted to see all the evidence. When we dragged the suitcase in, he said, "What kind of bullshit is this?" He told us we had about two seconds to open it up.

Tom replied, "The doctor has the key and was going to mail it to the expert in Vegas."

To which the boss replied, "Get the hell out of my office." We did, and headed straight to the airport before he changed his mind.

We got to Las Vegas that same day and immediately called the expert to ask where his office was. He told us to stand by and he would come to our hotel, which just happened to be the Four Queens.

He got there before we had a chance to unpack and took a look at the x-rays and the molds, and said that was good enough for him and that he concurred with Dr. Harold and would testify to those findings in court. He then said that if we needed anything in Vegas to call him, and with that he left his card and also left our room.

Total time from the time we got off the plane to now was about two hours into our five days. We looked at one another and said, "This ain't too bad."

We then called the Las Vegas Police Department and asked for the homicide unit and they put us in touch with a Detective Sergeant who was born and raised in Vegas, and he took care of us for the rest of our stay.

He wined us, dined us, and showed us parts of the town that only someone of his stature would venture into. He also introduced us to some businessman from Michigan who took us to one of the most lavish restaurants on the strip. The total bill for the four of us was almost eight hundred dollars, which included several bottles of wine and escargot for appetizers. What a way to live!

That whole evening Tom and I sat at the quarter slots and every twenty minutes or so the businessman would drop a roll of quarters in our tray. I actually thought I was going home with some extra money, but the minute the businessman left, so did the money. The machine got it!

We also found that the Coppers in Vegas have their own gin mill where they do all their drinking and gambling away from the crowds. The drinks were good, but their machines were no different than those on the strip. When we got back from our five-day mini vacation, we went to thank our boss; he slammed the door on us.

Now it was back to the real world and when we told the D.A. what the expert had to say, he issued a first degree murder charge on Luther John. We then served the warrant and took a brief statement from Luther John. He denied the murder, but did admit to being in the backyard about 1:00 a.m. the morning of the murder and said he heard some wrestling on the ground, but paid no attention to it.

Ironically, he also stated he was in the backyard with a guy by the name of Mark, who was the individual in the murder that I talked about earlier, where he implicated his brother and friends and later refused to testify. He was never charged, but I believe he was with Luther John at the time of the murder.

Two weeks later we had the preliminary on Luther John with an outstanding testimony from Dr. Harold. My testimony was limited to describing the scene and how Betty was found. The defense had only a few questions and Luther John was bound over for trial.

During the next several months the defense filed several motions to have the evidence and statements thrown out, but since the D.A.s involved in the case had done such a terrific job, all the defense motions were denied.

The jury for Luther John was picked on December 9, 1985. After opening statements by the defense and the prosecutor, (who now was Mary, because the original D.A. had left the office to teach at the university), the jury was taken by bus not only to view the scene of the murder, but also to get a general idea of the neighborhood and where in relation to the body Luther John lived.

The jury was then brought back to the courthouse and the first person to testify was the Medical Examiner. Several of the women on the jury had tears in their eyes and had their hands over their mouths during the description of the numerous wounds, bruises and teeth marks all over the victim's body. This took the better part of two days, and by the third day it was time for the two forensic odontologists to testify.

Dr. Harold and the expert from Las Vegas testified for about three hours with no objections from the defense. These two experts had the jury spellbound. My testimony was only about an hour and after that the prosecution rested. The defense didn't call any witnesses.

Closing arguments were the morning of December 12. The jury was out for an hour-and-a-half, including lunch, when they came back with a guilty verdict of first degree murder. The Judge sentenced Luther John to life in prison and he was on the way to the State Prison by two o'clock that afternoon.

This was one of the first cases in the Midwest where the suspect was charged and convicted with the only evidence being the bite marks, along with the fact that Luther John lived right next door from the murder scene.

There were two other jurisdictions from Wisconsin that sat in on the trial because they had similar cases. Within the next year one of those cases was brought to trial and they also got a conviction on bite mark evidence in which Dr. Harold was the expert. In fact, we made Dr. Harold famous and after these cases he began lecturing all over the country.

We saw him several times after that. In fact, we attended a death school where he was the lecturer and the Luther John case was the subject of his talk. Tom and I kidded him later that he should take us along on his lecture tour.

46. Officers Down... Again

I had taken about four or five days off and hadn't kept up with the news, so I was shocked when I came to work and found the whole homicide room filled with bosses. The day before, two Milwaukee Police Officers were shot and killed. A certain amount of fear goes through each Officer's mind every time he leaves his home. The thought is always there that he's going to meet a situation that he's not able to handle, and that's going to result in he or she getting hurt real bad or possibly giving the ultimate sacrifice.

In this case the Officers were well respected, well trained, well disciplined and doing just exactly what they were expected to do—make the city a better and safer place for all the citizenry.

The whole incident naturally was tragic, but what made it even worse was the fact that one of the Officers had just gone to the day shift. He had not worn his bullet proof vest because he thought the day shift was just not as violent as the many years he had spent on nights.

These Officers apparently found four suspicious youths standing by a building in a high crime area of the city and decided to talk to them. For whatever reason, the Officers must have relaxed for a moment and lost track of the hands of one of the youths. In an instant, one of the youths pulled out a small caliber gun and firing just two shots, took two lives, and changed the lives of several families forever.

One of the Officers was dead at the scene, and the second was conscious and talking to the responding Officers. In fact, he talked all the way to the hospital during which time the ambulance he was in broke down, and he had to be transferred to a second ambulance.

I wasn't at the hospital, but apparently the doctors did all they could, and were literally saturated in his blood, trying to save him. I was told later by the Medical Examiner that during the autopsy she discovered the small caliber slug had caused so much internal bleeding, that the Officer was as good as dead at the scene, and even if the doctors were with him on the scene he probably wouldn't have made it.

I knew both Officers and had dealings with them in the past, but was not involved in their personal or family lives. It was a tragedy that played out twenty-six times over my thirty-three-year career, each one no more or less soul wrenching than the other.

Every murder I ever investigated was always given a high priority and was always given the dignity that it required, but when it involved a fellow Officer, everything else stopped.

Within twenty-four hours the suspect was in custody, the gun recovered, and a full statement taken. Within four months the individual was tried by the D.A. himself and received two consecutive life sentences.

But, this was the day after the murders and all hell was breaking loose. By this time they had the name of the suspect and every jurisdiction in Milwaukee County and the surrounding counties were searching for him, and he was subsequently found and arrested in a suburb.

Once the whole sordid circumstances were related to everyone in the room, one of the general Detectives was told to attend the autopsy. Tears started forming in his eyes, and all he could say was that he had been partners with one of the Officers; he had known him and his family for years. The boss's eyes went around the room and all heads bowed.

Nobody wanted the job, and soon all the eyes searched for members of the Homicide Squad. I very, very, very reluctantly said, "Okay, I'll do it." I've seen death in just about every form, but when I walked in and saw the bodies of these two fine men that had literally given their lives in their line of duty, the feeling was almost overwhelming.

The autopsies lasted two hours and forty minutes according to my memo book. There was also the notation in my book that one of Officers was shot in the thorax and suffered a lacerated aorta; the slug was removed from the fourth lumbar vertebra on his left side.

The funerals were attended by hundreds of Officers from throughout Wisconsin and surrounding states. The slain Officers were laid to rest in front of their grieving, but yet gracious families. When Marlene and I got home we embraced and hugged the kids and I suppose said that, but for the grace of God, it could have been me.

47. More Interesting Investigations

In spring of 1985, a very young Police Officer assigned to night parking duty happened to see a car in an alley with the driver standing outside relieving himself. The driver pulled away and the young Officer stopped him. He immediately jumped out of the car and came back to the Officer. The young Copper was pretty sharp and immediately took the driver back to his car, and saw a woman slumped over on the passenger's side. When asked about her condition, the driver said they just had sex and she must have fallen asleep. The Copper called for another Squad and upon checking further, they found that the lady was dead and rigor mortis had started to set in.

By this time Tom and I had just arrived at work and were sent out to the scene. Everything was just as the Copper had found it. The paramedics had come and agreed that the passenger was dead, and they also agreed that there was no sign of a struggle or obvious trauma. When the Medical Examiner arrived, all the pictures had been taken; we helped get her out of the car and onto the gurney. We noticed blood on the back of her blouse, which covered a puncture wound. To make a long story short, our inept Medical Examiner could not find a cause of death, so a second autopsy was performed and the cause came back—manual strangulation.

The second autopsy would not have been performed if Tom and I hadn't taken the driver downtown and questioned him for several hours. This is what I wrote in my memo book and what the driver signed as his statement:

Vernell, Eric and David (the driver) picked up Barbara (the victim) about midnight and went to several taverns. They bought a pint of Canadian Mist and went back to Barbara's house and drank the pint. They then dropped off Vernell and Eric and went back to her house and sat in the alley and drank a pint of gin. They then drove around down by the lake and past a cemetery and into the alley. They agreed to have sex and Barbara pulled one leg out of her slacks and panties and they had sex. David then started to drive away and Barbara started to beat on him and call him a "fag m.f'r that didn't know how to screw." David then stopped the car and hit her several times in the face and she slumped against the passenger door. She then came up with a knife and tried to stab him and he knocked the knife out of her hand and it landed on the floor. She reached down for the knife; he picked it up and grabbed her by the throat and plunged the knife into her back. He said he doesn't remember pulling the knife out or throwing it away. (We later found the knife in the bushes.) He stated he got out of the car to take a leak and saw a car pull into the alley. He didn't realize it was a Squad until he saw the red light.

It turned out that the knife wound to the back was not the cause of death. David had just strangled Barbara to death. It took about three days of follow-up investigation and interviews of all the parties named by David, along with checking out the various residences with search warrants. The basic story David had told was pretty much the truth, but he left out all kinds of drug dealings and drug consumption details the night of the murder—apparently everyone was stoned.

David was charged with second degree murder and several months later pled guilty. He received twenty years in prison to be served consecutively with time lost on a parole violation. All in all, he was probably out by the time I retired five years later.

What a great system. It's no wonder that about twenty percent of murders go unsolved and of the eighty percent left, a good number aren't prosecuted for a variety of reasons. Of those left, a good portion are set free by juries that just don't listen to the evidence. They say it's the greatest system in the world and I suppose it is, but it sure gets frustrating at times.

Within the next several weeks I was involved in several murder investigations; two of them stand out and deserve being described.

The first occurred the later part of May in 1985, and involved the death of a seventy-year-old white female who was found on her bed. She had been obviously sexually assaulted, beaten in the face, suffocated, and bitten on her stomach and breast. I don't know what's with these bite mark cases. She lived in a fourteen unit apartment building in a poorer section of town, had been divorced for forty some years and had no children.

The newspapers found relatives who said she was an independent woman who cleaned homes for wealthy people in the suburbs for many years. They couldn't imagine the terror and pain she must have suffered by the hands of her killer. Actually we weren't working when the scene was investigated. When Tom and I came into work, the late shift had a suspect in custody that they had been talking to during the night. All they asked us to do was get saliva samples from him to check against the bite marks and sexual assault evidence. After doing this, we then went to the apartment building and started interviewing the tenants.

If there was anything I learned in any kind of investigation it was to talk to the same people over and over until they say, "Get the hell out of my life, I told you the same story each time we talked." And then, I usually gave them one more shot. Tom and I started questioning the same neighbors of the old lady, who had been interviewed just a matter of hours before. Suddenly, they remembered a disturbance four or five days prior to the body being found. The more we talked the more information came out that an individual either drunk or high was knocking on the doors and talking incoherently. They also said when they looked down the hall, they recognized the subject as visiting someone in apartment seven.

The lady in apartment seven was very helpful and said she remembered the knocking on her door several nights ago and realized who it was, but she knew he was either drunk or doped up so she didn't answer. She gave the name Jude and an approximate date of birth, and indicated he had a girlfriend on the south side.

With that information we got a photo of Jude and showed it to the other neighbors and they all identified him as being the one from several days ago. We didn't put a lot of faith into the identification because the late shift still had a suspect in custody, which was not Jude.

We checked with our Bureau of Identification and found out that the last time Jude was arrested he gave his contact person as Dawn, who lived on the south side. With this information we contacted Dawn, and she gave us some startling information that had both Tom and I shaking our heads when we left her home

She said she had known Jude for several years and was trying to break off their relationship because all the alcohol and drugs had affected his thinking, which wasn't that great in the first place. Then she dropped the bomb. She said he had come to her house several nights ago drunk and said he had tried to visit Janet (tenant in apartment seven) and she wouldn't answer so he went to a first floor apartment, broke an outer window, cut a screen, and crawled into the apartment. He said he found an old woman in the kitchen and took her to the bedroom where he threw her down and bit her on the right shoulder. He said he had sex with the old lady and then left her apartment. We were almost in shock.

We asked Dawn if she had been watching TV or read the newspapers, and she said all she had been doing was going to work and staying at home. When we told her about the old lady in Janet's apartment building, she broke down in almost uncontrollable sobs. She said she would do anything to help us and said that Jude had a very distinctive overbite, gave us the name of his dentist and told us that the last time she saw him he was on his way to Chicago. Dawn said since that time Jude had called her several times, and said he was going to hitch-hike to Florida.

With that information we went back to the bureau and found that the guy the late shift had been questioning had a good alibi. When we told them what we had, they released him. We then went to work.

We contacted the dentist Dawn had given us and he was going to respond to a subpoena we were getting for Jude's dental records. We got a search warrant to tap the phone lines in Dawn's house, which we then served, and we got her written permission and authorization for this phone tap.

We then set up camp in her house for the next four days—not a real exciting plant job. The house was clean, but Dawn was no mental giant and sitting for hours on end waiting for Jude to call and listening to her other conversations was a bit much. But, not all jobs are exciting.

Jude called all four days, sometimes two or three times. Dawn was terrific and played the game like a pro. She told him how much she missed him and wanted to be with him and tried to get him back to Milwaukee. He just kept hitch-hiking towards Florida and each time he would give a location we would teletype the jurisdiction and ask that he be picked up.

We later learned that the closest we came was in some southern state where the state Police were coming in the motel's front door, and Jude actually held the door open for them. Finally on Saturday he called and said he just got into Tampa and would wait for her if she could find a way down there. We had already made arrangements with the D.A.'s office for traveling, had expense money and three open-end plane tickets.

Sunday morning bright and early we were on our way to Tampa, Florida—Tom, Dawn and I. We had already contacted the Hillsborough County Sheriff's Department, who actually control the airport Police. They in turn contacted the Tampa Police Department who said they would have a Detective waiting for us.

The plan was for Dawn to walk a few feet in front of us wearing a red scarf and when she spotted Jude, she would take the scarf off. Almost like on TV.

We arrived in Tampa and the Detective met us at the plane. We then took a tram to the main air terminal. Tom, the Detective and I separated in the terminal and we let Dawn wander around carrying her overnight bag. We must have waited for a good forty five minutes and were getting nervous when all of a sudden we heard this wailing sound, "Dawn, Dawn, Dawn."

Out of the corner of my eye I saw this pathetic looking creature about five-feetseven-inches tall, wearing dirty baggy clothes with a ratty old blanket covering his shoulders. He not only was unshaven, but also looked like he hadn't taken a bath in several weeks—which he probably hadn't.

Here this poor little creep was standing in the airport after hitch-hiking half way across the country, looking at his girlfriend who he hadn't seen for a week, and was probably thinking of all kinds of romantic things they would do in a couple of hours. He was on about his fourth, "Dawn" when Tom and I jumped his ass and threw him to the ground.

Because we were in the airport, a crowd started to gather. Imagine how it looked, these two big guys jumping on this poor little man. What really made things worse was when the plain clothes Detective pulled out his big semi-automatic and pointed it at the three of us and yelled, "I got him covered." Well, the screams could have been heard throughout the terminal and all I could think of was, this wasn't the way it was supposed to work!

The Detective from Tampa arrested Jude and he was booked in the Tampa airport jail.

We then made arrangements for Dawn to visit some of her relatives in Tampa and also made arrangements for her to get home. We returned to the jail and during the booking and subsequent interview, we noticed what appeared to be bite marks on Jude's hands. Everything was moving fast. We arrived in the airport at 12:30 p.m., made the arrest at 1:15 p.m., got back to the booking area at 3:30 p.m., and then Jude refused to let us photograph his hands. He was handcuffed and placed in a cell under watch so he wouldn't cause additional damage to his hands.

We then contacted a Judge in Hillsborough County and he had a three-way conversation with a D.A. in Milwaukee and an assigned public defender for Jude in Florida. They all conversed and the Judge then issued a search warrant for Jude's hands.

By the time we got back to the jail it was only 5:15 p.m. and when we read the search warrant to Jude he relented and gave us written permission to photograph his hands, which by now were starting to scab over, but still had marks that gave distinctive bite mark impressions.

Now came the hard part. Even though the Judge had assigned a public defender to Jude, he stated it was strictly for the search warrant and had nothing to do with the arrest or pending interrogation during which we would advise Jude of his rights and he would have to ask for an attorney. I advised Jude of his rights and he said he understood them and made no request for an attorney, but he also denied the murder and denied being at the scene.

After laying out the facts and what the witnesses had said, especially Janet, he finally said he would tell us all about it. He then gave us some cock and bull story about how some black guys had threatened him and made him break into the old lady's apartment, but he denied killing her.

We let him sit for a short time, gave him some coffee and a sandwich and then gave him one more shot. We must have hit the right moment and this is what he told us, as is recorded in my memo book:

On May 26, 1985, he left work and went to Dawn's house but she wasn't there. He looked for her at several bars and hung around her house until 8:00 p.m. when she came home with a white male and he watched them go into her house. He knocked on her door and rang the bell, but she wouldn't answer. He then called the Police and they came and allowed him to get his clothes out of her house. He then took a cab to the area of 26th and State Street and started hitting the bars and drinking Jack Daniels and Coke. He tried to call Janet, but she didn't answer. He then went to her apartment and pounded on the front door, but also got no answer. He said he then pushed in a basement window and used a cigarette lighter to find steps. He found a chisel and used it to pry open a door to another apartment. He said it was dark in the room and he stumbled on a bed and found a woman lying there. He couldn't see her face, but she started to moan and groan so he started to hit her in the face, head, body and chest.

He started to bite her and she quit moving, so he had sex with her. He got up and went to the kitchen and saw his hands full of blood so he washed in the sink and then saw a rack of keys. The old lady must have been the manager, and he saw a key to Janet's apartment (apartment seven) and tried to use it on her door, but he heard her call out and ask who was there, so he ran out of the apartment.

He said he stayed in a hotel that night, and the next day bought some clothes and took a bus to Chicago. He called Janet, but could hear the Police in the background and hung up. He said he then hitch-hiked to Florida. That was it—a full signed confession. We called the boss back in Milwaukee and the next day we went to court in Tampa and Jude waived his rights and they issued an extradition warrant.

After flying back to Milwaukee, we took Jude to the D.A. and he charged him with first degree murder and two counts of first degree sexual assault. He pled guilty several months later and got life plus forty years, but I wouldn't be surprised if he was on the street today.

The press was always calling us and looking for some interesting news. In fact, they were waiting at the airport for us when we brought Jude back. We had to put a coat over his head and run through the airport because we still hadn't had a line-up for the witnesses. Not that I didn't like the high profile cases, but the press did get a little pushy once in a while and had to be put in their place.

Regarding the press, it was not unusual to pick out one or two reporters and TV people that you could trust and give them the scoop. But, usually the bosses took care of that.

The second murder in mid-summer 1985 that stood out was also one that caught a lot of press, but for different reasons. A young nineteen-year-old of Palestinian heritage had been behind the counter of his parent's inner city grocery store. He came to this country at age three with his six-month-old brother, mother and father. His brother, who now was fifteen, was behind the meat counter at the rear of the store, behind a wooden door that had been placed there for security reasons.

The young man later explained, "I was bending down when I heard about four or five gunshots coming from the front of the store. I looked up and saw my brother with blood coming from his head grab a gun from a man. The man then hit my brother's head with a meat cleaver, shot him, and then stabbed him in the back. Two men ran from the store. I hit the alarm and then held my brother in my arms while he said to say goodbye to his wife and to tell her he loved her—then he died."

The younger brother said he knew the robber and had seen him many times in the store causing problems. In the past, he and his brother had thrown him out, called the Police, and had the man arrested. He came back several times and 'swore vengeance.'

The young man also offered that he was born in Bethlehem in the Israeli Occupied West Bank and that, "In Bethlehem, if you kill somebody, they hang you in front of everybody." He said, "I'm in favor of capital punishment or torture, whatever you want."

The cause of death was bleeding caused by head injuries believed to have been inflicted with a meat cleaver. His left ear was severed and he was shot four times. With the description of the assailant, we looked up the history of the Police being called to the store, and within a few hours had the suspect in custody.

I questioned the subject for several hours during which time he stated he was a member of the BGD (Black Gangster Disciples), and he killed the store keeper because he came at him with a gun. The confession was relatively easy and signed by the suspect. He indicated everything was true and then initialed every page both top and bottom, which was important for the purpose of substantiating the validity of the statement.

The next day I took him to court and was bombarded by the press, because unknown persons had made threats against the suspect. When he was questioned by the D.A. he denied the confession. He said the only reason he said those things was because I said it looked like self-defense, and he would be released. The charge was first degree murder and he was held on $250,000 bail.

About seven or eight days later a preliminary hearing was held. The courtroom was guarded by extra deputies, metal detectors at the door and no spectators were allowed other than the family and witnesses—one being the person that entered the store with him, but left before the killing and was not charged with the murder.

The young victim's wife and mother stayed in the courtroom dressed in full length black dresses with veils and wept, while his brother described the murder scene in great detail, breaking down several times. When questioned by the defendant's attorney, the young man was a strong witness, telling how he had seen the suspect in the store numerous times and the night of the murder, saw his face as he was striking his brother.

After I read his confession, the Judge bound him over for trial and both the D.A. and I said it was a perfect case and that we should have little trouble getting a conviction—little did we know.

The case came up for trial about ten months later and the hallway outside the courtroom was filled with the victim's relatives (who had traveled all the way from Palestine), witnesses, the press, and deputies all over the place with their metal detectors. There apparently had been numerous threats by phone, and when I approached the victim's family, they firmly denied any threats, but made it clear that if the defendant went free, they would handle it themselves. Throughout the trial I got to know the victim's family quite well and they invited Marlene and I over to Palestine and said we would not have to have any fears, because their home is surrounded by walls and they have armed guards. You can just imagine what Marlene said when I told her where we could go visit!

The trial was about to start. When we entered the courtroom, the Judge, who had been reprimanded several times for his arrogance and dislike for the Police, was standing behind the bench dressed in his black robe; his arms folded, and announced with a loud voice to his deputies, "Search all those Palestinians for guns." Well, let me tell you that the trial went downhill from there. The Judge and defense attorney were Jewish, the defendant was black, the victim was Palestinian and the D.A. and I were white Gentiles. What a conglomeration.

I testified first regarding the scene with little reaction from the Judge or defense. The victim's brother testified next and did a great job. He testified how he saw the defendant, who he called by name, standing over his brother hacking him in the head with a meat cleaver and then shooting him in the back. He said that as the defendant ran from the store he was yelling, "BGD! BGD! BGD!," (Black Gangster Disciples).

The D.A. then showed him pictures of the scene without the body but pools of blood were evident; the witness started to cry and then stared at the defendant. The Judge called a recess and as the victim's brother left the stand, he started to attack the defendant and was pulled away by the deputies.

The Judge became enraged, he screamed at me for not doing something, he screamed at the D.A. for showing the picture and he screamed at the witness and threatened to jail him. When several spectators got up, he threatened to throw them all out of the courtroom.

I forgot to mention that this was a trial to the court; in other words, there was no jury. This was my first waiver of a jury for a murder trial and also the first for the D.A., who I had several trials with before, and who was head of the Homicide Unit of the District Attorney's Office.

I then testified about the confession the defendant gave that was written in my handwriting, but signed and dated by the defendant. All of the pages were initialed on the top, bottom and several times throughout the statement where corrections were made. It was a good statement and was upheld by several courts prior to the trial, so I had no problem when the Judge said he wanted to see it. He looked at it for several minutes, and then threw it at me and said that he couldn't read it and that if I didn't know how to write, I should use a typewriter.

He then started to scream at me and the D.A. and told me to go back and tell the Chief of Police that he ran a lousy Department and that, "Every grade school has a videotape machine, yet the Police Department doesn't have one."

The defendant then took the stand and said I had beaten the confession out of him and had slammed a table into him during the brutal interrogation.

During the rest of the trial the Judge constantly berated me, the D.A., all of our witnesses and every time the victim's family would move, he would berate them and call them refugees.

The trial lasted four days and it was a brutal four days. What started as a great case was looking bleaker by the minute. The defense had several witnesses that lied their asses off. The trial finally ended and the Judge said that the prosecution did such a lousy job that he was not going to make a decision until he came back from vacation.

The D.A. told the victim's family that he was pretty sure the Judge felt that they would not stick around for a week and he could then reduce the charge of first degree murder. The family not only promised that they would be back, but that they would fill the courtroom. They also said that the Judge didn't intimidate them in the least.

The Judge came back from vacation and again berated the prosecution. He praised the defense and stated it was with a great deal of reluctance that he found the defendant guilty of first degree murder and sentenced him to life in prison. Again he berated the family and called them refugees who dealt in stolen property in their stores and then referred to the book *Hajj* by Leon Uri, which apparently is a racist book. He then slammed the gavel down so hard that it actually bounced in the air and then he stormed off the bench.

The families all met in the hall and were extremely classy people. The question they asked of me was, "Where do we go to file a complaint?" The one that did the asking, I found out later, was a professor at Marquette University. I immediately took them to a relatively new position in the D.A.'s office called the Victim Witness Program. Once the head of the program heard all the details of their complaint, she immediately called for the D.A. himself; she was obviously shaken.

All the families thanked me for what I had done. They said they were all going back to their country to try and put their lives back together. They also indicated that as violent as their country may be at times, their punishment for crimes is much more just.

I really didn't pay too much attention to their complaint because I knew the Judge was a real asshole that I had also dealt with when he was as an Assistant District Attorney. It was not until probably a year later that the Judge was disbarred, not only for that complaint, which was a large factor, but many others. It was also several years later that the defense attorney in that case was disbarred and went to jail for drug dealing.

I read in my memo book and note that a John Doe hearing Tom and I had been working on occasionally for the past year came to an end. I say occasionally because that's how often we could find the witness. Several warrants were issued and when two of the suspects were picked up and were about to have their preliminary hearings, their two defense attorneys, who naturally were court appointed because they were indigent, laughed about the case because it was four years old and they said I would never find the witness. They both changed their attitude when I got on the stand and testified to a four-page confession that one defendant had given. I remember the look that the guy's attorney gave him and then just shook his head and waived the preliminary.

I remember that a lot of the, what I would call good attorneys, would get us on the side and ask, "Just how in the hell did you get that asshole to confess? He wouldn't even tell us the whole story."

Another case I noted was a murder trial that was starting. When it was originally issued, the issuing assistant D.A. was one of the really good assistant D.A.'s in the office. The case was based on eyewitnesses and the testimony of a co-conspirator that was given a deal. By the time it came to trial, the issuing assistant D.A. had left the office and became a federal prosecutor in Florida. The case was then assigned to a new assistant D.A. with a cocky attitude, who didn't need my help—which I could accept, but he wasn't prepared for the trial.

The trial lasted four days and the jury was out about six hours. When they came back with the not guilty verdict, several of the jurors looked at me and then put their heads down. I talked to the foreman and all he said was that I should really tell the assistant D.A.'s boss what a horrible job he did, and that even though they knew the defendant was probably guilty, the assistant D.A. most definitely didn't prove it.

I got Karl to go to head D.A., and he did call the new assistant D.A. and ask about his conduct, but by that time it was really too late and the young assistant D.A. left several months later. I'm pretty sure he went to the public defender's office in another city.

48. Inside Her Yard, Outside Her Fortress

I had a couple of days off and when I came back I got involved in a typical drug homicide. The victim was twenty-two-years-old with a lengthy record. He was found in an alley in the core area and had been severely beaten, shot in the top of his head, and his hands and legs were bound with banding wire. The late shift had the murder and two suspects were already in custody. We helped gather the evidence and got reports ready for the D.A.'s office, which took the better part of the day.

We were just getting ready to go home when we were sent to meet a uniform Squad that had been sent to check on the welfare of an old lady who had lived in the same neighborhood for the past sixty years. Her husband died several years ago and all the neighbors had moved out, but she had no relatives and no means to move. These are the really sad cases. All your do good politicians who want the best for everybody just close their eyes on these people because they're not going to bring them any publicity, so they just let them rot in these crime ridden neighborhoods.

When we got to the house we noticed that the rear door had been covered with metal screening and Plexiglas. The doorframe showed evidence of prior damage where actors tried to get in. There was a new hole in the Plexiglas that apparently allowed someone to enter the residence. All the rest of the doors and windows were securely locked. The yard was immaculate with the grass being freshly cut and flowers along the side of the house. The rear porch had been recently painted and the yard was clean, unlike the garbage strewn about the rest of the yards. The Officer led us to the bathroom where we found the old lady. She was lying on the floor and it was obvious that she had been dead for several days. Her stockings were pulled down to her ankles, but her undergarments appeared to be undisturbed even though her dress was pulled up to her neck. She had a pillowcase around her neck and she was wrapped in a blanket. Her face appeared to have numerous bruises, but much of the discoloration was from the purging of the body. Someone from the Medical Examiner's office came and conveyed the body. The preliminary examination did not reveal any trauma that showed obvious signs of the cause of death. The garbage was wrapped in newspapers from five days prior and we could not tell if the home was ransacked, or if the old lady was just a poor housekeeper. Also, there were four days of newspapers in the front door and at least four days of mail.

We started to make the neighbors and the first house I went to next door was the home of a lady that lived there with her six children. The children ranged in age from ten to nineteen with the eighteen—and nineteen-year-olds being a couple of real punks. The lady was on welfare and none of the older kids had jobs. It was obvious that the kids could have cared less about the old lady next door.

By the time we got our reports called in and all the evidence marked and packaged, it was midnight. We decided to take a break and get a fresh start in the morning—besides, our inept Medical Examiner still could not come up with a cause of death.

First thing the next morning before I even had my first cup of coffee, the phone rang. It was some anonymous good citizen that had been walking in the alley, in the area of the old lady's house, several days prior. He was approached by a black male, who had a box of property that he said he got from an old lady's house, who was dead.

I convinced the caller to meet us at a McDonald's, and after a few burgers and fries he gave the names of several people he had seen go into the victim's house. Within four hours we had about ten people in custody, including the punks next door. After interrogating the ones we thought had the most knowledge, but no direct involvement, we got it down to four that we thought had the answers.

The first one to crack was a juvenile who said the other three approached him four days before the old lady was found. One of the three said they had beat up an old lady and didn't know if she was dead. They wanted him to act as a lookout while they ransacked her house. He agreed and went to the old lady's backyard, where he saw her lying next to the back porch. Before he could say anything, he was handed a television out the back door and told to put it in the garbage cart. Several others then filled the garbage cart with articles from the house. He said he then saw the other three carry the old lady into the house.

He denied hitting the woman or touching her body, which as it turned out was probably the truth. With this information we really laid on the other three. They all admitted to burglarizing the house, but said they found the old lady in the bathroom lying on the floor.

What complicated the whole matter was the Medical Examiner said she could not rule out death by natural causes. It was not until after we told her that we had four people in custody who admitted they had beat her until she quit moaning, that she finally relented and made the cause of death: heart failure as a result of a physical beating. Several months later, and with two of the actors who were not involved in the actual death accepting a plea bargain to testify against the other two, the main two pled guilty to: second degree murder by conduct imminently dangerous to another and evincing a depraved mind.

For that they each received thirty years with an additional twenty years for burglary. I testified to the statements I received from the two main actors, including the neighbor, that they saw the old lady in the yard and said, "Let's get her." Then they jumped the fence and started to beat her. She swung a stick at them, but they grabbed the stick and beat her to the ground. They fled when they heard a car coming. Later on they came back and found the old lady still moaning. They kicked her until she stopped, and then dragged her into the house and put her in the bathroom.

The Judge said it was one of the most aggravated offenses of burglary he had ever seen and gave them the maximum sentence. When the neighbor said he was sorry, the Judge said, "You profess to be remorseful. It doesn't do much good for your victim for you to be remorseful now."

As an added note, my former partner Carl was now a Lieutenant and in charge of a newly formed Gang Crimes Unit. This was a group of uniform men and a few Detectives who responded to and investigated gang crimes all over the city. They were some of the most aggressive and hard working guys I had ever been in contact with. They all loved to work for Carl because he gave them free rein to do their jobs. They were all in plain clothes, used old cars and Squads, and anytime we were looking for someone, all we had to do was call the unit and they had our suspects within hours. That's how in the last case with the old woman we were able to immediately pick-up the eight or ten guys and clear the murder. Carl later became a Captain and headed the same Squad until he retired.

I should also mention that in the old lady murder I said the assailants put their loot in a garbage cart. What was commonly used to transport stolen property was, and probably still is, were the green plastic city owned garbage carts. The thieves would burglarize a house, put the articles in the garbage carts, and leave the cart in the alley. After the Police arrived and left they would come back for their loot. Pretty ingenious!

49. Arson, Drugs and Vagrants

It was now the end of 1985, and I was called to the head District Attorney's office. He said he had asked my boss if I could be given some leeway for a while to work on the Bembenek appeal. Her appeals and all my investigations of the murder of Christine Schultz, and all the trips involved could probably fill a book by itself. I think I'll just continue with my memo book and maybe if I find time when I'm all caught up, I might spend some more time on the Bembenek Case.

Actually, Tom and I spent the next five or six months almost exclusively on the Bembenek (Christine Schultz) homicide and all the follow-up investigation. According to my memo books, we were also involved in at least fifteen or sixteen other new homicides, none of which really bear mentioning. I don't know if that sounds callus or not, when a murder doesn't need mentioning, but the truth is that if I wrote about every case I was involved in, this book would be several volumes long.

I look in my memo book and recall that many times when crews were short, we got assigned to some of the more high profile cases that didn't involve murder. One such was the early part of 1986 when Tom and I were called into the Inspector's office and told to help the Arson Squad on a particular fire. One of the well-known watering holes that had been frequented by Coppers for the past twenty-five years, during which time many of the participants had risen through the ranks and now were in high command, had burned to the ground and was determined to be arson.

We reviewed all the reports with the arson Squad and determined, among other things, that the owner of the building and the tavern licensee had financial problems. During this whole investigation there was never any pressure put on us to look at them favorably. Tom, I and the Arson Squad were all under the same opinion, that whoever was responsible was going to jail.

I don't know if it was Tom or I that answered the phone in the homicide room, but the caller said that the fire was arson, the torch man had been burned badly and had gone to another state to get treated, and the driver of the getaway car was scared and would talk. We made arrangements to meet the informant, who turned out to be the getaway driver's brother, who turned his brother over to us. We took him downtown and he told us a story about how his friend 'Jimmy' had told him that he was a swamper (a janitor) at this tavern and had forgotten something there. He wanted him to take him there and wait while he went inside. The driver said he took Jimmy to the rear of the closed tavern and waited there for about twenty minutes while Jimmy was inside. Suddenly, there was this loud explosion that blew out the basement window and several minutes later Jimmy came out the rear door.

His clothes were smoldering and there was smoke coming from the top of his head. Jimmy was moaning, but told him to start driving back to his house. Once he got Jimmy back to his house and helped him inside, he could see how badly burned he was and saw the skin on his arms and face actually falling off. He said he ran out of Jimmy's house, called his brother and had been in hiding since. He also said he knew the reputation of the tavern and feared for his life.

Just as we were about to leave, he told us that while they were in the car, Jimmy told him that a third party, who was paid by the building owner to torch the place, had hired him. 'Jimmy' also told him that he went to the basement, spread gas all over the floor, broke off a gas pipe and then made a Molotov cocktail, lit it and threw it on the floor. The next thing he remembers is picking himself off the floor with excruciating pain to his face, arms, hands and legs.

Tom and I went back to the bureau just in time to take a call from the driver. He said he had just heard from Jimmy who gave him his phone number from where he was staying at in Illinois. Jimmy also said his face was starting to heal and he wouldn't be back until all the bandages were off.

While the Arson Squad guys left to find Jimmy in Illinois, Tom and I went to the D.A.'s office and obtained a warrant for Jimmy. When we had the warrant in hand, we got in touch with the arson guys and they picked up Jimmy. They brought him back to Milwaukee and put him in the hospital burn center.

The next day Tom and I went to interview him at the hospital, and found him bandaged from head to foot. Through the little opening by his mouth he made the statement that he swore to all the way to the State Prison. He said he had a key for the tavern because he was the swamper, and went there to get some booze. He said that as he was leaving the place there was a loud explosion that blew him out the back door. He denied everything else and no matter what we and the D.A. promised him, and what his attorney advised him to do, he kept the same story. He was found guilty by a jury and sentenced to ten years in prison. The driver moved out of state and there was never any further investigation. The whole matter was dropped.

I recall two murders that were connected and never solved. One was a male who was found in a vacant house, bound from head to foot with clear plastic tape that one would use on boxes. He suffered several gunshot wounds to the back of his head. It was a drug related execution and this was the death mask that we had at our table in the homicide room when we all decided to have chili.

We investigated that one for a long time and had a number of suspects. Just when we thought we might have a possible suspect, the suspect was found in the trunk of his car, wrapped in a canvas drop cloth, and also shot several times in the head. We even went so far as to have the paint spots on the drop cloth analyzed and found them to be consistent with paint buckets found in the possession of another suspect. We also found that the drug world was close-knit and run by fear and intimidation. After several months of banging our heads, the cases were put on the shelf for future homicide Detectives to take a look at. In all possibility they may criticize us for not looking further.

In all honesty, in most circumstances, time would not allow us to spend the needed time on frustrating dead-end cases. Smaller Departments that had one or two homicides a year had more time to spend on these types of investigations. This is a sad but true statement.

Speaking of smaller Departments, by now, as I mentioned previously, the Homicide Squad had increased in size to at least eight Detectives on the day shift and several on the early and late shifts. This allowed Tom and me to attend a two-week seminar in upper Wisconsin that is put on by the state twice a year.

The seminar was held at a Baptist retreat location which did not allow drinking. We were housed in several dormitories, and the main classroom was in one dormitory room that allowed crime scenes to be set-up in the adjoining wooded area. This was probably one of the best homicide seminars that I ever attended, but all the cases were based mainly on Milwaukee murders and most of them Tom and I had handled. The instructor always made the comment that, "This is how this particular investigation should be handled, unless it's in Milwaukee." Meaning that we handled so many cases that short cuts had to be taken, in comparison to smaller communities that would have maybe one murder a year or one in five years. They would call in the State Crime Laboratory to handle their investigation. They even brought up Doctor Harold to talk about our bite mark case that by now had given the doctor national recognition.

After spending two weeks in school I came back to work on the following Monday. Tom was on vacation and I was working with Rosie. The late shift had a homicide where two guys got involved in an argument over money and during the fight, one guy picked up a barbell and beat the other guy to death. That not being enough, he then poured a bottle of whiskey over the body and set it on fire. The suspect may have gotten away with the murder for awhile, but the neighbors called the Fire Department and when the suspect said the victim had accidentally set himself on fire, they called the Police and he was arrested.

This was a run of the mill murder, if there was such a thing, but naturally this one had a twist. The suspect didn't feel like talking to the late shift so they let him sit for a few hours, then Rosie and I gave him a shot. Usually Rosie was the dominant sort of Detective that was not afraid to take charge, but he may have had a bad night or whatever, because he just sat back and listened while I interrogated the subject for a few hours and then took a complete confession.

The suspect was subsequently charged with second degree murder and a few days later had his preliminary hearing and was bound over to Circuit Court.

This was just another typical murder and in about two months Rosie and I received subpoenas for a Miranda Goodchild Hearing. The defendant was challenging whether he was advised of his rights and waived them, and also was challenging his confession. I had testified in court hundreds of times and this was no different. I testified to the confession and advising of the subject's rights and I thought this would be the end of it.

The State rested and the Judge asked the defense attorney if he had any witnesses. To the surprise of the D.A., and me, the defense attorney called Rosie to the stand. Now you have to understand Rosie. He was a large African-American man that not only had a large build, but he also had a large ego. He was characterized by the media as one of the top homicide Detectives in the state. And he probably was.

Seeing as I had taken the confession and had already testified, Rosie found no reason why he would be called to the stand other than to question something I had said or done.

I was seated at the table with the D.A. when the defense lawyer approached us and threw a business card on the table indicating that he was showing the prosecution a piece of evidence that he was going to introduce.

I took one look at the card, sat back in my chair and said to the D.A., "This should really be good." The business card was printed with the name of Roosevelt Harrell, Attorney at Law, with the address of the Milwaukee County Safety Building on it. There were several grammatical errors, one of which was the spelling of Rosie's name.

You have to get a visual image of the courtroom. Rosie was on the witness stand, which was several feet higher than the floor that the defense attorney was standing on. This made Rosie about two feet higher than the attorney.

The attorney approached Rosie and handed him the card and asked, "Detective Harrell, isn't it a fact that you gave my client this card and pretended to be an attorney when you took his confession?"

Rosie took one look at the card, stood up, leaned over the witness stand rail and shouted in a voice that made the veins in his neck stand out, "I demand to know where you got this card! I have never seen anything like this in my life. I think this is an insult for you to present something like this to me."

He then grabbed the rail and at first I thought he was coming right over it. The defense attorney jumped back and stumbled, the Judge spun around in his chair and said, "Rosie, Rosie just settle down." That only set Rosie off more and he really went into a tirade.

The poor bailiff, who had been minding his own business and was cleaning his fingernails, almost fell off his chair. He started to come toward Rosie, but realized Rosie was more than he wanted to handle. Then they all looked at me and the D.A. said, "Do something!"

And all I said was, "Not this guy!"

Well, Rosie calmed down and the Judge adjourned the case. The defense attorney was about to say something to Rosie, but figured discretion was the greater part of valor and he packed his bags and left.

By the time we got back to the bureau, Rosie was fit to be tied. He went screaming into the Inspector's office who, in turn, called in Karl and told Karl and me to calm Rosie down.

The Inspector added fuel to the fire by telling Rosie that he could expect a full investigation into the allegations and if he had anything to do with the business card, he should say so now. Rosie went storming out of the office, followed by Karl and myself. This was one of the best homicide Detectives that the city had ever seen and they were taking the word of some scumbag against him.

Several months passed and we went to court again and I testified about the confession, which was upheld, and the defendant had his date set for trial. This time there were two extra bailiffs in the courtroom, but Rosie just sat at the table and glared. The Judge was a nice old man, very liberal, and was known to give very soft sentences. He said, "Good morning Rosie," but realized when he didn't get a response, that he shouldn't push it.

Several more months passed by and the press reports really upset Rosie. Finally, we received word from the D.A.'s office that the killer had agreed to plead guilty to second degree murder. He also admitted that the whole business card episode was phony, but all he would say was that he got the card from another guest in the County Jail while he was awaiting trial.

Rosie never got a response for his demand for an apology from the defendant, the public defender, the court, or the Police Department and this left him bitter for a long time. In fact, just to add a little irony to the whole episode, after I testified at the plea bargain, the public defender and I were talking in the hallway and he told me that he knew the card was a phony from the very start. He said he felt bad for Rosie, but couldn't go against his client.

We went to the D.A. with this information and asked for action to be taken against the public defender, but naturally the D.A. refused because the public defender denied making the statement to me and I had no witnesses.

What was even more ironic was the fact that the public defender was then appointed to the Fire and Police Commission. The union asked me to testify to the commission about the remarks the attorney had made about the business card and I agreed, but they never called me. That same attorney wound up being Chairman of the Fire and Police Commission.

Unbeknownst to Rosie and me, the Department was still conducting an investigation into the card and it wasn't until January of 1988, that they finally found a printer in Racine that admitted being hired by the killer's family to have the card printed. We tried to get the convicted murderer charged with perjury, but the weak D.A. said the guy was serving twenty years and that was enough.

This case just wouldn't go away and after I retired, I read an article in the newspaper in December of 1992, where the original Judge received documents from the defendant, who was in the State Prison. He said that the Judge had agreed to sentence him to ten years rather than twenty years, in exchange for his guilty plea. He also sent along two documents called 'Agreement and Plea Agreement' supposedly signed by the defendant, his attorney, the D.A. and the Judge. All parties agreed that the defendant apparently transposed their signatures from other documents and placed them on his 'Agreement.'

When the Judge was questioned by the press as to what he was going to do about it, the Judge simply said that he felt sorry for the poor guy and felt his incarceration made him desperate. Yeah, really! I loved the job, but some of the people who handled the judicial system made it very tough.

A few days later, Tom and I were sent to a homicide by the lake front. When we got there, we found the crime scene to be under a walkway that led from the top of the bluff overlooking the lake front to the lake itself. There were several uniform Officers at the scene and a good deal of spectators, both young and old, some carrying their beach toys and blankets.

What they saw was a man lying about 30 feet down a steep embankment next to the walkway. His dirty disheveled clothes were covered with blood and there was a gaping hole in his neck. Upon closer examination, and what would not have been in view of the spectators, was that a bottle of pills had been shoved into the neck wound.

We observed that the Officers had another apparent vagrant in handcuffs. The Officers told us that he was found sleeping under the walkway bridge and had mumbled something about his buddy being killed.

We told the Officers to disperse the inquisitive on-lookers and then instructed them to take their prisoner downtown to the bureau. It took us about three hours to conduct the examination of the scene, gather all the evidence, have the whole area photographed, and have the body removed. We then headed downtown to interview our victim's friend.

Without going into great detail, the vagrant gave us several versions of what transpired and we finally broke it down in writing that the two vagrants had been drinking at one of the local watering holes in the area the night before. After using their last dollar to purchase a bottle of rot gut wine, they returned to their roost for the night, which was under the walkway. They then took turns with the bottle and one of them got a swig more than the other did, and in their drunken stupor they began to fight.

The result was that our suspect broke the bottle over the victim's head, slashed his throat, shoved a pill bottle in the wound and then threw him down the embankment. The suspect then curled up under the walkway and slept until he was awakened by the Officers.

The suspect signed the confession and we took him to the city jail where we turned him over to uniform Officers who gave him a phone call. They recorded that he called his sister and told her that he had killed his friend, and felt real bad about it. The next day he was charged with first degree intentional homicide.

Even the D.A. and the defendant's court appointed lawyer agreed that because of the state of intoxication by both men the charge would be reduced to some other form of homicide. Case closed, right? Wrong.

Ten days later he was bound over to Circuit Court. After several motions to throw out his confession and the subsequent statement to his sister along with challenges to the evidence we had collected, the case went to a jury trial.

As I recall, the D.A. and I didn't spend a great deal of time picking the jury because we thought it was an open and shut case, and so did the defendant's lawyer. Even the defense attorney was surprised when the defendant came walking in from the holding cell to take a seat next to him, a female juror in the front row waved to the defendant. And that was only a start!

During the trial when I read his confession, I could feel the stares from the jury and the stares weren't good. The best shot was when the defense called a psychologist who had examined the defendant for a total of fifteen minutes while he was in the holding cell behind the court. The psychologist testified that in his opinion the defendant could not have killed anyone. The jury was out for forty-five minutes and came back with a not guilty verdict.

I tried to talk to two of the women and one of the men on the jury as they were leaving, and the one woman just said, "You should be ashamed of yourself. I don't know how you sleep at night."

This case had another irony. Several weeks later my partner Tom was cutting his grass and the killer came by his house, waived and said, "Hi Tommy."

50. Body Dump and 150 Hours Worked in Ten Days

It was now the end of September of 1986, and the Homicide Squad had increased by several more Detectives on the day shift and had expanded to the early and late shifts. Tom and I also lost the use of our personal cars and were required to start wearing suits and ties again. Karl had been promoted to Captain and we had several new bosses. It was a high profile unit to head and several bosses vied for the job.

I can't recall who all the new members of the Squad were, but I remember two black Detectives—named Ken and Kenny—who were not only outstanding investigators but good people who Marlene and I are friends with to this day. There also was Don, who after a stint on the Homicide Squad, received several promotions and actually retired as an Assistant Chief and was in charge of the entire Detective Bureau. And there was Dave, a really good guy that I think came to the Homicide Squad with some sort of injury. He took care of all the autopsies. Then there was Nick, a Hispanic Detective who probably had twenty-five years on the job and had gone undercover on the Vice Squad while still in the training school. This guy was one of the sharpest Coppers I had ever known and he knew someone in every part of the city. I could probably tell a story about all the guys on the Homicide Squad, but it would take volumes, so I'll try and limit it to my actual partners and cases in which I was involved with other Detectives. This brings me to a really interesting case. (Not that they weren't all interesting!)

I had just spent about eighteen hours the day before investigating a murder, gathering evidence, taking a confession, and getting all the reports ready for court. I came to work, punched in and was about to get a cup of coffee when the boss said, "Get your ass down to the river; they just pulled out a body."

I said, "I got a case going to the D.A. and they're all waiting for me, and besides, it's probably just a floater and no foul play involved."

To which he replied, "Not this one." He was right.

By the time Tom and I got there, they already had the woman pulled out. A black female who had been in the water five or six days, bloated beyond recognition, wearing a scarf around her neck and a pair of net pantyhose. Also obvious even past the decomposition of the body were numerous wounds.

The body was taken to the Medical Examiner's office where prints were taken and the victim was identified as a twenty-one-year-old female with a history of prostitution and drugs. The autopsy revealed forty stab wounds and a severe beating around the face, head and upper body.

All three shifts worked on the case for the next few days in between several new murders. After going through the victim's past arrests, which included the name of her current pimp, and paying a few bucks to get some information from some ladies on the street, the names of five suspects came up—four hookers and their pimp.

All the shifts started looking for the suspects and the word on the street was that they all left town. Finally the heat must have been getting to the current working ladies, because they apparently convinced one to turn herself in to a public defender.

Naturally, her story was that she didn't have anything to do with the murder and, in fact, tried to stop it. Her name was Jackie and her story was that Vanessa, the victim, had held out some money on her pimp, Michael. Michael then set his other ladies on her at his apartment. First they beat her with several ashtrays, lamps and other objects, burned her with cigarettes, and then stabbed her with a scissors. The pimp made sure that everyone did a little hitting and stabbing so that they all were equally involved. He stood back and watched and directed the blows and stabs, but didn't actually participate.

She gave the names of the actors involved and also the name of the pimp. She was then taken to the D.A. and charged with party to the crime of first degree murder with the understanding that her testimony would be needed against the others, and this would all be taken into consideration at her sentencing.

Several days went past and warrants were issued against Lisa, Michael, Michelle and Lydia for first degree murder and their names were entered in the National Crime Information Center (NCIC) database.

The next day Tom was off and I was doing follow-up on two new murders when the phone rang. It was a Detective from Ridgeland, Mississippi, who said he had Lisa in custody and that Michael had been arrested in Jackson, Mississippi.

I got that phone call on a Monday afternoon and that started the longest week I ever put in on the Department—even surpassing the riots of 1967! In fact, I recall that I worked one hundred and ten hours overtime in the next ten days—that included both my off days. That was on top of my regular forty hours. Also, I must have traveled at least twenty-five thousand miles.

The Detective in Mississippi said Lisa had admitted her part in the murder and had implicated everyone else, including Jackie. Lisa had waived extradition and said she had just talked to Lydia that morning by phone. She said Lydia was staying at the Park Plaza Hotel in Dallas, Texas.

I then made a call to a homicide Detective in Dallas and he checked the hotel and found that four people were staying in a room, including Lydia. He said no one was there at that time and they were planting on the room and would let me know the minute they made an arrest.

The only other homicide Detective working in Milwaukee that day was Don, who had taken part in the original investigation and knew everything about it. I told him the whole story, related it to our boss, went to the D.A. for authorization, and within three hours we were on a plane to Ridgeland, Mississippi.

Marlene was used to this and when I gave her a call and said to pack my bags, they were waiting when I got home. She already had canceled our plans for the next few days and like always, never complained about the inconvenience of the job.

We arrived late that night in Ridgeland, which was a small suburb of Jackson, with about ten Officers including a Police chief, two Detectives and a Sergeant waiting for us. First thing the next day they assigned the two Detectives to us, one white and one African-American. I make the distinction because as we were crossing a man-made dike with a lake on one side and swamp on the other, the black Detective remarked in a casual manner, "If they ever drain that swamp, all they would find is chains and bones." This was the deep South and even in the mid-eighties, in the next several days, I learned a few shocking things.

After breakfast the Detectives took us to the County Jail where they were holding Lisa and I knew right away why she had given a full statement and waived extradition. The jail was a big brick building with a front door and I assume a back door and maybe one barred window on each side. Inside the front door was a desk and behind the desk was a cot with dirty sheets and a blanket. The guy that got up from the cot looked like he hadn't shaved or taken a bath in a month, and only the uniform and badge gave me an indication that he was the jailer.

We identified ourselves and asked to see Lisa. The jailer hollered through an open door leading to a cell block and a few minutes later this disheveled, sickly looking black girl came through the door. She looked like she hadn't eaten or slept for a few days. We signed her out and took her to the county sheriff's building where we started questioning her. After she was advised of her rights and stated she understood and waived them, the first thing she said was, "I'll tell you everything. Just don't send me back to that jail." She said the cells were rat infested, the food was rancid and the doors weren't even locked, but she knew she'd be killed if she even stuck her head out. Then she gave a full statement, both written and verbal.

Naturally, all the blame went to Jackie, the snitch. She said Jackie was bi-sexual and got in an argument with Vanessa and started hitting her with a wooden ashtray. She then jumped on her and grabbed a scissors and started cutting Vanessa's hair. The rest of the girls and Michael joined in the beating, and then Jackie started stabbing Vanessa in the chest. Lisa denied doing any of the stabbing and said that after Vanessa was stabbed, Jackie pulled off Vanessa's boots and slacks and dragged her to the rear steps, pulling off her blouse and then threw her down the stairs.

She said by this time Michael was yelling at the girls, "You killed her; now you have to get rid of the body." But Lisa knew Vanessa was still alive because she could hear her moan.

Lisa said they dragged Vanessa outside and Jackie went berserk. Jackie started to beat on Vanessa and stab her as they threw her in the trunk of Michelle's car. Lisa said she had stuck a gag in Vanessa's mouth and Jackie tied it behind her head. Lisa said she could hear Vanessa moaning and crying in the trunk and at that time Michael said, "Now you bitches gotta kill her." Michael told Michelle, who was driving, where to go and the next thing Lisa knew they were going under a bridge and Michelle was backing the car toward a metal barrier by the river. Once the car stopped they all jumped out, Michelle opened the trunk, Jackie dragged Vanessa out and again started to beat and stab her.

At one point Vanessa grabbed Lisa by the leg and said, "I just want to go home."

And at that time Lisa felt blood gushing on her leg and Jackie was screaming, "Slash her throat! Slash her throat!"

Everyone was going wild. Michelle and Lydia were stabbing Vanessa while Jackie was dragging her toward the river and the next thing Lisa heard was Vanessa's body splash in the water. Everything went silent.

Lisa said they were all covered with blood so they got back into the auto and went to Michael's brother's house where they crashed all over the house, still in their bloody clothing. They got up the next day and Lisa and Michael went to a discount store and bought clothes for everyone. They then talked Michael's brother into taking them to Minnesota where another brother lived. On the way, somewhere around Madison, they had car trouble. When a State Trooper came by to help them, Jackie and Lydia each had a gun and they threw them in a field while the Trooper was walking back to his Squad. They then traveled to Minnesota, stayed a couple of days and then Michael and Lisa headed to Nebraska and the rest headed to unknown destinations.

While staying at a hotel in Nebraska, Michael called home and was told that Vanessa's body was found floating in the river. They then headed to Mississippi where they were stopped by the Police and arrested on the murder warrants that had been issued.

We took Lisa back to the jail and told her that we would probably head back to Milwaukee the next day. Then we headed to the Jackson, Mississippi City jail which was just a few blocks away and questioned Michael. He gave a somewhat different version of what happened, but what he said was enough to substantiate a murder charge.

He said that several of his girls were at his crib when Jackie brought Vanessa there. He said Vanessa got high and seeing she had her own pimp, he called him and said for him to, "Come and get his bitch." At that point Jackie and Michelle jumped on Vanessa, started to cut her hair, then started beating her and then stabbed her with the scissors.

He said he tried to stop the whole thing and even grabbed the scissors from Jackie. He said Jackie then threw Vanessa down the stairs and called the other girls to come and help her. By the time he got to the rear door they already had put Vanessa in the trunk and she was nude except for her net stockings. He did admit that when he saw Vanessa in the trunk he thought she was dead and admitted saying, "You all done killed the girl and now you got to get rid of the body." He said the only reason he went along in the car was to see where they were going to put the body. He denied telling them where to go but admitted he knew the area because it was on the way to his Parole Officer's office. Michael said he would waive his extradition because the jails in Milwaukee were better and besides that he wanted to make bail because he had business to take care of.

By the time we got back to the hotel and had a bite to eat, it was after midnight. We just started putting our notes together for the day when the phone rang. It was a late shift boss from Milwaukee who said they had been trying to reach us for several hours. He said that Lydia and Michael's brother had been picked up in Dallas and they didn't have anyone to go get them to bring them back to Milwaukee. They wanted us to fly to Dallas, pick them up, bring them back to Mississippi and then to Milwaukee.

Not only was it an interesting investigation but the dollar signs were starting to light up. The next two days were my off days and that was time-and-a-half for all the hours put in. As it turned out, I think I had about thirty-five hours worked in the next two days.

By 6:00 a.m. we were on the phone making connections to Dallas and by that afternoon we were checking into the Hyatt Hotel in downtown Dallas. We were within walking distance of the main Police building and after checking in the hotel we made contact with their homicide unit and were assigned to Detective Jim Gallagher—kind of close to my name. He immediately asked where our guns were and when we said back at the hotel, he said let's get them because no Police Officer travels in downtown Dallas without a gun. He then proceeded to give us a tour of their facilities and even showed us the area where Jack Ruby shot Lee Harvey Oswald as he was being taken for arraignment in the assassination of President Kennedy. I have to admit, I did get a strange feeling seeing the steps and doorway in the garage. I immediately recognized the area from watching the shooting on TV.

He then took us to interview Michael's brother Robert, who minimized his involvement in conveying Michael and the girls across several state lines and basically told us everything we already knew. In fact, after taking his statement, we told the Detective that we weren't going to take him back to Milwaukee because he agreed to cooperate and testify against his brother if needed—that, and the fact that we were accumulating too many prisoners!

We then questioned Lydia and after telling her what Jackie, Michael and Lisa had said, she admitted everything, including stabbing and beating Vanessa.

After we were done interviewing the suspects, Detective Gallagher took us to their union hall which contained a full bar on the second floor, closed to the public. There again I came in contact with those Texas Officers that all had big guns, big hats, little badges and could drink like fish.

After several cocktails and at the end of a very long day, my partner Don made this great statement to a table full of armed homicide Detectives: "I just want to let you know that I don't believe in the death penalty." I looked at him like he was some kind of a nut and immediately got up and sat at the other side of the table with all the hats and guns. They all gave him a strange look but let it pass when he bought the next several rounds.

Morning came too fast and by noon we were back on the plane with Lydia flying back to Mississippi, headache and all. We put her in the city jail and then went to find our two Detectives. Much to our surprise, one had been made a Sergeant when the Sergeant became the chief, and the chief was now a patrolman. I guess that's what you get with a ten-man Department.

They took us back to our hotel and before we could make arrangements for the flight back to Milwaukee, the phone in the room rang and it was another boss from Milwaukee. He said the third girl, Michelle, had been picked up in a small town outside of Nashville, Tennessee and he wanted us to get her and bring them all back. Now even the money wasn't looking that good, and it even looked worse when I called Marlene and she told me what I was missing with the kids. But, once again she never said a word when I said it would probably be a few more days.

By this time we were almost out of county money and were starting to spend our own. Besides that, Don had a new Discover credit card that he wanted to try out and he was buying all kinds of t-shirts for his kids. What he didn't buy was a pair of shorts and he washed that same old pair of red boxer shorts every night.

This whole thing started to get complicated so we called the boss and said we not only needed money, but we could use a female Milwaukee Detective to help with the women. Our Department agreed to have a female Detective meet us in Nashville with some more money.

We made arrangements to fly from Jackson, Mississippi to Nashville, Tennessee. When we got to the airport we got the five tickets and the local Detective got us through security with our guns and three handcuffed prisoners. They let us get on the plane first, but when we were going past the cockpit, the co-pilot stopped us and not only asked for our guns, but he also said no one could fly wearing handcuffs. He had this big book of flight regulations on his lap and I suppose I couldn't really blame him. I must have looked out of sorts by this time, because the pilot asked if we could handle the prisoners if they remained cuffed and we kept our guns in the cockpit. I said it would be no problem, but the co-pilot started pointing to his big book which upset the pilot because the pilot asked the co-pilot just who the hell did he think was in charge of the plane?

With that, the co-pilot slammed his book closed and we took our seats in the rear of the plane.

I have never been a real good flyer, but I was nothing compared to Michael, who was sitting next to me. He put his handcuffed hands over his eyes as we were taking off and never dropped them until we landed.

When we landed in Nashville, someone must have phoned ahead because we stopped way out on the tarmac. After a few minutes a van approached and they opened the plane door and brought up some portable steps. The passengers were all talking and when the stewardess brought Don, our shackled guests, and I through the plane there sure were a lot of gasps. This caused Lydia to look at one of the passengers and say, "What the 'F' are you looking at?" Real classy, but I suppose what else can you expect.

Now we had to wait for the plane to come from Milwaukee with our money and female Detective, so we walked our chained threesome through the airport, putting up with all the glances and rhetoric between the girls and bystanders. We were lucky that none of them had to go to the bathroom. We waited about two hours for the plane. When the passengers got off and we spotted our female escort, all I could say was, "Give me the money, and start taking these girls to the bathroom."

She replied, "Thanks a lot for the warm greeting," as she put five hundred dollars in my hand.

Not only did we have enough problems, Lydia, who was seventeen, announced that she was about five months pregnant.

We checked all the prisoners into the Nashville County Jail, who really didn't want to take our prisoners, and we had to appear in front of a Judge who issued a court order instructing the jailers to accept our guests.

We then checked into a hotel, had a nice meal, and then asked our female companion if she wanted a drink, to which she replied that all she drank was wine. So besides a long day, Don and I had to go out looking for a bottle of wine at midnight. Incidentally, that same female Detective was just promoted to Captain in the last week as of this writing.

The next day we traveled to some little town named Clarksville and there took custody of our fourth and last prisoner, Michelle. We questioned her and took a complete statement in which she implicated everyone, including herself.

We stayed overnight and bright and early the next day we picked up Michelle and drove back to Nashville. We had already made flight arrangements for the seven of us, and I called Marlene and said we hoped to be back in Milwaukee that evening. We went to the Nashville County Jail where Don stayed with Michelle, while the female Detective from Milwaukee and I went to get our other three prisoners. Easy enough I thought. Wrong!

By the time we found out where to go, we were informed by several irate guards that we had not told them that Lydia was not only a juvenile but also pregnant. They said the Judge that had issued the court order was really pissed off at us and we were lucky that this was his off day or he would probably hold us in contempt. We were now in a waiting area that was reserved for bounty hunters and all the doors were locked. Next, the female Detective made the classy statement, "Just give us our damn prisoners so we can get out of this filthy shit hole."

Now we pissed off everybody and I told her to keep her opinions to herself because if they threw her in jail, all I had was a credit card and I wasn't going to use it to bail her out.

The guard finally gave us Lisa, Michael, and Lydia, and when he opened the cell block door he was in a room several feet from the door. The female Detective turned and gave him a dirty look. He jumped up and went for the door. I grabbed our three prisoners and said, "Let's get the hell out of here." We hit the outside door and ran to the car, looking back to see the guard at the door giving us the finger. I know for sure that if he had gotten to the door before we did, he would have thrown all of us in the can.

When we got back to our car after several hours of what I considered to be an unwelcome experience, we found Michelle chained in the back seat and Don sunning himself on the trunk. When he said, "What the hell took so long?" all I could say was, "Get your ass in the car, drive and don't ask foolish questions."

I was really looking forward to an uneventful flight home, seeing Marlene and the kids and getting a good night's sleep in my own bed. But, this trip was one from hell. Even all the overtime was now starting to take its toll. When we checked in at the airport, the trip got worse. Again somebody must have either made a phone call or we were on the evening news or something, because the airport security approached us and asked who we all were. The chains and handcuffs didn't help, and then he asked, "Are these the four people wanted for murder in Wisconsin?" The handwriting was on the wall. He told us that all the airlines had been warned of our intentions and we were informed that all the airlines had the same policy—one prisoner and two guards per flight. In other words, we would have been flying back and forth from Tennessee to Milwaukee for the next four days.

I called Marlene and told her there was a glitch and not to look for me until she sees me coming in the door. Again, no real bad response from her, but I could tell she was getting a little agitated.

We called our boss and related our problem and he really had no solution other than to say, "Just handle it," so we decided to 'just handle it.' We already had a big four door car, I don't recall exactly what model, and all we had to do was convince the rental agency to let us drop it off in Milwaukee; however, I don't think we ever told them of our guests.

With that done, we bought a couple of pieces of secure luggage for our guns, locked them in the trunk and started out for Milwaukee, which was just short of six hundred miles away. So the seven of us—four prisoners and three Detectives—started heading north in the rental car.

The trip itself was fairly uneventful other than the frequent rest stops when each prisoner had to be unchained. This would wake the other three, causing a tirade of four letter words. We also had stops at various fast food places where we would walk in with our entourage and watch the stunned patrons.

The only real meaningful happening during the trip, which I have related numerous times in various talks I've given, occurred after several hundred miles. We had all been quiet for a period of time when suddenly this timid voice came from the back seat, "Jesus Christ is my Savior."

It caught me by surprise and I said, "Say that again." I then looked around and saw Lydia holding up a small green bible she had received in prison and she repeated the statement. Thinking back, I should have said more than, "He most certainly is." But the time didn't seem appropriate. I did, however, contact several people I knew in the prison ministry and they approached Lydia several times and her newfound faith did appear sincere.

I don't recall exactly how long it took us to get back home, but it was late the next afternoon. Before we checked the prisoners in, we took them all past Michael's house and had them show us the route they took to the river where they dumped Vanessa's body. No remorse was seen out of any of them.

We took them back to the building, wrote brief reports and headed home. One-hundred-ten hours overtime from Tuesday through the next week Thursday.

Their trials came up about six months later in front of a Judge, that all I can describe him as, is a nice old man who hated to send anyone to jail. Each one of the defendants would have accepted twenty years and several thought they would get life. Here's what they got after a plea bargain:

Lydia—second degree murder with a sentence of twelve years, even though she testified to stabbing Vanessa thirty times. The good Judge said he didn't think a pregnant seventeen-year-old would help throw the body in the river.

Michelle—second degree murder, sentenced to fourteen years, admitted stabbing Vanessa nine times and helped throw her in the river.

Lisa—second degree murder, seven years. On the stand she stated she didn't stab Vanessa and didn't help throw her in the river. It was pointed out to the Judge that she confessed to stabbing the victim but he said, "When you look at the whole picture, what difference does it really make?"

Michael—second degree murder, ten years. He could have stopped the whole act and he also told the girls where to throw the body.

I know that Lydia had her baby in jail and I kept track of her for awhile. I later one checked her record and found out she was arrested in 1996 for forgery and got one year in jail and five year's probation. She apparently wasn't on parole and must have only served a few years for the murder. What a justice system we have.

51. Skull Sightings

I don't know if I'm ever going to finish this book. I'm following my notes, memo books and scrapbook of newspaper articles and every time I recall an old case I remember how interesting it was and how it affected my life. I don't want any potential readers to think that my partners and I were totally absorbed in these homicides and didn't do or experience anything else. Actually, every morning for the first couple of years we started out with several cups of coffee and then about twenty minutes of trying to throw a paper wrapped ball into the wastebasket for a few bucks. After that got boring we bought a dartboard. But, once we were moved out of our cozy little room into a general section of the bureau, our relaxing antics came to a halt. We became a larger unit and our unlimited freedom more or less also came to a halt. There was still unlimited overtime and free days every once in a while, but we usually had something going just about every day.

My memo books show that after the trip, I took a vacation and had several uncomplicated murders and it was now coming close to closing out 1986.

It was a Saturday morning and Tom and I were looking forward to one of those relaxing days where we could catch up on some old reports when the good old phone rang. Again, someone anonymous wanted to give some information on an overdose. I was about to switch him to the Vice Squad when he said several guys helped the victim overdose and also helped dump the body. Now it was interesting!

He gave us the name of the victim and a couple of suspects who I'm sure were a couple of guys that ripped him off for drugs or short-changed him. I told him to call back in thirty minutes and started checking the missing persons. Sure enough, the guy the informant was talking about was forty-three-years-old and had been missing for several months. His parents had reported him missing but because of his age, no work was really done on it. He was a bartender at a bar right across the street from the *Milwaukee Journal* newspaper and the last time he was seen was at the bar.

The snitch called back about an hour later with added information that he believes the body was dumped in Waukesha County, which is adjacent to Milwaukee County. A quick call to that county sheriff revealed they didn't have an unidentified body, but they had a human skull that some dog was found playing with at a local farm.

We picked up the first guy the snitch had named and asked him to come downtown with us, to which he replied, "Is it about Brian being missing?"

Solving murders are not always easy, but every once in awhile all the little things come together just like a puzzle. Some puzzles are for kids and some for geniuses. This was a kid's puzzle.

I don't think we were all the way into the building before the guy told us that the missing Brian was a heavy drug user, but he was afraid of needles. What he would do is have one of his friends hold him down while the other would shoot him up. That's apparently what happened in the back room of the bar after it closed. Brian mixed his own needle full of whatever and Sam, our guest, held his arm while Paul stuck it in him. Brian almost immediately went into convulsions, passed out and after a short period of time, stopped breathing. They tried CPR without results and then tried to figure out what to do with the body. They wrapped it in a blanket, put it in the trunk of their car, drove to a secluded area in Waukesha County and dumped it down a hill by the side of the road.

We asked Sam if he had any idea where the body was and he said that he did. We still had no I.D. on the skull, but the Medical Examiner brought in our famous forensic odontologist who was comparing the teeth against our missing Brian and said he'd have something for us the next day.

We called Waukesha County and met one of their Detectives along with Sam who directed us down a bunch of country roads that by this time had changed in appearance with about two feet of snow. We passed a farm and Sam said it looked familiar, which brought a smile to the Waukesha Detective because that's the farm where the dog had found the skull. Sam finally said, "Stop!" And, said he thought it was in this particular area. This is where another part of the kid's puzzle was put in place.

Tom in his cowboy boots and slacks looked over the bank on the side of the road and said, "I can't believe this shit." He proceeded to take a step forward and slid on his ass to the bottom of the hill, cussing all the way. The way he explained it later, he reached the bottom, put his hand in the snow to push him up, grabbed something on the ground and came up with Brian's I.D., pants, jacket, shirt and some bones. But, no head. We already had that.

Waukesha took care of the remains and we took Sam back to the building where we booked him for murder, knowing full well that the charge would never be issued. We then went and picked up his buddy Paul, whom I immediately recognized as someone I had arrested probably fifteen years ago as an escapee, and at the time he had claimed to be B.D. Cooper. B.D. Cooper was the guy that parachuted out of a plane over some wilderness with a suitcase full of money. Some of the money was found but never B.D.

Anyway, Paul denied any involvement in the drug overdose because he was on parole and in trouble with his agent, who was looking to put him away—which he subsequently did. Over the weekend we must have interviewed a dozen junkies with the help of the Vice Squad, and they really were all quite cooperative. Almost all of them either knew what happened or had a pretty good idea.

By Monday morning we had everything put together and took the whole package over to our favorite D.A., Bob. He scratched his head and said he had a pretty good idea what to charge, but wanted to check with a few more D.A.'s just to make sure. One office led to another and by the time we got to the sixth D.A. they all agreed that the charges would be: concealing a death and failure to render aid to a crime victim. With the added charge of habitual criminality on our friend Paul, it almost guaranteed his parole revocation. Several months later both Sam and Paul plead guilty. I think Sam got a year in the House of Correction and Paul had his parole revoked until 1996.

That was actually the second skull I investigated. The first was a hooker whose decomposed body was also found in a field in another county and again a dog found the body. But, this time someone was with him and didn't allow him to play ball with the skull.

In that case we actually did get a cause of death that made it a homicide and since the body was found in an adjoining county, we considered it their homicide and the recovery of the body cleared our missing person's report. We did find witnesses that said she was picked up on the street in Milwaukee, but the case was never cleared and we never found where the murder had occurred. So, for the next several years we would meet for lunch with the Detectives from that county, and they would always insist that it was actually our homicide and that we dumped the body over the county line. Kind of a warped humor, but that was their first murder in two years.

52. And More Investigations Plus a New M.E.

I still had time in 1986 for several more interesting cases, including a case that involved a victim named Carol. We were sent to a house in the middle of the core area, where we met several uniformed Officers that had a little nine-year-old girl in their Squad. She was neatly dressed, very polite and told us that she had left for school in the morning with her brothers and sisters and that her father and mother were at home when she left. She was dropped off by the bus from school, entered through the front door and saw the furniture in the living room tipped over and some bloody clothing on the floor.

Just as a side thought, it never ceased to amaze me the trauma that these young kids faced almost on a daily basis. Here was this polite nine-year-old that lived in this house with five brothers and sisters, all by different fathers, and her mother. She didn't know who her real father was, but was told that he was in prison for armed robbery. She called the man that lived there 'father' because she really wanted one to tell her friends about. What she didn't tell her friends was that when her mother and father left their home, they carried a sawed off shotgun on a strap under their coats. What an environment.

Back to the story—she saw the basement door open and when she looked down the stairs she saw her mother lying with her feet on the bottom stair. Her body was lying at a funny angle, her head covered with a blanket and a large pool of blood. She ran to the neighbors, who went to her home, and then they called the Police.

It was now two o'clock in the afternoon and we must have been in the home until seven or eight at night. The first thing was to identify everyone that was in the house from the time the body was discovered by the little girl until I arrived with Tom. Then we split up with Tom doing interviews while I handled the scene. I usually called it 'interviewing the body' and I would start by having the photo guy shoot pictures of the body from every angle without moving it until the Medical Examiner arrived. The notes I took described what I saw and in this case it was a black female about thirty years old, five feet tall, one-hundred-forty pounds, lying at the bottom of the basement stairs partially on her side and back with her feet on the bottom stair. She was wearing white tennis shoes, black corduroy slacks, black stockings, white sweater pulled up over her breasts—possibly as a result of the fall down the stairs. Her head was wrapped in a yellow blanket with another blue blanket next to her. Her feet were to the north, right arm to the east, left arm to the west and she had a diamond ring and a wedding band on her left hand.

By this time the Medical Examiner arrived and the body was moved, all the while being photographed at every movement. Once the blanket was removed from the face there was a large gaping hole to the left side of her face. The body remained there for several hours until I had identified every article that I thought was necessary to take as evidence. That included various articles of bloody clothing found on the steps and swatches of hair and blood on several steps. It was obvious she was either thrown or fell down the steps, and after finding large areas of blood and a spent shotgun shell in the living room, it became apparent she was thrown. The body was taken from the scene and now the exhausting project of searching the first floor and collecting evidence started. The City Engineer was also called from home to diagram the entire house and all the furnishings.

By this time Tom was done interviewing all the neighbors and the victim's children, and got the name and description of the so-called 'father.' Now it was back to the building where all the evidence had to be packaged and inventoried—which lasted until about two in the morning. I still don't know how Marlene handled these hours.

The next day I spent in court so Tom and Rosie went to Gary, Indiana, looking for the victim's husband, because that's where he was from. They brought him back to Milwaukee and booked him for murder, but he had alibis in Gary that swore he got there early in the morning of the murder and without any other statements, he had to be let go. We knew we had the right guy, but it was another case that just went nowhere. That is until March of 1990, when I got a call from the Crown Point Police in Indiana who said they had arrested some guy that wanted to give information on a Milwaukee murder. Jimmy and I traveled to Crown Point and found a real good D.A. and met with several of his investigators. They lined us up with some guy that had been arrested for burglary and was looking for a break. This guy told us that Carol's boyfriend Alvin was a friend of his, and a couple of months prior, Alvin told him how he had shot Carol, threw her down the basement steps and then drove to Gary, Indiana to establish an alibi. We took a complete statement from the snitch, who also found us another witness, and then we proceeded to look for Alvin.

This was an experience in itself. The two investigators from Crown Point took us to the Gary, Indiana, Homicide Squad and introduced us to the Sergeant in charge. He was the only white person in the unit and he said he was retiring in a couple of months and was glad to get out. We told him who we were looking for and he said he would assign a Detective who knew everyone in the city. Well, this dude walked in and if I didn't know better, he and Michael the pimp could have been brothers. Here was this little black dude dressed in what appeared to be a tailored suit with rings on every finger and more jewelry than I had seen in a long time—and it all looked real. When told who we were looking for, he said he knew Alvin and his family and even went to school with Alvin. He also knew Alvin's hangouts and thought we would have him in a couple of hours. First, we had to buy him dinner, which amounted to steak and cocktails, and then he took us on a tour of about a half dozen joints in the city.

For the next three hours the only white people I saw besides Jimmy (the investigators had left and I know why), were two guys that were running across the street, jumped into their truck and took off. Jimmy and I knew we were being had by the third joint, because we would just be missing Alvin by a few minutes. We find out later that our Detective was calling ahead and said we were coming and if Alvin was there he should leave.

We left our Detective friend, went back to the motel and the next day called the investigators and told them what happened. They weren't surprised and said there was so much graft and corruption in that city it made Chicago look like a Boy Scout camp.

With the statements we had we went back to our D.A. who issued a charge of first degree intentional homicide on Alvin and with that we put his name in the NCIC—the National Crime Information Center. We were notified one month later that he was picked up in Atlanta, Georgia. Jimmy and I took a flight out the next day, which was Sunday, and after checking into our hotel we went to a small suburb of Atlanta where Alvin had been arrested. It looked like a nice sleepy little suburb and when we pulled up to the combination Police Station and City Hall, there was a podium on the steps and a large American flag. We thought we had come upon some civic celebration, but when we entered the station we were surprised, to say the least, when a dozen Officers in riot gear met us.

We identified ourselves and were told that the Ku Klux Klan was holding a meeting on the steps and that was what the podium was for. We asked what kind of crowd they expected and if we could stay around and watch, to which they responded, "Be our guest." With that they showed us to a room that had a full view of whatever was going to happen. Well, it sure wasn't anything like I had read about, because the Klan members were dressed in suits and numbered five or six and the audience was about eight or ten people who we couldn't tell if they were sympathizers or protesters. The big mucky muck of the Klan spoke his trash for about twenty minutes and then everybody left. I asked the Coppers if this was normal and they said this particular county had quite a reputation in years past, but things had really calmed down. We couldn't see Alvin that day because he had been taken to the County Jail and we wouldn't see him until the next day.

The next day we picked up Alvin, who had waived his extradition, and brought him back to Milwaukee. Several months later he was convicted of a lesser degree of murder and I think got about twenty years in prison, which meant he would be out in about six or seven years. Not much time for a cold-blooded killing.

I always wondered what happened to that little nine-year-old now that I have grandchildren that age, and I'm seeing firsthand how they're turning out experiencing a good and stable family life.

Towards the end of 1986, we investigated the robbery and murder of a Chinese restaurant owner who had been in the area for years. Marlene and I had eaten there several times until the neighborhood changed. The old man tried to protect the money in his register and paid for it with his life. Months later Rosie and I took a confession from one of the parties involved and apparently he took exception with the fact that it led to a long prison sentence. Several years later both Rosie and I were served with federal notices that we were being sued by the actor while he was in prison. He claimed that during the confession I pulled his hair out and Rosie kicked him off the chair he was sitting on. The suit was subsequently dismissed, but it required several depositions and a good deal of time.

Later we learned that prisoners in several State Prisons would file either appeals or other suits and send them on toilet paper and crumpled envelopes to the District Attorney's office. They apparently learned in their prison law library and from their jailhouse lawyers that if the State did not respond in a certain period of time, that their suit would automatically become valid. Their thinking behind the toilet paper was that it would probably be thrown away by some person thinking it was a joke, when they in fact had documented the sending of the letter. Maybe the days of hard labor weren't so bad after all. Apparently, there must be a lot of leisure time in prison.

Speaking of prisons, I've been in most of the prisons in Wisconsin, both federal and state, and in a great deal of prisons outside of the state. It always made me a little jumpy—especially at the State Prison in Waupun, when I would have to give up my gun and then be led through the yard by some little female guard. Sometimes I would get half way through the exercise yard, hear the clanging of the weights, and I would hear, "Hey Gauger, what the hell you doing here? How come you didn't stop to say hello?" All I could do was just wave, smile and hope he was there for life, and if he wasn't, I hope I treated him well.

The next case wasn't the first homicide of 1987; I think there were at least ten that preceded it, but it sure was one of the strangest. In fact, it would probably make a good two-hour mystery on TV. Tom and I came to work and the boss said we were assigned a missing person report. Naturally, there had to be a story behind this. Not that we were too good to handle a missing person, but the workload with homicides was more than we could handle. With that, the late shift took us to the back room where they had three brothers, all with different last names; one being a juvenile. Also, sitting on the table was a missing person report that must have had a good dozen pages attached, which meant it had to be at least a couple of weeks old. In fact, it was fourteen days to the day that it was reported. Now came the strange story.

Four brothers were in the basement of a business place in the core area. They said they were just looking around, but after we talked to them for about twenty minutes they admitted to breaking in. They then related that they were surprised by the apparent owner and several others, including a woman, so they all fled. Some went out the basement window and some up the rear stairs. When they hit the outside they all ran in different directions to their house. Once there they realized that their brother Joe, who was nineteen at the time, was missing.

They waited several hours and then went back to the area of the store looking for him, but everything was shut tight and no one was around. It took a couple of days after he was missing several times at the kitchen table, when his mother asked if he was in jail. The rest of the brothers didn't say anything so the mother filed a missing person's report. Seeing as the subject was older than eighteen, not a great deal was done other than a few reports filed by the uniform men. The polygraph examiner who was also assigned to homicides—he was Don, who I took the long trip with. He gave the brothers polygraphs and they all passed. It was now evident that something happened in the store basement and we had to get in there to look around.

The next day Tom and I went to the store and found the owner very cooperative. He had been in the grocery business in the core for a number of years at several different locations and had been burglarized and robbed several times at each place. He operated the store with his wife, son, and several other relatives. When we told him what the brothers had said, the guy was really cool. He denied knowledge of anything, including his place being burglarized. He said we could search the whole place, which we did, after getting his permission in writing.

We searched the whole first and second floors and found nothing suspicious. We then went to the basement and got around to the area where the brothers said these unknown people surprised them. We brought in some big lights and found a lot of stains, most of which probably had been there for years. We found an area in a corner that the stain appeared fresh, so we brought in a technician who fumed the area with a substance that, when looked at in the dark, brought out this huge bloodstain. There were stains from the basement window to the corner like something or somebody had been dragged across the floor.

This was enough to bring the owner downtown where after several hours of interrogation, and him giving a long list of alibis for the date in question, we had to let him go. He never asked for an attorney and said anytime we wanted him he was available. By this time the technician had taken several samples of the stains, and we got them ready for shipment to the crime lab. The crime lab confirmed that the stains were human blood. By this time we had checked all the owner's alibis and they seemed halfway believable, but without a body we really had nothing but a missing person.

The missing person was put on the back burner for several weeks because of new homicides. We were told that the three brothers apparently had forgotten about their missing brother and had been caught in another burglary. It was another grocery store and one of them was caught hiding in the freezer. We questioned them again for a couple of hours, but they still maintained their original story.

We then got involved in a really gruesome murder of an old couple who were found in their home beaten to death with a ball pin hammer—one of those with a sharp end and a flat other end that shoemakers use. The man was found in the basement work area and the poor old lady probably tried to run up the stairs away from her assailant. He caught her half way up the stairs, beat her to death and her head was down the steps and her legs up.

They apparently had been there for several days and she was almost completely bled out. Tom and I handled the scene, which took several days, including gathering and packaging all the evidence and attending the autopsies. What a tragic way for an old couple to end their days.

During one of our morning meetings with two shifts of Detectives going over all the evidence from the old couple, we were called out. They had found our missing burglar and I was to call some Detectives in Lake County, Illinois. They told me that the body, with our burglar's identification in his pocket, was found in a ditch off the side of a road just across the state line. He apparently showed signs of being tortured to death, and the actors poured a flammable substance on the body and set it on fire.

We headed down to Illinois and met the Detectives who were in charge of the investigation. They were very helpful, but just as in the case where the hooker from Milwaukee was found in another county, these guys were glad we were taking over the investigation. We felt sure that the murder took place in the basement of the store and the body was dumped alongside the road by the actors. We also felt sure that the storeowner was involved and even got a call from a snitch. He said the word on the street was that the storeowner, along with his father, girlfriend, and a nine-year-old, beat and burned the burglar after they found him in the basement of their store.

We thought we had this one nailed, but some of the best cases just never work out. We spent several weeks going over all the evidence, getting a new search warrant for the store and questioning all the parties we felt were involved. By now they had attorneys and refused to be interviewed. We never could type the blood that was found by fuming the basement—even though we knew it was human we could not find any evidence that they burned the body there. We even found paint on the body similar to some we found in the basement.

As a last resort we arrested the storeowner and took him and his attorney to one of our best D.A.'s trying to work a deal that we would charge him with a lesser offense and not charge any other family members. The guy knew we were grasping at straws and after holding him for two days, we had to release him.

That was one of those cases that just fell into that proverbial pit and never got cleared. It was tragic and yet prophetic in that the victim's brothers were arrested again a year later and finally went to jail.

I think I may have mentioned it before, but when the statistics come out and they show that our clearance rate was always in the high eighties or nineties; that also meant that ten or fifteen out of every one hundred murders went unsolved. It just shows how fragile life is.

It was also the first part of 1987 that the county hired a new Medical Examiner. He came from Hennepin County in Minnesota and was really a breath of fresh air for us; he was very professional and extremely knowledgeable. He was an expert in shaken baby syndrome, in which, as he explained it to me, meant that a baby's brain is surrounded by fluid and when shaken by the shoulder this allows the head to snap back and forth. The brain bangs back and forth against the skull causing hemorrhaging and bruising to the brain and also damage to the brain stem. I'm sure he would explain it better than that, but I'm also sure those are the basic details. I was quoted in the newspaper several months after he arrived and at that time I stated, "He's done a fantastic job. He's very professional and easy to work with. He comes to most murder scenes, which never happened before and he asks our point of view, which is important to us."

One of my first dealings with him was when I had to attend three autopsies in one day. It was his practice that he wanted a Detective to view the body before he started the autopsy and observe any external wounds or marks. He also wanted us to observe the initial cutting of the body and observe while he tracked any wounds. A bullet wound would be tracked with a probe and would follow from the entrance wound to where either the bullet was found or where it exited. A knife wound would be measured in depth and width. The three autopsies in question covered a variety of means of death.

The first was a stabbing of a fifteen-year-old, which was relatively simple. The second was a shooting death of a gang member, which was also quite simple as both slugs remained in the body. The third, however, displayed the Medical Examiner's expertise and involved the death of a two-month-old, who the father reportedly found not breathing when he checked on him in the morning. These autopsies were not my favorite to witness. They involved the opening of the top of the skull with a saw-type device and removing the brain. In this particular case the examiner pointed out five skull fractures of varying degrees, a swollen brain and hemorrhaging in the eyes. He said violent shaking of the child, that I previously described, caused the death of this child.

These cases are very difficult to prove and after bringing in the father and mother for several hours of questioning, the father did admit to shaking the baby because he would not stop crying, and he became angry because it prevented him from going out for the evening. He was subsequently charged with a lesser degree of reckless homicide and served only a short time in the County Jail. Its ironic how many people try for years to have children and spend thousands of dollars in the attempt, and some people just throw lives away because it interferes with their particular lifestyle.

I see, according to my notes, that a twenty-six year veteran of the Department was killed in a motorcycle accident. I also note that a nineteen-year veteran of the Department was being accused of commercial gambling in which another city employee had lost about thirty thousand dollars while 'making book' on the NCAA.

It was about this time that we set up a meeting with the new Medical Examiner and the assistant D.A.'s that handled the homicide trials. We wanted to rack our brains to see if we could come up with a reason why we lost four Homicide jury trials in a row. All we could strategize was that you could never figure out what's in a jury's mind. That's why they always say, "If you're guilty, take it to a jury and if you're innocent, take it before the court." That, and the fact that they changed jury duty from a month to a week. By the time jurors realized they were being scammed by attorneys, liberal Judges, and lying witnesses, they got the idea that maybe the guy was a defendant because he was probably guilty, they were no longer on the jury panel. With the shortened jury time the court is always working with a new jurist. Anyway, they still say that it's the best system in the world and I would probably have to agree if the jurors would just listen to the testimony and not let their emotions and personal agendas get in the way.

There was a case where several customers were waiting in line at a fast food restaurant in the inner city area. Someone cut in line, an argument ensued and the guy cutting in got shot in the chest. The shooter fled the scene with a female that had been in line. But prior to fleeing, and while the other customers fled, the female kicked the body on the floor, reached in his chest pocket, pulled out his bloody wad of money and then she fled the scene. How's that for your righteous liberals, who I imagine don't actually believe these things really happen.

The next day was Palm Sunday and when I came to work I had the autopsy of one of two friends that were arguing over a letter to a girl, when one of them stabbed the other through the heart and then cut his face from ear to ear.

We had a good suspect and a new program was just starting on a late news channel called *Crime Line Anonymous*. This was my first of many appearances on the program and it was kind of fun for the family to see me on TV. The actual programming only lasted for a few minutes while the moderator would interview me regarding a particular case. I would respond by indicating that we were usually either looking for a suspect or naming him or her. Throughout the years we got close to the reporter handling the program, and we actually made several good arrests from it.

This was part of a national program that I think was surpassed by the television program *America's Most Wanted*. The founder of the *America's Most Wanted* program is the father of Adam Walsh, the little boy abducted and killed in Florida. As I mentioned previously in this book, this was the crime to which Elwood Ottis Toole, while questioning him on death row, admitted to Tom and I that he killed the little boy.

It was now the end of May 1987, and we already had forty murders for the year, which was a new record. One of these murders involved a guy walking up on a porch, ringing the doorbell and when the guy he was looking for came to the door, he shot at him with a shotgun, missed and killed the guy's wife. I didn't handle the scene but became involved when they took the suspect in custody, but couldn't find the shotgun. Finding the shotgun was necessary because it was a circumstantial case. A snitch said the shooter threw it from a car into the bushes in a park. We searched every inch of the park, crawling through all the bushes and came up with a lot of cuts and scratches, but no shotgun.

The next day was Sunday. I had just gotten the newspaper and a cup of coffee when I got a call from a district commander that his men had found the shotgun on top of a garage. I went out to the scene and found two uniform Coppers and several citizens standing in the alley. One Copper, who was Tom's brother, said the shotgun was on top of the garage they were standing in front of, and they were waiting for a picture car. They had a ladder next to the garage so I climbed up to take a look. The garage was built into a hill so the side by the house was only about four feet off the ground. When I reached the top of the ladder, the garage roof was empty except for the shingles. I asked the Coppers if the gun was on the other side. They laughed and said I should quit screwing around and when I said there was no shotgun there and they checked for themselves; panic set in.

They swore there was a shotgun there just an hour ago and even one of the citizens who had originally found it, verified it. The picture car arrived and I told him he could take a picture of the shotgun that wasn't there, which the Coppers didn't think was funny. They called their boss, who was screaming on the phone, and said he would have their asses if they didn't come up with the gun.

Everyone started to fan out and search the area. I went to the house that apparently went with the garage and knocked on the rear door. No one answered but the door swung open, so I walked in. I walked up the back steps and knocked on the inner door and again did not get a response, but the door swung open. Not getting a good feeling, I pulled my gun and called into the kitchen—not knowing exactly what to expect. I got halfway into the kitchen when some guy came around the corner, scared the shit out of me, and I would imagine with my gun in his face, put some fear in him also. He asked me what the hell I was doing in his house and after identifying myself, I grabbed him by the collar, shoved him in a chair and said he better come up with the shotgun or his ass was going to jail. At first he said he just woke up and I should get out of his house. With that, for some unknown reason, I got my cuffs out and he said, "Okay, okay, I'll get the gun." With that he headed into a bedroom, reached under the bed and started pulling a shotgun out. I stepped on the gun and said to back-off, which he did. I then marched the guy outside carrying the shotgun and we were greeted by the uniform men, which by now had increased to about fifteen. They had smiles from ear to ear and would have given me their first-born, they were so happy to see the gun.

Now came the story that I had to tell my boss, who had already called the Inspector at home saying we had the murder weapon. My friend in the house tells me that people had been damaging his car that he parked in the alley. So the night before, he went out and got smashed, came home, got his gun and crawled up on the garage to wait for someone to mess with his car. The only problem was that he was so drunk he rolled off the garage and, being unable to get back up on the garage because of his intoxicated condition, he left the gun on the roof and went to bed. The next morning he got up and saw the Squad and Officers in the alley and could see the shotgun still on the roof. He sneaked out the back door, climbed on the roof from the yard side, retrieved his gun and went back to bed until he heard me in his kitchen. He had all the paper work to show it was his gun and being unable to think of anything to charge him with, other than stupidity, I let him go. Now all that was left was to satisfy the bosses. I let the uniform men handle their boss and I headed downtown to explain what had happened. My boss didn't say much, other than to say that if I let the murder weapon go, all my good work didn't mean shit and I would be back on general duty.

That's the way it used to be in the Department. We would come to work in the morning, after spending twenty hours the day before clearing some homicide, and we would get slaps on the back. Eight hours later when we were getting our ass chewed out for something, I would say, "What about this morning when we were heroes?"

To which the response was, "That was this morning and this is now, and right now you guys are lower than dog shit." I always wondered how that logic would go in the business world.

53. Squad 107M ... Body in a Bag

It was toward the end of summer if 1987, on a very warm Saturday, that I was working by myself and was sent to meet a citizen "holding property." Kind of an unusual job and it really didn't cause any special reaction until several minutes later when the dispatcher added, "Squad 107M, the property is in a plastic bag in the alley and appears to be a body." Now that made more sense.

By the time I got to the alley behind the address given, I had to almost push my way through the crowd of onlookers, news media, and curious uniform Coppers. I was introduced to a citizen who had a strange story to tell. It seemed that for the last week to ten days, every time he would open the garage doors in the morning and close them after work, he would be aware of this strange odor. He said the longer it lasted, the more repugnant it got. On this particular day he was coming home and parking his car, when he noticed a young boy jump over a wooden fence between his garage and the neighbors. The fence was quite high and when he checked, he realized that the neighborhood children had placed a piece of wood over a plastic bag and made it into a ramp so they could jump the fence. He also realized that the strong odor he had been experiencing was coming from the plastic bag. He tore a hole in the bag and much to his dismay saw a human leg covered with maggots. He took me to the garage and pointed to the fence and said, "Look for yourself, but don't ask me to look again."

My first thought was that it was a doll or a manikin, but that thought ended when I got about twenty feet from the fence. I knew from the smell that it was a decomposed body. The board was off the bag far enough and I wasn't completely sure that it was a leg I was looking at because of the maggots, so I opened the bag a little more and now saw not only a human leg, but two eye sockets full of the crawling creatures, staring at me. I called for a picture car and the Medical Examiner, and at the same time a uniform Officer came running up to me all out of breath and said, "I got a witness; you got to come with me."

With that the Copper took me to a house maybe fifty yards from the body, and introduced me to a mother, her 14-year-old son, and one of his friends. They said that about one and a half weeks ago they were walking past this Scott guy's house and he called them over and asked if they would help him dig a hole. When they asked him what for, he said to bury a body. They knew this Scott to be a little weird so they asked him what happened. Scott related that he was in his basement with some guy who pulled a gun on him, so he took the gun away and checked him. The two boys went their own way and didn't pay much attention to Scott. But several days later one of the boys was again approached by Scott who now related, "Hey, you and your buddy have to help me out, the body is starting to stink and I'll give you guy's twenty dollars every Friday from now on if you'll burn the garage down. I think it will take about three gallons of gas to do the job." With that, Scott took one boy by the arm and said, "Come on, I'll show you." They headed toward the garage where the body was found and the boy said the closer he got, the stronger this smell got. He pulled away from Scott and went home.

I took a complete statement from the boys and had them point out where Scott lived and then went back to the body in the bag. By that time the Medical Examiner had arrived and we pulled the fence away and after having pictures taken from every angle, we opened the garbage bag. It was hard to tell at first because of all the maggots, but it definitely was a black female, partially clothed and in a fetal position. The stench was unbelievable and I asked the examiner why anyone would want to go into his profession. To which he responded, "Look who's standing next to me," and I suppose he was right. I knew right then that it would be another call to Marlene to put out a robe in the garage so I could change clothes and take my suit and pants to the cleaners or this time maybe even the garbage. The decomposed body smell used to saturate my clothes and get into the hairs of my nose which sometimes would last for days.

Anyway, after the Medical Examiner was done with his exam of the body, the body and bag were taken to the Medical Examiner's office and an autopsy was started. While this was going on, several Coppers and myself went to Scott's house and talked to his mother who said he was at work at a car repair place on the south side.

I had a south side Detective team call me and had them check for Scott. A few minutes later they said they had him in custody and were bringing him downtown. I met them at the bureau and took Scott into one of the interrogation rooms, sat him down and read him his Miranda Rights. I told him we found the body in the bag that he threw over the fence, to which he responded, "I knew you would. I should have burned the garage down." So before I could even sit down, and before we even had an identification of the body, I had an incriminating statement.

Here's the story that Scott gave me. He said about three weeks prior to this date he was at a tavern down the block from his house. At the tavern he met this lady that was drunk and wanted to have sex. She said her name was Patricia and that she was having marital problems. He brought her to his house and took her to his basement bedroom where he started to get undressed, at which time she pulled out a gun and demanded his money and drugs. He said he practiced martial arts and took the gun away and gave her two quick shots in the head with his fist and killed her. He didn't know what to do with the body, so he put it in three garbage bags and hid it in the corner of the basement behind some boards. He checked on it every couple of days and noticed that it was starting to smell. His mother started to complain about the smell in the basement and asked him if he had rotten food down there. He said he got the guy upstairs to help him carry the body outside and they threw it over the fence. Then he said, "You guys would have never got me if I had burned the garage down." He gave a complete signed statement, but that's not where the investigation ends. I then went with a couple of uniform Coppers and had him point out the garage where he had thrown the body. How fast things change and how soon people forget. The area was still taped off and I still had a guard on the area, but the crowd had left and the alley was full of kids playing.

I then took him to his house and got written permission from both him and his mother to go into the basement. Once there, Scott pointed out the area where he killed the young lady and another area where he hid the body. It was in that area where I recovered some women's clothes, a belt and an address book. I gathered the evidence and took Scott back downtown, locked him up in the city jail and called the bureau of identification. They had taken prints from the body and had tentatively identified her as a female named Paulette. With that information and the address book, I got a good idea who she was and where she lived. By this time it was late in the evening and I again had to call Marlene and not only had her put clothing in the garage, but also cancel a dinner engagement. And again, never a word from her about how the job was interfering in our private lives.

By now the uniform Coppers had enough so they went home. I went to the last address we had on Paulette's criminal record, which contained some minor arrests like shoplifting and drug charges, and there I found her mother. She was a nice lady that knew immediately something was wrong. She asked if we had found Paulette and when I told her we had, she said, "Is she dead?" And when I told her she was, she started to cry and said Paulette was ending a bad marriage, had four children and really never had much of a chance in life. I had to tell her Paulette was murdered and then I stuck around until several relatives arrived.

The next day was Sunday and I spent several hours at the Medical Examiner's office during the autopsy. The body, clothing and plastic bag had been put in refrigeration so the odor wasn't really that bad. After the autopsy I took all the clothing and bag back to the property bureau, packaged and sealed it all in plastic bags and then put it in one big box that would contain most of the evidence gathered. This was the normal procedure in homicide investigations, but this was not a normal homicide.

I went home at the regular time that evening and had plans the next day to get all the paperwork ready to take Scott to the D.A.'s office. I went out with Marlene for a nice dinner and watched TV. During the evening news we heard how the case was cleared by excellent work by the Police. Remember that saying about being lower than dog shit in a matter of hours? Well, the phone rang at five in the morning. The caller was a supervisor in the property bureau and he was so furious he could hardly get the words out of his mouth. He said that I should get my ass down there right now. With the added sarcastic remark, "And bring your gas mask," as he slammed the phone down.

The minute I walked into the building the same stench that was in the alley permeated the whole first floor. The supervisor was at the door and was livid. He said half a dozen people on the early and late shifts had already gone home and they had a private cleaning firm on the way to see how the entire first floor could be fumigated. I guess the clothing and plastic bag had defrosted and because the bags were sealed and evidence in a homicide, they didn't know what to do. The boss's question was kind of direct when he said, "Got any ideas, asshole?"

It's a good thing I had a good rapport with the Medical Examiner because he let me store the evidence in their refrigerated locker until it was sent to the crime lab, by which time it had stabilized and lost most of its odor. Needless to say, that incident was the talk of the bureau for several days and I took a lot of shots over it.

I was on the way to the D.A.'s office and was told that the press and cameras had been waiting for several hours, when I got a call that a couple of guys in the city jail wanted to talk to me about Scott. Apparently Scott didn't realize that there's no honor amongst thieves. Scott had spent several hours bragging about his exploits with Paulette to two guys in cells across from him. I brought these two guys from the city jail over to the bureau and. In fact, I knew one of them personally from arresting him several years prior and was responsible for sending him to prison.

We exchanged greetings and the one I had arrested some time ago said there were no hard feelings. He wondered if the information he had might help him on a parole revocation that he had pending from the time I had put him away. I told him it depended on what he had and assured him that I would let his parole agent know.

As a side note, I think I mentioned before how important it was to follow through on any promise that you made, no matter how bad the guy was. In this particular case when I told him I would tell his agent he said, "I trust you because you treated me square the last time."

The two were separated and both gave the same story, which indicated that they both must have been conversing with Scott. Scott told them that he had picked up Paulette in a bar, and she said she was leaving her husband after a bad relationship. They went to his basement bedroom where they snorted cocaine both before and after sex, and then said she was leaving. He told her she wasn't, then beat her, strangled her and put her body in plastic bags which he kept in the basement for several days. He also told them that he told the Cops she had a gun but she really didn't and that he'll tell the D.A. that he threw the gun into the lake. He told them that a Spanish guy that lives upstairs from him helped carry the body outside, and he was going to hire someone to take care of this guy so he wouldn't testify against him. He also told them where he had hidden some of Paulette's jewelry in the basement rafters. They said he seemed really cocky about what he had done and how he figured he would beat the case by saying it was self-defense.

Can you imagine the look on Scott's face when I brought the two snitches back to their cell and at the same time another Copper was taking Scott to talk to his lawyer? These two guys had been around the mill and definitely weren't intimidated by a punk like Scott. One gave him the finger and the other said, "So long M.F.'r! See you in Waupun!" I then got a search warrant for Scott's house and found the jewelry right where they said it was.

The next day I took Scott to the D.A. where he was charged with first degree intentional homicide, second degree sexual assault and concealing a body. His attorney was with him in the D.A.'s office and told him not to say anything but he looked at me and said, "You know those two guys were lying." And all I could do was smile and give him a thumbs-up.

The trial was several months later and he tried to plead guilty to a lesser charge but Bob, the D.A., wouldn't allow it. Scott testified at the trial and said the cocaine snorting and sex was consensual. Paulette then pulled a gun and tried to rob him, so he grabbed her by the neck until she dropped the gun, then realized he had killed her. After the Medical Examiner's testimony, my testimony, and our two witnesses' testimony, the jury was out one hour and came back guilty on all counts. He got life plus a bunch of years and believe it or not, he probably is still in prison. The jury was interesting because I really didn't pay any attention when their names were pulled from a box. They answered the usual questions that are posted such as occupation, area where they live, relation to law enforcement or any lawyers involved. My ears perked up when I heard a woman's voice say, "I know Jim Gauger very well from church." Sure enough, I hadn't seen the woman walk in or take her place in the jury box. I immediately told the D.A. that I see the woman and her husband every Sunday in church. The Judge also questioned her about how well she knew me and could she still stay unbiased to which she answered yes.

Much to my surprise she actually stayed on the jury and I was able to talk to her the next Sunday about the case, seeing as the trial was over. She said the case was very interesting and yet very sad. She couldn't see how I could do this on a regular basis and how Marlene could handle it. She also said the whole jury, the Police and D.A. did an outstanding job and that's why the jury stayed out only one hour.

54. More Murders and Snitches

The murder investigation of Paulette and the follow-up on the case lasted all week and probably a good seventy hours. I had off the weekend and came back Monday morning thinking of spending a couple of days updating all my reports and books. No chance. Four murders over the weekend, two cleared and Tom and I had the other two. One we cleared the next day. It was some white kid and his girlfriend that went to a teen dance, and when some black kid cut in and grabbed his girlfriend the white kid invited the black kid outside. The white kid apparently thought they would have a fistfight and that would end it. Before the white kid could even attempt to throw a punch, he was shot twice in the chest and died on the spot. That's what happens when you bring your fists to a gunfight. There were a dozen witnesses for both kids and after the suspect was picked up, he was charged with homicide by reckless conduct. Several months later after all the witnesses testified, he was found guilty and got three years in jail. What a waste of a life.

The other murder was a south side murder that involved two Hispanic gangs. Someone flashed the wrong sign and a gang member was pulled out of his car and shot in the head right there on the street. There had to be thirty or forty witnesses that saw nothing and after several weeks of questioning dozens of people, we came to a dead end and had to move on. I made notes on this one and what amazed me most was the filth that these little kids were living in, and how gangs controlled the entire neighborhoods. I suppose it's starting to hit home again because now when I see these poor kids it reminds me of my first granddaughter, Elizabeth, and how fortunate she is to have loving parents and a good home. In my opinion, these other kids absolutely don't stand a chance in life and will ultimately be victims of either violent deaths or prison.

I spent most of my career in the inner city and I'll take the African-American community any day over the Hispanics. It seems that the Hispanic gangs not only hate and despise the Police, but also truly hate each other; so much for trying to make sense out of nonsensical situations. Maybe I was starting to get too old for this stuff.

A few days later Tom and I got a call from one of our best snitches ever. I think I told the story about Tasha and how she cleared several murders and recovered murder weapons for us, and how we got her a down payment for her house from the feds. Well, this time she called and asked about a murder that happened about nine months ago that Tom and I had nothing to do with, but knew the circumstances. It involved a random shooting on the street and several suspects were brought in and released and nothing more had been done on the case. It was still on our homicide board but was one of those that

I'm sure would have been erased on New Year's Day. The victim's name was Harry and Tasha said he was a friend of hers and the guy that killed him was staying at her house. She also said that if we put a little pressure on him she was sure he would kick in. She also said he was at her house right now and that if we came there and the drapes were open we should come through the front door and he would be sitting next to her on the couch. She also said she had taken his gun away and hid it in a closet. We had absolutely no doubt that she was telling the truth, but still took a Tac Squad with us.

Sure enough, as we passed the house the drapes were open. We parked down the block and had the Tac Officers go through the front door without causing any damage because we knew it was open. Just as she said, she was sitting on the couch with her arms around this guy that couldn't believe what was happening. We followed the Tac Squad Officers into the house and arrested the guy, who was known as M.C. along with Tasha and took them both to downtown.

Once downtown we locked M.C. in an interrogation room, got Tasha a cup of coffee and asked what the hell was going on. She said MC had come to her house several times and was talking about this guy he "wasted." She really didn't pay much attention to it until she realized the victim was her friend Harry. She also said she was sure that the gun she took from M.C. was the murder weapon.

We also wanted to keep everything on the up and up so we got a search warrant for the residence and sure enough, we found the gun in the closet exactly where she said it would be. And sure enough, the ballistics results several days later showed it to be the murder weapon. We had to get the murder file and go through it as best we could because the Detectives with the most knowledge of the case were from another shift and were off that night. We then started our interrogation of M.C. and after two hours we had him admitting to everything but the murder. He said he really didn't want to go back to jail and he was madly in love with Tasha. We took a break and had a cup of coffee and asked Tasha what she had done to this guy because he said he would do anything for her. That's all she had to hear. She asked if she could talk to him in private. We had nothing to lose, so we put her in a room with M.C. and watched through a two-way mirror.

This lady was something else. She pulled her chair next to his, put her arm around him and started to sob uncontrollably. Tom and I couldn't believe what we were watching. This whole scene went on for about fifteen minutes during which time they hugged, kissed and cried. She then pounded on the door and we let her out, sobbing hysterically, and took her to another room. She was priceless. The tears and sobs were replaced by a big smile and she said, "He'll tell you all about it." I said what the hell did you tell him, and she said that she told him that we were charging her with party to the crime of murder, and he said he could never see her go to jail.

We went back in and within minutes took a complete signed confession that wound up getting him twenty years plus habitual criminality that added another ten years.

We waited until the original Detectives came back to work to put the whole thing together and make sure he wasn't confessing just for Tasha's sake. There were witnesses to the murder and he was identified in a line-up. And, not only did the gun match as the murder weapon but we definitely linked the gun to M.C. Tasha was unbelievable and didn't want anything for her information and even said she would testify at M.C.'s trial if we needed her.

I think that was the last time I had personal contact with Tasha but I did get several calls from Detectives even after I retired asking if they could trust her. I would always say, give her anything she wants because she's worth it. And it always was. The last I heard was that she gave some good information and all she wanted was a job with the county, and the Coppers involved obliged her.

55. Hospital Operating Rooms

It was right about this time that several doctors in emergency wards of area hospitals, which handled most of the gunshot cases, were being called to testify about the handling of evidence. The defense knew they were causing problems by subpoenaing the doctors and having them sit in the courtroom for hours, just so they could say they removed the bullet from the victim and what they did with it. It is called the chain of evidence and was rarely if ever challenged. The doctors didn't want to waste their time in court, so they decided that a Detective handling the case had to be in the operating room and they would hand the slug, missile or whatever the object was, over to them personally. This little inconvenience didn't last very long until the D.A.'s office and the hospitals came to an agreement. I became involved in several of these situations, some of which were quite interesting and to say the least, amusing.

It was a quiet Sunday morning until the boss got a call from a local hospital. They were going to operate on a female with a bullet wound to the head. She was under Police guard, but they wanted a Detective there to recover the bullet when it was removed. The boss said even though it wasn't my case, he wanted me to do him a favor, just run over to the hospital, get the slug and come back. I remember him saying, "One hour at the most." Sure. When I got to the hospital I knew immediately why the uniform boss wouldn't let the guard recover the slug. First, I had to get rid of all my gear, gun, handcuffs, books, etc. Then I had to dress in this hospital garb including a jump suit, mask, head gear and foot covers. I had to go into the operating room where they were playing rock music and watch the operation for a full hour, maybe longer. Even though I was experienced in watching dead bodies being carved up, I really didn't care to get this close to a real operation on someone's skull. The doctor wanted me right next to him. He was really a nice guy and probably thought he was doing me a favor, and for some sadist it probably would have been interesting.

The woman he was operating on was in her mid-thirties and apparently the night before tried to rob two guys. These guys had not only an alternate life style, but were quite proficient in taking guns away—because that's exactly what they did. Then they shot her in the head. The bullet entered just above and behind her left ear and by the time the surgeon had placed his clamps and other paraphernalia around the wound, what started out to be a hole about one inch, now appeared to be about three inches. The doctor kept probing in the hole and pulling out small pieces of bone and dropping them into a pan. He then suddenly declared, "A-ha! I got it!" He pulled out his fingers, told me to put on some gloves and said, "Here, put your finger in there and you can feel the bullet."

To which I said, "No thanks, I'll take your word for it."

I really don't think he was trying to embarrass or impress me because he just said, "Okay, I'll get it," and proceeded to remove the slug, dropped it in a small jar and handed it to me.

I politely said, "Thanks," got his name and left the operating room.

One other time, I went to recover a bullet at County General Hospital. I went through the same procedure, had to undress and put on their garb and lock my clothes in a locker. This time the doctor simply reached out the door of the operating room and handed me the slug. Unfortunately when I went back to the locker room, the key didn't fit the lock in the locker. The nurses, who unfortunately I knew, said this would be no problem and I could sit in their lounge area until a maintenance man came to open the locker. This was great except it took him three hours to get there during which time all the nurses came to see this poor Detective that didn't have any clothes to wear. Adding more insults was my boss, who called me for a job, and went into hysterics when I told him of my predicament. Such were the hardships of the job.

56. Repeat Offender—for Murder

In 1977 the decomposed body of Carolyn, who was a teenager, was found in an empty boxcar in Glendale, a suburb of Milwaukee. The girl had one child, one miscarriage and was pregnant again. After several months of investigation, Carolyn's seventeen-year-old boyfriend, Tommy, was arrested for the murder. He claimed that Carolyn met him after her class at a local high school and they went to the boxcar to have sex. During the sex act Carolyn accused him of seeing another girl and slapped him several times. He became enraged, grabbed her by the throat, and strangled her with the strap from her purse. He left her body in the boxcar and after she was reported missing, he went back to her body, which by now had started to decompose, and covered it with a piece of cardboard. Three months after the murder a railroad worker discovered the body. Tommy pled guilty to second degree murder when the District Attorney thought he could not prove intent. On April 17, 1978, the Judge gave him twenty years, which was five less than what the D.A. recommended and added that Tommy, "Seemed to have no feeling of guilt or remorse." Tommy was paroled on December 19, 1986, after serving eight-and-one-half years and was denied parole on six prior occasions.

The parole board said, "Tommy's release would no longer be a threat. He has met the board's requirements for minimum security. He appears ready to return to society."

The psychologist and probation Officer in charge of Tommy said, "Tommy is not a dangerous person and is a prime candidate for rehabilitation and there appears to be a minimal likelihood of possible harm to another human being by the subject." They added that, "There would appear to be little or no merit for him to spend a long period of time in any prison."

In November of 1987, Tom and I were sent to a homicide scene in the central part of the city. The house was a two-story bungalow flat, which was well kept. There was a uniform Officer guarding the door and as we entered, lying on the couch in the living room, which was off the front vestibule, was the body of a young woman. She was lying on her back with her right hand across her chest and her left hand on top of her head. She was fully clothed and apparently had been shot through her left hand and into the top of her head. She was married, had a small child, and was discovered by her husband when he came home from his third shift job. Her name was Arlene, and after all the photos were taken and the evidence surrounding the body was recovered, the Medical Examiner removed the body. I then proceeded to search the entire house while Tom questioned the neighbors. Ironically, I found numerous pieces of stereo equipment in the attic that Arlene's husband said he had purchased at a local store. I took down all the serial numbers and a later check showed that they were all taken in a burglary, which put an unusual twist to the case. But now we were more interested in the murder.

Tom had made the neighbors and found several that saw a male leaving the house carrying pieces of stereo equipment. They also said that the subject was familiar in the area and had been seen at the home of the victim on several occasions. With this information we questioned the victim's husband at great length. He then reluctantly admitted that he suspected his wife of carrying on a relationship with someone she had gone to school with. The man had been in prison and his wife Arlene had written to him several times. He came to see her when he was released. His name was Tommy.

The next day we got Tommy's record and spoke with his Parole Agent, who had nothing but praise for him. I told him what I suspected Tommy had done and he responded there was no way Tommy could possibly be involved. We had a photo made of Tommy and included it in a photo array that we showed Arlene's neighbors. They all made a tentative, identification but wanted to see him in person.

Tom and I went to Tommy's home and talked to his mother who said she didn't know where he was or when he would return. That same evening Tommy came to the bureau on his own and was questioned for several hours and denied everything. The Detectives couldn't contact the witnesses, Tom or me, so they had to let him go.

The next day I worked alone and first thing in the morning I went to Tommy's house. When he came to the door I identified myself and he said, "I turned myself in last night, why are you bothering me?"

I told him, "This time I'm arresting you." With that we went back to the bureau and by this time the witnesses had been found and a line-up was held. Tommy was positively identified as being in the neighborhood the day of the murder.

Now came ten straight hours of interrogation. He was advised of his constitutional rights and never asked for an attorney, phone call or anything else. We went through his whole life from his childhood, through his high school years and went over every aspect of his first murder. Only after he was convinced that several children had seen him by the victim's house did he finally admit that he was at the house, but left after Arlene told him she was leaving her husband. She also told him that the baby she just had was actually his. I then confronted him with the fact that I found his present girlfriend and she told me that she had seen him with a gun. He responded that Arlene had bought him a gun when he told her he had been mugged. He stared at me for a long period of silence and then suddenly said, "Give me some cigarettes and coffee and I'll tell you all about it."

This is the most crucial part of any interrogation. If I was to jump up and leave the room he might change his mind. If I sat back and told him to tell me first, I might upset him and he could go back into his denial mode. Whatever is done at this particular time can always be second-guessed and the results are never the same. This particular time I went to the door and asked a uniform Officer to get some cigarettes, coffee and sandwiches. I then sat back and nothing was said until the uniform Officer returned. Tommy just stood by the window motionless.

He had a couple of cigarettes, a cup of coffee and a few bites of the sandwich—all the time staring at me. I finally said, "Okay, that's enough; let's talk about it."

He put out the cigarette and said, "This is how it went down. Arlene and I had known each other since high school and we wrote to each other while I was in prison. When I got out I started seeing her when her husband went to work. I think I'm the father of her second child. I went to her house and carried the gun she had bought for me. told her that I was moving in with another woman and we argued about it. She was lying on the couch with the back of her head towards me and her left hand on top of her head. I had the gun in my right coat pocket and was sitting in a chair behind her. My jacket got caught in the crack of the chair, and when I reached down to pull it out, I grabbed the gun. She was saying that she was never going to let me go and was going to leave her husband. Something came over me and I just pulled out the gun and shot her in the head. I never stabbed her—at least I don't think I stabbed her."

That was it. He asked for more coffee and cigarettes and while he was smoking and drinking we went over the whole statement again as I wrote it down. When it was all done we read it over together and he signed it. I was quoted in the newspaper as saying that he, "Showed remorse after the confession and was very intense." I don't really recall his exact actions but I always wonder how these Judges, psychologists, and caseworkers can sleep at night. This guy absolutely, positively, should not have been on the street.

His trial came up in February of 1989, and before the trial he pled guilty to first degree murder. He was given the mandatory sentence of life, which was to begin after the ten years he got for violating his parole. During the sentencing the Judge said, "He has forfeited his right to ever walk the streets again as a free man."

Tommy was given a chance to address the court and he said, "Life is a valuable thing and it's not something you can take away. A lot of people look at me as cold-blooded and don't think I have any feelings, but they are wrong. Life is God's gift. The only thing I can say now is I'm sorry for all the families involved."

It's been more than thirteen years since the murder and he's almost forty-oneyears-old and has spent almost twenty-three years of his life behind bars, that's if he's still locked up. I wonder what his feelings are now. I wonder if he's back on the street. These liberal-minded people have short memories.

57. Bembenek Publicity and Motions

I see, according to my notes, that I made *People Magazine* for the first time. They ran a story about Bembenek and they referred to me being assigned to the investigation. The D.A. called my boss and me over to his office and wanted me to do all the follow-up on her appeals. Her lawyers had just filed another motion for a new trial, and I had to read the entire court transcript along with Bob, the D.A. in charge. The motion made all kinds of references to either new evidence or evidence that we had missed. This went on for as long as I was on the job and I think I indicated that if I found the time I would tell my whole story about the Bembenek case. In fact, this motion made reference to statements made by Fred Schultz, who you may recall was Bembenek's husband and Christine Schultz's ex-husband.

By this time Schultz had divorced Bembenek and made statements that he now was convinced she killed his ex-wife. He had moved to Florida with his oldest son and the D.A. wanted us to go to Florida and interview him. They also wanted us to try and find Bembenek's first attorney, who by this time had lost his license to practice law in Wisconsin and also moved to Florida. Along with that, the Identification Bureau had a new machine to search for fingerprints and had matched one from a 1983 homicide. After a check it was found that the suspect lived in Florida, we were to find him and question him about the 1983 case.

Once again Tom and I packed our bags and headed to Florida. We were able to plan this trip out so it didn't cause a big conflict at home. The only one left at home was my son Jeff, and I really didn't care to travel without Marlene.

It took us a couple of days to find the murder suspect. We eliminated him when we found that he had worked at the house and was not even in the same state at the time of the murder. We then located Fred Schultz and went to interview him and his son. They lived in a beautiful home that Schultz had built himself. Fred was the same old egotistical self-centered person he had always been. However his son, who I think was about eighteen or nineteen, was just a perfect polite young man. Fred told us that he was absolutely convinced that Bembenek had killed his ex-wife, but he couldn't really add anything new. His son, who had given tearful testimony at the trial that he thought the killer was a man with a ponytail, now was convinced of Bembenek's guilt and stated that he would not hesitate to come back to Milwaukee and testify.

After taking their statements we met Bob, the D.A., who had flown down, and proceeded to find Bembenek's attorney at his fifth floor condo on the beach in Miami. The place was beautiful, with big picture windows overlooking the ocean. The attorney was a perfect gentleman and didn't give us anything that we could use because of his lawyer-client privilege. All in all, a week in the sun in February was not bad and was one of the perks of the job.

Actually, it was another three months before the motions came before the court. Bob the D.A. had been conducting an inquest the week before and counted on me for most of the preparation. We were both amazed at how poorly Bembenek's current lawyer was prepared. This actually was her third or fourth attorney. Anyway, Bembenek testified and really put on a show. She wore no make-up, sandals, white socks and a prison jump suit that was at least two sizes too big. She even cried at the right time on the stand. I thought she did a lousy job, but Marlene was in the courtroom and said she drew a lot of sympathy from the spectators. Her first attorney was brought back from Florida and he, too, really put on a show. A flamboyant guy that hadn't changed from the original trial, which I thought he lost not only because of the insurmountable evidence, but because he didn't take into consideration that Milwaukee, at that time, was fairly conservative and didn't like his Hollywood actions. Her attorney then called a legal scholar from the public defender's office who testified that her attorney definitely had a conflict of interest between Bembenek and Schultz, because Schultz hired him and was himself a suspect. The motions only lasted a half-day and then Bembenek's lawyer asked for a new trial. The Judge said he would give it some thought but not to count on it. The next day the motion was denied.

I remember at that time that Tom and I had spent at least seventy or eighty hours on preparation for the motions including the trip, reading the file, and interviewing witnesses. I'm sure Bembenek was prepared all by herself to testify, and had looked forward to the motions for months. What amazed me was how unprepared her attorney was. Maybe all the publicity that went along with the case clouded his thinking. I told the D.A. what I thought and he told me it was basically none of my business; all I had to worry about was that I do my job. Which I did.

58. Confession in Colorado Case

I spent almost the whole first month of January, 1988, in court with several jury trials and follow-up on the Bembenek motions. The day after I got back from Florida I had my choice of two homicides. One was a cab driver who was found dead in a driveway and his abandoned cab located several miles away. The other was a twenty-one-year-old who raped his sixteen-year-old girlfriend's seventeen-month-old baby girl and then beat her to death—all because he was high on coke. I took the cabby because at that time the baby was only a month younger than my granddaughter, Elizabeth. learned to handle most anything, but the boyfriend had already been arrested and I really didn't think I could question him without beating his ass. So I took the cab driver who was killed by two hookers, who wanted to rob him for money to give to their pimp. It was cleared in one day with a full-signed confession.

Right after that I got a call from a Denver, Colorado homicide Detective who related a strange story. It seems some guy called the Detective from a fast food restaurant on a Saturday night, and said his conscience was bothering him. He said he was from Milwaukee and had beaten his friend to death in Milwaukee in 1981, and moved to Colorado to live with his sister. He said he was having, "Bad dreams and a guilty conscience," and wanted to go back to Milwaukee and serve his time. Nothing really ever surprises me and that's what made this job so interesting.

The Detective gave me a name and when I ran it through the system, all I could find was a missing person's report that was cleared when the guy was found dead in a park. He had been missing from December to February and when he was found he was badly decomposed. The Medical Examiner, who at that time was our incompetent person, couldn't decide if it was an accident, suicide or a homicide. The victim suffered a blow to the side of his head that left him in a coma and she listed the cause of death as hypothermia.

The next day Tom and I were on our way to Denver. We toured the city with the Detective and then went to question our man with the guilt complex. We talked to him for several hours and he convinced us that he and his good friend had gone out for the evening and had gotten into an argument over a pool game. They left the tavern and were walking through a park when they started to fight. The suspect said he picked up a branch and hit his friend in the head, knocking him to the ground. He then asked his friend if he was alright and thought he got a response of some sort, so he went home. He thought their friendship had ended and never heard from his friend again. Several months later he read in the paper that the body was found, so he left town and moved in with his sister.

We called a D.A. back in Milwaukee and related the story. He said for us to bring the guy back and he would charge him with something, but didn't know exactly what. We brought the guy back and the D.A. charged him with second degree murder. It was later reduced to some sort of negligent homicide after he pled guilty, served sometime in the House of Correction and then probation. Really not much of a penalty for taking a life, but the death would never have been solved if he hadn't come forward.

Life is so strange; I wonder how many other people are out there with a guilty conscience. As I said before, with an eighty percent clearance rate, twenty murderers out of a hundred get away with it.

59. More Cases . . .

While having breakfast with some of my old partners, they reminded me that by 1988 the Homicide Squad had expanded to all three shifts with about thirty-six Detectives, and several Lieutenants and a Captain. Both Rosie and Ray made lieutenant before I retired, but I was the first Homicide Detective to retire from the Department. They had moved us out of our secluded back room and put us in the general assembly with just a few portable walls. I remember one of the ways we kept track of the homicides. We made little grave markers out of paper and hung them on the wall with the homicide number, date, victim, and if it was cleared. We also had a large life-size cardboard figure of 'Elvira' in her black outfit, and we placed the current grave marker right on her chest. This figure always sat next to my desk and lasted for years, until the new Chief of Police came past one day and remarked, "That's disgusting! Get rid of it." Apparently, he came from a very small Department that had maybe one or two homicides a year and had no idea how stress was relieved in our Department. Absolutely no harm was meant and all it showed was that the Chief was never really a Policeman's Policeman.

I remember when I was a young Copper, there was a family that lived in the district and they had several children, including twin boys. These two boys were the scourges of the neighborhood. They were professional burglars by the time they were eight years old and were considered too young to be detained at a juvenile facility, so each time they were caught they were simply returned home. When they were old enough to be locked up, it only lasted several days and they were out again.

Once I got to the Detective Bureau I happened to hear their names mentioned, which were Chester and Lester. They were involved in just about everything and eventually one of them was killed in a drug deal. This was not surprising to me and the only reason I mention it, is that in 1988 I was assigned to a six-week-old baby's death, who the Medical Examiner was calling a homicide.

I did a background on the name and found that it was Chester and Lester's brother. I had never met the father, but when I interviewed him I could hardly believe what I was hearing. He admitted fathering at least twenty-six children to the best of his knowledge, and had no idea where most of them were. He also nineteen grandchildren, was forty-four-years-old and living with some woman who was the mother of about half of his children. I then did a further check on his record and found that he had a seven-page record with the F.B.I. and that he and his wife had killed a child in 1975 by beating and burning him to death. The coroner's inquest showed it was a homicide

but couldn't prove who was responsible, so they both were freed. He also had a record for sexually abusing most of his daughters, but had only spent a few months in the House of Correction. I further learned that his first wife and three of his children had died in a suspicious fire at his home while he was separated from his wife and living alone.

I attended the autopsy of the current victim and the Medical Examiner removed his brain and showed me all the discoloration that he said was due to violent shaking. He said the child was shaken so violently it caused hemorrhaging inside his spine and at some point the damaged nerves simply told the brain to tell the heart to stop—layman's language. Once again an inquest was requested by the District Attorney and after two days of testimony, the Judge ruled there probably was negligent handling of the child at times, but not enough to issue charges of negligent homicide. As far as I know, the guy is still on the street and still producing kids.

One of the ironies to the whole thing was that this latest homicide apparently caught the eye of some national press. About a week after the inquest I got a call from someone on the *Oprah Winfrey* show. They said they were looking for the man that fathered twenty-six children and wanted him on their show, but couldn't locate him. Once I realized it was a legitimate call, I asked the caller if they knew the whole background on this guy and when they said they hadn't, I laid out all the facts to which the caller replied, "Forget I called."

Tom and I spent the next full week in a jury trial. While this was not that unusual, the case itself caught quite a bit of press. It was a murder from almost a year ago where the victim was found shot to death in a garage. Besides being shot he was beaten almost beyond recognition. He was a well-known drug dealer and the suspects were all drug dealers and sons of former drug dealers. All the witnesses had endless criminal records and we had to give immunity to several people who were at the scene of the murder, but didn't take part in the beating or killing. I mention this case because Tom and I put a considerable amount of time into the preparation. We again had Bob as the D.A. who agreed with us that in order to get the shooter, we had to work a deal with the beater, even though he helped drag the body out of the house and covered it with a mattress in the garage. The deal was to charge them both with first degree intentional homicide and in exchange for his testimony the guy that did the beating would be allowed to plead to a lesser charge.

The trial was so intense that metal detectors were placed outside the courtroom and the Judge was given an escort home every night. The jury was picked from outside the county and their identities were kept secret. Now that I think back, the only ones that never received any protection were the Coppers involved. The thought never even crossed my mind and I often wonder what Marlene must have thought when I would come home and tell her how petrified the witnesses, Judge, and jurors were. It never crossed my mind that she might feel some danger, but just like always she never showed concern, but just let me do my job.

As I recall from my notes, the jury was made up of twelve plus two alternates. There were four women, ten men, one African-American, thirteen white, five from Milwaukee and nine from the suburbs. They ranged in age from twenty-two to sixty with three teachers, four factory workers, an ex-nun, three housewives, two secretaries and one clerical aid. Six were single and eight married with between zero to six children. The trial lasted seven days, with Sunday being an off day, and the jury was sequestered the whole time. The twelve jurors were selected and while we were waiting for their verdict, we had a chance to talk to the two alternates who said without the co-conspirator being charged, they would have found the one guy not guilty. Now we were a little worried and when the jury was out into the second day, we really started to worry. But, they did come back with a guilty verdict and the guy got life.

What made the whole case a little gratifying was that the Judge told us to get our boss and meet in his chambers. This Judge was not particularly known as being pro Police, so we really didn't know what to expect. When we entered his chambers he was very business-like but then told our boss that he was really impressed with what he said was our tenacious handling of the case and without that and a good D.A. it would have been lost.

On the way back to the Bureau, I said to the boss, "That comment should be good for a couple of days of relaxation."

To which he replied, "Get a good night's sleep and let Marlene and the kids know what a great job you did, but when you come in tomorrow, it's like it never happened."

The *Milwaukee Journal* did a long article on the Homicide Squad, brought on by a series of elderly murders. By this time the day shift had grown to Tom and me, Rosie and Ray, Mac and Kenny and Dave. Bill was still our lieutenant, Al was the Captain and I think I already mentioned that Karl was promoted to Captain and left the Homicide Squad. The day shift was still the primary shift and received most of the publicity, most of the good trips and most of the follow-up on the good unsolved cases.

Right after this article appeared, *People Magazine* did a piece on Bembenek who had now been in the State Prison for about five years and had recently lost her first appeal for a new trial. My name was mentioned several times in the magazine and I soon received a letter from a lady in Canada who said she had the same last name as I, and wondered if we were related. It seems her relatives came from Germany and settled in Milwaukee.

As I am a first generation American and my dad came from Germany at the turn of the century, I responded to her. She also wanted to know my feelings on the Bembenek case and when I told her of my family background, I also included what I thought of the case. Apparently we didn't agree because I never heard from her again. All this publicity made good reading for the kids and Marlene, but I'm really a low-key sort of person and not used to that.

It had been one and a half years since the robbery and murder of a Chinese restaurant owner and the actor was just coming to trial. The case involved a great deal of circumstantial evidence along with witnesses who weren't sure of what they saw—couple that with a language barrier and several people going back to China. We also went through four different D.A.'s until we found one that really took an interest in the case, and that was only because he was fairly new and wanted to get some experience. The more he looked into the case, the more involved he got and realized that the case wasn't the strongest, but we had the right guy—now just to prove it!

The defendant was obnoxious and also went through several public defenders until he was forced to accept the last one or try the case by himself. Because of the long time it took to prosecute the defendant, he was out on $10,000.00 personal recognizance.

The jury was picked and after opening arguments the defense attorney came out in the hall and said that in twenty-five years of defense work, this was one case that he really wanted to lose. Well, he may have wanted to lose the case but he sure put on one hell of a defense. The trial lasted one week and the jury was out a day and a half and came back with second-degree murder and armed robbery. They said they had trouble with first degree because they couldn't determine intent, even though two shots were fired into the victim. It took a conscious effort to pull that trigger two times. They also said they had trouble linking the defendant to the actual shooting, which was immaterial because he was charged as party to a crime.

Anyway, he got thirty years and is probably out by now. In fact, this guy sued me and a few other Detectives involved in the case several years after I retired. I was accused of several things including deliberately and callously aiding and abetting in unlawful seizures that resulted in his arrest. I was accused of conspiring with Tom and Officers of another jurisdiction in an effort to fabricate his identification. Rosie and I were accused of unlawfully pulling out his hair and placing the hairs in a cap that was used to connect him to the crime. Rosie was accused of knocking him off a chair during an interrogation. I don't think he was asking for a new trial at this time, just a monetary settlement of a few hundred thousand dollars. I made several appearances to give statements under oath and it took nearly a year for the suit to be dismissed.

It wasn't the first time I had been sued and as I mentioned before, incarcerated individuals have the best available law books at their disposal and attorneys that are more than willing to take their cases. But that's our system and we just have to live with it.

The city went thirty-two days without a murder, which was a record since I had been on the Homicide Squad. Things got a little boring so they gave Tom and me a kidnapping and sexual assault case. Apparently, this guy had been watching his neighbor's wife at night through the window and became so enamored at what he was watching that he failed to hear the husband sneak up behind him. The next thing he knew he was in the trunk of a car and was being driven around the city. This went on for several hours and then the neighbor dragged him out of the trunk, beat him up pretty good and then took him into the house, laid him on a bed and stripped him. The husband and his buddy then rubbed the guy down with Vaseline and showed him all kinds of objects that they threatened to insert in various parts of his body. The guy screamed and pleaded so they wrapped him in a sheet, took the keys to his house and car, and put him in the trunk of his own car.

The husband and his buddy then went and burglarized his house, returning to the car with a stereo. When they couldn't start his car they left the stereo in the back seat and the keys in the ignition. They then called the Police and said someone was trying to steal the car. When the Police got on the scene they found the keys in the ignition and thought they heard something in the trunk so they opened it and out jumped this naked guy. He scared the Cops to the point where they almost shot him. When he told the whole story the Coppers arrested the neighbor and charged him with all sorts of crimes which were later reduced to several counts of disorderly conduct on all three parties, because no one wanted to complain. Actually, by the time we got to the scene the uniform Coppers had everything pretty well wrapped up and all we could do is watch this poor idiot standing in the street wrapped in a sheet and listen to the neighbor say he made a mistake and just should have beat his ass and let him lay. I really couldn't disagree.

Every time I think I have seen just about every type of crime, I'm usually surprised by the next call. It was a beautiful Sunday morning and Tom was off. I spent the first few hours preparing for the next week which included going to the D.A.'s office with several cases. I was just going to take a lunch break when my boss called and had me meet him at a very nice residence in a nice area of the city. He was standing in the backyard by a tree and when he said, "This is a new one even for me." I figured it would be new for me also.

Here's how the story went. A very nice hard-working couple of modest means had adopted several children of different ethnic origins. One was a sixteen-year-old girl who, because of her large physical appearance, had hid the fact that she was pregnant. When the rest of the family went on a brief vacation, the sixteen-year-old had her baby in the bathroom. She cut the umbilical cord with scissors and flushed the placenta down the toilet. She then cleaned the baby up and breast fed it. This went on for two days when she started to panic. She realized that not only had she not wanted to get pregnant, she only saw the father a couple of times and she didn't have the vaguest idea where he was and didn't even know if he knew he was going to be a father. That, along with the fact that her parents were coming home the next day, and the fact she was terribly ashamed, made her take drastic action.

She went to the backyard, dug a hole next to a tree and buried the baby in the hole. I know how cruel and inhumane this sounds, and it is. She must have been really desperate to do such a horrible thing. She not only was ashamed of her body and the situation she had put herself in, but was totally overwhelmed by the whole traumatic situation.

The next day her family returned from vacation and she began to hemorrhage. On the way to the hospital she collapsed and told her parents the whole story. She was admitted to the hospital and the family immediately called the Police and their family attorney. The family and their attorney were in the backyard when we arrived and it was obvious that the attorney did not want to be there. His practice was limited to wills and probate and had never handled a criminal case. The Medical Examiner's office arrived and the parents told us the general direction that we should dig.

When I was seventeen-years-old I cut grass at a local cemetery and when the grave diggers went on strike I helped dig a few graves. I also was involved in the exhumation of several bodies, but they had been buried in caskets. This was the first time I was asked to dig up human remains that had been recently buried.

The digging went slow. I dug with a small spade and after digging down several inches, human remains became evident. I put on rubber gloves and cleared the area by hand. To say the least, it was a ghastly sight. My notes indicated the body was found six inches from the surface and was lying at a forty-five degree angle with the right arm extended up and the left arm under the torso. The body was taken to the Medical Examiner's office and after the autopsy was performed, I was told that the baby had been born alive. It had been fully developed and had been fed. The Medical Examiner could not say if the baby was buried alive, but said the death was not natural. This was a very strange investigation in that I never did get a chance to interview the girl and only talked to her parents and the lawyer. The parents were devastated to say the least and the lawyer was sorry he was there and never objected to anything. I filed all my reports and was then off for two days.

When I came back to work Tom and I were immediately given two new homicides and when I asked about the baby, I was told that some other Detectives had handled the case and it was turned over to the juvenile authorities. I knew that without an exact cause of death and without the family's cooperation, the death would never have been discovered or reported. That was another very tragic death.

A few days later I came to work and was given follow-up on a homicide from the night before. This guy had worked at a factory for a few weeks, got injured and was subsequently off of work. He was home sleeping when he got a call about 11:00 p.m. His wife woke him, and then she went to bed and fell asleep. About 1:30 in the morning she heard a loud noise outside in the alley. She put on her robe and went outside. She found their car up against a pole opposite their garage, completely engulfed in flames with the motor roaring and the back wheels spinning, even after the tires had been burned off. She couldn't tell if anyone was in the car because of the smoke, flames and steam. Someone must have called the Fire Department because they came down the alley and put the fire out. It was at that time they said there was someone in the front seat and she saw the person's remains, realized that it was her husband and then collapsed. By the time I got the follow-up the autopsy was already done. The cause of death was a large wound to the left side of the neck, with a full load of shotgun pellets found in the wound. The victim also had a few hundred dollars in his pocket, so we ruled out a robbery.

We must have worked that case for at least a week. One neighbor said when he heard the tires squealing he looked out his bedroom window, and saw three black males running down the alley. Just then the car burst into flames and he called the Fire Department. He could only give a vague description. We then concentrated on the victim and his past history. His work record wasn't the greatest and he had a minor drug record. His friends said he had pretty much cleaned-up his act once he got married, but still liked to hit the local taverns.

The way it turned out, when his wife woke him the night he was killed, it was his buddy from work wondering if he was going in the next day. He told him no, that he had been hurt and then hung up. He must have decided that as long as he didn't have to go to work he would go to the local gin mill for a few drinks. We found the tavern, and the bartender remembered him coming in, having two beers and leaving.

The case was going nowhere and to make matters worse, some lousy neighbor got mad at her boyfriend and made a call that he was the killer. That took a full day to straighten out and by this time we had two more murders, so the guy in the alley was put aside. It must have been two weeks after the murder that we got a call from a Madison Detective. He said they had someone in jail on a misdemeanor shoplifting charge, and the guy said he wanted to talk to Detectives from Milwaukee about a guy in a burned car in an alley that was shot to death.

Just to show you why, to this day, nothing ever ceases to amaze me. The next day Tom and I went to Madison and found this twenty-one-year-old black male who had been arrested for shoplifting. He would have been given a ticket and released, but he was wanted on another misdemeanor warrant in Illinois, so he was being held for them. As it turned out, Illinois didn't even want the guy. We took him to a side room, advised him of his rights, and he gave us this story that he was from Chicago and belonged to a disciple's street gang. He put down this big drug dealer who was paying off the Police in a suburb of Chicago. In fact, he said he had paid the Police Chief five thousand dollars himself and now a contract was out for him and he couldn't go back to Illinois. He then asked what he would get in Wisconsin if he confessed to a murder. We told him up to life, but we had to have all the facts and make sure we knew what he was confessing to.

He then said he and two buddies (that he said he would never name), were walking down an alley in Milwaukee when this car came by and was pulling up toward a telephone pole, like the driver was getting ready to back up into a garage. The driver rolled down his window and hollered something to the three black males that they couldn't understand.

The guy we were talking to said he went up to the car window and asked the guy what he said, to which the driver responded, "What are you niggers doing in my alley?" This guy said he pulled out the sawed-off shotgun he had under his coat, put it up against the driver's neck and pulled the trigger. He said the tires squealed as the car leaped forward and slammed into the telephone pole. All three ran down the alley and when he looked back the car was still up against the pole and had just burst into flames. He said they ran for several blocks before throwing the gun in some bushes.

The guy also kicked into four armed robberies of filling stations, two before the murder and two after. Besides not wanting to go back to Illinois, he said he was having a hard time sleeping at night and actually thought maybe he was being bothered by the thought of the murder. He said he had done just about everything but murder and maybe he actually had a conscience, which I doubt.

We took a complete signed confession and said we would be back the next day to bring him back to Milwaukee. The next day Tom and I went back to Madison and after getting his misdemeanor charges dismissed, brought him to Milwaukee. On the way back I again advised him of his rights. He led us right to the alley and right to the garage where he had shot the guy. The telephone pole was new because the other one burned down, but there were still scorch marks in the pavement. He then directed us to the area where he threw the shotgun, but this would have been too much to ask for if it was still there, which it wasn't.

We took him to the D.A. and had him charged with first degree murder, armed robbery and habitual criminality. Once again this case had an irony because several months later I was called to testify in a Wade Goodchild Hearing, in which the defense was challenging the confession. I testified that I took the first confession after advising him of his rights, and again advised him the second day on the way back from Madison to Milwaukee. The Judge hearing the motions was a little twerp who didn't particularly like Coppers. I had several run-ins with him and I don't think he particularly liked me, and the feeling was mutual. He ruled that the first confession was good, which was all that was needed to convict the guy. But, he ruled the statements he gave Tom and I the next day and the viewing of the scene violated his rights, because it was his word against mine that I advised him of his rights. Tom hadn't testified because the D.A. didn't think it was necessary. Here was this scum bag robber, killer and gang member, and his word was better than mine. As soon as the Judge made his decision he jumped up and left the courtroom. I was fit-to-be-tied. I headed for the Judge's chambers and the D.A. grabbed me and said I should calm down because the Judge would like nothing better than to throw my ass in jail.

I couldn't believe what I was hearing and went immediately to get our boss, Karl. I explained to him what happened and he said let's go see the head D.A. He was in his office and apparently had heard how upset I was and met us at the door. Right off the bat he said, "Don't get so excited Jim. We really don't need that part of the evidence to convict the guy." Telling me that only made me angrier. By now the whole D.A.'s office and several Coppers had gathered.

I told the head D.A., "This asshole Judge called me a liar and I'm just supposed to stand here and take it?" I went toward the hallway leading to the pressroom where several reporters were that I really got along with. I said, "Let's see what they have to say about the whole thing." Karl was shaking his head but wasn't stopping me; but, the head D.A. pleaded for me to stop and said he would try and get the Judge to explain his decision. By this time I already had about seventy hours in that week and just said, "Screw all you people," and walked out.

By the time I got back to the Bureau I had calmed down and we all had a good laugh about it. Those were the days when a Copper could blow off a little steam and the Chief would stand by you. But thinking back to some of those instances makes me wonder about the whole judicial system and how some of those egotistical self-centered obnoxious people were allowed to become Judges. I suppose they weren't qualified for anything else. What's even more amazing is that this Judge then went on to the State Court of Appeals and carried his reputation with him.

However, life goes on and I got quite a few shots from some of the D.A.'s over the next several weeks. They all agreed that the Judge was wrong, which gave me some satisfaction.

60. Sentenced to Death Three Times and a Fresh D.A. Fizzles

Before I get into a real interesting case, Marlene mentioned it was about this time in my career that it became popular for Officers to seek counseling every time they had a traumatic experience. They tried to have a psychologist interview Tom and I after we had three homicides and several autopsies in one work week. We told the boss that if that was the way they were going to handle future investigations we wanted off the Squad, because we thought it was a waste of time.

It seemed that stress on the job had become quite popular as a way to get a disability. I always thought that if you can't handle the job, get a different one. There are hundreds of interesting areas in Police work.

I also noted in one of my memo books that the *Milwaukee Journal* newspaper did an article, sometime in 1989, on how the inmate population in Wisconsin was aging. They gave two examples with these two old codgers in Waupun State Prison standing next to each other. One by the name of Ervin Moss was serving a life term for murder and the other guy, Theodore Thompson, was serving seven years for a vehicular homicide. They were both 76 years old and looked like a couple of nice old timers. Well, I don't know about Thompson, but I put Moss away and he had quite a history.

According to the statement he had given me, when he was a youngster he killed someone in New York and received the death penalty in Sing Sing State Prison. This was apparently reversed and he was re-sentenced to life. He served his life sentence and was freed only to kill again, and he received another life sentence. After he served out his second life sentence he came to Milwaukee and obtained a mail order certificate making him a minister. He then opened a storefront Church and became involved in an argument with one of his parishioners and you guessed it, he shot him to death in an alley. He claimed self-defense but was convicted of first-degree murder and got his third life sentence. He was a tough old coot and may be on the street again. He would only be 88 years old after serving his third life sentence and who knows, maybe there's some sort of record he could try for. You sure would think that after three times, life would mean life.

Jumping ahead a little in my scrapbook, I found a newspaper article from May 26, 1996, and my friend Ervin is still in prison and still waiting for parole. He was trying for the third time and said if he got out he would move to Tennessee and live with his daughter. Who knows, this old timer just might make it out one more time. This is 2001 and I'll have to check and see if he ever did get released. It's kind of funny how I still get calls on old cases and still read in the newspaper about people I put away and who got out just to commit other crimes and go back to prison.

I came to work on a hot Sunday morning in July and was the only one working in the Homicide Unit. The minute I sat down with my cup of coffee I was approached by two Detectives from the late shift. This was their story. There had been a brutal murder in Oconto County in northern Wisconsin. An Indian woman was found in her trailer in a remote area. She had been beaten so badly that at first they thought she had been shot in the head, but the hole had come from some sort of blunt object. Her car was missing and later found in Shawano County. A second car was found about a mile from the trailer, all burned. The plates on the burned vehicle were traced to a home in Milwaukee and two people were subsequently picked up and brought in for questioning.

One of the guys was a twenty-nine-year-old white male who denied any involvement in the murder, but did state that he had been in prison and had been corresponding with the victim for several months. When he was released he visited her several times at the trailer, but had a pregnant girlfriend in Milwaukee and stopped seeing the victim several months ago. The other guy was a passenger in the car with the twenty-nine-year old and was also brought in for questioning. The two Detectives told me they had been talking to both men all night and had come up with nothing. They felt both men probably had something to do with the murder and wanted me to give them a try.

I entered the interrogation room of the twenty-nine-year-old white male who said his name was Danny. I introduced myself like I normally did, tried to get a background and set the mood for the questioning. The guy came from a broken family, which wasn't unusual, seemed fairly intelligent even though his schooling was less than nothing. He spent five years of his youth in a home for boys, two years in a locked juvenile facility and nine years in our State Prison. So that adds up to sixteen years locked up out of his first twenty-nine. We must have talked for about two hours, just about generalities, families, his girlfriend, who just had a miscarriage, and the guy he was arrested with. Now it was time for giving him his rights.

I told him that I was going to advise him of his rights, which he probably knew better than me; he acknowledged with a nod. I read him his rights from a card that I carried and asked him if he understood them, to which he said "Yeah." I then told him that with his background and being on parole, he probably was going to get revoked and would serve out the remainder of his sentence. He didn't seem to be ignoring what I was saying so I kept working on the fact that he really didn't have to talk, but must have some sort of conscience. He just kept staring at me, not saying a word. I must have talked for another hour and was just running out of words when he said, "How about a sandwich, coffee and some smokes?" I said that was a good idea and supplied him with what he wanted.

He smoked three or four cigarettes and ate the sandwich during which time we just had small talk about his life in prison, when he suddenly said, "Leave me alone for awhile and I'll think about it." I left the room and the late shift Coppers asked how things were going; I said I didn't have the vaguest idea. I left Danny alone for about fifteen minutes and then went back into the room. I sat across the table from him and was totally shocked when he said, "Okay, I'll tell you all about it."

He said he had become acquainted with the victim when she wrote him in prison and they became pen pals. He contacted her when he got out on parole and they had a relationship together. He also had a girlfriend in Milwaukee that was pregnant with his child and one day he, his girlfriend and another couple, (the other man arrested with him and in another interrogation room), went to the victim's trailer. When he took his pregnant girlfriend into the trailer the victim naturally became upset and they started to quarrel. Danny slapped her a few times and she bit him on the arm. Danny said the other guy with him, who was named Travis, gave him a tire iron and he struck the victim in the head, threw her to the floor and strangled her. He said she was still alive when Danny grabbed the tire iron and finished her off.

Later on in the investigation I took statements from the two girlfriends who were waiting in the car. They heard struggling in the trailer and one said to the other "Something's going on in that trailer. I hope they're not killing her."

The other girl replied, "I know my Travis wouldn't kill anybody." I got a good signed confession from Danny and then took him in the other interrogation room where he told Travis to tell the truth. Travis gave a statement, but was a little vague when it came to the beating. He later led the deputies from Oconto to where they threw the tire iron.

I called the authorities from the little berg up north and within a couple of hours two deputies and their local D.A. showed up at the Bureau. The two deputies were really nice guys, but the D.A. was new and thought this case was a piece of cake and a feather in his cap. I tried to tell him that the one confession was really good, but the other needed a lot of work, to which he replied, "Are you trying to tell me how to do my job?"

How right I was! Several weeks later both Danny and Travis waived their preliminary hearings and were bound over for trial. Danny went to trial first; he was the guy on parole and the trial lasted about four days. The trial was held in the small northern town and the jury was picked in Green Bay because of all the publicity. It was a good jury and with the confession there was little doubt. That, along with blood samples taken from Danny's clothing that matched the victim's, the jury was out about two hours and came back with first degree murder—for which the defendant got life.

By this time the young D.A. was really pumped up and was ready for the second trial. I told him not to expect the Danny to be ready to testify against his buddy, because he still had to spend a good deal of his life in prison and didn't want to be labeled a snitch. I tried to get him to let Travis cop out to second degree or some sort of reckless homicide. The D.A. didn't listen to a word I had to say and the second trial started.

Again the jury was picked from a different county because of the prior publicity. I had been involved with enough juries to recognize some weeping do-gooders that thought jails were not proper places for anyone. In fact, they just glared at me when I read the fist Danny's confession and nodded in agreement when he took the stand and said he did all the striking with the tire iron and Travis just watched. I could see the handwriting on the wall and made one last attempt to talk to the D.A. and see if he still could work a deal, but he just turned his back to me.

This time the jury was out less than two hours and sure enough, the foreman stood proudly and announced, "Not guilty."

I was seated in the back of the courtroom and wasn't really that surprised, but what immediately got my attention was when one of the victim's family members jumped to his feet. He started screaming and jumped over the railing separating the court proper and the spectator section. He lunged at the defendant, two deputies grabbed him, and his attorney rushed him out of the courtroom. Now all hell broke loose. The Judge was pounding his gavel, the deputies were struggling with several family members, the jury was screaming and two women fainted. The hero foreman tripped over the fallen jurors while trying to get out of the courtroom and now the victim's son put his arm through a glass door as the deputies were trying to arrest him. All I did was sit in the back of the courtroom and watch the whole pandemonium. By now the ambulances were arriving to treat the jurors; the Judge and the D.A. were in a huddle trying to make sense out of what happened. At one point during their huddle I did catch the D.A. look my way and got the impression maybe he realized that he wasn't as good as he thought he was. Always an irony!

It's now 2001, and I read in the newspaper that some guy convicted of killing two court Deputies was up for a parole hearing. Just two days before his hearing he stabbed another prisoner with some make-shift knife, his parole was denied, and he was charged with the stabbing. The stabbing victim? Danny.

61. Another Statistic

It was late in 1988 that Tom and I got involved in one of those murders that just didn't make any sense, not that any of them really did. But this one was really a tragedy. A young twenty-two-year-old man was walking home after getting off the bus from night classes at the University of Wisconsin-Milwaukee. He had just arrived at the front sidewalk of his home when he was shot in the chest; he died right there on the sidewalk. His body was found by a passer-by who went to the house and knocked on the door to ask the occupants to call the Police. The family called the Police, then went out and found their son dead. What a tragedy. I spoke to the family the next day and through their tears and anguish, they told me what a clean cut All-American boy he was. Good student, faithful church-goer, computer whiz and just a perfect son. Not a known enemy in the world and absolutely no reason for him to become another statistic.

The investigation went on for several days and hundreds of neighbors, friends, fellow students, teachers, and even several bus drivers were interviewed. Still nothing! The Medical Examiner had no idea from what distance the shot had been fired, but it had entered at such an angle that we finally surmised that it was a random shot, possibly someone firing a shot in the air. As remote as that sounds, shots in the air have to land somewhere.

I think the real irony of the investigation came several weeks later when I received a call from a minister at a church, quite a distance from the victim's home. He had asked for the Homicide Squad and when I answered, he asked if I was working on the lad that was found shot on the sidewalk. When I responded that I was, he said he might have some information for me. I asked what church he was at and Tom and I went right out there.

It was a large non-denominational church on the far northwest side of town in a decent neighborhood. The minister introduced himself and led us to his office. He announced that a young girl called by phone and he thought he recognized her voice. She was hysterical and said she thinks it was her boyfriend that shot the young man on the sidewalk. She said it was an accident and her boyfriend had just pulled out a gun and fired it into the air. She became concerned because it was the same night and about the same time as the murder. The girl then said her boyfriend was coming in the door and she hung up. The minister said he thought he recognized the voice but wasn't sure. He thought she might be in a youth group in the church. I told him that was great, for him to give me her name and let us handle it. To which he replied, "I can't tell you."

To which I replied, "What?"

He said that he would contact the girl and if she wished to talk to me he would arrange an interview; otherwise, it was his pastoral obligation not to divulge her name or the contents of their conversation.

I thought Tom was going to climb down his throat. Not being as subtle as me, Tom said, "What the hell is the matter with you? We have a dead kid that may have been caused by a tragic accident and you won't help us?" You know what the minister did? He turned around, went into his office and shut and locked the door.

We went back and told our boss about it, who called his boss, who said we should run it past a D.A. The D.A. referenced the state statutes and couldn't come up with a defining reason one way or the other. He suggested that we wait a few days and call the minister and see what he says. I couldn't believe what had transpired in the past few hours. We waited three days and went back to the church. The minister said he would talk to me, but not Tom. Tom was furious but relented, and I went into the minister's office where he closed the door. He then announced that the whole thing was a mistake and that he didn't want to talk anymore. I asked him if he found the girl, to which he wouldn't respond. I then asked him why he called in the first place and his response was great, "I just wanted to do my duty as a citizen."

I couldn't believe what I was hearing and when I told Tom, he went into a tirade. The minister came out of his office and said we should leave and not come back. This whole matter was discussed at great length with several D.A.s and our boss. The conclusion was that we could actually start a John Doe hearing and subpoena the minister. This was presented to the head D.A., and he said his office would handle it and let us know what they found out.

After several months and numerous inquiries of the D.A.'s office, we were told that their investigation did not warrant a John Doe and we should drop the whole subject. To this day I believe the murder is still unsolved and has never been worked on since.

It's kind of funny that I keep writing about all these murders and what a tremendous job I had, and I kind of let slide that my personal life was still going on. The kids were getting older. Karen and Kristie were married and Liz, our first granddaughter, was born. We were very involved in a great church and life was really good. The one thing which will never cease to amaze me is that Marlene kept this whole family focused and was able to manage the disruptive nature caused by my job. When I think back, I realize there may have been many stressful situations with the kids growing up, especially with Karen and Kristie dating and staying out late at night. But once again, Marlene handled everything and any traumatic experiences during that time were far outweighed by all the good times our family had, and continue to have to this day.

Back at work, Tom and I were sent to a military reserve base in the city and were taken by several uniform Officers to a shed on the base. Inside was a uniformed soldier lying on his back with a huge hole in his left chest, and a large forty-five-caliber gun lying by his side. The whole investigation didn't take but a matter of a few hours, and the poor soldier just became another statistic. What really happened was that he was from Illinois and his wife had multiple sclerosis and he couldn't get a transfer to a base nearer to her. That, along with mounting medical bills, not being able to be with his children, and some emotional problems overlooked by the service, was more than he could handle. He wrote a letter to his Commanding Officer, checked out the forty-five and took his life. It was another bureaucratic mistake and just another statistic easily forgotten. Very sad.

The next day I was sent to a local hospital to investigate a baby that was dead and covered with bruises. The baby was three weeks old and all the marks on the body didn't really look like bruising to me, but the Medical Examiner's investigator, nurses, doctor, and someone from the Youth Aid Bureau said they were bruises, so who was I to argue. After ten hours of investigation, interviews and the autopsy, it was decided the bruises were mongoloid spots from birth. The mother was single with four other kids, on welfare, a lesbian with a live-in partner and being treated for syphilis. She was also pregnant by some guy she slept with one night in Chicago and the baby in question also had syphilis. The baby actually died of Sudden Infant Death Syndrome (SIDS), but in reality it was probably a blessing because what chance did she really have in life?

I'm going through my memo books and scrapbook of newspaper clippings of many of my cases and now am trying to bring this writing to an end. I went through half of a memo book and counted sixteen additional murders that I worked on and fourteen additional autopsies that I attended. That, along with all the court time and trying to keep a somewhat normal family life, was starting to take its toll. Probably the fact that I was fifty-three years old at the time and had planned on retiring at fifty-two, had something to do with it.

The job just could not have been more interesting and we had a great boss in Bill, but I recall I think I was starting to burn out and thinking of maybe looking for something else. I do recall that Tom and I had the best of everything and some of the younger Homicide Detectives on other shifts made several comments wondering when I was planning on retiring. Once again Marlene never put any pressure on me one way or the other.

62. Continuous Custody

It was now 1988, and I had three big trials coming up that needed a lot of work. It seemed these cases took forever to come to trial, mainly because the defense knew that witnesses would either disappear or in many cases become victims themselves.

Prior to these trials the D.A. would always have us locate the witnesses, go over their testimony and let them read the reports we had filed, sometimes two years prior, to refresh their memory. Many times these weren't your normal type good citizen witnesses, and usually they had a criminal past and only became witnesses to save themselves. Anyhow, it was a busy time with the holidays coming and I really didn't want another big case.

Sure enough, we got a call from the State Prison that someone wanted to talk about a murder. I spent a great deal of time in prisons throughout the United States and they all pretty much were the same. Everybody wanted to rat on someone else so they could get some sort of a break. We would always go to these interviews somewhat apprehensive because the snitch usually didn't want to testify, but always wanted something in return for information.

This guy was different. He was a petty thief that was going to get transferred to a work camp in a couple of months and by summer would probably be on the street. He didn't ask for anything and just said that he was getting tired of hearing this guy brag about killing this old man with a crowbar and never getting caught, even though he left a cigarette lighter on the scene. He gave us the guy's name and said the murder supposedly happened around this guy's house and occurred just a short time before he went to jail. We had several open homicides and nothing he said sounded familiar, so we said we'd look into it and get back to him. The snitch said that's all he knew, wouldn't testify to anything anyway, and really never wanted to see us again.

It took Tom and me about three days of searching open homicides, in between several other death investigations, when we found the one we were looking for. It was a seventy-five year old man on the south side who lived alone. He was found by a neighbor lying on his bed covered with blood and a crowbar across his chest. The rear door had been forced open and the place ransacked. The only thing the neighbor knew for sure that was missing was a TV the old man had in his kitchen.

Now that we had the right murder, we had to prove who did it. Tom and I had nothing to do with the original investigation so we took a day to read over the whole file. We then went to the Property Bureau and checked what evidence was recovered at the scene. Much to our surprise we found a cigarette lighter that could not be identified as the victim's and the crowbar, which was the murder weapon.

With this information we went to the Probation and Parole Department with the name of our suspect, Steve, and they supplied us with the names of Raul and Hector who were his known associates. We then checked the prison system and found that both Steve and Hector were locked up in two different prisons and Raul was out on the street. We checked the records for Raul and found that he was on probation. When we contacted his Probation Officer and told him the circumstances he immediately put a probation hold on him. That gave us the authorization to pick him up without a warrant.

When we got to work the next morning, the late shift had picked up Raul and he was all primed for us. We walked into the interrogation room and Raul jumped up and blurted out, "I had nothing to do with killing the old man."

I said, "What the hell are you talking about?"

And he said, "I knew this was gonna happen and all I did was drive the car and get rid of the TV." Some confessions take hours and some take minutes.

Raul said he took Steve and Hector to a house they wanted to burglarize. It was early in the morning and they were only gone for a short period of time. When they came back to the car, one of them was carrying a TV and the other had some sort of ring. Hector said, "I think we killed the old guy. Let's get the hell out of here!" Raul drove to his house and said that by this time he was really scared. He said he and Steve went to a drug house with the TV and traded it for a half ounce of coke, went back to his house and smoked it up. The next day they saw the murder reported on TV and even saw a Detective carrying out the crowbar that belonged to Steve. Raul then took us past the drug house where he traded the TV for the coke. We then checked with the Vice Squad and not only did they have a record on the drug house, but it was knocked off two days after the murder and the TV was taken as evidence. No one could ever find the owner of the TV. It was just about to be disposed of by the Property Bureau when we took Raul down there and he identified it as the one he got from Steve.

We took Raul to the D.A.'s office where he acknowledged the statement he had given Tom and I. He then was given access to a Public Defender and a deal was worked out where if Raul testified against Steve and Hector, he would be charged with a felony, but the jail time would be stayed with the condition that he stay out of trouble. I think I mentioned it before, how these supposedly tough criminals would prey on helpless victims, but would sell their soul, their mother, their unborn child, or their best friend to save their hide.

Now with Raul's statement and our other physical evidence, we made arrangements to go to the two State Prisons to interview Steve and Hector.

Steve was first; he was in the maximum security prison. We had called ahead and he was waiting for us in the Administration Building. He was a little guy who thought he was pretty macho and definitely had an attitude. We introduced ourselves, and after a little small talk, advised him of his rights, to which he gave a classic response. "I know why you guys are here and I've already done nine years of hard time in my life so you're not fooling anyone. I've just decided to tell you the whole story." He then proceeded to give us a full confession with a couple of variations that would come out later in court. He blamed the whole thing on Hector and said he tried to stop Hector, but the situation got out of control. That was good enough for us. Just his admitting being on the scene was good enough for a conviction, along with the physical evidence and Raul's testimony.

Next, was Hector who was in a medium security prison a few miles away. We talked to him the next day and once we showed him the statement Steve gave us blaming Hector, we couldn't stop him from talking. He also gave a full confession and even admitted holding the old man down while Steve beat the old guy with the crowbar. Hector had just gotten three years for burglary and the only thing that worried him was if I thought his girlfriend would wait for him. I said, "If she's got about twenty years to waste, I suppose she will."

To which he replied "I think I'll hang myself."

To which I replied, "Whatever turns you on."

Steve and Hector were both charged with first degree intentional homicide and burglary. The D.A.'s office was all excited about the confessions taken in prison because it challenged a Supreme Court ruling regarding "Continuous Custody." In other words, could we go to prison and take a confession without their lawyers being made aware that we were talking to them? The case was good without the confessions so the D.A.'s office was going to push it all the way. There were so many pre-trial motions regarding the confessions, rulings, and appeals, that the actual trial didn't take place until after Tom had died. Raul got probation and Steve and Hector both got life. I wonder if his girlfriend waited.

63. Prison Interviews

Seeing as how I'm getting closer to the end of my stories, this might be a good time to tell about a few experiences that I had interviewing people at various state and federal prisons. One of the first federal prisons I went to was in Stillwater, Minnesota. It wasn't really my case, but the Homicide Squad had just started and Pat, my partner, had someone there to talk to. What amazed me was not only the size of the prison, but when we talked to several inmates, they all agreed that it was just like living in a hotel, except they couldn't leave and tour the countryside. They said the food was excellent, the recreation was anything they wanted, including first run movies and if they didn't want to work, they weren't forced to. Now these were some hardened criminals that had spent considerable time behind bars.

The next federal lockup I visited was in Virginia, again with Pat, and again with the same opinion from the inmates that they had basically all the comforts of home.

State and local holding prisons are somewhat different, especially in some of your southern states, where conditions could best be described as the guests knew that they were there because they committed a crime, and the best that they could ask for was to come out of there alive. Say no more.

Some interviews were conducted in well-lit comfortable rooms that created a good atmosphere, while other times we were cramped in three by three foot rooms and talked through glass on a phone. Sometimes we got excellent cooperation from the prison officials and sometimes, like in the Cook County Chicago Jail, we were purposely stymied in our interviews.

I remember going to Chicago with Mack and talking to a killer pimp drug dealer named Shorty G. The jailer brought Shorty G into the Captain's office and sat us around a table. The Captain came into the room, said nothing to us and told Shorty G to, "Keep your mouth shut, and don't tell these assholes anything." With that he turned around, walked away and the jailer came in and said our time was up. Who knows what was going on, because other times I went down there and got great cooperation. I probably do know, but just don't want to put it in writing!

Our State Prisons were entirely different; we always got great cooperation! We would call, make reservations for a specific time, and our guest would always be ready for us. That's one thing about prison interviews, you always knew where the interviewee was and he or she was always available. I remember going many times to the woman's prison in Taycheeda, especially during the Bembeneck years. These were some tough ladies that used strong language and didn't particularly care how they looked or what they said.

When going to the prisons for men, security was always tight with lots of guards, metal detectors, steel doors and security cameras. After going through all these checks, they would assign a little female guard to walk us through the yard to the Administration Building. In that yard you could find all sorts of things—like a group of Indians sitting around in headdress pounding on a drum, or ball games, or the most common exercise, lifting weights.

I remember going to this one prison about five or six times in a two-week period. We got to know the guards in the front office. One time they had the metal detectors set so tight that I was just about naked and the alarm still went off. I finally took my shoes off and sure enough, it was the metal eyeholes on my shoes that set off the alarm.

We always placed our guns in lockers before the metal detectors and the next time I went there, they said that because of the shoe incident, I should just come around the detector. We all had a laugh and then started to go through the various areas where the doors were controlled by a guard behind thick glass. One door would open and the second door would not open until the first door was closed. Well, we got through the first door when I suddenly stopped and whispered to the guard with us, "I forgot to leave something back in the locker."

He casually asked, "What?"

And when I said, "My gun," I thought he was going to have a heart attack. He motioned for the guard to open the first door again and after we got into the locker area and I put my gun in the locker, he held his fingers about an inch apart and said he came about that close to losing his job.

Anyway, during the time I spent on the Homicide Squad, I hit just about every state and federal prison in the area. It was usually interesting and always good for a few hours of overtime.

64. A New Year—Clean Board; First Murder of the Year

The whole month of December 1988 was spent either in the D.A.'s office getting warrants or testifying in court. I was on vacation from December 23rd through January 1st so when I came in on the 2nd I was well rested and ready to get started on a new year. The homicide board had been wiped clean. I was having my first cup of coffee and everything was right with the world.

By 9:00 a.m. we were all in the back room listening to the start of another violent year. It sure didn't take very long. Apparently, one hour and fifteen minutes after midnight on January 1st, five or six guys walked into an after-hours joint in the core area where about 250 people were drinking and dancing. They opened fire with handguns, which were returned by the armed security guards, and when the smoke had cleared the count was incredible. One dead security guard, seven patrons shot and at the hospital, and an unknown amount had fled and were treated at local hospitals or at home. Besides that, while everybody was running and shooting, dozens of purses were stolen along with several fur coats and eleven hundred dollars that the doorman had taken in. Six people had been arrested, but as of that time, there had been no identifications of all the shooters. Apparently, just about everybody had a gun and this happened even though the doorman was armed and everyone had to pass through a metal detector. Maybe they should have checked the batteries in the metal detector. It really was a shame because ninety-five percent of the people probably were just there for a good time.

I was working by myself and spent the next twelve hours interviewing victims. The confirmed victims were: one dead, one shot in the head and released, one shot in the buttocks, one shot in the right leg, one shot in the right leg, arm and shoulder, and two shot in the left foot. Kind of ironic that the only one released from the hospital the same day he was shot was arrested and brought downtown. I questioned him, and naturally he didn't know who shot him, didn't want to complain, didn't want to be a witness, and just wanted his lawyer. His name was Porter and I remember part of our last conversation. He considered himself invincible because he had been shot several times before. Well, his invincibility ended eight days later when he was at another after-hours joint. About fifteen armed men came in; they hit one man over the head with an Uzi, grabbed Porter and dragged him outside. They threw him into a van and drove away followed by several other cars. The van slowed and he was able to jump out and run.

An eyewitness said he started running down the street when the van and car doors opened and men started to open fire at him. He was struck several times and stumbled to a porch, crawled up and began scratching at the screen door. When he couldn't get in the house, he got on his hands and knees and pleaded with two guys. They opened fire and blew him away.

You know what's really amazing? This didn't occur in some far off third world country where people live behind closed and bolted doors. This was happening in my city where I was born and raised and where my family lives and my kids go to church and school. This is what our liberal self-serving society has allowed to happen. They're so afraid that someone's rights are being violated that they fail to realize that's just a small section of society and the vast majority have to suffer because of their thinking.

When the Police arrived on the scene they found him in a pool of blood. The only things in his pockets were several bullets, but no gun, no money, and no identification.

He had been shot several times in the right eye, forehead, back of his head, shoulder and left side. When we went to the scene, we recovered casings and live rounds from 45 and 380 caliber weapons. The front door and front porch also had a couple dozen bullet holes. What was really unusual was when Tom and I started to make a few of the neighbors, we found a single mother with several kids who said she saw the whole thing from her bedroom window across the street.

The autopsy showed that Porter had been shot ten times with two shots from less than two inches and one being a contact wound, meaning the gun was placed up against his head and the shooter just wanted to make sure he was dead.

I think what I'll do is recall this whole case right through the trial because the entire investigation lasted off and on for almost nine months. I should also mention that Carl—Ernie's and my partner for many years, and a close friend to this day—had made Captain. He had spent time on the Early Shift Holdup Squad and now was assigned to the day shift during which time he commanded the Violent Crimes Task Force. This was a group of mainly uniform men who had been hand-picked by Carl and a Sergeant to travel in plain clothes and react to violent crimes that were starting to prevail in Milwaukee. Part of this was due to two groups of African-American males. One named The BOS, which stood for Brothers of the Struggle and the second was the BGD, which stood for Black Gangster Disciples, and had their origin in Chicago.

Carl, my former partner, had an amazing group of guys that we used all the time. No matter who we were looking for or wanted, they always found them. Carl was the Captain in charge of this group which was called the Violent Crimes Task Force. It was a tremendous group of very dedicated Coppers that loved to work for Carl because he was not only a great boss, but he gave them free rein to operate. Up to that time the city had been relatively free of any organized drug dealing, or so we thought. But, these two gangs taught everyone some lessons in violence.

As an example, several weeks after the Porter execution, one weekend turned in six shootings, which resulted in three murders, all drug and gang related. Two of the murders were in a housing project where three gang members walked into a drug distribution house, shot the lady doorman in the throat and proceeded to the second floor bedroom where they assassinated two dealers. They left ten thousand dollars and large amounts of cocaine, indicating the murders were hits. Lots of witnesses, but all were too scared to talk. We even tracked down one customer of the drug house who had a big job with a local college. He lied his ass off to protect himself and said he was just a casual user and was a first time customer.

Anyway, back to our eyewitness in the Porter murder. This was our first time involved with the Witness Protection Service of the Sheriff's Department. Our witness and her children were hidden so well that anytime we wanted to talk to them we had to go through the Sheriff's cover people. We didn't have the vaguest idea where she was hidden. By this time Carl's guys and the Feds (F.B.I.) had been doing wiretaps and came up with the names Earl and Milton. Carl's guys picked them up and Earl was positively identified by our witness as being one of the shooters of Porter. Besides that, we had come up with another witness who was in one of the cars that followed the van with Porter and had actually seen Porter being gunned down. On top of that, Earl called Tom and I to the County Jail and gave us a half-ass confession in which he admitted being at the scene of the shooting, but said he tried to stop the shooting of Porter. The statement was self-serving, but it at least put him at the scene.

It was just amazing what these guys would say and who they would put down just to save their own hide. The Feds had found one of the big guys in the whole drug operation that they really had a strong case on. He not only turned snitch on the street, but he swore as a confidential informant to numerous search warrants and even helped Carl set up a wiretap that was conducted on both the BOS and BGD for over a year. And after all that, he still got forty years of federal time a year later. I suppose this was better than the life with no parole that he was almost certainly guaranteed if he didn't cooperate.

Earl and Milton were charged in the murder of Porter and naturally they came up with all the best criminal lawyers in the state and the whole investigation and court appearances lasted months. In fact, I remember during this period of time the defense lawyers complained to a Judge that they felt their client's jail cells were being bugged and their telephone calls tapped. They also said we were paying informants in the jail to trap their clients into making incriminating statements. This was a time in the history of Milwaukee that drug dealers were a huge part of the criminal activity and several John Doe Investigations were started by Carl's men and the Feds.

During this time we did a lot of work with the DEA (Drug Enforcement Agency), the criminal section of the IRS and the F.B.I. I remember going with a search warrant to Earl's house where he lived with his mother. It was a modest single family home in a changing part of the city's north side. This was a lesson in how crime pays—at least for a period of time. We started in his second floor bedroom closet, which conservatively contained two hundred pairs of tennis shoes that averaged about $150.00 a piece, then thousands of dollars of jewelry and hundreds of dress and sport shirts. Added to this was endless stereo and TV equipment that must have cost thousands. We then went downstairs and I remember seeing a pile of suits that must have been at least four to five feet tall lying on a table. Almost all of them were silk or of equal quality, and a majority still had the price tags attached averaging five hundred to a thousand dollars apiece. There were at least a dozen full-length men's fur coats and just as many fur hats.

These are just the things I remember and don't recall if any drugs or money were found. One IRS agent, who was also a CPA, individually accounted for all these items. I was told that the reason for the accounting was to show Earl's financial worth, because he had never filed tax returns and never held a job.

You know, actually the real story behind the BOS and BGD were that they were nothing more than a bunch of street punks that just got lucky dealing drugs. At least they were lucky for a while, but sooner or later they all wound up either dead or in jail. But, punks or not, while they had the money and the drugs they ruled a large section of the inner city.

I remember sometime during the investigation, word came that one of the bigger suppliers to these guys was picked up in Dallas, Texas. From the wiretaps he was also suspected of being in one of the cars involved in Porter's death. At the last moment I was sent down there to talk to him to see if he would cooperate. Supposedly, no one knew I was going to Texas, so when I went to their County Jail and was led to this lounge where he was with this silk suited lawyer, needless to say I was shocked, not only to see the lawyer, but that they even knew my name. The drug dealer talked freely, but only in self serving terms. He put the finger on several small dealers in Milwaukee, but really gave me nothing of importance.

Now, here was a guy waiting to be tried for murder. He had never been arrested, was thirty-three years old, a college graduate with a good job, never did drugs, only dealt them. I talked to him and his lawyer for several hours and then flew back to Milwaukee. I was off that weekend and when

I came back, I got a call from this guy's lawyer who said he now wanted to cooperate and would give me the whole story, including putting Earl and Milton down for the shooting. Our D.A. wanted me to fly back down and take the statement, but the D.A. in Texas said to hold off because it would cloud their whole trial. I learned later that he was convicted in Texas and got sentenced to life.

This whole case was getting interesting with Carl's guys and the Feds putting pressure on the drug dealers and they were all trying to make deals. Everybody was snitching on everybody else to the point where it was getting hard to keep track. We thought we had put a good case together and after all the legal maneuvering and motions to suppress just about all the evidence and statements, the trial started in August of 1989. Earl had a good local attorney that I knew and got along with quite well. The D.A. was one of the better D.A.s that I thought handled the case as well as anyone could have. There was considerable publicity in the case so the defense requested a change of venue. The jury was picked in Madison and brought back to Milwaukee for the trial.

I remember going to Madison to pick the jury. The courtroom was full and the only minority in the whole room was Earl. This didn't make any difference because there were so many do-gooders in the room that I knew we would have a hard time finding anyone that would just listen to the testimony and leave their personal opinions behind. Even though they all said they would keep an open mind, I had my doubts. Out of 150 potential jurors and after about five hours of voidiring them (questioning potential jurors by both prosecution and defense), we finally had the fourteen people needed, twelve plus two alternates. Believe it or not they included a doctor who had been disbarred and was now studying law and had two brothers who were Public Defenders, two students from the University of Wisconsin and one older female that thought she could find someone guilty but would have a hard time sending them to jail. That's what we had to deal with, along with a Judge who was not known to be a great friend of the Police and prosecutors.

The jury was brought back to Milwaukee and under heavy guards, was sequestered in a local hotel. The opening statements were given and we then boarded a city bus to go to the crime scene. The after-hours joint where everything started was our first stop. The street was loaded with sheriffs, local Police, bystanders and tons of news media. You could tell that the jurors had never experienced anything like this except for TV shows and they were rightly quite concerned. We entered the after-hours joint through a heavy wooden door that had been covered by a previously opened barred door. The door and surrounding outside wall showed numerous bullet holes, some old and some new. We entered the dimly lit main room that was approximately

50 feet by 50 feet. Several deputies turned on some floodlights they had brought along, and the first thing I saw was the astonished faces of the jurors. The place was a rat hole, ceiling tile hanging down, broken light fixtures, broken tables, chairs, and bottles, wires all over the floor leading from a broken stage and shell casings that jurors couldn't believe they were stepping on.

The Judge asked me to point out all the areas of concern, such as where Porter was standing when he was dragged out the door and a few other areas. You could see that this was the last place in the world those jurors wanted to be and I thought it was a good lesson for them. We then loaded them back on the bus and followed the route the car and van took to the place of Porter's demise. Again we were followed by the media and curiosity seekers. I don't know how you would feel if Squads pulled up in your neighborhood and a bus full of people arrived and a handcuffed man was taken out of a Squad, but it surely would cause a big disturbance—but not in this neighborhood. People right next door and across the street just came out of their houses, got into their cars and drove away. Again the Judge had me point out where, according to witnesses, the car and van stopped and Porter was chased up on the porch and then executed.

The first full day of testimony was from the first Coppers on the scene, the City Engineer who diagramed the scene and several witnesses who were awakened by the gunshots. Most described the car and van and several men chasing a man down the street and up onto a porch. Some even described how he was shot in the street and crawled to the porch and appeared to be pleading for his life when the final shot was administered. We even had the homeowner on the stand who testified that she was awakened by shouting and gunfire and realized that people were on her porch. She could hear more gunfire and someone hollering, "Please don't kill me." She was asked if she looked out the window or opened the door and all she said was, "Are you crazy?" None of these witnesses could make any identification.

The Medical Examiner testified to the cause of death and stated that any number of the wounds could have been fatal, including one shot that came from a gun that was placed against his head.

Our first main witness was the young lady who lived across the street and who we had in protective custody. She was brought into the courtroom by several members of the Witness Protection Program and was obviously scared to death. She gave her testimony in such a low voice that the Judge continually told her to speak up. She testified that she was in her first floor bedroom facing the street when a sound woke her up and she looked out her bedroom window. She saw a car and a luxury style van in the street and five or six men. She then heard gunshots and saw the men chasing another man toward a porch across the street. It looked like he fell several times in the street and more or less crawled up onto the porch and was lying down, scratching at the screen door. She said it was at this time that she saw a man walk up to the figure lying on the porch and shoot him at close range.

She was then asked if that person was in court and she pointed to Earl and said, "That's him." She wasn't the greatest witness, but taking into consideration she was born and raised in the city, had several children and lived by herself and even though Witness Protection set her up in another city, she still had relatives here. The defense attorney was pretty decent with her and just tried to cross her up on a few of her statements and the fact that she was looking through a window. He insisted that the street was dark and tried to change her identification of Earl. She was excused, left the courtroom under guard and I never saw her again.

I testified for the next several hours about my experience on the Homicide Squad, this particular investigation, my experience with gangs, my arrest of Earl and the statement he gave me and Tom. I also testified to recovering 50 to 75 shell casings on the street outside the after-hours joint and at the murder scene, just to show how violent the whole episode really was. The only statements I gave under cross-examination were that Earl turned himself in with his attorney, was cooperative and denied the actual shooting. He admitted being on the scene and witnessing the shooting, but said he tried to stop others, who he named, from killing Porter.

We then brought in one of Porter's friends who was at the after-hours joint the night of the killing. He was brought in under federal guard as he was serving federal time for numerous drug convictions. He testified that on that particular night Earl and about fifteen other men came storming into the joint flashing Uzi submachine guns and other weapons. They opened fire into the ceiling, grabbed Porter and dragged him out the door.

The next witness was a young black male who was actually in one of the vehicles that carried Porter from the joint. He testified that he was in the back seat and the two vehicles headed south on 6th Street. Porter jumped out and was chased down the street by several males including Earl and they all started shooting at Porter. Porter crawled up on a porch and several of the men opened fire. He said Earl was one of them and that after the shooting they all got back into the vehicles and fled.

It was obvious to the entire courtroom that this kid was absolutely terrified. He had refused witness protection and Tom and I had to find him several times and drag him off the street to get him into court. Besides everything else, he lived in the core neighborhood and realized the potential of what would happen after his testimony. He also testified in such a quiet voice that numerous times the Judge and court reporter asked him to speak up.

I'm sure that the jury didn't hear half his testimony and appeared indifferent to what he was saying.

That was our case. The defense didn't call any witnesses. There were four full days of testimony and several hours of closing statements and instructions by the Judge to the jury. Speaking of those instructions, they always include the Judge telling the jury that they should only consider the testimony from the stand and the evidence that is admitted by the court. They should leave their own personal opinions to themselves. What a crock that is.

I've talked to many jurors after the trial, and they mostly all had personal opinions of the Judge, attorneys, Police Officers, and especially witnesses who testified that they were at the scene of the crime and might have participated in the crime and were given a break for their testimony. I would imagine that's not only human nature, but also why so many guilty people go free. Of course, that is my biased opinion.

Tom and I had spent about 2,000 hours on this investigation and the jury went out for deliberations at 11:10 a.m., broke for lunch, and returned their verdict at 2:30 p.m. NOT GUILTY. I couldn't believe it. White liberals from a liberal county, that didn't have the vaguest idea of what life in the inner city is all about made this great deduction. Their reasons?

"We all thought that Earl was guilty, but the state failed to prove it conclusively. If they had shown that he was a big drug kingpin, we would have found him guilty. We had to weigh the facts and there was a clear lack of evidence. It's really very frustrating to not say what you really feel." Give me a break! What kind of stupid logic is that?

Even the Judge could not believe it. He called all the jurors into his chambers along with myself, Earl, the D.A. and defense attorney and said, "Where have you people been for the last four days? Didn't you hear anything that came from the witness stand? I'm thoroughly ashamed of you." With that he walked out of the room and the jurors were taken back to their county where drugs are a way of life, apparently.

But that wasn't all for Earl. Several months later he and two others were tried federally for drug conspiracy and money laundering. This guy had unbelievable luck. All three beat the conspiracy charge but Earl was found guilty on the money laundering. One of his co-defendants, who beat the charges, was killed in a drug house several months later.

The federal Judge in the case—who was known for his heavy sentencing—gave Earl twenty-five years in Federal Prison and a fine of half a million dollars. The Judge also stated that there was no doubt in his mind that Earl was involved in cocaine dealing at a very high level and couldn't believe how the jury could acquit him on the murder charges with all the credible evidence. He referred to the jury as "a blind chicken that picks up a kernel of corn by accident." But he also said they were free to do that under our system.

It was a busy day for Earl because after the federal sentencing, he went back to Circuit Court to be sentenced on state drug charges and received another thirty years.

65. Tom

To make things worse, putting in all those hours and working every day with Tom, I never realized until he told me, that he had lost fifty pounds. He was about six five and skinny as a rail and when he mentioned it, I really took notice. He said he had a doctor's appointment the next day and a couple of days later we were sitting in Training School. I asked him about the doctor and he said it wasn't good. He said he was diagnosed with terminal cancer and they gave him about a year. What do you say to someone you've spent the better part of eight years of your life with? Our social lives were opposite, but he was an unbelievable good Copper and excellent partner.

May 30th of 1989 was the last day I worked with Tom. He had gone to confession for the first time in many years and had made his funeral arrangements. Then suddenly he got a second opinion and some doctor told him that all the cancer was in one lung, and if they took it out he had a good chance of recovering. Tom was really excited, as were all the guys on the Squad.

It was about a week after he told me this and a few days before the operation that I was at a party with one of the Medical Examiners. I told him the story and was shocked when he said, "I sure hope to hell the doctor's wife doesn't need a new fur coat." He was right. Tom wasn't out of the hospital two weeks. We were sitting in his living room when he got the call from the doctor's office that said the cancer had spread throughout his whole body. I saw him practically every day until September 15th when he died. He was forty-nine years old, and the funeral was attended by hundreds of friends and Police Officers. A year later his brother, who was also an Officer, died of cancer, also at the age of forty-nine.

66. A Death in Custody

For several months prior to Tom's death, I mostly worked alone. During one of those days I got a call from Shelby County in Memphis, Tennessee. They had picked up a guy I had gotten a murder warrant on for a tavern holdup shooting. I flew down there and was told that the F.B.I. had made the arrest. Before interviewing the guy I went to the local F.B.I. office and found the agent in charge giving a press conference telling how his office had made the arrest. He was telling about the great job they did tracking down this individual and turning him over to the local authorities. After this I went to interview the guy, and was told by the local Police that one of their Officers had stopped him on the street, checked him out, found the open warrant and arrested him. He was handcuffed to a chair in the station and the F.B.I. was called. So much for the F.B.I.'s great arrest!

The guy gave me a full signed confession and I was just making arrangements to bring him back when my boss called and said the same county had arrested another fugitive from our city. He was flying down another Detective and I was to wait for him and bring back both prisoners. I think it was about this time in my career where all the traveling and motels was starting to get old. I was missing a lot of family life and even though Marlene and the kids never complained, it was the first time I had considered doing something else. I was fifty-three years old and was starting to realize it was a young man's job.

It became even more apparent when I came home from Tennessee. Marlene and I had planned a nice vacation and I was going to work a half-day on Thursday, go home at noon and help pack and leave Friday morning. I remember calling her about 9:00 a.m. at the church (where she worked) and said everything looked good and I should be home by 12:30 p.m. Well, I had the time right but it was 12:30 a.m., not p.m. when I got home. I had just hung up the phone when the boss said to get over to one of the District Stations on the south side. They had someone that died while in custody. Everybody in the Homicide room had either court or something else to do so just the boss and I went. When we got to the station, the entire assembly was filled with Coppers from the late and day shift.

Apparently at about 7:30 a.m., just as the shifts were changing and Coppers were arriving and leaving, some goof that had been smoking coke since Monday came running down the street half-naked. That wasn't bad enough. When he got in front of the station he started running across the hoods of several of the Coppers cars. To say the least they were a little perturbed and tackled the guy and threw him to the ground. They realized what they had when he started to throw Coppers off his back like they were little bugs. The more he threw off, the more Officers came out of the station. Several civilian witnesses said it was the wildest fight they ever saw. After what seemed like an eternity, but was probably only fifteen or twenty minutes, they had the guy handcuffed and strapped to a cart of the ambulance they had called. It was while they were placing him in the ambulance that someone suddenly realized that he had stopped breathing. The ambulance was only two blocks from a hospital and after giving him CPR they conveyed him to the hospital where he was pronounced dead. It seemed like a fairly simple investigation, interview a few Coppers, take statements from the witnesses, call in the reports and be home by 2 or 3 p.m.

I failed to realize how times had changed. I had been handling shootings involving Coppers for the last several years and thought I had a good reputation for being fair and open-minded. I also thought that I got along well with the union in those situations. This one was different. I went into the assembly with a homicide D.A. that had just arrived and asked the first of sixteen Coppers involved, who wanted to be interviewed first. I told them I had talked to the witnesses and they all said everything was handled properly. I even talked to the guy's girlfriend who said they had been smoking coke for three days straight, without sleeping, in some motel not too far from the station. She said all of a sudden her boyfriend jumped up, ran outside and down the street and started to jump on cars. He then jumped into the passenger's seat of her car and she drove away. She got about two blocks from the Police station when he jumped out, ran down the street and that's when the Coppers tackled him. She said she had been doing coke for five years and her boyfriend did coke for ten years. She lived with her mother, had one child, and was on welfare. She also said that all the Coppers handled themselves with a lot of restraint and she didn't know why they just didn't beat her boyfriend with clubs.

The first guy to raise his hand was a Copper I had known for several years. He was a good, hardworking Copper and when he announced, "We all want to speak to our union lawyer first," I was shocked. I had run into this on several prior occasions, but usually where there was some doubt that the Officers acted properly. This incident was cut and dried. Not only was I shocked, but also the D.A., who was Bob and who was as "pro Cop" as they come, was fit-to-be-tied and I fully agreed. I kind of put it into the perspective of going to the scene of a crime and every witness telling you they want a lawyer. Just at that time the head of the Police union came into the room. Not only did I know him personally, but he also represented me, because I was part of the union. I took him on the side and gave him the background on the situation, telling him that by the Coppers being uncooperative, it made the incident look like there was more to it than there was. He said he understood where I was coming from, but the union lawyer had been notified and we had to wait for him. Well, I had great respect for the union Chief, but on several of the past dealings I had with the lawyer, he came to the scenes smelling of alcohol. I didn't think this would happen because it was in the morning, but when it took several hours for him to show up, his breath didn't surprise me. Now not only was the D.A. teed-off and started to make threats about an inquest and cover up, but by now some of the Coppers just wanted to tell what happened and go home—especially when they saw who was representing them.

I called Marlene and tried to give her some sort of timetable and like always she just said she would get everything packed and ready to be loaded in the car. Her last words were, "We are going tomorrow, aren't we?"

So after all the interviews and reports I finally went home. It was not until I got back to work ten days later that I found that the guy was so full of cocaine, that the exertion from all the running and jumping on the cars and fighting with the Coppers was just too much for his heart. The Coppers were not at fault and the case was ruled a sudden death and closed. I was also told that his girlfriend, who I had interviewed and who had tons of problems herself, overdosed three days after the incident and died in a motel room all by herself. What a waste.

67. Death—A Stinking Disposition

It never ceased to amaze me what people would do because of drugs. I got sent to one of the filthiest houses I had ever been in. It was home to eleven people, including two brothers, their girlfriends, and a whole variety of kids. It seemed that one of the girlfriends bought two quarter packs of coke on the street, brought them home and wouldn't share with anyone but her boyfriend. Her boyfriend's brother threatened her with a two-by-four and her boyfriend intervened—so naturally one brother hit the other over the head with the two-by-four knocking him cold. They couldn't wake him so they called an ambulance. When the paramedics arrived the guy woke up and refused treatment so they left. He passed out two other times and both times the paramedics were called and again he refused treatment. Finally, he and his girlfriend went to bed and several hours later she woke and found him not breathing. She called for his brother and the first thing his brother did, when he realized he was not breathing, was to go through his pockets, take his money and coke and run out of the house. When I got there the body was still in the bedroom along with tons of cockroaches. The smell was devastating, and after the body was removed and my investigation was completed, I went downtown to call in some reports and suddenly realized everyone was staying clear of me.

Throughout the years I came to realize the smell got into the hairs in your nose and you didn't realize how much you stunk. I put off the reports to the next day and called Marlene and told her to put a bathrobe and a plastic garbage bag in the garage. She must have been getting used to it because all she said was don't let the kids smell you. This one was so bad that I couldn't even take the clothes to the cleaners. I just scratched one sport coat, pants, shirt and underwear. What a job!!!

It was now the middle of the summer of 1989, and the heat must have made everybody a little touchy. Monday morning I was greeted with three autopsies, six interviews and follow-up on four homicides that occurred over the weekend. The unit was also starting to get a lot of press coverage because of the unusual number of homicides and a new Police Chief. The new Chief apparently was never a street Copper and came up through the ranks doing administrative work so he really had no particular use for the Detective Bureau. In fact, the only time I ever talked to him was when he came through the Bureau during his first month on the job. It's hard to explain Police humor, but like I explained before, I always had a large cardboard figure of "Elvira" next to my desk. For those of you that don't remember "Elvira," she had long black hair and was dressed in a long black gown. She was very buxomly and showed a lot of cleavage. Well, we used to hang a paper tombstone right over the cleavage with the current number of homicides and how many were cleared. The new Chief came past my desk and never said hello, goodbye or go to hell. He just pointed at the figure and said, "Get that disgusting thing out of here." That more or less set the tone for what kind of Copper's Chief he was and the feelings didn't get any better until he left the job. I'm sure "Elvira" is in some Copper's rec room, right next to the bar, and probably still has the homicide number in its proper place.

It's a good thing he was never our direct boss, because he really didn't care about the Bureau or any of the Detectives. We really never saw him and what he thought of us really didn't matter. It was important, however, what our immediate bosses thought, and they were great. I remember Vince and Bill being interviewed and they said, "I believe some of the Detectives are tired, but I don't see it affecting morale. They all work very enthusiastically. They're dedicated Officers. They're professionals. They extend themselves, and that's why they're on the homicide unit. Homicide investigation demands a meticulous approach. It demands that it be done in a religious fashion, and you have to maintain that."

They were also asked how these brutal murders affected the individual investigators, to which Vince responded, "Some are bothered more than others, especially when you see the elderly or the very young or the handicapped victimized. We'd be less than human if we weren't affected."

I tell you truthfully, I never had a bad boss, except one when I was a young uniform Copper, and I never had a bad partner. I think that's what made the job so tolerable; that and the mind-boggling way of life for some people.

68. Rookie D.A.

I remember by the first part of October 1989, the city already had ninety-five homicides with eighty-one of them cleared and I had personal participation in the investigation of sixty-three of these. By the end of the month the total was one hundred and one and the overtime was unlimited. Most of the murders were drug related and between that and just trying to keep up, the hours were endless.

One of these was a typical street shooting where one guy had a shotgun and the other had a rifle. The shotgun won. And as soon as the guy fell face first on his porch, someone from inside ran out the door, didn't see how the victim was, didn't call the Police, just grabbed the rifle and went back inside. This was a little bit different because a man from the suburbs, who had about 17 core rental properties, saw the whole thing. In fact, the shooter ran right past his car. The guy gave me a great description; the only problem was that he absolutely didn't want to get involved. He didn't mind having all those rundown shacks in the core that he got good welfare money for, but he didn't want to testify against anyone. Needless to say, the damage was already done. He gave me a statement and I was going to make sure he followed through on it. As soon as a good suspect was arrested, I personally went to his mansion in a suburb north of the city and brought him down for a line-up. This guy was terrified when he viewed five guys through a one-way glass window. It was obvious from the look on his face that he recognized the guy we suspected of the shooting. When I looked at the identification card I had given him and saw that he had marked "none" under anyone identified, I said to him, "You got to be shitting me! I know damn well you recognized the guy."

To which he replied, "I know, but I'm just too scared, I got a wife and kids to support."

Because he was the only really reliable witness I had, I had to promise him all kinds of protection—that and pointing out his civic duty and all the money he was scamming from the system and the publicity he might generate, he agreed and changed his identification card.

That was just the start of my problems. When I went to the D.A.'s office the next day expecting to see one of my favorite Homicide D.A.s, I was introduced to a young lady who was new on the team. They apparently wanted her to get her feet wet with a fairly typical murder that would challenge her and yet not be a catastrophe to lose. They also wanted an experienced homicide Detective to hold her hand. She seemed like a nice enough lady that really seemed to appreciate what they were asking me to do. I also knew her slightly from the D.A.'s office and she had a good reputation, so I didn't cause a fuss. I should mention now that she subsequently spent a lot of years prosecuting homicides until she transferred to the Feds and became one of the top federal prosecutors in the state. In fact, she ran for Judge but was beat out in the primary. Anyhow, I gave her all the facts in the case and brought in several witnesses and after two days, which was a long time, she issued a felony murder charge.

Several days later the defendant waived his preliminary hearing and I should have known this case would not be easy when the D.A. handed me a lengthy list of things she wanted done. I informed her as politely as I could that this was not my only case, to which she responded that this was her big chance and she didn't want to blow it. She was nice about it and I suppose I felt a little sorry for her, so in between other deaths, court appearances and other investigations, I finished her list. It was several months later that the trial started and she asked me to find the witnesses her office couldn't find, and serve them with subpoenas. Naturally, these are all the ones that didn't want to be found. One I was told moved to some unknown town down south and had been approached by the defendant's family and was bought off for a book of food stamps, a chicken, a box of Rice-a-Roni and a one-way bus ticket. Two others disappeared and I found out later they were hidden by an investigator for the Public Defender's Office who was an ex-Detective. In fact, I knew him well and had worked with him several times. But apparently he found no problem with selling his conscience and soul.

The closer the trial date came, the more the D.A. had me running. The only reason I put up with all her requests is that she was really nice and was really trying her best. Every request was always please and thank you. Two days before the trial was to start she called me into her office. My first thought was that she found some more little quirks that she wanted checked out. But when I saw her I realized that something was really wrong. She apologized and said that the head D.A. didn't think she was ready for the trial and assigned a more senior D.A. to the case.

I still wonder to this day if some deal wasn't worked out with the Public Defender's Office because the D.A. that was assigned was one of the most useless D.A.'s I had ever encountered. I don't know if I wrote earlier about a certain D.A. that I went to his boss and complained about some years ago, but this was the same one. He had no use for me and the feeling was mutual. He didn't appreciate it when I told him that the D.A.'s office must feel the case is a loser, because they sent him and he could screw up any case. He complained to my boss and I complained to his boss and everyone said we should just try and get along. That lasted until the day of the trial. I arrived in court with all the evidence and found the D.A. in a huddle with the Defense Attorney talking about a plea bargain. I couldn't believe it! I grabbed the D.A. by the shoulder, spun him around and said, "Just what in the hell are you trying to do?"

He just pushed past me and said, "It makes no difference anyhow, you put together such a shitty case that I tried to plea bargain it down but they wouldn't take it." I was furious, but the Judge called the case and we picked a jury. The D.A. did a lousy job, but the young lady that he replaced had put a good case together and it looked like a real winner. Four days of trial and the jury went out for deliberations.

They were out for several hours when they asked the Judge for some clarification of instructions and this asshole D.A. sent a piece of evidence into the jury room that wasn't allowed. When it became apparent what he had done, the Judge was furious and the defense called for a mistrial. Rather than accepting a mistrial, the Judge allowed the defendant to plead to a five year felony, knowing full well that he had lost his case. The jury was told that a deal had been worked out and they were dismissed. I met the Jury Foreman in the hallway and he asked me what happened. I told him and he said, "That's too bad because we were coming back with second degree murder." What a job by one of the most incompetent Assistant D.A.'s in that whole office! And you know what, twelve years after I retired, he was still there.

69. Verdict: Not Guilty

Going through my notes I remember that same summer of 1989, when I was sent to meet some uniform Coppers in the heart of the core. They were by a back porch, standing over what I thought was a small pile of clothing. Looking closer I saw it was a dead child that almost looked like a newborn.

I found out later, by making the neighbors and finding the mother, that the body was one of her twin sons. She couldn't wake him in the morning and thought he was dead, so she walked down the alley and placed him on some rear steps and covered him with his jacket. What I thought was a newborn was actually a 6-month-old boy who weighed 18 pounds, with the coat and diaper. In this day and age, with Milwaukee having the second highest welfare rate in the US, this baby looked like what you see on TV where the children are dying in some godforsaken third world country. And yet, rather than teaching these indigent mothers how to care for their children and how to stop becoming punching bags for these gang bangers, this liberal society just throws them more food stamps and welfare money and thinks that's the answer. Then they sit back, pat themselves on the back, go to church and say what a great job they've done in the inner city and how many people they've saved.

I was still working by myself most of the time after Tom died, when I had a particularly quiet day. I called Marlene and said I should be home on time. I just hung up the phone when the boss said all the guys from the next shift were in court and could I take a stabbing. I called Marlene back and said I would be a couple hours late. By the time I got to the apartment building, which was actually only about a mile from my house, all that were left at the scene was the Fire Department. They showed me into the bedroom, which was covered in blood. The bed sheets were drenched in so much blood that whoever was lying there had to be dead. Lying on the floor was a hammer and a knife, also both full of blood. The fireman at the scene said that the paramedics had conveyed a 26-year-old very pregnant white female who had been stabbed in the abdomen and hand, and struck twice in the head with a hammer. He said she was still alive and told him that she was lying in bed when she heard the patio screen door open. She then saw a black man peek his head around the corner and told her to close her eyes and not move. The next thing she knew, she looked up and saw a hammer coming down on her head. The man then stabbed her in the stomach. She said she rolled out of bed and was crawling to the kitchen when her seven-year-old son came in, found her and called 911.

When the first paramedic came on the scene and started treating her, he asked her who did it and she said, "It might have been my boyfriend, but I don't know for sure." By this time another team of investigators arrived and took over the scene and I headed to the hospital. The victim was in the operating room and the nurses allowed me to dress in some scrubs and go in. The operating room was no different than the woman's bedroom—which was also covered with blood. The only difference was that here they were pumping blood in as she was losing it and finally they stopped the flow. The surgeon said she was sedated and would be out for several hours and then in intensive care. He also said that the baby she had been carrying was stabbed through the neck and was dead.

By the time I got back to the scene the other Detectives were just finishing up. By the time I got back downtown and called in my reports it was 10:00 p.m.

The next morning I went out to the hospital and surprisingly found the young woman sitting up in bed. I found her to be of average intelligence, but on the naïve side. She came from a good family in another county and had become pregnant, married and divorced shortly after her first son was born. She lived for a while with her folks and then moved to an apartment in Milwaukee and got a job. Somewhere along the line she got tangled up with a loser who not only had her supporting him, but he got her pregnant and used her as a punching bag through most of their relationship. This was before the domestic violence law and every time she would call the Police, her boyfriend would talk her out of complaining.

On this particular morning, her boyfriend got out of bed and was in a crabby mood. He did some work around the house using a hammer that they kept in the kitchen. He walked out about 1:00 p.m. and told her to get her ass up or he was leaving without her. By the time she got dressed and to the back door, he, and her car were gone. She remembers her son being in the backyard. She went back to the bedroom and lay down on the bed and started to doze when she heard the screen door open. She looked up and saw a black male with only half his head showing, around the corner. She thought it was her boyfriend, Don, but wasn't sure. She said, "I see you peeking" and then the next thing she saw was the hammer coming down on her head. She said she saw the same green shirt Don had worn that morning and she said, "Don, what are you doing?"

He said "Shut up and don't look." By this time she was lying on the floor and he kicked her in the stomach.

She said, "Don't you know I'm pregnant?"

I kept asking her, "Are you sure it was Don?"

And she kept saying, "I think so, it was his face and he was wearing the shirt that I had just ironed that morning." She said he then left the bedroom and came back seconds later with a knife and stabbed her in the stomach and hit her in the head with the knife handle.

I kept saying, "You must have gotten a good look at his face."

And she said that her eyes were full of blood, but she was sure it was Don.

I left the hospital and went to see a D.A. that handled the sexual assaults for the county. I really never had a great deal to do with him, but I knew he had a great reputation with the Vice Squad. He listened to everything I had to say and then said to go back to the hospital the next day and if she stuck to the same story, he would issue a complaint against Don.

The next day I went back and she gave the same story and identified a photo of Don. With that the D.A. issued attempted first degree murder and first degree sexual assault. He couldn't be charged with the death of the baby, because at that time, in this great state, the baby has to have been born and taken a breath. Don was picked up that night and the next morning I talked to him for several hours. He was the loser that I thought he was, but I still had reservations that he was involved. He admitted leaving in the morning and slapping Joan around. But he denied stabbing her. His alibi was that he was at a rummage sale several blocks from the apartment at the time of the assault.

Even though there was a lot of follow-up on this case, his preliminary hearing came up and Joan testified that she was absolutely sure Don was the assailant. She convinced the Judge and Don was bound over for trial.

During the next several months when I had time, I worked on this case and even found the rummage sale he said he was at. The women at the rummage sale remembered him and the approximate time he was there and what he bought. There also was a great deal of animosity between Joan's family and Don, and I sometimes wondered if that didn't play a part in her identification. The trial came up several months later and I must admit I still was uncertain. I was glad to see the same D.A. handling the case that issued the complaint and knew he also had reservations. He suggested to the Defense Attorney that Don take a polygraph exam and if he passed, he would drop the charges. Don and his attorney agreed and I couldn't have been more pleased. Needless to say, I was totally surprised when the results came back that Don had flunked the polygraph miserably. In fact, the examiner said it was one of the worst he had ever seen. I have to give all the credit to the D.A. because not only was this case a loser, but he was in the midst of running for a Judgeship and didn't need the bad publicity.

It wasn't surprising that after three days of jury trial, they came back with a not guilty verdict. I can't blame the jury for that, but they wanted to talk to the Judge and told him the investigation was flawed. When he asked what they were talking about, they came up with all kinds of things that not only had been done, but had been testified to, which showed they really weren't paying attention during the trial. I didn't mind loosing the case, but what irked me was the fact that the jury failed to appreciate the brilliant job the D.A. did even in a losing cause. He gave a great made for TV opening argument, dynamic cross examination of Don and an outstanding closing argument and this jury never understood a thing he said.

That jury was typical of the jurors that are called for one week and usually sit in on only one trial, if they're lucky. They have no experience and all want to save the world and rehabilitate everyone. They lose sight of the fact that the state only gets one kick at the cat. Not guilty is forever. Whereas if we get a conviction, that can be appealed forever. I also believe juries play too much on the instructions from the Judge when he talks about "finding someone guilty beyond a reasonable doubt." Many jurors by their own admission take this to mean "any doubt."

My immediate boss, Bill, who was an unbelievable boss who treated me as well as I could possibly imagine, came to me and said he had a new partner for me and asked what I thought. I didn't even ask who it was and said it really didn't make that much difference to me, because I was starting to feel the pangs of retirement. I know I could have gone back to a regular Squad and cut down tremendously on the overtime. But, when you've worked hard to get the best job around, you hate to take a step back. Anyway, he asked me what I thought of Ken as a partner. I knew him from the job but never had worked with him. He had a reputation as being a good investigator who was really anxious to get on the Homicide Squad. I told Bill I had no objections and Ken became my partner for the rest of my time on the job. He was a good steady partner and I can't think of us ever having a disagreement, at least any that I can remember. He was a few years younger than I was and even after I retired, he continued to be one of the top investigators on the Squad.

70. *Verdict: Guilty*

It was the fall of 1989 and I had a vacation scheduled so Ken and I decided we would start working together when I came back. It was the day before my vacation that I was sent to homicide number ninety-three for the year. Some affect you a little more than others or maybe it was getting time for me to quit. Dorothy was a nice little old lady in her 80's who had been widowed for a number of years. She lived by herself in a little cottage, in a nice but changing neighborhood. Neighbors described her as an indefatigable woman who often was outside tending her flowers, cutting the grass or shoveling the snow in the winter. She was completely independent and the only thing she did wrong in her whole life was to stand by her front steps with a garden tool in her hand and say, "Hi" to a young black man that came by.

Several minutes after this seemingly innocent encounter, she went to her garage where this same individual laid in wait for her. It must have taken a great deal of courage to attack this frail little old lady, but that's exactly what he did. He not only attacked her, but he strangled her, sexually assaulted her, and then took a clothes line, and strung it from the rafters to make it look like she hung herself. There were other marks on her body that showed he must have tortured her before she took her last breath. This apparently was because her house was locked and he wanted her keys. Her slip was torn where her assailant ripped her keys from her garment that she had pinned the keys to, so as not to lose them.

This brave individual, I can't even call him a man, then went into her house and ransacked this immaculately kept home. He not only did it on that day, but he and his friends came back at least two more days. They even brought a truck to haul all their loot. Each time, they first entered the garage, poked around on the body with a screw driver, pushed her on the rope until it broke, and then entered the house and stole furniture and keepsakes that had been this lady's treasures.

A neighbor in the house behind hers and across the alley became concerned when he didn't see her for a while and called the Police. The uniformed men arrived, secured the scene, and called for the Bureau. When I arrived the uniform man was standing outside the garage and all he said was, "You're not going to like this one."

I spent the next six hours in the garage, three hours with the body until the Medical Examiner had it taken away. Many people have said that seems cruel and inhumane to leave a body like that and photograph it from every angle prior to it being removed. But any evidence that you see and move before it is photographed can never be put back in the same spot. Besides, if you're a Christian like I am, you know that the soul has gone and all that's left are the earthly remains.

Once the photographer, City Engineer, Medical Examiner, Identification Bureau and I were done, the garage was locked and sealed and we started to process the house. Total time on the scene was a good eight hours during which time the uniform men were making all the neighbors for two blocks in each direction.

One of the neighbors across the alley actually saw the truck that was used to haul Dorothy's belongings away and took down the license number. Another neighbor, when told what happened, said he actually saw several black males around the truck and in her yard and thought maybe Dorothy had hired them to do some work. The reason he said this was because they were there during the day, seemed relaxed, and were even joking around with each other.

The next day I went on vacation and learned about the arrest from the newspaper. Apparently, the license number was checked out and when they approached the house, the truck pulled up in front. It was driven by an old man who had loaned the truck to his daughter's boyfriend. He gave the name and address and within a couple of hours Carl's guys had the suspect in custody. He in turn gave the name of the guy that told him about the murder and took him to the scene. By midnight of the second day all the suspects had been arrested and had given statements. Even our hero, who committed the murder, gave a two-page written confession. He was then positively identified by the neighbor.

The murder got a lot of press and naturally the killer, who had a lengthy record, got a good attorney from the Public Defender's Office. Actually, the case came to trial over a year later, just before I retired and was the last jury trial that I chaired with the D.A. There were numerous motions to suppress everything from the evidence collected to the statements made by all the defendants. Most of the defendants had pleaded guilty to burglary and were going to testify against the killer.

The motion to suppress the confession lasted two days with the defense stating that his poor client was rigorously interrogated and tortured for fifty-two hours. We had a good Judge that saw through the bullshit and denied all the motions.

The day of the trial came and we felt we really had a good case. But, jury trials are never a guarantee. The jury was picked and the D.A. and I were particularly pleased that the defense had left an old woman in her late seventies on the panel. We had thought for sure that the defense would strike her. Well, the trial lasted a full week with many of the jurors being questioned in the

Judge's Chambers about any pre-trial publicity and the potential gruesome photos that they may have to view.

This asshole actually took the stand and denied not only the crime, but blamed it on his co-conspirators and denied that he had signed the confession. I was even ordered by the Judge to have a handwriting examiner check the defendant's handwriting to the signature on the confession—which was done and which came back positive.

The case went to the sequestered jury and I became concerned when they were out for the rest of the day and were coming back in the morning. Finally, just after noon on the second day they came back with a guilty verdict. I couldn't believe how long they took and noticed two of the male jurors kept looking at me. After the Judge thanked them for their duty, I went out into the hall and saw these same two guys waiting. They approached me and immediately said they wanted to apologize for taking so long. They said once they had picked a foreman, they took a vote and it was eleven to one for conviction on all the charges. One person held out for all that time and her reason was that she couldn't believe that anyone could do that to a human being. Do you know who the holdout was? The little old lady we were so proud to have on the jury.

The Judge was and still is one of the better criminal Judges and sentenced the twenty-five year old to life in prison with no parole until 2060, and if he is still alive, he would then start serving his thirty years for the sexual assault and burglaries. The only good thing to come out of the trial and sentencing is the knowledge that even the inmates in the State Prison have no use for a killer of children or the elderly; especially when torture was involved. What is the real shame is that this nice old lady, who had lived all those years had to suffer such a humiliating and degrading experience before her tragic death.

71. Cab Ride—A Statistic?

Tom's funeral was on September 18th of 1989, and Ken and I started as partners on September 19th. I think the first five days we worked together we had four new homicides and endless overtime. Ken couldn't believe how busy we were, but he was a good partner and more than accepted his share of the work and hours. He was also a big hunter and outdoorsman and I really didn't see him much until the end of November.

I see from my notes in my memo book that on one of those Mondays in late November, the courthouse was buzzing. They had five first degree murder trials set for one day. It really caught my attention because I was involved in four of them with Tom. Tom and I had taken the confessions in two of them and one by myself. With Tom's death it meant that I would have had to testify in all three.

As usual with jury trials, two got adjourned, one pled guilty and the fourth was a five-day trial that ended in a guilty verdict. So all in all, it was a good week, the only thing wrong was Thursday and Friday were my off days and I spent both days in court. On top of that the bosses assigned me with a young Detective from the early shift to work with the D.A.'s office and several suburbs on six elderly murders that occurred a few years ago. That whole investigation is a story in itself and if I find time later I'll write about it. Actually, the suspect in the murders finally came to trial after I retired. How fast time goes, the young Detective from the early shift was promoted to Captain and headed the Homicide Squad for a period of time. He then retired and having had his Masters Degree, landed a job heading a local University's Criminal Justice Program.

One of the last homicides Ken and I had in 1989 was that of a cab driver. Thinking back and reading my Memos, I recall that at first it was listed as a fatal one car accident. Apparently, the cab dispatcher heard a call over an open mike early in the morning that said, "Don't hurt me, don't hurt me!" She asked all the cabs to respond to her and the only one that didn't was the cab being driven by a young black man from Nigeria who had been in this country for only five years. He was married, had two small children and went to school during the day. The Fire Department was sent to the accident and found the cab on its side up against a pole. They had to cut the top off the cab to get the victim out and found that the gearshift had gone through his face, severing his spine. We got involved because the Medical Examiner called us and said the cause of death was a dissection of the spine, but he also found several knife cuts to his head and small puncture wounds to his back.

Ken and I went back to the cab and found a bloody knife under the front seat. We then went to the victim's family and tried to get a background on him. We talked to his wife, and family, who were completely devastated. The whole family was cab drivers and most all drove for the same owner. All they were doing was trying to make a living to support their families. No welfare, no other assistance, just hard work and a lot of hours. The case was being carried as a fatal accident and we had a hard time convincing anyone that it may have been a robbery gone bad.

The family said he usually dropped off his money during the night and this time failed to do so. He only had about twenty dollars in his pocket and he should have had more.

Both Ken and I had several jury trials set for the next two weeks, but first we found the time to get blood samples from the back and front seat and also hair samples from the windshield. We sent these samples to the Crime Lab along with samples the Medical Examiner took and by the time we were done with our trials, the results came back. There was foreign blood in the back seat and foreign hair on the windshield. This meant there was definitely a passenger in the back seat and possibly an assailant. Besides that, Ken and I made a few of the neighbors and found an off-duty Paramedic that heard the crash, looked out his door and heard pounding coming from the inside of the cab. He called the Police and then went back to bed, saying he doesn't get paid for getting involved off duty. Nice guy, really dedicated; good thing he's the exception on the Fire Department.

For the next several weeks, when we had time, we checked all the local hospitals to see if anyone was brought in with serious injuries from a possible car accident. We also checked whether he had been a victim in the past and found that he had been the victim of a robbery in 1986, and after a jury trial in which he testified the suspect was sentenced to nine years in prison. We disregarded that guy because it was only two years later and very seldom are the same suspects found robbing the same victim, especially cab drivers. After that the death just became another statistic.

The total for 1989 was one-hundred-sixteen homicides with seventeen being open and the cabbie being one of them. Actually, the statistics were pretty good, about an eighty-five percent clearance rate. But that percentage doesn't mean anything to the families of the seventeen murders that were unsolved.

Looking ahead, it was sometime in October of 1990 that we got called to the House of Correction. Apparently someone wanted to snitch on somebody in exchange for us talking to the D.A. on his own charge. These guys in jail are constantly bragging about their crimes. I don't know if it's just stupidity or if they think these other prisoners really care about what they did. Anyway, we were amazed at this guy's story.

Apparently, a buddy of his came to his door about 4:00 a.m. and was all banged up. He was bleeding from the face and head and was limping badly. He told him he had just robbed a cab driver and while they were struggling, the cabbie rolled the cab and smashed it into a tree. We were stunned. The guy went on to say that he took his buddy to a hospital in Racine where he registered under a different name, and when they saw a uniform guard looking at them, they left. He then took his buddy to a hospital in the city of Kenosha where he was admitted and spent about three days recuperating. We walked out of there and couldn't believe what we had heard.

The guy in prison gave us his buddy's name and after running it through records, discovered it was the same guy that had robbed the cabbie in 1986, and got nine years in prison in 1987. Even with good behavior and all that bullshit he did, he should have still been locked up. But no, apparently the prisons were a little crowded and this guy fell through the cracks and got an early release. We found his Parole Officer (P.O.) and he said he remembered his client coming in back in 1989 with a swollen face and limping. He told his P.O. that he was the passenger in a car that was involved in an accident, and they left it at that.

The Parole Officer was pretty good and when we told him the story he put a parole hold on the guy. We found the hospital where he was treated under another name and got a search warrant for his blood type. Sure enough, they matched and a warrant was issued for him just before I retired. Who knows, maybe he got another nine years.

72. The Cost of a Murder

Well here it is, 1990—an important year for a lot of reasons. The first homicide of the year was a strange one! It was followed by another one hundred-sixty-four for a new record; and, I retired. But let me get at several of the hundred-sixty-four that I was involved in and were really interesting, starting with the first.

Ken and I came in that morning and were given a homicide from the night before. About 3:10 a.m. on January 4th, a white male named Mike was found lying in the gutter in the core area and had been stabbed to death. The late shift did a nice job and even though it was obvious the guy had been robbed and his pockets turned inside out, they not only identified him, but also found his car parked six blocks away.

We started at the scene and were led in the wrong direction, because the flop house where he was found in front of had a bunch of drunks and coke heads in it that had gotten in a fight the night before. To make matters worse, there were knives involved and there was blood trailing to an upstairs apartment. There was no heat or electricity in the place, so we brought everyone downtown and questioned them for a few hours and decided that they had no connection to the body. Even to this day it still amazes me. Here this body was lying in the gutter in front of their house and they just left it lay there while they drank and shot-up.

Anyhow, we found that the white guy worked on the north side, lived on the east side, was divorced and liked to hang around in black taverns. Ken and I went back to the area where his car was found and saw that it was parked just a half block from a tavern. We went into the tavern late in the afternoon and naturally were the only white guys in the tavern, obviously Cops and not particularly welcomed. After spending the better part of my life in the inner city, I bought a few drinks for a couple ladies that looked like regulars and before we knew it, we were part of the crowd. It took a couple of hours, but the ladies said they remembered the victim and thought they had seen him in the tavern the night before he was found. They had about six or eight guys they figured who knew what was going on, and as long as the drinks were flowing the tavern was our interrogation room. Each time they would bring up a name that they thought we should talk to, I asked where to find them. Immediately they would get on the phone and all we could hear was, "Get your black ass down here because the Police want to talk to you." Within minutes the door would fly open and some of the guys would actually be out of breath when they staggered in.

Whatever these young ladies had on these guys must have been good, and it wasn't their bodies because they each tipped the scales at close to three hundred pounds. We spent the next several hours in the place and shared a couple of cocktails when a young lady walked in, walked up to us and said, "I think I know who you're looking for." After a few drinks she gave us the following story.

She frequents this particular bar because they allow her to apply her trade. She had been arrested several times for prostitution, lives with her seven children by five fathers, and collects $879 in welfare and $398 in food stamps a month. On this particular night Mike was really drunk and flashing a lot of money. At closing time she and her sister drove home with her sister's boyfriend. They passed Mike on the street and he was so drunk he could hardly stand. They went home and she went to her lower flat and her sister and boyfriend went to the upper flat. She talked to her sister the next day and her sister said her boyfriend left and came back several hours later and mentioned something about a robbery, but she didn't pay any attention to him. She also said she really feels bad that Mike was killed and thinks her sister's boyfriend might be involved.

The next day we picked up the boyfriend, brought him downtown, advised him of his rights and told him his girlfriend had put him down. This was one of those easy ones—within an hour we had a full signed confession. He said Mike was flashing money all night and when he saw him staggering drunk on the corner he decided to rob him. After his girlfriend went into the house he took her car, found Mike on the street and asked him if he wanted a ride to where he could get him some lady and a little coke. Mike got in the car and they drove to the flop house apartment and before entering, th guy demanded money from Mike. Mike refused and they struggled and t' guy stabbed Mike in the side. When Mike was on the ground the guy to fifty dollars from Mike's pocket, put the knife in his pocket and drove ho He did say that when he left Mike he was standing in the gutter muml something and holding his side. The guy even said he lost the knife c street because it fell through a hole in his coat pocket.

We then went back to his girlfriend's house, told her what ha and got permission to search her house. We found the guy's black l(and sure enough, it had a hole in the pocket with a stain that lo(blood. We then got a city crew to search the sewers in the area bu find the knife.

The next day we took the case to the D.A.'s office and char with felony murder and armed robbery. Good investigation, case closed, right? Nothing is certain regarding homicide inves nothing surprised me ever since Ernie and I got the Indian (charge. This latest guy was bound over for trial and his Public already talking about copping a plea. About two weeks after hearing, I came to work and the Vice Squad was at my desk. They told me that they had picked up a hooker overnight and she was trying to get a break because she was on probation for the same thing. They said she had information on the murder of the white guy that was found in the gutter by this drug house. I told them the case was cleared, the guy confessed, was bound over for trial, and was probably going to plead guilty. They asked me if I wouldn't at least talk to her.

I went back to the interrogation room and this young hooker said she was sure her boyfriend Barry had killed the white guy because the white guy didn't have any money. She said Barry was bragging around town about what he did and was so spaced out on drugs that she was sure he would talk. She even said if we picked him up and he didn't talk, she would let us wire her and she would get him to talk while she applied her trade. I'm glad we didn't have to go that far because I think the bosses would not have looked too kindly on that sort of statement.

Our hooker snitch told us where to find Barry and the next day we picked him up, took him downtown, and within a couple of hours, here was his story. He was broke and going to this drug house where he hoped to get a nickel bag on credit. Much to his surprise, he sees this drunken white guy in front of the drug house standing in the gutter. Barry walked up to him, pulled a knife and said, "Give me all your money." Poor Mike must have thought, "How many times can I get robbed in one night?" Barry said the guy pulled his pockets inside out and said all he had was a quarter and with this Barry stabbed Mike, took the quarter and fled the scene. Ken and I couldn't believe what we were hearing but it sure sounded possible. We had Barry sign his confession and then took him back to the scene where Mike was found and Barry pointed to the exact spot where Mike's body was found.

The next day we took Barry to the same D.A. that handled the original case and he charged Barry with second degree murder and armed robbery. He also called the attorney for the original guy charged and said he was dropping the murder charge, but letting the armed robbery charge stand. This was all fine with us and sounded like a good deal for everyone. But, I note in my memo book, that months later Barry was found guilty of second degree murder and got ten years. I also found that the first guy's case was now being handled by one of those D.A.s that was just a useless piece of shit. He not only dropped the murder charge, but also dismissed the armed robbery. He made the decision that he would have a hard time proving armed robbery and that we should be satisfied that we had the real killer.

At that time in my career I had a good reputation with the D.A.'s office as well as with several reporters and TV news people. I went to the head D.A. himself, who called in the Assistant D.A. that had the charges dropped and we had a big pissing contest right there in his office. If I remember right, I won the battle but lost the war. The D.A. chewed out the assistant but didn't feel they could reopen the case because of the way the assistant had it dismissed. I accepted this but still made my point by dropping a dime to the press and TV. They gave the Assistant D.A. the bad publicity he deserved. I never had dealings with him again, which didn't break my heart, but at the time of this writing, I think he's still an Assistant DA in the same office.

What made this case even more interesting, if that's possible, was that after I retired, the *Milwaukee Journal* published an article entitled, "The Cost of a Murder." The reporter happened to pick this particular case because it was the first murder of 1990. He broke out the estimated costs to the taxpayer for this crime, and here's how it was reported:

$ 297.50	Emergency people on original scene
2,700.00	Medical Examiner cost, autopsy, etc.
5,400.00	Police cost, Detectives, court time
650.00	Burial paid by County
1,800.00	Court costs for charging conference
769.00	Preliminary Hearing
12,258.00	Trial cost
1,500.00	Public Defender
11,331.06	County Jail waiting for trial, 219 days
218,840.33	Prison costs, received 20 years, mandatory release 13.3 years $1371.18 per month, $16,454.16 per year
$255,545.89	GRAND TOTAL

Take into consideration that was the first homicide of the year followed by one-hundredsixty-four more. That's over 42 million dollars—in 1990; incredible statistics!

This same article was followed by the pictures of all one-hundred-sixty-five homicide victims from 1990. Considering I left the Department in November of that year, was out six weeks with an operation, had four-weeks of vacation and had at least eight long-lasting jury trials, I still was involved in twenty-nine of those cases.

It's 2002 and I've been gone from the job for twelve years now, and I have only great memories about all the years that I spent on the Department. But, looking at my notes and memo books, I must have been getting ready to call it quits. This is what I wrote at the end of January, 1990: "All we have heard for months now is how concerned the U.S. government is with the drug wars in Asia, Panama, Columbia, etc. using the military and billions of dollars. Actually, we can't d anything right here at home in Milwaukee.

I just read in my notes where another jury found my old friend Earl not guilty on drug conspiracy charges. These were federal charges and the Feds were so sure they had a conviction that they told me they would show his involvement with the Porter murder at his sentencing. I just can't believe the not guilty finding.

During the trial they showed Earl and all his friends in their full length mink coats, diamonds, gold jewelry, big cars, and no jobs, but still with top highly paid defense lawyers. I think our jury system is truly failing and needs a complete overhaul—either that or we need to start spending some big money on good prosecutors. We are definitely loosing the drug war and yet these same jurors will be the biggest critics of the Police; never the Judges, prosecutors or themselves. I think it's almost time to get out. I'm starting to take these things personally. Don't these jurors ever consider that maybe because the defendant is sitting where he is, that there's the vague possibility he did something and that they should give maybe the slightest bit of edge to the prosecution? But every jury I have ever been involved in always looks for some "out" for the defendant. I know they all have Constitutional rights, but give me a break—I have rights too! The right to live in a decent society!

73. Whodunit?

There was never any time to rest on our laurels; the bosses and press gave us accolades, but we never had time to enjoy them. That last year I spent on the job was total chaos, endless hours and endless interesting cases. I'll try and describe just a few so I can finally finish writing this book. I think by now my children, grandchildren, and anyone else that's reading this book may be becoming bored!

It was February of 1990 when Ken and I were sent to meet some uniform Officers who had been sent to a "sudden death." This could have been anything from an overdose to a death that had some strange twist that they wanted the Detective Bureau to have a look at. Well, this case not only had a bizarre twist, but a strange conclusion. We met the uniform men who said, "If this is a suicide, it's the strangest one we've ever seen." The scene was an older two-story brick building on a main street in a changing area of the city, but still not a high crime area.

The lower portion of the building had a store and one apartment and the upper had three, one-bedroom efficiency apartments. The Officers led us to one of these three, which was at the far end of the building without a porch. We entered the living room, which was modestly furnished and it showed nothing out of order. We then proceeded to a small kitchen area and there seated at the table was this little, sixty-four-year-old lady named Celia, covered in blood. There was a kitchen knife in her left hand and her head was lying on her right arm, which was on the table. She had obviously been dead for some time as her bowels had let loose and there was no sign of rigor mortis (the body going stiff)—which generally takes twelve hours to set in and then twelve hours to reverse it. The amount of time "in and out" depends on temperature, position of the body and other variables. Anyhow, it was obvious she had been dead for at least a day.

By the time the Medical Examiner came we had all our pictures taken, interviewed the subject's landlord, sister, and brother-in-law, and searched the entire apartment for any obvious evidence. Then we examined Celia's body closer and discovered that she had been stabbed at least fifty times between her neck and stomach, and once in the head. All these wounds were through her clothing, and there didn't appear to be any defensive wounds or any sign of a struggle. The Medical Examiner later found that none of the wounds were deep enough to be fatal, and that she actually bled to death.

Her sister said Celia was born with crippled legs that had been getting worse, along with arthritis setting in and other ailments. Celia had been divorced since she was twenty years old and lived on social security and rent assistance and had very little extra money. She apparently felt very secure in her apartment and never answered the door without looking through the peephole. Celia's sister called the landlady when she couldn't get in touch with Celia and the landlady unlocked the dead bolt from the outside, entered the apartment and found the body.

The only evidence we found was a cut telephone cord, several wigs, some with glass particles in them, and we also discovered that the keys for the apartment were missing. She had her false teeth lying on the dining room table, which apparently was common. She could not drive, had no male friends, did not go to church and seldom left the apartment.

We then brought all the tenants from the building down to the Bureau and after several hours, determined that they all had alibi's that eliminated them as suspects for the time being.

During the next two days I worked alone and went back to the apartment several more times and gathered miscellaneous items, including her private phone book. I then started calling all the numbers and determined that she had no hidden wealth or any unusual life and just seemed to stay to herself. It's a good thing we had a temporary lull in murders because otherwise I wouldn't have spent this much time on the case, which looked like either a bizarre suicide or a real whodunit.

Because we had a little extra time, all three shifts were involved in contacting her friends. I came in that next Sunday and was told to meet the late shift at one of these friends's house. When I got there it didn't look good because there were several Bureau cars along with a Rescue Squad and the Medical Examiner. When I approached the house the late shift Detective met me and once again announced the adage, which was getting all too familiar, "You're not going to believe this." This Detective and his partner had waited for daylight and went to the front door of a couple whose address was listed in Celia's personal telephone book. They rang the bell and after several minutes an older white man looked out the front window and when he disappeared they thought he was going to answer the door. Instead, much to their surprise, they heard two shots come from inside the house. They broke down the door and found an old couple on the front room floor with the man still taking some last breaths. He still had the gun in his hand and the Detectives apparently had interrupted a murder suicide. It had been well planned, including a suicide note that described the funeral arrangements they wanted.

After dealing with the victims and having the bodies removed, we searched the entire premises with one thing in mind—finding any evidence about Celia's murder, but nothing showed up. This had to be one of the strangest cases I ever worked on. We thought of maybe a suicide pact between all three and also the possibility that they told Celia about their plans and she became a victim. We also realized that while looking at that angle, we may have overlooked two isolated incidents and Celia's murder may have had nothing to do with the murder suicide. Besides that, the next several days produced another rash of murders and time was running short on solving Celia's murder and I knew that in a short time, she would become just another statistic.

The old couple's names were Viola and Clinton. Ken and I found their son and daughter-in-law to be very cooperative in the whole investigation. They apparently had gotten together with Viola and Clinton the day Celia's body was found and the old couple acted strangely. Clinton said, "Wait till you read what happened in the paper and see it on TV." When they asked what he was talking about, both Clinton and Viola became quiet. They also didn't want to go to Celia's funeral and when Clinton's son checked their assets after their deaths, he found that Clinton and Viola had charged over six thousand dollars worth of things on their credit cards—none of which was ever found. They also couldn't find Viola's purse or her address book, which she always kept with her.

I believe the case involving Celia remains open to this day. In all probability the three may have had either a suicide pact or Viola and Clinton wanted to relieve Celia from all her pain and then take their own lives. Whatever happened the day Celia died will probably stay a mystery until the end of time. Who knows, some stranger may have gotten away with murder, just like thousands of others. Needless to say, some of these cases are stranger than fiction and become just another statistic that's filed away as a memory. That's what makes these types of crimes so unique and so final.

74. Discretion with Affair

By April of 1990 I already had five jury trials and four trips out-of-state to either question suspects or bring them back to Wisconsin. I remember I had just gotten back from Atlanta, where I picked up a prisoner from a case I talked about earlier, when I was sent to an armed robbery and shooting. Usually we didn't get these cases, but the clerk was shot in the head and was supposed to die, which he didn't. Anyway, the whole crime was caught on a video surveillance camera and when we developed the film, we saw either a witness or an accomplice standing by the cigarette machine during the whole incident.

We had his picture blown up and shown around the motel where the shooting took place, and he was identified as a regular customer. In fact, he was in his usual motel room at that time. I can't remember who I was with, but when we knocked on the door and showed our badges to a startled man in his late fifties, he immediately stepped into the hall—I figured there was something a little out of the ordinary about this. In the first place this guy didn't fit in this particular motel in this particular part of town. And, when we insisted on interviewing him in the motel room, the scenario became obvious. His partner in the room was about twenty years younger and after some reluctance he introduced us to his secretary.

A little discretion is usually used in these instances unless the guy turns out to be a complete asshole and then a call may become necessary. But I can't ever remember having to make such a call. This guy was very cooperative and even made a positive identification of the shooter. He did, however, plead with us that unless he was absolutely desperately needed, he wished to stay anonymous. As it turned out he didn't have to testify, but I did have to subpoena him and when I went to this very large insurance company and saw his secretary, she sure turned red.

75. Close Call

You would think that after all these years, which was approaching thirty-three, that an experienced Copper would have all the savvy necessary to protect himself from getting hurt or killed. Not so. That's why you still read in the papers how older Officers get themselves in situations that result in their deaths.

It was in June of 1990 and murders number fifty-nine and sixty had occurred overnight. Ken and I had been briefed on both of them and had a list of follow-up work on both of them, but first we had some old business to take care of. We went to a house in the core looking for a female suspect in a homicide, not expecting to find her or her boyfriend—who was the actual shooter. We got into this second story flat and suddenly realized that not only was the female suspect there, but also a half-dozen friends and her six small children. Another man we had been looking for confronted us and by this time the whole situation was starting to get a little testy, to say the least.

I was standing in front of a closed bedroom door that must have contained something not meant for my eyes because everyone was starring at the doorknob. Discretion being the greater part of valor, I was able to contact the dispatcher and asked for a backup Squad. Much to my dismay the dispatcher asked if I was calling for an assist or just a backup. An assist would have brought half the Department and I didn't think we were ready for that, so I said we just needed a Squad to cover us in a touchy situation. To which the dispatcher replied, "Not a Squad available in the city, but keep us informed."

Well, Ken was a good sweet talker and after a few tense minutes we told the male and female they were key witnesses and we wanted them to look at some pictures downtown. They must have believed us because they both got into the Squad, even though their friends said they would be sorry these white honkies were taking them to jail.

We must have gotten half-way downtown when the woman suddenly exclaimed, "You know the guy that did the shooting was in the bedroom with an automatic! If you had opened that door he would have shot you. He had told everyone that no Copper was going to take him alive!" Close call!

The good Lord was once again watching over me as he had been so many times during my career. Now that my Police career has ended and I'm able to write these memories for my family, I have to mention how much my faith played a part in the job. I can't possibly recall the many moments I spent in prayer during my career. Walking the dark alleys, entering the houses where I knew the possibility of death was there, and especially the Homicide Squad. It was not unusual to pray with men and women confessing their crimes; or each time I watched an autopsy or entered a vicious crime scene, I would say a silent prayer that I could handle the situation and not embarrass myself, my partner, or the office I represented.

76. We-Tip/Crime Line Anonymous

I don't know if I ever had the chance to talk about *Crime Line Anonymous*, which was a very popular TV show in the eighties. I think later on, "America's Most Wanted" show started and *Crime Line Anonymous* faded away. But during its heyday it was a very popular show. It was based out of California and televised locally with a local reporter using local crimes.

When the program was aired, anyone could anonymously call the tip line in California, which would then send the tip to the appropriate local Police Department. If the information was used by the Department, we would fill in an amount of reward—up to $1,000. The form would be sent back to California where the informant had been given an anonymous number that was not available to us. The outfit in California would then award an amount to the informant. I recall several times I pleaded with the local reporter to try and get the informant's name and location because without it, the information was useless. The reporter's name was Allen and he tried unsuccessfully to get the names, but was told that strict confidentiality was required. Anyhow, Tom and I did a lot of television *We-Tips*—the local program for *Crime Line Anonymous* and in fact, became very good friends with the reporter and his cameraman. I remember my kids getting a bang out of seeing me on TV and Marlene would usually record the program.

The reason I bring this subject up is not only to tell about the *We-Tip* program, but to also show how racially divided we were even in the late 1980's and 1990's. One such case was a typical example. Two white couples walked out to the end of the government pier on Lake Michigan one warm summer evening. While they were standing there, according to witnesses and statements from the assailants themselves, three African-American men eighteen to twenty years old approached the couples. One of the males came up behind the couples and said, "Don't you like me?" And with that he began to smash a white man's head (Silas was his name) into a concrete wall. When Silas tried to run away, the assailant chased after him calling him a "honky punk" and telling his friends to "get him." While trying to get away, Silas jumped into the lake and disappeared. The assailant later said he threw a life preserver into the water at the spot where Silas jumped in, but Silas never came back up. The assailant's buddy said he could hear Silas calling for help and thought he was trapped under the pier.

All the assailants fled the scene and the next day Silas's body was recovered by divers who said he probably was sucked under the pier by the water current and couldn't get loose. The cause of death was ruled a drowning, but he also suffered blunt force trauma to his head. The death was then ruled a homicide and that's how I got involved.

About two weeks after the assault and murder, the case was still unsolved, so I did a *We-Tip* with Allen, filming from the end of the pier and showing where Silas had jumped in. Allen tried to get me to say that the crime was racially motivated, which it was, but the whole Department was so intimidated that I had to settle for a, "No comment" response to his questioning. And even for that I was later criticized as being too insensitive. In fact, this was at the same time that several white males had chased an African-American man onto the freeway in New York where he was struck and killed. That incident drew national news, protests and marches by the NAACP and demands for a federal investigation. Our murder rated just a small article in the local paper.

The *We-Tip* paid off and we arrested the three males who gave complete statements, including the fact that they started the whole altercation and included that it was racially motivated. Actually, they were arrested after their lawyers brought them in. Apparently, the three had all graduated from high school and one in particular was a good athlete and had a scholarship waiting for him.

Now is when it became interesting. I was off the next day and the Detective that took them to the D.A. fully expected some sort of homicide charge and also requested an enhanced charge, because we thought it was a hate crime. When I came back the next day the Detective was just shaking his head. The case had been reviewed by one of the better female Homicide D.A.s and she said they needed more time and more investigation and all three were released on their own recognizance—meaning just a signature bond. It got worse after that, and the three were subsequently charged with aggravated battery that carried a maximum prison term of two years. When I heard this I immediately went to the D.A., who I knew very well and had a lot of respect for, and questioned her decision. All she said to me was that I should just stay out of it and mind my own business just as she had.

Apparently, the handwriting was on the wall and the decision had been made right from the top of the D.A.'s office, and there would be no further discussion. I wondered what would have happened if the races of the victim and the assailants had been reversed. I always thought justice was supposed to be blind and equal. Apparently that's not always the case. Why should this surprise me?

77. Time to Get Out?

The Homicide Squad had really changed since it first started. All three shifts were now involved and the young guys on the late and early shift were just waiting for an old timer like me on the first shift to retire. They would love to go days and get all the good trips. Maybe it was getting time for me to start thinking of retiring. To this day I always said that it was unusual to have such a tremendous job for so many years, and maybe it was time for me to leave while I still had a passion for the job.

I told Marlene that I was thinking of leaving and again she put no pressure on me, but said that I should do what I thought was best. I remember that I had planned to have another job all set by the time I was fifty-two so I could leave, and here I was close to fifty-five and still hanging in there. I still thought I might go to the D.A.'s office as an investigator and even had several D.A.'s pushing me for the job. But, there were always budget problems and the job never became a reality until after I left the Department.

The action never stopped. Every morning was either planned the day before or was taken up by a new homicide from the night before. The only break would come when I would spend several days in court with trials, and these, in fact, were occupying a great deal of my time—or when I had the luxury of taking a trip, which was also getting to be quite regular.

I had just come back from a trip to Atlanta, Georgia with Jimmy when I was scheduled to testify in Federal Court at the sentencing of two members of the BOS, who had been found guilty of federal drug charges. In fact, the prosecuting Federal Attorney became a local talk show host. Anyway, I was shocked by the federal system that allowed me to testify to several unsolved murders that the two defendants were suspected of. Even though there was not enough evidence to try them in our Circuit Court, I was able to testify in their sentencing that they, in all probability, were involved. (I believe this testimony was later ruled inadmissible by the Supreme Court.) There were no objections from their lawyers and all they could do was listen for several hours while I testified how bad they were. I would imagine the Judge already knew their records because they each got thirty-five years. I really like the federal system. I think in the state courts all the defendant has to serve before he or she is eligible for parole is one third of the sentence and mandatory release after two-thirds of the sentence. At least that's what it was at that time. While under the federal guidelines they got only about fifty days a year off for good behavior. This meant that if they got ten years, they had to serve better than eight.

The murders just kept coming in; there was no stopping, and each one had its own little twist. I think I'll just mention a few before I bring this to an end.

There was Darbie, the twenty four-year-old that was collecting $617.00 per month in welfare, plus food stamps, plus rent assistance. She was having sex with so many guys that her caseworker couldn't keep track. She really must have upset one of them because we found her naked with Vaseline all over her body and her bra stuck in her mouth. She was strangled manually. The house was a shit hole with no food and very little furniture. We arrested about a dozen guys over the next several days and had to release them all. This is one that is probably open to this day unless some nut has a guilty conscience, which I doubt. There's always a sad side, and that is the children Darbie left behind. Any chances that they had, or will have, of leading a normal life are probably non—existent. And when they grow into either career criminals or someone with emotional or psychological problems, I wonder if society will take their childhood into consideration.

Then there was Pamela, who was shot to death trying to protect her sister from her sister's abusive boyfriend. Kelvin went to the house with handcuffs and a gun to kidnap Pamela's sister, Phyllis. When Pamela got in the way she was shot and her sister was dragged away by Kelvin. Phyllis was in a motel for two days and beaten and raped before she was released. Kelvin was arrested by us and sentenced to seventy years in prison. His statement to the family at sentencing was, "I'm sorry I hurt you."

Or the drunken man that left the bar at closing and then went back and asked the drunken female bartender for another drink. Rather than the drink, she shot him in the head, went back behind the bar, had another drink and waited for the Police.

Or the time Ken and I got a call from the mother of a murder victim who was approached by her neighbor, who had seen a suspect fleeing the scene of a murder that happened twenty-four years ago. The neighbor said she was hypnotized to help her stop smoking and the hypnotist said he could help her recall the incident and maybe identify the suspect. We went and talked to the hypnotist who seemed legitimate and said he could put the witness under and show her some pictures of suspects and she could possibly make an identification. It sounded a little far off the wall and when we ran it past one of the D.A.s, I thought she was going to fall off her chair. So much for hypnosis!

Then there are the tough ones to investigate. The ones that really hit home. An African-American male walked up on a car at a stoplight and shot the driver through the head. Definitely drug related and when we interviewed the passenger, he told us who his dad was and we both knew him as one of the better narcotics Officers on the job. We went and talked to his dad, who was standing by his son, but we could see the pain in his face. We could never connect the son to the murder, but the event almost destroyed the father. How thankful I am that my family was never corrupted by my job.

Or the street shooting where the only witness was a sixteen-year-old boy. He gave an incredible account of what happened and said he was just standing on the corner when this car pulled up and the passenger asked him for some dope. The kid ran across the street, pulled out his gun and started to shoot at the car. The guys in the car shot back and then drove away. The final answer was that the passenger in the vehicle actually shot the driver as he was trying to shoot the kid. Before we could get everybody arrested, a group of druggies came back and shot up the kid's mother's house in broad daylight. The final tally was three arrests for homicide, party to a crime.

Or the case of the two guys going to a tavern and getting drunk and thrown out. They drove away and were stopped by the Police and the driver was arrested for drunken driving. The passenger was also drunk, but the Coppers told him to take a bus home. Well, the guy got on the bus and when he made a transfer to another bus, he started to hassle four African-American males with a stick, poking them and making racial slurs. You know the old story; don't take a knife to a gunfight! Taking a stick is even worse. As the drunk was showing the bus driver his transfer, one of the males shot him in the back and the drunk became the first homicide on a county bus.

It took us a couple of days to find the shooter, but with four involved it was only natural that someone would drop a dime. This is the case where the family hired a lawyer to turn the suspect in because they thought he was innocent. When we arrested the guy, the lawyer told him to cooperate, which he did. He gave a full confession and said the only reason he shot the guy was because his friend handed him a gun as the guy got on the bus. While I took his confession, his mother and sister were waiting out in the hall and the lawyer had left. When I told them what their son and brother had said, they wouldn't believe me and demanded that they see him. I already had a signed confession and they really seemed like nice people, so I brought them back into the interrogation room where he again confessed to the shooting. The emotional scene between mother, son, and daughter, was not one of my more pleasant memories.

I can't help but write about Rodney, who I arrested in May of 1990 for a drive-by shooting. He was charged with first degree intentional homicide along with his buddy Jeff. They were both bound over for trial and Jeff was the first one to face a jury, with the trial being held in October of that year. I remember this one because after the jury was picked, we had spent a day taking testimony. After the trial was over I was told by one of the jury members that one of the female jurors announced on the first day of the trial that she thought Jeff was innocent and she wasn't going to listen to anymore testimony. Apparently from that point on she didn't talk to anyone and when they finally went into deliberations she just sat there and knitted. She announced then that she had all her Christmas shopping done and she would hold out forever with her not guilty vote. After two days of deliberation the jury came back hung—eleven to one. A month later Jeff was tried again and got life!

But back to Rodney—I retired in November of 1990 and didn't testify in his trial until sometime in 1993. During that time he sat in jail for almost three years, got married and divorced twice while locked up, watched the construction of a new jail and saw his buddy Jeff go through two trials and serve a year and a half of his life sentence. He also went through two attorneys, two Judges and seven trial dates. After all this time it took the jury only two hours to come back with a guilty verdict. The only consolation Rodney had was that all his time spent in the County Jail would go towards his total incarceration time.

78. The Murder of Sara

I suppose I can't complete my book without mentioning the murder of Sara. It was the beginning of June 1990 and I was on vacation. It was a Sunday night and whatever we had been doing during the day must have taken its toll because I fell asleep watching TV. Marlene woke me with a start saying, "Jim, wake up, Sara was murdered."

I can't personally remember ever talking to Sara unless it might have been a, "Hi" while I was talking to her parents. But I knew her parents very well, as they were members of our church. I immediately sat up and on television saw a red car parked in the street, uniformed Officers walking around, and a picture of Sara flashed on the screen. I just caught the last part of the news that said she was found dead in her car parked on a city side street, and that one person was in custody.

It was probably 10:30 at night when I called down to the Homicide Squad and talked to Kenny, not my partner, but one of the best homicide Detectives and interrogators on the Squad. I told him I knew the family of Sara really well and wanted to know what was going on. Kenny said she was found dead in her car and it appeared she had been strangled. The Medical Examiner hadn't given a cause of death yet, but the car was locked, there was no evidence of a struggle, her clothes were not disarranged and her personal property looked like it had not been touched.

He also said they had her boyfriend in custody and they had him in tears and on the verge of confessing. He said I should give him a call the next morning and by that time they'd have more information.

Marlene and I sat back and talked for awhile trying to put some thoughts together about the family. Marlene had been the secretary of the church for about nineteen years and knew practically everybody. I knew Sara's folks very well but only recalled Sara as a child and then suddenly she grew up and was now a very attractive young lady. I had seen her in church with her folks and her older brother and I knew that the family was very close and that both children had been adopted. I believe she was about twenty-one when she was killed and my immediate thoughts were how the family must have been reacting to such a cruel fate to someone so young and vibrant.

The next day I gave Kenny a call and asked if they got the confession. He said they had to let him go. He said he really felt they had him right on the verge of confessing and there was no doubt in his mind that they had the right guy. I asked what went wrong and he said he and his partner were taking a break and getting them and the suspect something to eat, when a well-known criminal attorney appeared at the Bureau saying he was hired to represent the suspect and demanded to see him and to stop any interrogation of him.

The person the attorney talked to should have known that the demand for a lawyer has to come from the person in custody, and if he does not make the demand, no one can do it for him. In other words, the interrogation could go on for as much time as would be determined to be reasonable and once it stopped and the suspect was given a telephone call he could call anyone he wanted to. But as long as he was advised of his rights, which he was, and he made no demands for a phone call or an attorney, the interrogation could go on.

Well, this attorney kept ranting and raving and demanding to see his client and the Chief of Police for so long that he must have intimidated someone enough that he was allowed to see the suspect for a few minutes. Naturally that's all he needed because the first words out of his mouth were shut up and don't say another word. That not only ended the interrogation and possible confession, but it brought the whole investigation to a halt at a crucial time. And by the next day the suspect's mother came up with twenty-five thousand dollars in cash to bail him out.

The next day I came in and got the whole story. Apparently, once the body was found, and after several hours, they traced the plates and subsequently found Sara's parents, who told them about the boyfriend that she would stay with sometimes.

They found the boyfriend in an upstairs flat above a very fancy restaurant located about a block outside the city. They learned that the boyfriend's mother was a long time employee of the restaurant and when the Detectives brought her son downtown for questioning, she approached the restaurant owner. He felt sorry for her and gave her ten thousand dollars as up-front money to hire the big time criminal defense attorney. Not only that, but he also subsequently gave her the twenty-five thousand to bail him out.

Kenny and I were briefed on the case and viewed the Medical Examiner's report that indicated Sara had died of suffocation in that her airway was constricted and she lost consciousness, and as a result died. There were marks on her neck that indicated she might have been pressed against a hard object causing her to pass out. It was then that the continued pressure caused the death. These marks were consistent with the frame of a waterbed that was found in the boyfriend's apartment and by his own statement used by him and Sara the night before her body was found. He had admitted being with her, but said she left to go to her parents house early the next morning and that was the last time he saw her.

Sara's car had been towed from the scene and Kenny and I went down to search it for any possible physical evidence. It had already been checked for prints so the only thing left was to go through the personal property. Sara apparently had just gotten back from being out-of-state and was getting ready to move into an apartment, so the car was completely loaded, both the trunk and back seat.

After going through miscellaneous articles for about an hour, I came upon a box of papers that revealed a startling note. It was an old report card type pamphlet that Sara had received for perfect attendance when she attended Sunday school as a child. The ironic thing was that it was signed by me when I was the Sunday School Superintendent of our church. The irony was so great that we mentioned it to our boss who subsequently leaked it to the press and months later I was interviewed about the report. The press did a nice job and the headlines were, "Detective hasn't forgotten case, parents think they know killer."

Prior to this—and after the body was identified and released to the family—Marlene and I attended the funeral. It was a heart-breaking scene. The funeral home was so crowded with young people that the Police had to direct traffic. Sara's mother gave a soul-searching memorial that touched everyone and when she looked at me and said, "And I know Jim will find the killer that took our beloved Sara," it was a heart wrencher.

I spent a great deal of time on this particular murder for obvious reasons and regret to this day that the killer was never brought to justice. There is no doubt in any one's mind that the killer is the boyfriend who was arrested and subsequently released. He was re-interviewed several times later and always referred all questions to his lawyer. His mother, who many think may have been a co-conspirator and picked up her son where he parked Sara's car and body, has also been questioned many times and remains silent. I even did a *We-Tip* segment on TV and was shown walking down the street where Sara's car was found, asking for any information anyone may have. This didn't provide any new information. But, there was in fact, one witness who happened to be up feeding her baby when she saw this red car go by her house in a jerky motion. Sara's car had a manual transmission and it was a known fact that her boyfriend could not drive the stick shift. She also gave a good description of the driver, but when Kenny brought her down to view the boyfriend in a line-up; it was after he had been released. His lawyer had him all decked out in nice clean clothes, a short hair cut and was clean-shaven. The witness said he looked like the driver of the car but she couldn't say for sure.

Sara's family had no real money, but they managed to scrape together ten thousand dollars for a reward. This still didn't bring any new clues or shake the conscience of the boyfriend, his mother, or any friends who may have known what happened. In fact, some time later the restaurant owner—where we suspect the murder occurred (in the boyfriend's flat above the restaurant) and who put up the bail money—contacted the family and apologized for what he had done. He had fired the mother and felt that he had done a discredit by providing the bail money and the high priced criminal lawyer. He also offered to supplement the reward money, which I don't know that he ever did.

Throughout the years several Milwaukee Homicide Detectives would reopen Sara's murder case and contact the family, who always appreciated the new interest. But, it would always lead to the same suspect who apparently never told anyone about his involvement and until he does, the crime will remain unsolved. Even Sara's mother went to her grave knowing that her beloved Sara's killer was still at large. Very, very, very sad.

79. A Phone Call to Retirement

It was now September of 1990 and I was having lunch with Leo, who was my Insurance Agent, and also a good friend. He asked me an interesting question. He said, "When are you going to get out of this rat race and spend more time at home with Marlene, the kids and grandkids?"

I said, "When you find me a good job that's as interesting as the one I've got." With that he told me to get him a resume and he would contact the big insurance company he worked for.

It was a couple of weeks later that I was called for an interview, so I showed up at this insurance office and was first interviewed by some young lady in human resources who was much younger than my daughters. We had a pleasant conversation about my past thirty-three years. I then met with people from the Special Investigation Unit of the company. After meeting with two men for about an hour I went home and told Marlene that if there was ever a job I would retire for, this was it. I also told her there were a lot of applicants and I held little hope to be called back.

Well, strange things happen and on November 14th, my boss Bill and I were getting ready to go out for breakfast when I got a call from the insurance company. They offered me the job. I accepted and I turned around to Bill and said, "You're not going to believe this, but I just retired."

And he said, "Let's celebrate."

I then went to the church where Marlene was the secretary, walked in and told her the same thing. To my amazement I didn't get much of a response because she didn't believe me. In fact, it took several days for me to convince her that I was leaving the only job I had held for our entire married life. And true to her low-key attitude that she always had and her confidence that I was doing the right thing she said, "I know you did the right thing."

So that was it. Thirty-three years and thirteen days from the time I was sworn in as a Police Officer it all came to an end. I officially retired on January 19, 1991. It was the greatest job in the world and to this day I feel privileged that I was allowed to be an Officer and Detective and experience all the things that make up this world of ours. I actually spent the next nine years working as a Fraud and Arson Investigator for the insurance company and that could be another whole story. It was a great period of time and I enjoyed it tremendously.

By this time Karen, Kristie and Jeff were all married and I was blessed with four grandchildren and by now that number has grown to ten with three great-grandchildren. As of this writing, Marlene and I have been married fifty-two years and without her continued patience and understanding I would never have been able to be the Officer that I felt I was. I hope that in the years to come that my writings will be read by my family to show them what an interesting life they allowed me to lead.

Presented To
JAMES O. GAUGER
Detective, Homicide Division – M.P.

Outstanding & Dedicated Servi[ce]

Your fellowship will long be remembered.

Day Shift Homicide Division
Capt. T. PEREWITZ   Det. N. SANDOVAL
Lt. W. VOGL   Det. K. MORROW
Det. D. SLIWINSKI   Det. K. McHENRY
Det. K. DOBESH   Det. J. KOSZUT
Det. D. MURPHY

December 16, 1990

CONGRATULATIONS
JIM GAUGER
ON YOUR RETIREMENT OF BEING A MEMBER OF THE FIRST HOMICIDE SQUAD OF THE MILWAUKEE POLICE DEPARTMENT

1982 to 1991

CAPTAIN CARL RUSCITTI
LIEUTENANT ROOSEVELT ROOSEVELT
LIEUTENANT RAYMOND SUCIK
LIEUTENANT BILL VOGL

IN MEMORY OF
TOM JACKELEN

These plaques were given to Jim upon his retirement. Below are signatures from co-workers.

850 murders later, officer calls it quits

Dec 1990

By DAVID DOEGE
Sentinel staff writer

Jim Gauger made a career out of trying to solve murders.

He poked around so many homicide scenes and talked to so many killers that he's not really sure how many murders he helped solve. He thinks the number is somewhere around 850.

Now, Gauger has retired from his specialty to work for an insurance firm.

But as natural as it might seem, Gauger didn't leave because he was burned out or bummed out.

"It was time," he explained. "I don't know how much longer I could have kept up at this pace.

"I wanted to go when I still felt good about my job."

And 850 murders after he began, Gauger, 55, still felt good about his job.

"It's a fascinating type of crime," he said. "I feel privileged that I've been able to live a life like this."

Gauger left a factory job in 1958 to become a police officer and followed a route through the department typical for those days. He began work on a police ambulance — delivering seven babies — walked a beat, and became a detective in 1973.

Back then, detectives were assigned to "general duty." They investigated whatever came their way, including homicides.

It wasn't until 1982 that the department formed a homicide squad.

Gauger, a tall, broad-shouldered, easy-going man, frequently spent his time inside the courtroom, seated beside the prosecutor as the lead investigator on cases.

But the path from the murder scene to the courtroom isn't always easily followed, and Gauger has many of them burned into his memory.

Take, for example, the path that Gauger and his longtime partner, Tom Jackelen, took from a North Side back yard where the partially clothed body of Ione Sychosz was found in 1984.

A forensic odontologist determined that bite marks on the victim's body indicated her killer had a missing rear molar and a twisted front tooth.

During that investigation, Jackelen and Gauger visited the home of one of the victim's neighbors, Robert Lee Stinson. They left a short time later, but only momentarily.

"Tom said, 'We got the guy,'"

Gauger recalled. "We went back inside and he told him a few jokes and the guy started laughing.

"When he laughed, sure enough, there were those teeth."

Stinson denied any involvement, but was summoned to a John Doe proceeding, where an impression of his teeth was taken in a judge's chambers. It linked Stinson to the killing and he eventually was tried, convicted and sentenced to life in prison.

Jackelen and Gauger worked together on cases from the day they joined the homicide squad until the day Jackelen died last year from cancer. They traveled throughout the country checking details and suspects.

Among them were Henry Lee Lucas and Ottis Elwood Toole, a bizarre pair of death row inmates in the Southern United States who claimed in the mid-1980s to have killed hundreds of people while drifting throughout the country.

"We spent a week in Monroe, La., where they had a big seminar for detectives from all over the country," Gauger said. "We had all kinds of maps and case files we took down there."

They also spent a week talking with Lucas in Texas and another week with Toole in Florida. Lucas, Gauger said, was a con man. He described Toole as a "transvestite pyromaniac."

"We showed Toole a picture of a woman," Gauger said. "He said he picked her up in a bar, took her home, had sex with her, strangled her with a telephone cord then set the place on fire.

"That's exactly what happened in the case. Toole never was charged with the crime, however, because his statement was the only thing authorities had. It also hurt that Toole had no idea where Milwaukee was and when he supposedly was here, Gauger added.

"You feel bad when you can't solve them," Gauger said, "especially in the cases, where you know who did it, but you can't tie them to it."

One such case pained him each month. That's how often a woman whose daughter was killed several years ago telephoned Gauger.

"She'd call every month and ask what was new," he said. "She's a very nice lady, but there was nothing we could tell her."

Gauger treated her like everyone else, politely. Killers, victims' relatives and snitches were treated the same.

"If you treat people well, they'll treat you well," he said. "In this business, you never know whose you're going to need that guy on the street.

"Even after you get a confession, you treat them well. It's not uncommon to have a defendant wave at you in court."

Article printed in the Milwaukee Sentinel December, 1990.

Born in 1935 as a first generation American to German Immigrants, Jim Gauger was raised in Milwaukee, Wisconsin. He attended parochial and public schools and worked as a laborer until he joined the Milwaukee Police Department at age twenty-two. He married Marlene the same year and they just celebrated their fifty-second wedding anniversary. He spent forty-two years investigating crimes for both the Police Department and a major insurance company. He is retired and spends his time reading, woodworking, traveling and with his children, grandchildren and great grandchildren. He still resides in the Milwaukee area.

The Memo Book is written in a matter-of-fact, police report style where true emotions and heartfelt opinions emerge in poignant situations. Jim Gauger investigated numerous crimes—some horrifically gruesome—described in detail, giving the reader a view of days in the life of a police officer. We owe much to these men and women who risk their lives—homes and hearts—for citizens of their precinct. Gauger is truly courageous yet humble and unabashedly honest; his dedication and love for his family is evident. It was difficult to choose which of his 800 murders cases to write about—presented is a glimpse of some interesting and bizarre situations. My dad remains the most positive, optimistic person I know with truly deep, deep faith; he is amazing! He has always said he had a fantastic job that paid the bills and his job paid him—in many ways.

—*Kristie Jorgenson*

Edwards Brothers Malloy
Oxnard, CA USA
November 10, 2014